Hideaways Golf

Hideaways Golf

DIE SCHÖNSTEN HOTELS UND DESTINATIONEN DER WELT
THE WORLD'S MOST BEAUTIFUL HOTELS AND DESTINATIONS

KLOCKE VERLAG

GOLFHOTELS FÜR GENIESSER

Unsere exklusiven HIDEAWAYS-Bildbände erfreuen sich großer Beliebtheit als Nachschlagewerke für anspruchsvolle Weltenbummler oder als unterhaltsame Lektüre, mit der man sich einmal zu den schönsten Hotels der Welt träumen kann. Auf vielfachen Wunsch unserer Leser haben wir jetzt erstmals auch eine Sonderedition HIDEAWAYS Golf zusammengestellt, die sich auf Hotels spezialisiert hat, die entweder über einen eigenen Golfplatz verfügen oder in deren Nähe sich außergewöhnliche Golfplätze befinden. Packen Sie Ihr Golf-Bag und folgen Sie uns zu *fairways to heaven* an die Costa del Sol in Andalusien, die sich wohl zu Recht seit kurzer Zeit auch „Costa del Golf" nennt. Mehr als fünfzig atemberaubende Plätze bieten hier mit 320 Sonnentagen im Jahr einzigartige Spielbedingungen. Nicht minder beliebt als Golfdestinationen sind die Algarve oder Mallorca, wo mit dem Real Golf de Bendinat ein „königlicher" Parcours auf ambitionierte Spieler wartet. Absolute Paradiese für Golfer sind auch Südafrika, Dubai und die Bermudas. Natürlich darf in solch einem Bildband auch Schottland, die Geburtsstätte des Golfsports, nicht fehlen. Hier waren wir zu Gast im legendären St. Andrews Old Course Hotel, wo vor mehr als sechshundert Jahren der erste Ball abgeschlagen wurde, und in Loch Lomond, einem der exklusivsten Clubs der Welt. Doch auch in Frankreich, in der Schweiz, in Österreich und auf zwei der besten deutschen Plätze laden wir Sie zu faszinierenden *tee-times* ein.

Our exclusive HIDEAWAYS coffee table books have either proved extremely popular reference books for discerning globetrotters or served as a relaxing read for those who seek to escape the daily grind and dream of the worlds most beautiful hotels. Due to popular demand of our readers we have now published a special edition HIDEAWAYS Golf, featuring hotels that either possess their own golf course or are situated near exceptional golf courses. Pack your golf bag and follow us on the "fairways to heaven" to the Costa del Sol in Andalusia, now appropriately called the "Costa del Golf". Over fifty breathtaking courses offer unique golfing opportunities during 320 sun drenched days. Other popular golf destinations are the Algarve or Majorca, where the Real Golf de Bendinat provides a "royal" parcours to challenge any ambitious golfers. Further paradise like locations for golfers such as South Africa, Dubai and the Bermudas are also featured in this volume. Naturally, any serious golfing book has to include Scotland, the birthplace of golf itself. There we were guests of the legendary St. Andrews Old Course Hotel, where over six hundred years ago the first ball was teed off but we also visited Loch Lomond, one of the most exclusive clubs in the world. Finally we would also like to invite you to tee off in France, Switzerland and Austria as well as two top German golf courses.

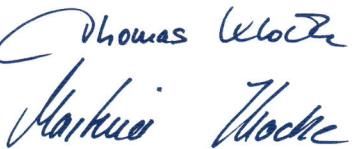

Thomas und Martina Klocke
HERAUSGEBER / PUBLISHER

Hideaways
GLF

Die schönsten Hotels und Destinationen der Welt

Klocke Verlag GmbH
Höfeweg 62 a, 33619 Bielefeld, Telefon: 05 21 / 9 11 11-0, Telefax: 05 21 / 10 96 96
Internet: www.klocke-verlag.de, E-Mail: info@klocke-verlag.de
1. Auflage 2001

Nachdruck, auch auszugsweise, nur mit Genehmigung des Verlages.
Alle Rechte vorbehalten, insbesondere die der Übersetzung, Vervielfältigung,
Übertragung durch Bild- oder Tonträger, Mikroverfilmungen oder Übernahme in Datensysteme.

Titelfoto:
Stefan von Stengel

Fotos:
Ydo Sol, Klaus Lorke, Jürgen Gutowski, Martina Gutowski, Ulrich Helweg, Freddy Peterburs

Texte:
Thomas Klocke, Günter Ned,
Jürgen Gutowski, Gundula Luig, Sabine Herder, Bernd Teichgräber

Art Direction:
Nicole Lucas

Grafische Gestaltung:
Sabina Winkelnkemper, Thomas Kacza, Sabine Flöter, Manuela Kley

Lithographie:
Klocke Medienservice: Holger Schönfeld, Werner Busch

Produktion: Claudia Schwarz

Vertrieb: Stephan Klocke

Druck: Graphischer Betrieb
Ernst Gieseking GmbH, Bielefeld

Gedruckt auf Profimago

Printed in Germany

ISBN-Nr. 3-934170-09-9

Golf in Andalusien

ALMENARA
16

KEMPINSKI RESORT ESTEPONA
26

LAS DUNAS
36

Golf auf Mallorca

OFRA HOTEL
48

ARABELLA SHERATON SON VIDA
56

Dorint Golf Resort & Spa
64

Reserva Rotana
72

Golf an der Algarve

Quinta do Lago
86

Vila Joya
94

Vila Vita Parc
102

Golf in Dubai
BURJ AL ARAB
118

Golf in Südafrika
FANCOURT
130

Golf in Mexiko
LAS VENTANAS
140

Golf in South Carolina
LITCHFIELD PLANTATION
154

Golf auf den Bermudas
CAMBRIDGE BEACHES
162

Golf in Schottland
ST. ANDREWS
172

SKIBO CASTLE
180

LOCH LOMOND
188

Golf in Frankreich
LES BORDES
198

Golf in der Schweiz
GRAND HOTELS BAD RAGAZ
208

Golf in Deutschland
MARGARETHENHOF
218

SONNENALP
226

Golf in Österreich
SCHLOSS PICHLARN
238

REISEINFORMATIONEN
246

SPIELRAUSCH UNTER SPANI-SCHER SONNE

Blissful golf under the Spanish sun

GOLF IN ANDALUSIEN

Nicht ohne Grund wird die Südküste Spaniens, die Costa del Sol, auch Costa del Golf genannt. Auf über 70 Golfplätzen findet man reichlich Platz für meisterhafte Birdies und Eagles. Erfahrene Golfer aus der ganzen Welt treffen sich vor allem am westlichen Küstenabschnitt, der mit über 40 Kursen als das europäische Golferparadies schlechthin gilt. Geprägt von der faszinierenden andalusischen Landschaft, phantastischen Ausblicken auf die Küste von Afrika und die Felsen von Gibraltar und jeder Menge spannenden Greens hat jeder Platz seinen ganz eigenen Charakter. Und wie es sich für ein richtiges Paradies gehört, scheint hier natürlich auch die Sonne, und das über 3000 Stunden im Jahr. So kann man auch im Winter ungehemmt sein Handicap verbessern.

It's not for nothing that the south coast of Spain, the Costa del Sol, is also known as the Costa del Golf. There is plenty of space on more than 70 courses for masterly birdies and eagles. Experienced golfers from all over the world meet primarily on the western part of the coast which has 40 golf courses and is anyhow known as the European golf paradise. The fascinating Andalusian landscape characterizes them all. The fantastic views of the African coast and the rock of Gibraltar and any number of demanding greens lend each course its distinctive character. And, as befits a heavenly place, the sun shines for 3000 hours throughout the year so its possible to improve one's handicap in winter too.

Der Golfplatz von Almenara ist spektakulär, die Höhenunterschiede sind gewaltig, man spielt vor einem Panorama aus Gebirgen und Wäldern mit Blick bis zum Meer.
The Almenara golf-course is spectacular and the differences in altitude are massive. One plays against a panoramic backdrop of mountains and forests with a fantastic view to the sea.

Abschlag an der Costa del Golf
Tee-off on the Costa del Golf

ALMENARA
GOLF HOTEL & SPA

Text: Jürgen Gutowski • Fotos: Jürgen & Martina Gutowski

The eternal interplay of light and shade, the dazzling brightness and the deep violet are integral parts of the beautiful scenery which has given the glorious coastline of Andalusia its names – Costa del Sol, Costa de la Luz. The lives of countless artists, Chagall, Miró, Dalí have been influenced by this sunny part of the world around which winter makes a detour. Even the airport at Malaga has been named after Picasso and is traditional-

Andalusische Poesie – das ewige Wechselspiel aus Licht und Schatten, aus gleißender Helle und violetter Dunkelheit, hat dieser Küste ihre strahlenden Namen gegeben: Costa del Sol, Costa de la Luz. Unzählige Maler sind von diesem Sonnenland, um das sogar der Winter einen Bogen macht, ihr Leben lang beeinflusst geblieben: Chagall, Miró, Dalí – nach Picasso wurde gar der Airport von Malaga benannt, traditionell das Tor zur „Costa del Golf", wie das südspanische Dorado des Golfsports mit seinen fast 50 Plätzen auch genannt wird. Hier im „Goldenen Dreieck des Golfs" setzt sich die Poesie fort: Die Spieler von Almenara wandern nicht einfach nur von Loch zu Loch, sondern sie schreiten auf exzellent gepflegtem Rasen vom „Mozartschwung" zum „Honig König Salomons", vom „Traum Josefs" zu den „Säulen des Herkules". Der Parcours ist spektakulär, die Höhenunterschiede sind gewaltig, man spielt vor einem Panorama aus Gebirgen und Wäldern, das in der Alten Welt seinesgleichen sucht. Dass man hier mit der Scorekarte gleich den Schlüssel für den Elektrowagen bekommt, macht Sinn. Die ersten neun Loch sind noch bequem zu bewältigen, dann beginnt die Golf-Erlebnisreise. Bergauf, bergab, über Schluchten und an Seen entlang. Wer nicht mit jedem Schlag schnurgerade ist, der sollte sich gleich ein Dutzend mehr Bälle einstecken! Der Platz ist besonders großzügig angelegt. Das Prädikat „Spitzenklasse" trifft zu, auch wenn hügelige Bahnen und sehr große, schnelle Greens mit vielen Wellen das ganze golferische Können herausfordern. man tut gut daran, die Soft-Spikes mitzubringen. Almenara, 18 Löcher, Par 72, wird übrigens derzeit auf 27 Loch ausgebaut, die ersten neun Bahnen dienen dann vorwiegend der Golf-Akademie. Erst 1998 eröffnet, gehört der von David Thomas gebaute „Spielplatz" mit seinen grandiosen Bunkers inmitten wunderschöner Gartenarchitektur neben dem benachbarten, weltberühmten Valderrama und drei weiteren Top-Grounds zu den

ly regarded as the gateway to the "Costa del Golf", the name coined for this golden corner of southern Spain because of its numerous golf courses, now nearly fifty in number. Golfers in this Golden Golf Triangle of Almenara don't simply wander from hole to hole but stride across beautifully cultivated lawns from the "Mozart's Swing" to "King Solomon's Honey", and from "Joseph's Dream" to the "Pillars of Hercules". The course is spectacular and the differences in altitude are massive. One plays against a panoramic backdrop of mountains and forests the like of which would be difficult to match in the old-world. Here you are given your key for the electro-buggy along with your scorecard, and it makes sense. The first nine holes are easy to negotiate but

then your golfing experience begins in earnest. Up and down hills, across ravines and alongside lakes – if you don't hit the ball with absolute accuracy you would be wise to take a dozen extra balls along with you. The course has a very spacious layout and really does deserve its top quality reputation. Even if the hilly fairways are very wide, and the greens fast and undulating, one's golfing skill is tested to the very limit and it is always a good idea to take along the soft-spikes. Almenara is currently an 18-hole par 72 course which at present is being extended to 27 holes. The first nine holes will then be used primarily by the Golf Academy. The course with its grandiose bunkers and beautiful garden architecture, was designed by David Thomas and only opened

Der von David Thomas designte Golf-Course von Almenara gehört neben dem legendären Valderrama bereits jetzt zu den Top-Plätzen Andalusiens.

This of David Thomas designed Golf Course of Almenara belongs beside the legendary Valderrama to the top places of Andalusia already now.

Schöner kann ein Tag nicht beginnen – Frühstück auf der eigenen Terrasse mit Blick auf den Golfplatz.
There is no better start in a day – breakfast on the own terrace with gaze on the golf course.

Verschlungene Gässchen führen durch die idyllische Hotelanlage.
Devoured alleys lead through the idyllic hotel.

Stilvoll und elegant – die Hotellobby.
Style and elegance – the hotel lobby.

in 1998. Located right next to the world famous Valderrama and three other first class courses, it is one of the best in the world. Obviously Almenara has the full range of practice possibilities including its own German and English-speaking golf academy with Astar swing video analysis equipment, a floodlit driving range, and putting and pitching greens. A pro shop rounds off the facilities on offer. In the middle of the golf course, high up on a green hill blessed with views of the fairways and the Mediterranean and surrounded by 11½ acres of gardens with olive and eucalyptus trees, is a sunny little village where the Andalusian style bungalows of the Almenara Golf Hotel welcome their guests. Going past a waterfall, little lakes and a spacious pool landscape are properly surfaced little access roads lined with orange trees heavy with fruit which lead to each of the hotel's 150 houses – including the ten suites with two bedrooms and a separate living room. Although the hotel has four-star status, the interiors would certainly do credit to some five star establishments. The unpretentious simplicity of the furnishings which have a modern, ethnic look have been carefully thought out to the very last detail, and many there are. The bathroom mirror doesn't steam over because it is heated, a feature only found elsewhere in hotels like the Oriental in Bangkok, and the air conditioning can be personally adjusted to regulate heat or reduce it. There are three telephones and a

besten der Welt. Klar, auch an Übungsmöglichkeiten fehlt es Almenara nicht, eine eigene deutsch- und englischsprachige Golfschule mit Astar-Video-Equipment zur Durchschwunganalyse, dazu eine Flutlicht-Driving Range, Putting- und Pitching Greens in der Nähe des Pro Shop runden das Angebot ab. Mitten auf dem Golfplatz, hoch oben auf dem grünen Hügel, gesegnet mit Ausblicken auf Fairways und Mittelmeer, steht ein kleines sonnengelbes Dorf. Im andalusischen Stil inmitten eines 46 000 Quadratmeter großen Gartens mit Oliven- und Eukalyptusbäumen begrüßen die Bungalows des Almenara Golf

Hotels ihre Gäste. Durch gepflasterte Strässchen, an denen Orangenbäume reiche Früchte tragen, vorbei an einem Wasserfall, kleinen Seen und einer großzügigen Poollandschaft, erreicht man eines der 150 Domizile des Hotels, darunter auch zehn Suiten mit zwei Schlafzimmern und separatem Wohnzimmer. Obwohl offiziell ein Vier-Sterne-Hotel, gereichen die inneren Werte der Räume so manchem Fünf-Sterne-Haus zur Ehre: Die unprätentiös-schlichte Einrichtung im modernen Ethno-Look stimmt bis ins Detail, und derer gibt es viele: Der Spiegel im Bad beschlägt nicht, denn er ist beheizt, was man sonst nur in Häusern wie dem Oriental in Bangkok findet. Die Air Con dient wahlweise als individuell regelbare Kühlung oder Heizung, drei Telefone plus Modembuchse und der ins TV integrierte Internetzugang mit drahtloser Tastatur, die selbst Bett-Surfen erlaubt, erfüllen alle modernen Kommunikationswünsche. Gut bestückte Minibar, kinderleicht zu bedienender Safe, Haartrockner mit Powerluftstrom, Kabel-, Satelliten- und Pay-TV & Video – alles auch auf Deutsch und Englisch – eine TV-Playstation sowie Spot-Leselampen am Bett verraten, dass bei der Planung dieses Hotels der anspruchsvolle Gast kompromisslos im Mittelpunkt stand. Die beiden Twin-Betten sind groß und bequem, die Bettwäsche wird jeden Morgen gewechselt und jeden Abend

modem connection. Internet access is integrated into the TV which has remote control enabling you to surf the Internet from your own bed. The very latest in modern communication is provided leaving no desire unfulfilled. A well-stocked mini-bar, an easy to use safe, a hair dryer with power air flow, cable, satellite and

Die beeindruckende Wellnesslandschaft „Elysium" wurde nach den griechischen Inseln der Seligen benannt.
The impressive Wellness oasis "Elysium" was named after the Greek island of the blissful.

Die in unprätentiösem Ethno-Look gestalteten Zimmer lassen keine Wünsche an modernsten Komfort offen.
The rooms shaped in casual Ethno-look leave open no wishes at most modern comfort.

Die gesamte Anlage des Almenara Golf Hotel & Spa wurde wie ein andalusisches Dorf gestaltet.
The entire facility of the Almenara Golf Hotel & Spa was shaped like an Andalusian village.

pay-TV & video in English and German, a TV play-station and spot reading lamps attached to the bed are all features which reveal that the guest was the primary focus of all deliberations when this hotel was at the planning stage. The twin beds are large and comfortable, the bed linen is changed every morning and turned down every evening, the bath towels are huge and as soft as the bath robes which are available in various sizes. The bathing experience doesn't end there. The sparkling cascades of the "Showers of Sensations" in the Almenara Spa called "Elysium" after the Greek abode of the blessed, must be the most spectacular ever seen in Spain. To induce perfect harmony of body and mind there is a Finnish sauna, a Turkish bath, jacuzzi, warm and cold water pools, Kneipp baths, a body-building studio with the latest equipment and much else. What is more over 50 treatments using Sisley cosmetic products are on offer and are applied by a professional spa team managed by the expert Frauke Behrens. They include seven different massage techniques, eight kinds of facials, a whole range of body treatments such as body peeling, thalgo applications, cellulite treatment, algae and saline baths, see grass and mud packs, electrotherapy and aroma therapy baths.

geöffnet, die Badetücher sind riesig und genauso weich wie die Bademäntel, die in verschiedenen Größen zur Verfügung stehen. Das Badevergnügen setzt sich spektakulär fort mit „Showers of Sensations" und den wohl sprudeligsten Kaskaden, die Spanien bis jetzt gesehen hat, im Spa des Almenara, nach den griechischen Inseln der Seligen „Elysium" benannt. Zur Glückseligkeit tragen bei: Finnische Sauna, Türkisches Bad, Jacuzzi, Warm- und Kaltwasserbecken, Kneipp'sche Bäder, hypermoderner Kraftraum und vieles mehr. Rund 50 Behandlungsmöglichkeiten mit kosmetischen Produkten aus dem Hause Sisley werden vom professionellen Spa-Team unter der Leitung der Expertin Frauke Behrens außerdem angeboten, darunter sieben verschiedene Massagen, acht Formen der Gesichtsbehandlung, vielfältige Body-Treatments wie Body Peelings, Thalgo-Anwendungen, Zellulitebehandlungen, Algen- und Salzbäder, Seegras- und Schlammpackungen, Elektrotherapie und Aromabäder. Selbst ärztliche Untersuchungen und Schönheitsoperationen können vorgenommen werden. Das Hotel verfügt über drei Restaurants, eines befindet sich etwas entfernter im Almenara-Beach-Club am privaten Strand von Sotogrande: Im „La Cabaña", der ehemaligen Finca des legendären Gründers von Sotogrande, Joseph Mac Micking, kann man in gemütlicher Atmosphäre traditionelle andalusische und internationale Spezialitäten genießen. Vom benachbarten hoteleigenen Reitstall „Stables" können die Gäste zum Ausritt am Strand starten. Oder man macht sich von hier auf den Weg zu den beiden Restaurants auf dem Hotelgelände. Im „Vein Tee Ocho", ein informelles Bistro mit

Das Gourmet-Restaurant steckt den anspruchsvollen Rahmen für die erlesene mediterrane Küche.
The gourmet restaurant puts the selective framework for the exquisite mediterrane cuisine.

einer geräumigen Panoramaterrasse, direkt oberhalb der Greens gelegen und den ganzen Tag geöffnet, genießt man leichte italienische und spanische Ciabattas, Salate, Tortillas, Nudelgerichte und Steaks. Um 19 Uhr öffnet dann das Gaia Restaurant im ersten Stock des Hauptgebäudes die Pforten zum Dinieren im edlen Ambiente festlich gedeckter Tische zwischen Säulen in zarten Rotbrauntönen und hohen kirchenähnlichen Rundfenstern, die den Blick auf die Kaskaden vor der Lobby und die hohen Königspalmen freigeben. An der Wand finden sich Beispiele der berühmten andalusischen Fliesenkunst, weiches Licht aus kunstvoll arrangierten schlanken Lampenschirmen und Kerzen beleuchten die gediegene Atmosphäre des mediterranen Lukulliums, leise Musik umspielt die Gäste, die es sich bei Königsgarnelen, Hirschfilet, Seezungenrouladen oder japanischen Thunfischsteaks bis spät in den Abend gut gehen lassen. Das Servicepersonal ist, wie auch an der Rezeption, in der Bar und beim Housekeeping, aufmerksam, dezent und ausgesprochen freundlich. Almenara – eine andalusische Poesie aus Genuss, Gesundheit und Golf.

Medical checks and cosmetic surgery are also available. The hotel has three restaurants, one of them a short distance away at the Almenara Beach Club on a private beach of Sotogrande. At the "La Cabaña", the old finca that once belonged to Joseph Mac Micking, the legendary founder of Sotogrande, one can relish traditional Andalusian cuisine and international specialities in a cosy atmosphere. The neighbouring hotel has its own riding stables called the Stables, a good starting point for a ride along the beach. Alternatively, guests can make their way from here to the two restaurants in the hotel grounds. The informal "Vein Tee Ocho" bistro which is open all day long has a spacious panorama terrace overlooking the greens, and serves light Italian food and Spanish ciabattas, salads, tortillas, pasta dishes and steaks. The Gaia Restaurant on the first floor of the main building has a very distinguished ambience and opens its doors for dinner at 7 p.m. Its beautifully laid tables are placed between pastel-coloured red-brown pillars, and the high church-like circular windows afford a view of the cascades in front of the lobby and the tall palm trees. The walls are decorated with examples of the famous Andalusian tiles and the tasteful Mediterranean surroundings are illuminated with soft light from artistically placed lamps and candles. Quiet music envelops the guests as they enjoy their king prawns, filet of venison, sole, or Japanese tuna steaks until late in the evening. The staff, whether at reception, in the bar or busy about the house, are attentive, discreet and extremely friendly. Almenara combines all that is good about Andalusia – enjoyment, good health and golf.

Im Almenara zeigt sich die „Costa del Golf" von einer ihrer schönsten Seiten.
At the Almenara appears the "Costa del Golf" at one of her most beautiful sites.

Kempinski Resort Hotel Estepona

Viva España

Andalusien, Spaniens sonnenverwöhnter Süden, zieht seinen besonderen Zauber aus feinsandigen Stränden, einzigartigen Naturerlebnissen, phänomenaler Kultur, temperamentvollen Nächten und aus über 40 Golfplätzen. Im vom Massentourismus noch weitgehend verschonten Estepona, Marbellas historischem Nachbarstädtchen, entführt das luxuriöse Kempinski Resort Hotel Estepona in die Vielschichtigkeit Andalusiens und auf herrliche Greens, die zu den schönsten der Welt gehören und bedingt durch das konstante Klima an der Costa del Sol das ganze Jahr über Golfvergnügen pur versprechen.

Estepona, the historical small town neighbouring Marbella, which is still relatively untouched by mass tourism, the luxurious Kempinski Resort Hotel Estepona entices visitors to explore Andalusia's diversity and the magnificent greens which are amongst the most beautiful in the world and, because of the even climate on the Costa del Sol, promise pure golfing pleasure all year long.

Text: Sabine Herder · Fotos: Ydo Sol

Die strahlend weißen Dörfer im Hinterland hängen wie Nester an den steilen Bergwänden.
The gleaming white villages in the hinterland cling like nests to the steep mountain walls.

Rechts: Im „Private Wing" kann man den Luxus des Grandhotels in den eigenen vier Wänden in Anspruch nehmen.
Right: In the private wing, Grand Hotel luxury can be enjoyed from your own four walls.

"Valderrama" – the very sound of this name makes golfers' hearts beat faster. The stunningly beautiful golf course in Andalusia is one of the best in the world and in 1997 was the venue for the Ryder Cup. This event was held for the first time in Europe on the greens of Valderrama.

„Valderrama" – allein der Klang dieses Namens lässt Golferherzen höher schlagen. Der wunderschöne Golfcourse in Andalusien gehört zu den besten Plätzen der Welt und war 1997 Austragungsort des legendären Ryder Cups. Der ursprünglich von Robert Trend Jones kreierte Kurs war mit Blick auf den Ryder Cup, der auf den Greens von Valderrama das erste Mal in Europa stattfand, von Seve Ballesteros, dem spanischen Champion, so umstrukturiert worden, dass manche der spektakulären Tees in die Golfgeschichte eingingen. Doch Valderrama ist nur einer von über 40 Golfplätzen – weitere befinden sich noch in der Planung – an der Costa del Sol, die seit dem Ryder Cup auch offiziell den aussagekräftigen Namen Costa del Golf trägt. Verwöhnt von über 3000 Stunden Sonnenschein im Jahr und einem überwiegend konstanten Klima sind die Freunde des kleinen weißen Balles in Andalusien das ganze Jahr über bestens aufgehoben. Selbst wer nur ein paar Tage Zeit hat, seinem Hobby zu frönen, schätzt den Süden Spaniens nicht nur wegen des Wetters und der schnellen Erreichbarkeit. In Andalusien knubbeln sich fast alle Attraktionen, die die Iberische Halbinsel seit Jahrzehnten an oberster Stelle der Urlaubshitliste halten: quirlige Badefreuden an sonnigen Küsten, grandiose Naturerlebnisse im bergigen Hinterland, phänomenale Hinterlassenschaften

Der anspruchsvolle 18-Loch-Course Valderrama ist durch den Ryder Cup zur Golflegende geworden.
The demanding 18-hole course at Valderrama became a golfing legend as a result of the Ryder Cup.

der Mauren, temperamentvolle Fiestas, herrliche Greens und dazwischen – immer wieder Raum für stillen Genuss und Entspannung.

„Individuelle Entspannung für die Gäste", dies ist auch die oberste Prämisse des Geschäftsführenden Direktors Willi Dietz, auf die er sein engagiertes Team seit der Eröffnung des Kempinski Resort Hotels Estepona im März 1999 eingeschworen hat. Die außergewöhnliche „Hardware" dafür gab ihm der Architekt Melvin Villaroel an die Hand. Villaroel ist für die Integration seiner Projekte in die natürliche Umgebung weit über Spaniens Grenzen hinaus bekannt und so fügt sich auch das Kempinski am Stadtrand von Estepona, Marbellas historisches Nachbarstädtchen, trotz seiner Größe harmo-

The course, which was originally created by Robert Trend Jones, was restructured by Spanish champion Seve Ballesteros for the Ryder Cup in such a way that many of the spectacular tees entered golfing history. But Valderrama is only one of forty golf courses (and more or being planned) on the Costa del Sol, which since the Ryder Cup is also officially referred to as the Costa del Golf, a sobriquet which speaks volumes. Basking in more than 3,000 hours of sunshine a year and with a predominantly even climate, Andalusia is an ideal venue for golf fans all through the year. Even those with only a few days to spare for their hobby value the South of Spain not only for its weather but also for the speed with which it can be reached. Andalusia combines almost all the attractions which have kept the Iberian Peninsula at the top of the holiday favourites list for decades: exhilarating bathing on sunny costs, natural grandeur in the mountainous hinterland, a phenomenal heritage from the Moors, lively fiestas, magnificent greens, yet always room for quiet enjoyment and relaxation between times. "Individual relaxation for the guests" is the key priority of the Managing Director Willi Dietz, to

18-Löcher mit Tücken: Almenara in Sotogrande.
A treacherous 18 holes: Almenara in Sotogrande.

Spektakuläre Aussichten auf das Mittelmeer und die Felsen von Gibraltar begleiten das Spiel auf dem Golfplatz Alcaidesa in San Roque.
Spectacular views of the Mediterranean and the Rock of Gibraltar are the backdrop for a game on the Alcaidesa golf course in San Roque.

HIDEAWAYS 29

Auf der Terrasse der Lobby Bar genießt man den Tag.
Savouring the day on the terrace of the Lobby Bar.

which his committed team has been sworn since the opening of the Kempinski Resort Hotel Estepona in March 1999. The outstandingly attractive setting for this was provided by the architect Melvin Villaroel, who is famous far beyond the borders of Spain for the integration of his projects in the natural surroundings. On the edge of Marbella's historical neighbour town of Estepona, the Kempinski – despite its size – blends harmoniously into the coastal landscape of the Costa del Sol, and the colours of Andalusia set the tone of the exterior as well as the interior of the building complex. Even on

nisch in die Küstenlandschaft der Costa del Sol ein, und die Farben Andalusiens prägen nicht nur das Äußere des Gebäudekomplexes. Schon beim ersten Schritt in die Halle ist man von der einzigartigen, sehr stimmigen Atmosphäre des Resorts gefangen. Durchflutet vom Licht Andalusiens, eingerichtet mit edlen Möbeln und üppigen Pflanzen, öffnet sie sich mit großen Glasflächen zur Meerseite. Durch die Glastüren erreicht man die Terrasse der Lobby Bar, von

Eingebettet in den Garten Eden schillern die drei Außenpools wie wertvolle Türkise.
In their setting in the Garden of Eden, the three outdoor pools shimmer like precious turquoises.

Die Werke des Künstlers Stefan Szczesny durchdringen alle Lebensbereiche des Resorts mit Kunst.
Works by the artist Stefan Szczesny permeate all interior areas of the resort with artistic flair.

der man bei guter Sicht einen herrlichen Panoramablick über das Mittelmeer hinweg auf Afrika und die Felsen von Gibraltar hat. Zwischen dem hoteleigenen, einen Kilometer langen sauberen Strand erstreckt sich der Garten, ein subtropischer Traum von sieben Hektar. Tatkräftig unterstützt durch Jürgen Sauer, Initiator und Visionär der weitläufigen Anlage, hatte Villaroels schon in der Planungsphase sein besonderes Augenmerk auf die Gestaltung des Gartens gelegt. Über 1500 verschiedene Palmensorten waren in Containern aus der ganzen Welt gekommen, um hier eine neue Heimat zu finden. Im Einklang mit alten Olivenbäumen, unzähligen exotischen Pflanzen – auf die jeder botanische Garten stolz wäre –, Wasserfällen, weiten Rasenflächen und der Architektur hat er eine Oase geschaffen, in der die Gäste nur zu gerne verweilen. Hier im Garten Eden, umgeben von Palmen, Sonne und Meer, rücken selbst das angestrebte Handicap oder die kulturellen Highlights Andalusiens schnell in den Hintergrund (schließlich ist morgen

Frische Produkte aus der Region und ein Hauch Exotik erwarten den Gast in „The Restaurant".
Fresh produce from the region and an exotic touch await guests in the Kempinski Restaurant.

„Cuisine légère" nennt Küchenchef Markus Herbicht seine weltoffenen und leichten Zubereitungen.
Chef de cuisine Markus Herbicht calls his internationally inspired light dishes "cuisine légère".

auch noch ein Tag). Dies ist genau die richtige Einstellung, um sich von den versierten Damen im zentral eingebundenen Polly Mar Wellness Center einmal so richtig verwöhnen zu lassen. Auf 1000 Quadratmetern tragen der Fitnessraum, der beheizte Innenpool, tägliche Trainingsprogramme, das umfangreiche Massageprogramm, Thalasso Deluxe, Rasul und vieles mehr dazu bei, dass Körper und Geist wieder in Einklang kommen. Das Konzept der exklusiven Beautybehandlungen ist von der faszinierenden Landschaft und Natur Andalusiens inspiriert und verleiht ein frisches und strahlendes Aussehen, mit dem man leicht zum Star des Abends avancieren kann.

Um sich rundherum wie ein Star oder vielleicht eher wie ein verwöhnter spanischer Aristokrat zu fühlen, sollte man sich nicht zu spät in die bequemen Korbstühle auf der Restaurantterrasse niederlassen. Während man an einem erfrischenden Aperitif nippt, zeigt sich im weichen Abendlicht die Pracht des subtropischen Gartens und der feinsandigen Bucht von ihrer

their first step inside the lobby, guests are captivated by unique atmosphere and ambience of the hotel. Flooded with Andalusian light, lavishly furnished and beautifully decorated with luxuriant plants, it opens onto the sea through large windows. Passing through glazed doors they emerge on the terrace of the lobby bar, from which – if visibility is good – there is a wonderful panoramic view over the Mediterranean towards Africa and the Rock of Gibraltar. Between the hotel and its own spotlessly clean beach, which extends for more than half a mile, there is a dreamy subtropical garden covering seventeen acres. Actively supported by Jürgen Sauer, the visionary initiator of the extensive development, Villaroels placed particular focus on the garden design in the early planning. More than 1,500 different types of palm were imported in containers from all over the world to this new habitat. In harmony with old olive trees, innumerable exotic plants – which any botanical garden would be proud of – waterfalls, extensive lawns and the architecture of the buildings, Villaroels created an oasis in which guests love to relax. Here in the Garden of Eden, surrounded by palms, sun and sea, your target handicap or even Andalusia's cultural highlights are put in perspective: tomorrow is another day. This is exactly the right mood to get in tone in the hotel's Polly Mar Wellness Centre and relax in the expert hands of its female staff. With a floor area of around 1,000 square metres, fitness room, heating indoor pool, daily training sessions, extensive massage programmes, Thalasso Deluxe, Rasul and many more facilities, the Centre caters for your mental as well as your physical well-being. The exclusive beauty treatments provided are inspired by the fascinating countryside and nature in Andalusia: they ensure a fresh and radiant appearance which may well make you the star of the evening. If you want to complete the feeling of being a star or perhaps a spoilt Spanish aristocrat, you should arrive in time to secure a place on one of the comfortable rattan chairs

Auf der Speisekarte steht das, was die Saison zu bieten hat – vielleicht Langustinos mit Gurken-Tomaten-Tatar und Shiitakepilzen oder eine kross gebratene Rotbarbe auf Tomaten-Couscous und eingelegten Zucchinis.
The menu includes the best that the season has to offer – perhaps langostinos with cucumber-tomato tartare and shiitake mushrooms or a crisp pan-fried barbel on tomato couscous and marinated zucchinis.

Warme Farben und exklusives Interieur stecken in den luxuriösen Zimmern den Rahmen für anspruchsvollste Wohnkultur zum Wohlfühlen.
In the luxurious rooms, warm colours and exclusive interior design set the tone to make demanding visitors feel pampered.

Im Polly Mar Wellness Center sorgen ausgebildete Therapeuten mit Kosmetikbehandlungen, Massagen, Thalasso und Rasul dafür, dass Körper und Geist wieder in Einklang kommen.
The well-trained therapists from Polly Mar Wellness Center cater with beauty treatments, massages, thalasso and rasul for the mental as well as the physical well-being.

schönsten Seite. Und fast könnte man die Mauren, die vor über 1000 Jahren vom historischen Wachturm direkt neben der Terrasse die gleiche Aussicht hatten, ein bisschen bedauern, denn die Grünanlagen, die diesem Ort seinen besonderen Zauber geben, kamen erst durch die Visionen der renommierten Hotelgruppe Kempinski und des Initiators Jürgen Sauer hierher. Bevor man bei einem Glas Sherry die armen Mauren bedauert sollte man nicht versäumen, am Golfdesk mit María Uceda Muro ein Schwätzchen zu halten. Die liebenswürdige Gästebetreuerin ist im Resort die Muse aller Golfer: Sie kennt alle Plätze – für die wichtigsten bestehen ermäßigte Greenfees – persönlich, organisiert von den Abschlagszeiten bis zur Mietausrüstung alles rund um ungetrübtes Golfvergnügen – Insidertipps natürlich inklusive. Während María sich um lästige Details kümmert hat man Zeit, die Lobby noch mal ganz in Ruhe zu betrachten. Hier, wie im ganzen Haus, selbst in allen Zimmern und Suiten, hat der Kölner Künstler Stefan Szczesny mit über 100 keramischen Bildern, großformatigen Leinwandarbeiten, zahlreichen Grafiken, Keramikvasen sowie Malereien auf Glasätzungen dem Kempinski Estepona einen unverwechselbaren Stempel als Gesamtkunstwerk aufgedrückt.

Sobald der abendliche Aperitif beendet ist, trägt der versierte Service die Speisenfolge auf: Zweierlei von roten Gamba auf fernöstlichem Mangosalat mit Joghurtdressing, gebratener Seehecht mit Artischocken, Kaviar und Nussbutter, Kalbsrücken aus Avila im Bananenblatt auf rotem Curryschaum und Buddhistischem Gemüse und zum Dessert geeiste Ananassuppe mit Minzeis. Als „Cuisine légère" beschreibt Küchenchef Markus Herbicht seine weltoffenen und leichten Zubereitungen. Dass bei ihm nur

on the restaurant terrace. Sipping a refreshing aperitif, you can enjoy the views of the subtropical garden and the sandy beach at their best in the soft evening light. You might feel slightly sorry for the Moors – who took in the same view more than a thousand years ago from the historic watchtower – because the gardens which now look so magical were created only through the vision of the world-famous Kempinski Hotel Group and the initiator Jürgen Sauer. Before you start to feel too sorry for the Moors – as you sip a glass of sherry perhaps – you should

beste Zutaten zum Einsatz kommen versteht sich bei dem sternerfahrenen Saarländer von selbst. Die Liebe zu fernöstlichen Aromen hat er aus seiner mehrjährigen Tätigkeit in Thailand mitgebracht. Mutig, aber stets köstlich, kombiniert er das Mediterrane mit den bekannten und unbekannten Aromen Asiens, die auf jedem Teller eine perfekte Geschmacksharmonie eingehen. Wer eher die typische andalusische Mittelmeerküche schätzt kommt im Beach-Restaurant auf seine Kosten. Dort kann man bei Tapas & Co die ungewöhnliche Architektur des ganzen Gebäudes, die mit dem Preis „für die beste

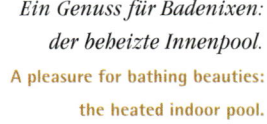

Ein Genuss für Badenixen: der beheizte Innenpool.
A pleasure for bathing beauties: the heated indoor pool.

Ein Kilometer feinsandiger Strand für die Hotelgäste ganz allein.
Hotel guests have 600 yards of fine sandy beach all to themselves.

Auf dem privaten Balkon ist der phantastische Meeresblick inklusive.
The fantastic sea view from the private balcony is part of the package.

Architektur eines Luxus-Resorts" ausgezeichnet worden ist, bewundern, und mit Blick auf den „Private Wing" mit seinen zwischen 60 und 200 Quadratmeter großen 89 Suiten kann man sich dem aufkeimenden Neid kaum verwehren. Die Besitzer der privaten Appartements, von denen leider nur noch ein paar zum Verkauf stehen, können in ihren eigenen vier Wänden den ganzen Luxus des Resorts zu Sonderkonditionen nutzen. Beneidenswert, zumal im angeschlossenen Medico-Resort ein internationales Fachärzte- und Therapeutenteam für diskrete und erstklassige Behandlungen in den Bereichen Orthopädie, Voice Chaping, Allergien, Hals-Nasen-Ohren-Heilkunde, Gynäkologie, Urologie, Dermatologie, Homöopathie und Akupunktur sorgt. Doch erst einmal im eigenen Zimmer angelangt, ist das Fünkchen Neid schnell verflogen. Denn das Zuhause auf Zeit glänzt mit großartigem Fünf-Sterne-Komfort: Klimaanlage, Sat-TV, Radio und Computer/Fax-Anschluss ebenso wie private Balkone mit postkartenreifem Meeresblick und anspruchsvollste Wohnkultur zum Wohlfühlen.

not miss the chance of a chat with María Uceda Muro on the golf desk. This popular member of the guest-service staff is a muse for all golfers: she is personally familiar with all the golf courses – reduced green fees can be arranged for the best courses – and organises everything to ensure trouble-free golfing from tee-off times to equipment hire, including insider tips. While María deals with the details, you have time to take a closer look at the lobby. Here and throughout the hotel, including all the rooms and suites, the Cologne artist Stefan Szczesny has placed his unmistakable overall stamp on the Kempinski Estepona with more than a hundred ceramic pictures and large-scale canvases plus numerous graphics, ceramic vases and paintings on glass etchings.

When you have finished your evening aperitif, the professional service personnel might present the following menu: red gamba served on a Far Eastern mango salad with yoghurt dressing, pan-fried sea pike with artichokes, caviar and nut butter, rack of veal from Avila in banana leaf with red curry sauce and Buddhist-style vegetables and, for desert, iced pineapple soup with mint ice-cream. The famous chef de cuisine Markus Herbricht, who comes from the German Saarland, describes his internationally-inspired light recipes as "cuisine légère". He uses only the finest ingredients and fell in love with Far Eastern aromas and flavours when he worked in Thailand for many years. Adventurous but always delicious, his recipes combine Mediterranean elements with familiar and unfamiliar Asian aromas, creating a perfect harmony of favour in every dish. The Beach Restaurant caters for those who prefer the typical Mediterranean cuisine of Andalusia. Here the unusual architecture of the building – which won the prize for the "best architecture in a luxury resort" – can be admired over tapas and other Andalusian specialities. The view of the private wing with 89 suites of around 650 to 2,150 square feet in size makes it hard to resist a growing feeling of envy. The owners of the private apartments, of which there are unfortunately only a few still for sale, are able to use the entire luxury facilities of the resort from their own four walls. Particularly enviable because in the adjoining medical centre an international team of specialists and therapists provides discreet first-class treatment in the field of orthopaedics, voice chaping, allergies, ear-, nose- and throat therapy, gynaecology, urology, dermatology, homoeopathy, and acupuncture. But when you arrive in your own room you will quickly forget the little flush of envy which you may have felt. Your home for the period of your stay is full of dazzling five-star luxury. Air-conditioning, satellite television, radio and computer / fax connection plus private balconies with postcard views of the sea. Living conditions which are bound to make you feel pampered.

Las Dunas

Traumresort im Golfparadies Andalusien
A golfer's paradise dream resort in Andalusia

Text: Günter Ned · Fotos: Klaus Lorke

Las Dunas ist eines der exklusivsten Luxushotels an der Costa de Marbella. Swimmingpool und Gärten reichen bis zum Strand, das Haus zeigt die Pracht einer andalusisch-maurischen Hazienda, am Horizont sieht man Nordafrika und den Felsen von Gibraltar – ein traumhaftes Refugium mitten im Golfparadies von Andalusien.

Las Dunas is one of the most exclusive hotels on the "Costa de Marbella". With views of North Africa and the rock of Gibraltar on the horizon and a swimming pool set in landscaped gardens right down to the beach, this magnificent house aptly displays the splendour of an Andalusian-Moorish hacienda – a true fantasy getaway in the golfer's paradise of Andalusia.

Traumrefugium im Stil einer maurisch-andalusischen Hazienda.
Dreamlike hideout in Mooresque-Andalusian hazienda style.

The spectacular success of Las Dunas since it's launch onto the hotel-scene between Marbella and Estepona, can be easily gaged by the fact that only three months after it opened in February 1996, Las Dunas, was already a member of the Leading Hotels of the World. A measure of how, since it's inception, Las Dunas has striven to ally itself with the sport of golf can be seen in the accolade of being the official hotel of the Ryder Cup, held at the famous golf course of Valderrama; this only six months after the resort opened. Since then this haven of style on the seafront has become a premier location for all those who seek to indulge their passion for that game with the small white ball in Andalusia – which, as its generally known, one can do all-year-round. Whereas with the onset of winter, rain and snow would make many golf courses in northern Europe inhospitable, the mild climate of southern Spain offers ideal conditions in which Las Dunas can spoil its guests with a tailor made all round service. The resorts' golf department, managed by Vivian Menton, is equipped to cater to any requirement, wish or demand of its guest golfers. This would start with trifles such as supplying those guests with complete set of first class equipment who chose not to bring their own down to Spain; these include high quality equipment by Callaway and other famous brands. Golf clubs and shoes are polished free of charge. Naturally other forms of assistance are more crucial. The region around Marbella enjoys the highest golf course density in Europe. Vivian attends and takes care of all reservations. She has excellent relationships with 28 regional golf courses including priority booking for the best tee-off times as well as a host of discounts. The scope of golfing opportunities range from Seve Ballesteros's course Alhaurin and Las Brisas (designed by Robert Trent Jones and also a past location for the Spanish Open and World

Wie spektakulär Las Dunas bei seiner Eröffnung im Februar 1996 in der Hotelszene zwischen Marbella und Estepona auftrat, wird schon dadurch deutlich, dass es bereits ein Vierteljahr später Mitglied der Leading Hotels of the World war. Und wie sehr sich Las Dunas von Beginn an dem Golfsport verbunden fühlte, zeigt eine andere Auszeichnung. Bereits ein halbes Jahr, nachdem die ersten Gäste kamen, war Las Dunas offizielles Hotel des Ryder Cups. Austragungsort: der Golfkurs von Valderrama.

Seither ist das stilvolle Refugium am Meer eine erste Adresse für alle, die in Andalusien ihrer Leidenschaft für das Spiel mit dem kleinen weißen Ball nachgehen – und das bekanntlich übers ganze Jahr. Während Regen und Schnee viele Plätze im Norden Europas unwirtlich machen, wenn der Winter kommt, bietet das milde Klima Südspaniens ideale Bedingungen. Las Dunas verwöhnt seine Gäste mit einem maßgeschneiderten Rundumservice.

Anlaufstelle ist das Golf-Department des Hotels. Leiterin Vivian Menton ist fit für alle Bedürfnisse, Wünsche, Anforderungen, die golfende Gäste mitbringen. Das beginnt bei Kleinigkeiten: Wer sein eigenes Equipment nicht mit nach Spanien schleppen will, kann sich bei ihr vor Ort komplett und erstklassig ausrüsten,

Das Las Dunas zeigt die Pracht einer andalusisch-maurischen Hazienda.
Las Dunas displays the splendour of an Andalusian-Moorish Hazienda.

Impressionistische Wandmalerein in der Gauguin-Halle.
Impressionist mural paintings in Gauguin Hall.

Cup), as well as the Links course of Alcaidesa (architects: Peter Allis and Clive Clark). The ultimate golfing experience can be found at Valderrama, one of the top championship clubs on the European continent. All courses can be reached from Las Dunas within 10–40 minutes. An especially close working relationship exists with the nearby La Quinta Golf & Country Club. Here golfers have the opportunity to train with a pro: La Quinta has it's own golf academy. Bookings can be easily arranged.

Las Dunas caters hand and foot to golfers, as golfers, but also as hotel guests. You will live, relax and regenerate yourself in a surrounding that can offer all of what one might expect of a luxury resort: stylish and comfortable interiors, a first class cuisine and appendant to it, especially important for sports

Die Rezeption im Trompe-l'œil.
The reception in Trompe-l'œil.

HIDEAWAYS 39

people, all the body care facilities like swimming pool, beach and spa. Architectually Las Dunas presents a reference point to the unique cultural landscape of southern Spain. The regions beauty and charm, exemplified in Marbella with its mix of styles, lies in its history. During the centuries of Muslim rule Moorish and Spanish architecture blended into what

auf dem Qualitäts-Level von Callaway und anderer renommierter Marken. Schuhe und Schläger werden gratis geputzt. Entscheidend aber sind natürlich andere Hilfen. Die Region um Marbella ist die Gegend mit der größten Golfplatzdichte Europas. Vivian kümmert sich um alle Reservierungen. Sie hat beste Beziehungen zu 28 Plätzen in der Umgebung, hat bevorzugten Zugriff auf Abschlagszeiten und kann reduzierte Preise anbieten. Die Spielmöglichkeiten reichen vom Seve-Ballesteros-Kurs Alhaurin bis zu Las Brisas (desigat von Robert Trent Jones, hier wurden schon die Spanish Open und der World Cup ausgetragen), vom Links Course Alcaidesa (Architekten: Peter Allis und Clive Clark) bis zum Platz von Valderrama, d. h. der absoluten Spitze auf dem europäischen Kontinent. Alle Parcours sind vom Las Dunas innerhalb von 10 bis 40 Minuten erreichbar. Eine besonders enge Zusammenarbeit besteht mit dem La Quinta Golf & Country Club in

unmittelbarer Nähe. Günstig für Spieler, die gerne mit dem Pro trainieren: La Quinta hat eine eigene Golfakademie. Termine können jederzeit vereinbart werden.

Golfer werden also im Las Dunas auf Händen getragen, als Golfer, aber natürlich auch als Hotelgäste. Das bedeutet: Sie wohnen, relaxen, tanken auf in einem Domizil, das alles zu bieten hat, was man von einem Luxusresort

Maurische Eleganz in den Zimmern und Suiten.
Moorisch elegance in rooms and suites.

Fitness in edler Ambiance.
Fitness in luxurious ambiance.

erwartet: stilvolle, topkomfortable Interieurs, erstklassige Küche, dazu – gerade bei Sportlern wichtig – alles, was den Körper pflegt, Swimmingpool, Strand, Spa. Letzteres präsentiert sich im Las Dunas mit ganz besonderem Profil.

Die Architektur ist eine Referenz an die einzigartige Kulturlandschaft in Spaniens Süden. Seine Schönheit, etwa der Reiz einer Stadt wie Marbella ist einer Stilmischung zu danken, die die Region von der Geschichte geschenkt bekam. Während der jahrhundertelangen Herrschaft der Muselmanen flossen maurische und spanische Baukunst ineinander und begründeten Andalusiens Flair. Ein Flair, von dem sich Architekt Cesar Leiva und Interior Designer Massimo Cocchi durch und durch inspirieren ließen, als sie Las Dunas bauten. Wie sich die Anlage mit ihren flamingofarbenen Fassaden, mit den subtropischen Gärten und dem großen Swimmingpool zum Meer hin öffnet, gleicht sie einer imposanten Hazienda. Und doch sind überall maurische Formen eingebaut, schmückt sich die Ambiance überall mit arabischer Handwerkskunst. Um nur ein Stilmittel zu nennen, das muselmanische Baumeister gerne einsetzten, das Acht-

became the Andalusian style and flair.

This same flair inspired architect Cesar Leiva and interior designer Massimo Cocchi when they built Las Dunas. The resort with its flamingo coloured walls, its subtropical gardens and large swimming pool bordering onto the sea resembles that of an imposing hacienda. But Moorish features have been incorporated throughout, creating an ambient decor with fine arabic craftsmanship. The octagon is one stylistic device Moorish architecs used to employ. It has been used in the spa, restaurant lido, entrée area; even the fountains by the pool present themselves as octagons. The décor of all 73 rooms and suites has a strong mediterranean flair. White walls provide a backdrop to a host of soft and vibrant colours complimented by the light filigree rattan furntiure. Trompe-l'œil-

Lichtvolles warmes Ambiente überall, bei Tisch wie für Mußestunden in üppigen Sitzecken.
A luminous, light drenched ambience greets you everywhere; at your table or relaxing in luxurient seating areas.

Bühne frei für andalusische Nächte.
The stage is set for Andalusian nights.

landscapes by Belgian artist Marie de Troostembergh, scattered throughout the complex, magically give the walls a transparent feeling. Luxurious too are the bathrooms of marble and Andalusian tiles complimented by Nina Ricci's luxurious toiletries. The epitome of comfort can be found in the suites Clematis and Alfonso XIII, which can on demand be transformed into one Presidential suite. The suite lies separate from the main building, has its own lift, and like so many corners of Las Dunas it offers breathtaking sea views. Even the restaurant Lido's octagonal salon opens onto a semicircular terrace where diners can enjoy a direct view of the rock of Gibraltar. Inside one is surrounded by floor to ceiling windows and one of Marie Troostberghs' red and gold trompe-l'œil. The Lido's kitchens are overseen by the accomplished 3 star chef Heinz Winkler, known for his Cuisine Vitale in Aschau, who has created Cuisine Vitale Méditerranéenne especially for Las Dunas. This cuisine prepared by resident chef Peter Knogl won the Lido a Michelin star award. Ewald Fichthaler caters to the connoisseurs of European-Asian cuisine with his East-meets-West creations in the Piano Bar & Bistro Felix, naturally also a tempting place for international drinks and cocktails as well. Guests who prefer to relax on the beach after their 18 hole rounds of golf need not do without appetising food. The beach club El Chiringuito would offer them a Mediterranean buffet, paella, grilled – and other Andalusian delicacies' s well as a view of the North African coast. The beach however is not the only place at Las Dunas where body and soul can be reunited. Many guests, golfing or not, count the spa as one of its major attractions. This is no surprise seeing the array of services on offer: gym, hydrotherapy, Dr. Schultes World of Beauty (inclusive an innovative technique of skin-rejuvenation) and

eck: Spa, Restaurant Lido, das Entree, ja selbst der Brunnen am Pool präsentieren sich als Oktogone.

Das Ambiente der 73 Zimmer und Suiten ist voll von mediterraner Atmosphäre. Weiße Wände setzen das kontrastierende Spiel von sanften und kraftvoll leuchtenden Farben in Szene. Für die Möbel wählte man leichtes filigranes Rattan, zauberhaft hier wie überall im Haus die Trompe-l'œil-Landschaften, mit denen die belgische Malerin Marie de Troostembergh die Wände transparent macht. Luxuriös die Bäder aus Marmor und andalusischer Keramik, ein erlesener Akzent die Kosmetikserie von Nina Ricci. Der exklusive Komfort erreicht den Gipfel in den Suiten Clematis und Alfonso XIII, die nach Bedarf zur Präsidenten-Suite verbunden werden. Sie ist separiert vom übrigen Hotel, hat einen eigenen Lift und wie so viele Winkel im Las Dunas einen phantastischen Blick hinaus aufs Meer. Das Restaurant Lido zum Beispiel. Der achteckige Salon öffnet sich auf eine halbrunde Terrasse. Wer dort speist und nach Westen blickt, hat den Felsen von Gibraltar vor Augen. Innen ist man von raumhohen Fenstern

Die Küchenchefs kennen den Gusto der Golfer und sind für mediterrane Sternecuisine so fit wie für Spezialitäten aus Andalusien.
The chefs know the tastes and gusto of golfers and are as prepared for Mediterranean star-cuisine as for Andalusian specialities.

Mediterrane Keramikkunst am Brunnen neben dem Boule-Platz.
Mediterranean ceramic art at the fountain beneath the boule square.

und von Marie de Troostemberghs rot und gold leuchtenden Trompe-l'œils umgeben. Was aus den Küchen von Las Dunas kommt, trägt der bekannten Tatsache Rechnung, dass Golfer gerne köstlich speisen. Den Küchenchefs ist dabei klar, dass sich auf den Fairways unterschiedliche Geschmäcker Appetit holen. Entsprechend vielseitig ist das kulinarische Profil, mit dem die Direktion des Hauses, Han C. A. Browser und Felix von Bodman, ihre Gäste verwöhnt.

Die Küche des Lido schmückt sich mit einem brillanten Supervisor. 3-Sterne-Cuisinier Heinz Winkler, berühmt für seine „Cuisine Vitale" in Aschau, kreierte für das Las Dunas eine raffinierte „Cuisine Vitale Méditeranéenne". Peter Knogl, Küchenchef vor Ort, hat dem Lido damit bereits einen Michelin-Stern erkocht.

Ewald Fichthaler ist der richtige Mann für Liebhaber der euro-asiatischen Küche. Schauplatz für seine feinen East-meets-West-Kreationen: „Piano Bar & Bistro Felix", ein verlockender Ort auch für internationale Drinks und Cocktails. Wer es vorzieht, sich nach seinen 18-Loch-Runden am Strand zu entspannen, der muss selbstverständlich auf Gaumengenüsse nicht verzichten. Im Beach Club „El Chiringuito" labt er sich am mediterranen Buffet, an Paella, Grill- und andalusischen Spezialitäten, die Aussicht bis zur afrikanischen Küste inklusive.

Der Strand ist nicht die einzige Gelegenheit, will man im Las Dunas Körper und Seele in Einklang bringen. Für viele Gäste, ob Golfer oder nicht, zählt das Spa zu den wichtigsten Attraktionen. Kein Wunder, das Spektrum kann sich sehen lassen: Fitnesscenter, Hydrotherapie, Dr. Schultes World of Beauty (unter anderem mit einem innovativen Verfahren zur Hautverjüngung), Regina Sol Kurklinik (Anti-Stress-Programme nach dem Motto „Vorbeugen ist besser als heilen", diagnostischer Gesundheits-Check-up, Serum-, Hydro-Colon-, Ozon-Sauerstoff-Therapie und vieles mehr). So empfiehlt sich Las Dunas als bezauberndes Refugium mitten im Golfparadies. Schon mancher Gast hat sich in den sonnenverwöhnten Flecken an der Costa de Marbella so verliebt, dass er sich am liebsten vom Hotelgast zum Residenten verwandeln würde. Auch da kann die Direktion inzwischen helfen. „Las Dunas Park" ist fertig gestellt, ein Areal mit Residenzen der Top-Kategorie. Idealer kann ein Golf-Fan nicht wohnen: In den eigenen vier Wänden, dazu verwöhnt von den umfassenden Wohltaten, die Las Dunas Beach Hotel & Spa im Angebot hat.

the Regina Sol health clinic (anti-stress programmes, diagnostic health checks, serum-, hydro colonic irrigation, ozone-oxygen therapy and many more treatments). Thus Las Dunas commends itself as an enchanting retreat set in a golf paradise. Some guests have been so taken with this sun-drenched resort on the Costa de Marbella that they would love to become residents. With the completion of Las Dunas Park, a complex of first class residencies, the management can now cater to these desires. No golfer could live in a more perfect way; surrounded by their own four walls but spoilt by the comprehensive benefits that the Las Dunas Beach Hotel & Spa has to offer.

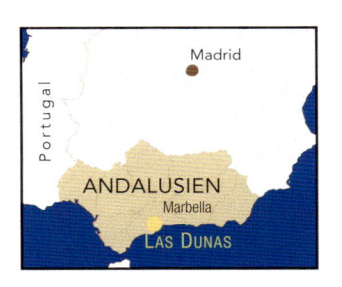

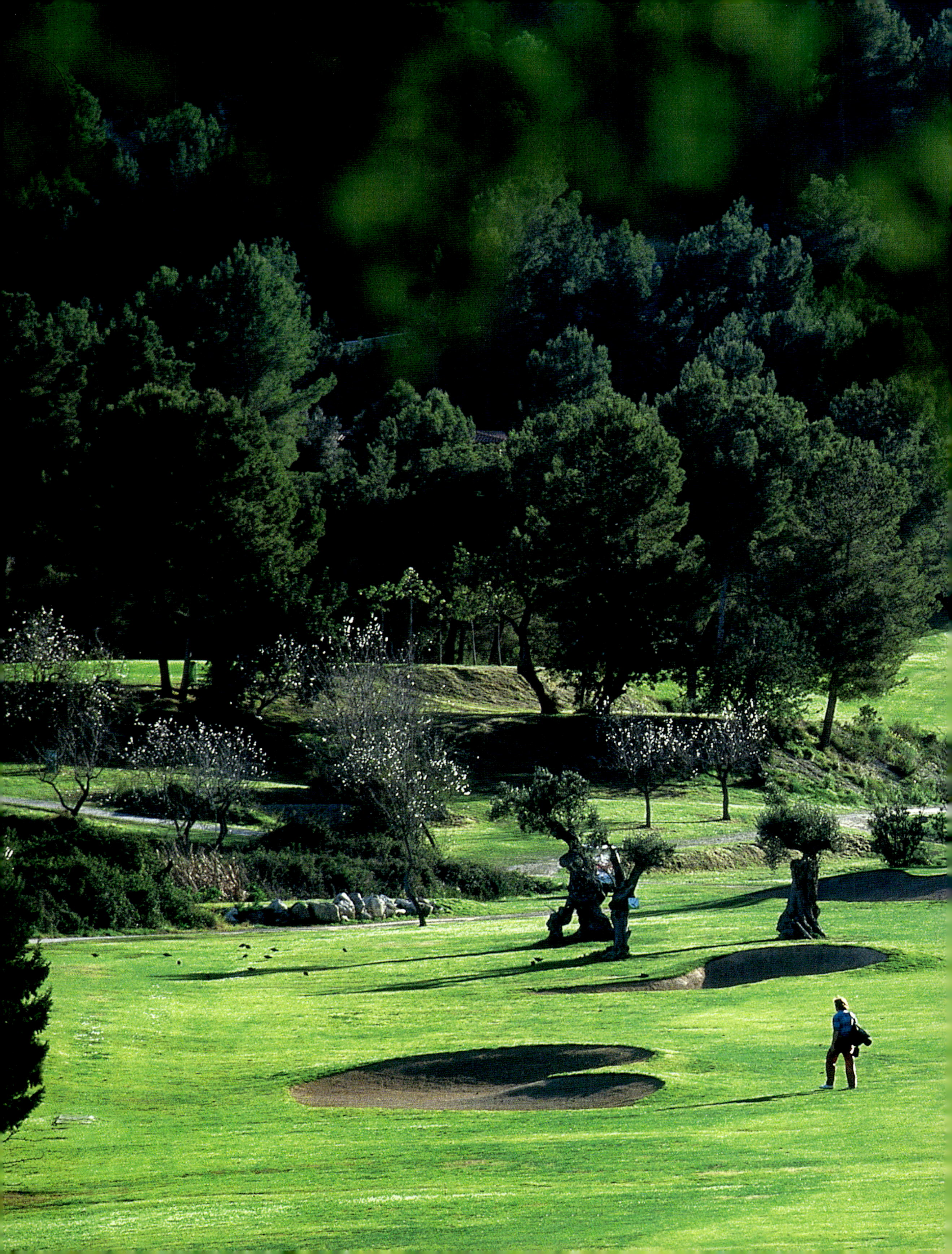

REIF FÜR DIE INSEL

Ready for the island

GOLF AUF MALLORCA

Mallorca entwickelt sich auch immer mehr zu einem Paradies für Golfer. Obwohl in den letzten Jahren zahlreiche neue Plätze entstanden sind, ist für viele der Golf Club Son Vida immer noch die Nummer eins der Insel. Der 18-Loch-Golfplatz, der 1962 von Fürst Rainier von Monaco eröffnet wurde, gehört zu den ältesten und traditionsreichsten Parcours der Balearen. Vier kleine Seen, alter Baumbestand sowie unzählige Mandelbäume und Palmen entlang sanfter Hügel geben ihm sein unverwechselbares Gesicht.

Majorca is fast developing into a golfers' paradise. While numerous new courses have appeared in recent years, for many the Son Vida Golf Club is still the number one course on the island. The 18-hole course which was opened in 1962 by Prince Rainier of Monaco is one of the oldest on the Balearic Islands and richest in tradition. Four small lakes, its old stock of trees and countless almond trees and palms on its gently undulating hills have given it an unmistakable profile.

Foto: Stefan von Stengel

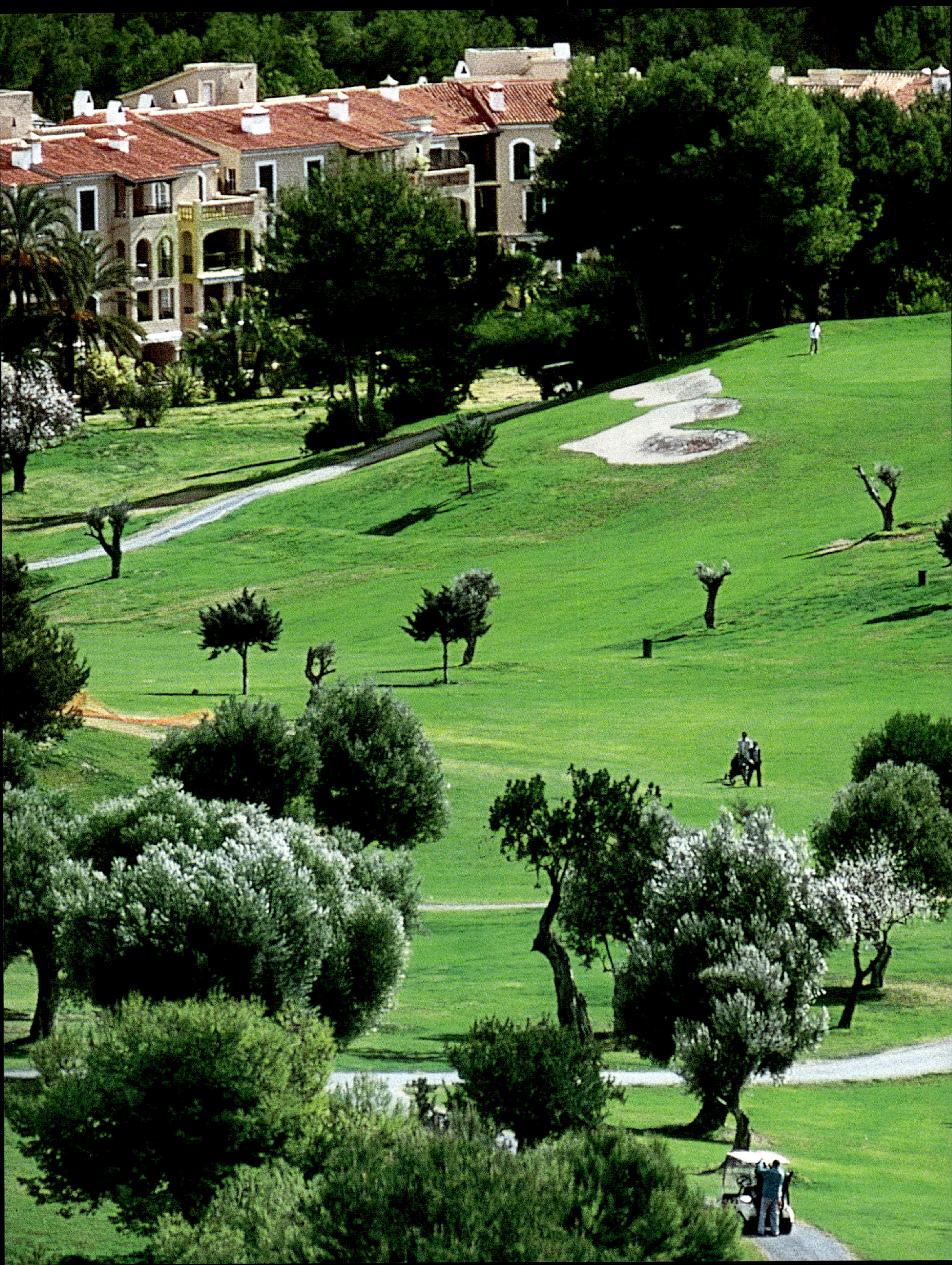

Spaniens König Juan Carlos ist Ehrenvorsitzender des Golfclubs „Real Golf de Bendinat". Mallorcas „königlichem" Parcours.
King Juan Carlos of Spain is honour president of the golf-club "Real Golf de Bendinat", Majorca's "royal" course.

Foto: Stefan von Stengel

Inmitten der königlichen Greens

Ofra Resort Hotel Mallorca

In the middle of Royal greens

Nur wenige Kilometer trennen die elegante Villenurbanisation Bendinat von Mallorcas Hauptstadt Palma und vom Promi-Yachthafen Puerto Portals. Sie liegt außerordentlich idyllisch in einem weitläufigen Tal mit altem Baumbestand an den Hängen oberhalb des Urlaubsorts Portals Nous und zählt zu den Hochburgen des grünen Sports. Hier, auf Mallorcas königlichem Golfplatz, dem Real Golf de Bendinat, schlagen Mitglieder aus ganz Europa ab. Und wer keine Villa in der Nähe besitzt, kann im komfortablen Ofra Resort Hotel mitten zwischen den Greens residieren.

Only a few miles lie between Bendinat, the elegant residential quarter of Palma, the capital of Majorca, and the yachting harbour of Puerto Portals. Its location is idyllic. Situated in a broad valley with old trees on its slopes, it overlooks the holiday resort of Portals Nous and has a superb reputation for golf. Members from all over Europe come here to play on Majorca's Royal Golf Course – the Real Golf de Bendinat. Those who don't already own their villa nearby can stay at the luxurious Ofra Resort Hotel located right in the middle of the greens.

Text: Gundula Luig • Fotos: Ulrich Helweg

Überraschend: Feinster Kolonialstil empfängt die Gäste in der Hotelhalle.
Guests enter a hotel lobby built in grand colonial style.

The elephant and two giraffes standing on guard at the entrance of the new Ofra Resort Hotel Mallorca signal what lies behind the door ahead. Obviously the animals are not real but bronze sculptures, popular symbols of Africa. Inside the hotel the guest is surrounded by African flair: dark mahogany, raffia covered walls, solid furniture with leather upholstery, old trunks, hunting trophies, and old photos and books. Even the paintings on the walls depict African scenes. They were specially commissioned for the hotel and painted by Adam Marian Pete, an artist who lives on the island. One would hardly have expected to find a grand colonial style hunting lodge here, yet it is precisely this that makes Ofra so delightful. To stand out from the others and to surprise again and again in a positive sense – this is its achievement. No wonder then that the hotel is not beside some beautiful beach or other, but right at the heart of the Royal Golf Course encircled by tees three, four and seven.

Ein Elefant und zwei Giraffen bewachen das Entree des neuen Ofra Resort Hotels Mallorca, stimmen schon von außen ein auf das, was uns hinter der Eingangstür erwartet. Natürlich sind die Tiere nicht lebendig, es handelt sich vielmehr um Bronzeskulpturen, symbolische Boten Afrikas und eindeutige Sympathieträger. Drinnen dann umweht einen das Flair des schwarzen Kontinents: dunkles Mahagoniholz, bastbespannte Wände, schwere Ledergarnituren, alte Reisekoffer, Jagdtrophäen, historische Fotos, Literatur – sogar die eigens für das Hotel gemalten Exponate des auf der Insel lebenden Künstlers Adam Marian Pete sind ein Bilderbuch Afrikas. Kolonialstil, den hätte man an diesem Ort nun wirklich nicht erwartet. Aber genau das macht die Konzeption des Ofra ja so reizvoll: Anders zu sein als die anderen. Immer wieder zu überraschen, im positivsten Sinne, versteht sich. Wen wundert es da noch, dass das Hotel nicht an irgendeinem schönen Strand, sondern direkt im Herzen des königlichen Golfplatzes liegt? Umrundet von Tee drei, vier und sieben. 65 Hektar umfasst die Gesamtfläche des Real Golf de Bendinat, dessen Ehrenvorsitzender Spaniens Monarch Juan Carlos ist. Vor allem wegen seiner zahlreichen, prominent besetzten Wohltätigkeitsturniere und den öffentlichen Veranstaltungen „Konzerte auf dem Rasen" macht der Platz immer wieder von sich reden. Vor 16 Jahren als 9-Loch-Anlage

Koloniale Elemente auch in der Architektur.
Colonial elements have been integrated into the architecture.

Umrundet von üppiger Blumenpracht.
Surrounded by an abundance of flowers.

The grounds of Real Golf de Bendinat whose honour president is the King Juan Carlos of Spain, encompass an area of 161 acres. The course has gained a high profile primarily because of its charity events, matches between celebrities and VIPs, but also because of the public Concerts on the Lawn. Established sixteen years ago as a challenging 9-hole course, it was developed into an 18-hole course in 1995 by golf architect, Martin Hawtree. It was his job to lay down the course across the broad valley with an old stock of trees, a valley now transformed by beautifully maintained tees, fairways and greens. The natural surroundings provide the golfer with a whole range of different conditions – gentle undulations, smooth areas, and fairly steep inclines. The river sand in the bunkers was replaced recently with

Elegant und vom Licht verwöhnt präsentiert sich das umgebaute Clubhaus des Real Golf de Bendinat.
The converted Club House of Real Golf de Bendinat is elegant and full of light

angelegt, hat man den sehr anspruchsvollen Kurs 1995 auf 18-Loch erweitert. Golfarchitekt Martin Hawtree oblag die Gestaltung des weitläufigen Tals mit seinem alten Baumbestand, das nun von gepflegten Tee's, Fairways und Greens durchzogen wird. Die natürliche Landschaft bietet den Spielern jede Menge Abwechslung, präsentiert sich mal sanft hügelig, dann wieder flach und geht mitunter ziemlich steil bergauf. Die Seesandfüllung der Bunker wurde jüngst gegen Flusssand vom Festland ausgetauscht. Das erleichtert das Herausschlagen

Überragt die königliche Golfanlage majestätisch: das Castillo de Bendinat.
The Castillo de Bendinat towers majestically over the golf course.

Einputten an Loch 11: Im Parque Natural wurde die Landschaft weitestgehend natürlich belassen.
Putting at the 11th. In the Parque Natural, the landscape was left untouched for the most part.

sand from the seashore because it makes hitting the ball out of the bunker considerably easier. The fifth hole is particularly challenging. Lying between high pines, it is very narrow, and certainly requires golfing experience and ability if one isn't to make a fool of oneself! It's why the handicap for men has been set at 28 and for women 36.

Jorge Pando who manages the course accompanies me in an electro-buggy on my tour across the grounds. We steer past Bendinat Castle towards the Parque Natural, the part of course which has been left virtually untouched, a challenging alternative for the golfer but paradise for flora and fauna. Many birds and plants have become established on the course, one of the

des Balls erheblich. Als besondere Herausforderung gilt das Loch fünf. Es ist eng, liegt zwischen hohen Pinien und man braucht schon Erfahrung und spielerisches Können, um sich nicht zu blamieren. So ist denn auch das Handicap bei Herren auf 28 und bei Damen auf 36 festgeschrieben. Jorge Pando, der Direktor des Platzes, begleitet mich im Elektrobuggy bei meiner Tour quer durchs Gelände. Ein Netz von Wegen schlängelt sich durch die Landschaft, vorbei am eleganten, neu ausgebauten Clubhaus, das mit umfangreichen Serviceeinrichtungen und einem Restaurant mit Blick über das 18. Green aufwartet. Vorbei am Schloss von Bendinat steuern wir zum Parque Natural, dem Teil des Kurses, der nahezu naturbelassen blieb. Eine anspruchsvolle Alternative für jeden Spieler und dazu ein Paradies für Flora und Fauna, denn viele Vogel- und Pflanzenarten haben sich auf dem Parcours angesiedelt. Mit ein Grund, weshalb der Real Golf de Bendinat

Öko-Golfplatz für Mensch und Tier: der Real Golf de Bendinat.
Eco-golf for man and beast – the Real Golf de Bendinat.

Öko-Förderung von der EU erhält. Diesem Selbstverständnis als naturverbundener Golfplatz entspricht auch das neue Streckenheft, das nicht nur dazu dient, die Spielergebnisse festzuhalten, sondern in Wort und Bild die dort vorkommenden Tier- und Pflanzenarten porträtiert.

„Eine feine Sache, die von unseren Gästen hervorragend angenommen wird", kommentiert Birgit Angele, Direktorin des Ofra Resort Hotels. „Wir gehören zwar nicht zum königlichen Golfplatz dazu, pflegen aber ausgezeichnete Kontakte dorthin. Unsere Gäste erhalten vergünstigte Greenfees sowie garantierte Startzeiten, wir organisieren den Transfer zum Clubhaus und unterhalten im eigenen Haus einen

Bagstore und Umkleidekabinen." Sollte jetzt der Eindruck entstanden sein, das Ofra wäre nur eine Residenz für elitäres Golfpublikum – weit gefehlt. Die luxuriöse Anlage ist ebenso ein ideales Domizil für den gepflegten Paar- und Familienurlaub. Für alle, die Ruhe und Erholung in außergewöhnlichem Ambiente schätzen, aber ebenso gern das Nachtleben Palmas genießen. Beides ist im Ofra möglich, denn Mallorcas quirlige Metropole pulsiert nur sieben Kilometer entfernt.

Anders als die anderen will sich das Ofra charakterisiert wissen. Und auch wenn es wie eine Plattitüde klingen mag – es stimmt. In völlig unverkrampfter Atmosphäre kommt die Wohlfühlstimmung von ganz allein. Kultivierte Lockerheit bestimmt die Regeln, gibt dem Hotel Persönlichkeit und seinen unverwechselbaren Charme, mischt sich unter das internationale Publikum wie prickelnder Champus in einen Cocktail. Fast fühlt man sich wie in einem privaten Zuhause bei Freunden, so herzlich und aufmerksam kümmert sich das Ofra-Team um seine Gäste. Sogar um die Jüngsten. Denen steht nämlich der Bendiclub offen mit eigenem Spielplatz, Kinderpool und qualifizierter Betreuung. Derweil lassen es sich die Eltern am großen Swimmingpool gut gehen, spielen eine Runde

reasons why the Real Golf de Bendinat receives a European subsidy for its promotion of a sustainable ecology. This ecological aspect is also featured on the scorecard which has information about the plants and animals in the grounds and illustrations. "It's a fantastic arrangement, and really appreciated by our guests", says Birgit Angele, General Manager of the Ofra Resort Hotel. "We don't actually belong to the Royal Golf Course, but we have excellent contacts with it. Our uests get reduced green fees and guaranteed starting times, and we organize the transfer to the clubhouse. We have a bagstore and changing rooms on our own premises."
Yet, any impression that this is a residence reserved for the golfing elite would be false. The luxurious hotel is ideal for couples and families who want a sophisticated holiday. In fact, it's perfect for all who welcome the peace and relaxation of an ambience which is out of the ordinary, as well as its proximity to Palma's nightlife. Both are available at Ofra because Majorca's pulsating capital is only seven miles away. Ofra wants to stand out, and even if it sounds like a platitude, it does. The feeling of well-being comes automatically in its relaxed atmosphere. It sets the tone, imbuing the hotel with its distinctive personality and charm. For its international clientèle it's like the tingle of champagne in a cocktail. The Ofra staff are so welcoming and attentive, within a very short time guests feel as if they really are at home with friends, even the youngest of them. Children have their own Bendiclub which has its own playground, children's pool and qualified child care assistants. In the meantime parents can go to the big swimming pool, play a round of golf or enjoy Ofra's wide range of activities. Alternatively they can visit the inviting Fitness & Wellness centre which is designed like a ship with teak planks, and adorned with the most wonderful trompe l'oeil painted by the artist

Viel Raum in den schönsten Farben: eine Junior-Suite.
Plenty of space and a most attractive colour scheme: a Junior Suite.

Wohnambiente vom Feinsten: die Mallorca-Suite.
The Mallorca Suite – an ambience of exquisite taste.

Teakplanken zieren den ansprechenden Wellness- und Poolbereich.
Teak boards line the sophisticated wellness and pool areas.

Superbes aus Schwaighofers Cuisine: Rotbarben-Lasagne mit Spinat an feiner Orangen-Zitronen-Sauce.

Schwaighofer's cuisine includes a superb lasagne with spinach and an orange-lemon sauce.

Viel beachtet bei den Mallorquinern: das Restaurant Es Romaní.

The Es Romaní restaurant is highly regarded by Marjorcans.

Viva Mexico! Die Poolbar Chumbo sorgt für Stimmung und kulinarische Abwechslung.

Viva Mexico! The Chumbo Pool Bar has a real atmosphere and provides culinary choice.

Carde Reimerdes. Her sailing ship on the high seas decorates the end wall of the attractive swimming pool. Portholes look out on to the modern fitness room. One floor down sauna enthusiasts can relish the pleasures of the Caldarium, the Hamam or the Finnish sauna, then cool off under one of the special showers or in the jacuzzi. The guest can then relax on a lounger in the quiet area where one can gaze in delight into the wise eyes of the many dolphins of the underwater wonderworld.

For those who feel inclined there is ayurvedic massage, or, if the sun isn't out, the solarium. On the other hand one could indulge in a whole day of beauty treatment in the capable hands of beauty specialist, Aileen Mees, at the Beauty & Hairdressing salon which she runs. Architecturally, the symmetry of the complex is very pleasing - three linked buildings grouped around the outdoor pool and surrounded by carefully tended gardens. The colonial style of the main building has a charm of its own. In contrast, the colour schemes of the 100 rooms and suites have been inspired by the bright hues of southern climes, blues, reds and greens. The exclusive furnishings, mostly made of brushed and limed pine, have been supplied by the Westphalian furnishing house of Ewald Beyer (Maison). The accommodation is spacious and the bathrooms tiled with local tiles are beautiful. The balconies and terraces, the Sat TV, modem connection, telephone, minibar and self regula-

Golf oder genießen das abwechslungsreiche Freizeitangebot des Ofra. Beispielsweise den einladenden, wie ein Schiff mit Teakholzplanken gestalteten Fitness-&-Wellness-Bereich, der von der Künstlerin Carde Reimerdes mit wundervollen Trompe-l'œil-Malereien verziert wurde. So wiegt sich ein Segelschiff in tosender See an der Stirnseite des reizvollen Innenpools. Bullaugen geben den Blick ins moderne Fitness-Studio frei. Eine Etage tiefer erwarten einen Saunafreuden im Caldarium, im Hamam und der finnischen Sauna, anschließend kühlt man den Körper unter einer der Erlebnisduschen oder im Jacuzzi, um dann genüsslich auf einer Liege im Ruhebereich zu entspannen. Dort blickt man in die Wunderwelt unter Wasser und schaut entzückt in die klugen Augen von zahlreichen Delfinen. Wer Lust hat, gönnt sich eine der ayurvedischen Massagen, tankt Sonne, wenn das Wetter mal nicht so mitspielt, im Solarium oder legt einen kompletten Schönheitstag ein. Im Beauty- und Friseursalon von Star-Friseurin Aileen Mees ist man in besten Händen.

In architektonischer Hinsicht überzeugt die Anlage durch ihre ausgewogene Symmetrie, gegliedert in drei Gebäude, die sich um den Outdorpool gruppieren, sowie von einem liebevoll angelegten Garten umgeben sind. Bezaubert das Hauptgebäude noch durch seinen kolonialen Stil, so kontrastieren die 100 Zimmer und Suiten mit ihrer strahlend frischen südländischen Farbwelt, mal blau, mal rot, mal grün inspiriert. Die exklusive Inneneinrichtung, überwiegend gebürstete und gekalkte Pinie, stammt vom westfälischen Einrichter Ewald Beyer (Maison). Großzügige Grundrisse, sehr schöne Bäder mit landestypischen Fliesen, Balkone und Terrassen, Sat-TV, Telefon, Modem-Anschluss,

Minibar und individuell regelbare Klimaanlage begünstigen den Wohlfühleffekt spürbar. Einen entscheidenden Beitrag dazu leistet ganz sicher auch Michael Schwaighofer mit seinem Team. Der österreichische Küchenchef hat sich bereits nach wenigen Monaten ein Stammpublikum für das Restaurant Es Romaní herangezogen. In einer Mischung aus mediterran-kolonialer Ambiance verwöhnen dort internationale Cuisine und natürlich die verschiedensten Facetten der spanischen Küche. Ob Jabugo-Schinken mit Tomaten-Ramilette, Olivenöl, mallorquinischem Brot und Knoblauch, ob Suprême vom Steinbutt mit Rotweinsauce und Haselnussöl oder Confit vom Spanferkel im Ofen gebacken an Honig-Thymian-Sauce – die Zubereitungen sind exzellent, der Service aufmerksam zuvorkommend, aber unaufdringlich. Ganz andere Stimmung, nämlich die einer mexikanischen Bar, erleben Gäste im Poolrestaurant Chumbo. An rustikalen Holztischen sitzend, mundet Herzhaftes wie Tapas Variadas, köstliche Spare Ribs mit Barbecuesauce oder eine der zahlreichen Tex-Mex-Spezialitäten: Quesadilla, Burrito & Co. Besonders stimmungsvoll wird es abends im Chumbo, wenn Barkeeper Andreas Rousseau, der zweimalige Weltmeister im Cocktailmixen, seinen Auftritt hat. Schon allein seine Zubereitungsrituale sind einen Besuch wert, weshalb die Ofra-Gastronomie auch bei Mallorquinern sehr angesagt ist. An den Mixkünsten Rousseaus kann man sich auch in der gediegenen Golf-Bar im Hauptgebäude erfreuen. Bei Livemusik, einem Gin Fizz oder Planters Punch kommt man leicht ins Fachsimpeln. Und ganz gewiss wird man morgen sein Handicap verbessern.

Gediegen und ein wenig Englisch: In der Golf-Bar werden die besten Drinks gemixt.
The Golf Bar where the best drinks are mixed is quiet English in style and rather sedate.

ted air-conditioning all enhance the feeling of well-being. An especially important part in all this is played by Michael Schwaighofer and his team. It has only taken a few months for the Austrian chef to attract a regular clientèle to the Es Romani restaurant who love the Mediterranean-colonial ambience of the place, and relish the international cuisine and the wide variety of Spanish dishes. Whether the Jabugo ham and tomato ramilette, olive oil, Majorcan bread and garlic, the turbot suprême with a red wine sauce and hazel nut oil, or the baked marinated sucking pig with a honey-thyme sauce, all dishes are superb. The discreet and attentive service is also excellent. The atmosphere at the Chumbo pool restaurant which is like a Mexican bar, is quite different. Guests sit at rustic wooden tables eating their tasty tapas variadas or delicious spare ribs with barbecue sauce. Also on offer are numerous Tex-Mex specialities – quesadilla, burrito & Co. The Chumbo has a fantastic atmosphere in the evenings when barkeeper, Andreas Rousseau, twice World Champion in cocktail mixing, arrives on the scene. His cocktail-mixing rituals alone merit a visit, indeed it is one of the reasons why Ofra gastronomy is popular amongst Marjorcans themselves. Rousseau can also be seen doing his thing at the sedate Golf Bar in the main building. It's so easy to talk shop against a background of live music, and it goes without saying that one's handicap will improve in the morning.

Charmante Gastgeberin: Direktorin Birgit Angele.
A charming hostess. General Manager Birgit Angele.

Sein Stil kommt bestens an: Küchenchef Michael Schwaighofer.
Chef Michael Schwaighofer – his personal style is much appreciated.

Golfurlaub unter Palmen
ArabellaSheraton Golf Hotel Son Vida

A golf holiday beneath the palms

Das Fünf-Sterne ArabellaSheraton Golf Hotel Son Vida auf Mallorca liegt oberhalb der Inselhauptstadt Palma im noblen, landschaftlich bezaubernden Villenvorort Son Vida. Das im Stil spanischer Herrensitze errichtete Haus wurde vom spanischen Tourismusministerium zum besten Hotel der Balearen gekürt.

The five-star ArabellaSheraton Golf Hotel Son Vida in Majorca is located above Palma, the island's capital, in the enchanting and exclusive residential area of Son Vida. The house, built in the style of a Spanish manor house, has been named by the Spanish Ministry of Tourism as the best hotel in the Balearic Islands.

Text: Thomas Klocke • Fotos: Arabella Sheraton

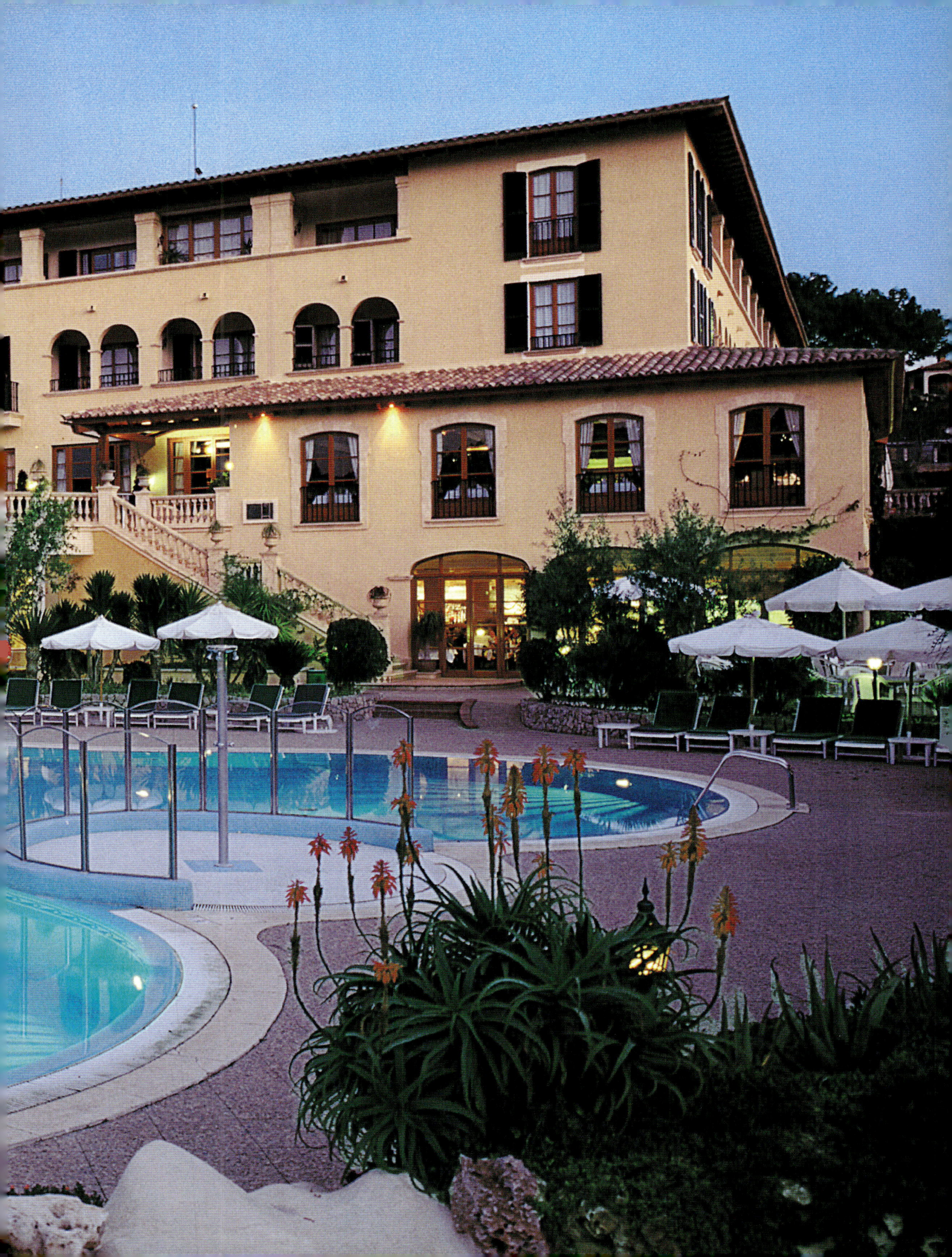

When you are playing the last nine holes on the Son Vida golf course – the gem among the golf courses of Majorca – and gradually approaching the Club House along glorious fairways, the whole beauty of the ArabellaSheraton Golf Hotel hits you at one glance. Uniquely surrounded by about 3 acres of garden with palms, carob trees and olive groves, the hotel with its typical Mediterranean architecture harmoniously blends into its Mediterranean background. The 93 rooms are on two floors, of these 24 are suites with one Presidential Suite. Guests can choose from nine different kinds of room with exquisite, high class interiors and thoughtful details. SAT TV, safe, self-regulated air-conditioning, hairdryer and trouser press are all conveniences provided as a matter

*B*espielt man den Golfplatz Son Vida, Mallorcas Perle unter den Golfplätzen der Balearen, und nähert sich auf den zweiten neun Löchern auf reizvollen Bahnen wieder dem Clubhaus, so genießt man die ganze Schönheit des Arabella-Sheraton Golf Hotels auf einen Blick: umgeben von einem einzigartigen, 13 000 Quadratmeter großen Garten mit Palmen, Johannisbrotbäumen und Olivenhainen schmiegt sich das Hotel mit seiner mittelmeertypischen

Gourmet-Restaurant „Plat d'Or" bietet exquisite Mittelmeerküche und feine mallorquinische Spezialitäten. Im zweiten Restaurant, dem „Foravila", genießt man auf der Terrasse den Blick auf den Pool und den Golfplatz. Hier werden Tapas, Snacks und sonstige kleine Köstlichkeiten serviert. Zum Aperitif oder zum Absacker trifft man sich bei Barchef Luis Ochoa, der in der Bar „Portico" mit ständig guter Laune und vorzüglichen Cocktails für beste Urlaubsstimmung sorgt.

Nach sportlicher Anstrengung ist das auf fernöstliche und Naturkosmetik spezialisierte Schönheitsparadies „Beauty & Holistic" genau die richtige Adresse, um Körper und Geist zu entspannen. Bei Aromatherapie mit Körpermassage kann man auf einer entspannenden Duftreise durch mediterrane Gärten

of course. The exclusive multi award-winning restaurant "Plat d'Or" serves delectable Mediterranean cuisine and fine Majorcan specialities. From the terrace of the second restaurant, the "Foravila", one has a view of the pool and the golf course. It serves tapas, snacks and other little delicacies. Guests meet up in the "Portico" bar for an aperitif or drinks served by the ever cheerful head barman, Luis Ochoa, whose excellent cocktails keep everyone in holiday mood.
After having exhausted oneself with sport, the "Beauty & Holistic" treatment centre which concentrates on Far Eastern and natural

Bauweise harmonisch in die mediterrane Umgebung ein. Über zwei Stockwerke verteilen sich 93 Zimmer, davon 24 Suiten und eine Präsidentensuite. Gäste haben die Wahl zwischen neun verschiedenen Zimmertypen mit erlesenem, hochwertigen Interieur mit liebevollen Details. Sat-TV, Safe, individuell regelbare Klimaanlage und Heizung, Fön und Hosenbügler gehören zu den selbstverständlichen Annehmlichkeiten. Das exklusive, mit vielfachen Auszeichnungen prämierte

treatments is just the right place to relax body and mind. One really can let go while one is pampered by aromatherapy and getting a complete body massage which feels like a restful aromatic journey through Mediterranean gardens fragrant with the perfume of lavender, balm and mimosa. Or one can succumb to the magic of oriental perfumes like ylang-ylang, mochus, pachuli or jasmine. General health can be improved by Dr. Edward Bach's therapy of flower essences. It prescribes taking drops of flower essences to stabilize the mood swings which trigger ill health. Other methods of relieving stress and restoring inner harmony are also available, such as iris diagnosis combined with molecular massage, and the Japanese Reiki healing method. However, well tried and tested treatments are also available at the beauty farm such as electronic and manual lymph drainage, foot reflexology, shiatsu and much else. Complete beauty treatments are an absolute must, whether a facial, a manicure or anti-cellulite treatment which apply top products such as Shiseido and Mary Cohr. The range on offer is rounded off by a fantastic pool landscape with indoor and outdoor pools, separate children's pool, a sauna, solarium, steam bath and a whirlpool. Yet the ArabellaSheraton Golf Hotel Son Vida is not still the hotel of first preference for golfers on the island's just because it offers a wide spec-

mit Lavendel-, Melissen- oder Mimosenduft so richtig die Seele baumeln lassen oder sich durch die Magie orientalischer Düfte wie Ylang-Ylang, Jasmin, Moschus oder Patschuli verwöhnen lassen. Die Bachblütentherapie nach Dr. Edward Bach stärkt durch Einnahme von Blütentropfen die Gesundheit und gleicht Gemütsschwankungen als Auslöser von Krankheiten aus. Irisdiagnose kombiniert mit Moleculare Massage und die japanische Heilkunst des Reiki sind weitere Methoden zum Stressabbau und zur Erlangung neuer, innerer Harmonie. Daneben bietet die Schönheitsfarm auch bewährte Methoden wie elektronische und manuelle Lymphdrainagen, Fußreflexzonen- und Nervenpunktmassagen und vieles mehr. Obligatorisch sind komplette Beauty-Anwendungen von der Gesichtspflege über Maniküre bis hin zur Anti-Cellulite-Kur, die von so hochwertigen Marken wie „Shiseido" und „Mary Cohr" unterstützt werden. Abgerundet wird das Angebot durch eine traumhafte Poollandschaft mit Innen- und Außenpool, separatem Kinderbecken sowie Sauna, Solarium, Dampfbad und Whirlpool.

Das ArabaellaSheraton Golf Hotel Son Vida ist nicht nur wegen der vielseitigen Sport- und Freizeitmöglichkeiten für Golfer nach wie vor die Nummer eins auf der Insel. Hier hat man sich in allen Belangen auf die Liebhaber dieses Sports eingestellt, was bei den beträchtlichen Greenfee-Ermäßigungen oder gar einer kostenlosen Runde Spiel täglich in bestimmten Golfarrangements anfängt und mit den zahlreichen qualifizierten Golftrainern, die selbstverständlich perfekt deutsch sprechen, noch lange nicht aufhört. Mehrmals im Jahr können sogar Kurse bei Carlo Knauss, dem Bundestrainer des Deutschen Golf Verbandes, gebucht werden. Das Ausleihen kompletter Schlägersets, ein Pitch- &-Put-Platz, fünf hauseigene Quarzsand-Tennisplätze, ein Croquet-Platz sowie ein Jogging-Track setzen weitere Maßstäbe im sportlichen Angebot. Obwohl der Golfplatz Son Vida einer der schönsten der Insel ist, bei dem man vom 6. Tee einen herrlichen Ausblick auf die Bucht von Palma und auf die Kathedrale genießen kann, steht mit dem soeben eröffneten, ebenfalls firmeneigenen 18-Loch-Golfplatz „Son Muntaner", der ausschließlich den Hotelgästen und den Bewohnern der „Residencias Mardavall" vorbehalten ist, eine weitere attraktive Spielmöglichkeit zur Verfügung.

Das ArabellaSheraton Mardavall Spa & Resort setzt neue Maßstäbe im Mittelmeerraum

Im Frühjahr 2002 wird das Son Vida eine firmeneigene Konkurrenz bekommen: dann eröffnet in unmittelbarer Nähe zum mondänen Yachthafen Puerto Portals und direkt am Meer gelegen das zweite Fünf-Sterne-Deluxe-Resort der ArabellaSheraton Hotels auf Mallorca: das ArabellaSheraton Mardavall Spa & Resort. 126 Demi-Suiten mit 60 Quadratmetern, 12 Einzelzimmer mit jeweils 24 Quadratmeter und zwei Präsidentensuiten mit jeweils 200 Quadratmetern und Butler-Service lassen keine Wünsche unerfüllt. Durch die besondere Bauweise des Hauses – das Hotel wird aus vier getrennten Bauten bestehen – sind alle Zimmer direkt aufs Meer ausgerichtet und verfügen über großzügige, drei Meter tiefe Balkone.

Ein Gourmetrestaurant, ein Tagesrestaurant mit Showküche und eine Poolbar werden auch die anspruchsvollsten Gaumen verwöhnen, die Smokers Lounge wird zweifellos zum Treffpunkt der Cigaren-Afficionados avancieren.

trum of sports and leisure activities. It has tailored itself completely to the needs of golf fans, starting with greatly reduced green fees and sometimes a daily free round as part of some packages, to the numerous qualified golf coaches who of course speak fluent German. But it doesn't stop there. Several times a year it is possible to book courses with Carlo Knauss, national golf coach of the Federal German Golf Association. The possibility to hire complete sets of clubs, a pitch and putting green, five hotel silica tennis courts, a croquet lawn as well as a jogging track set new standards in the range of sports facilities.

While it is true that the Son Vida golf course is one of the most beautiful on the island affording heavenly views over the Bay of Palma and the cathedral, the recently opened 18-hole Son Muntaner golf course belonging to the same company provides a further attractive opportunity for golfers. It is however reserved for hotel guests and residents of the Residencias Mardavall.

The ArabellaSheraton Mardavall Spa & Resort
Setting new standards in the Mediterranean

In the Spring of 2002 the Son Vida will have competition, albeit from the same company because a second five-star deluxe resort of the ArabellaSheraton hotel group, the ArabellaSheraton Spa & Resort, will be opened very close to the smart yachting harbour of Puerto Portals. 126 demi-suites each with a floor area of approx. 645 square feet, 12 single rooms with 258 square feet of space and two Presidential Suites of approx. 2,150 square feet plus butler service leave nothing to be desired. Owing to the specific design of the building – the hotel will consist of four separate buildings – all rooms face the sea and will have spacious, three metre wide balconies. A gourmet restaurant, a restaurant for daytime with a show kitchen, and a pool bar will pamper the palates of even the most discriminating and a Smokers' Lounge will no doubt become the rendezvous for cigar enthusiasts.

The 51,000 square feet of spa and wellness area in the future deluxe resort will certainly be unique in the Mediterranean. The inner zone with an area of 13,000 square feet will be occupied by a beauty farm along with ten separate treatment rooms, a "temple of experience" with a sauna, a Hamam bath, various Kneipp baths, ice grottos, aroma showers, a liquid sound pool, a brine bath, a cardio-room and yoga room. Outside in nearly one acre of grounds, a heated freshwater pool

Einzigartig im Mittelmeerraum wird sicherlich der über 4700 Quadratmeter große Spa- und Wellnessbereich des künftigen Deluxe-Resorts sein: im 1 200 Quadratmeter großen Innenbereich reihen sich eine Beautyfarm mit zehn individuellen Behandlungsräumen, ein Erlebnistempel mit Sauna, ein Hamambad, verschiedene Kneipp-Bäder, Eisgrotten, Aromaduschen, ein Liquidsound-Pool, ein Solebad, ein Cardio- und ein Yoga-Raum aneinander. Der 3 500 Quadratmeter große Außenbereich lockt mit beheiztem Süßwasser- und einem Freiluft-Salzwasserpool. Der Schwerpunkt des Spa-Bereichs wird auf Thalasso-Anwendungen liegen. Mehrere Konferenzräume für bis zu 200 Personen, ein Business-Center und verschiedene Smart-Meeting-Rooms mit ISDN-Docking-Stations ergänzen das Angebot.

Damit man auch im Urlaub immer erreichbar ist, verfügen sämtliche Zimmer und Suiten über ISDN- und Modem-Anschlüsse. Direkt neben dem Hotel entstehen die luxuriösen „Residencias Mardavall", rund sechzig private Ferienwohnungen zwischen 160 und 320 Quadratmetern Größe. Die Bewohner der Appartements können sämtliche Angebote und Einrichtungen des Hotels mitbenutzen.

ArabellaSheraton Golf Hotel Western Cape

Ihre Kompetenz in Sachen Golf und Wellness stellen die ArabellaSheraton Hotels zukünftig nicht nur auf Mallorca unter Beweis, sondern auch im Golfparadies Südafrika. Rund einhundert Kilometer östlich von Kapstadt, an der größten Lagune Afrikas „Bot River", in der Nähe von Hermanus gelegen, öffnet im Frühjahr 2001 mit dem ArabellaSheraton Golf Hotel Western Cape ein neues Luxushotel seine Pforten. Dieses *hideaway* wird über insgesamt 145 Zimmer, darunter zwei Königssuiten mit 200 bis 250 Quadratmetern und zwei Präsidentensuiten, verfügen. Dazu kommt ein über 1 000 Quadratmeter großer Spa- und Wellnessbereich, ergänzt durch eine Außenbadelandschaft mit Wasserfällen in einer großzügigen Gartenanlage. Das Interior-Design ist so gewählt, dass der Gast sofort das „Out-of-Africa-Feeling" bekommt und sich mit dem Land identifiziert. Die dezenten Farben der Umgebung, eines der attraktivsten Naturschutzgebiete Afrikas, spiegeln sich im ganzen Hotel wider. Alle Zimmer geben den Blick frei auf die idyllische Lagune, die direkt vor der Tür liegt. Unmittelbar neben dem Hotel beginnt der 18-Loch-Championship-Golfplatz „Arabella Country Estate Golf Course", der bereits im Dezember letzten Jahres eröffnet wurde. Geplant vom südafrikanischen Golfplatz-Designer Peter Matkovic, gilt er schon heute als einer der besten Plätze Südafrikas. Anlässlich der South Africa Open im Januar erhielt der Parcours die Auszeichnung „Best new Golfcourse in South Africa during 1999". Ein weiterer 18-Loch-Platz befindet sich in Planung.

Doch nicht nur für Golfer, auch für Naturliebhaber ist das Arabella Country Estate ein Eldorado: in der Bot River Lagune und den umliegenden Bergen leben über 130 seltene Vogelarten. So kann man hier beim Bird Watching unter anderem Flamingos, die seltenen weißen Pelikane, Löffelreiher, Graureiher und vieles mehr beobachten.

Das neue ArabellaSheraton Golf Hotel Western Cape wurde in die Luxury Collection von Starwood aufgenommen und wird nun zusammen mit weiteren ausgesuchten Hotels dieses exklusiven Kreises vermarktet.

and an open-air seawater pool will appeal to visitors. The main focus of the spa area is to be its thalasso-treatment. Several conference rooms for up to 200 persons, a Business Centre and various Smart Meeting Rooms with IDSN docking stations complete the range of facilities on offer. All rooms and suites will be equipped with IDSN and a modem so that one can be contacted even on holiday. Adjacent to the hotel are the luxurious Residencias Mardevall, about 60 private holiday apartments of approx. 650 to 3,440 square feet in area. Residents of the apartments benefit from all the special offers and facilities of the hotel.

ArabellaSheraton Golf Hotel Western Cape

Majorca is not the only place where the ArabellaSheraton hotels are demonstrating their expertise in matters of golf and wellness, but also in South Africa, a golfers' paradise.

Roughly one hundred miles east of Cape Town beside the largest lagoon in Africa, Bot River near Hermanus, a new luxury ArabellaSheraton hotel will be opening its doors in Spring 2001 – the Golf Hotel Western Cape. Altogether this hideaway will have 145 rooms including two King Suites with approx 2,150 to 2,700 square feet of space, and two Presidential Suites. In addition there will be a spa and wellness zone of over 10,760 square feet complemented by an outside pool area with waterfalls laid out in extensive gardens. The interior design has been specially chosen to give guests an "out of Africa" feel, to help them identify with the country. The muted colours of the surroundings, one of the most beautiful conservation areas in Africa, are reflected throughout the house. All rooms overlook the idyllic lagoon very close by, and adjoining the hotel is the 18-hole Arabella Country Estate Golf Course which was opened last December. Planned by the South African golf course designer, Peter Matkovic, it has already earned the reputation as one of the very best in South Africa. On the occasion of the South Africa Open in January, the new course was awarded the title of "Best new golf course in South Africa during 1999". A further 18-hole golf course is at the planning stage.

Yet the Arabella Country Estate is not only an Eldorado for golfers but also for nature lovers. In the Bot River Lagoon area and surrounding mountains there are 130 species of rare birds. If you go bird watching you might see flamingos, the rare white pelican, spoonbills, grey herons and many more. The new ArabellaSheraton Golf Hotel Western Cape has been included in the Starwood Luxury Collection and will now be marketed together with other exceptional hotels of this exclusive circle.

Dorint Golfresort & Spa Camp de Mar

Hommage an Mallorca • *Homage to Majorca*

Vorbei sind die Zeiten, in denen Mallorca auf Massentourismus setzte. Heute steht der natürliche Charme der Insel wieder im Focus der Experten, das Ursprüngliche, die Natur. Neue Hotelkonzepte sprechen den Individualisten an, einen Gast, der die Schönheit der Insel mit Respekt zu würdigen weiß, der sich durch Kultiviertheit und Sportsgeist auszeichnet und zu genießen versteht. Mit dem Dorint Royal Golfresort & Spa Camp de Mar hat Mallorca eine neue Fünf-Sterne-Ferienanlage bekommen, die Urlaubsträume auf höchstem Niveau realisiert.

The age when Majorca entirely depended on mass tourism is over. Once again experts are focusing on the island's inherent charm and natural environment. The new idea for hotel design is that it should appeal to the individualist – the guest who appreciates the beauty of the island, has sophisticated tastes, and enjoys sport. Majorca now has a new five-star resort, the Dorint Royal Golf Resort & Spa Camp de Mar which truly fulfils one's holiday dreams.

Text: Gundula Luig • Fotos: Dorint GmbH

Die Architektur verschmelzt mit den Terracotta-Tönen der Erde und der Vegetation.
The architecture merges with the terracotta-colours of the earth and vegetation.

"An island encircled by shimmering seas, with olive groves and pines, with fig trees and cacti ... this is eternal paradise". The Guatemalan writer and Nobel Prize winner for literature, Miguel Àngel Asturias (1899–1974) was effusive in his work "The Sea of the Balearics". The region around Andratx truly lives up to this typical picture book image of Majorca, the like of which would be hard to find elsewhere on the island. The lush gardens, the almond tree plantations, the gnarled olive trees and the characteristic pines of the island's fertile plains extend right down to the very edge of the sea. This is the real Majorca, a magical place inspiring the holiday dreams of so many which, since November 2000, has been the scenic backdrop of a top class hotel, the Dorint Royal Golf Resort & Spa Camp de Mar, Majorca. Just over three miles south of Andratx, in the beautiful bay of Camp de Mar, Dorint has found the optimum location for the group's leading hotel in the sun. An extra-

„Das Meer, das spiegelnd diese Inseln pries, zeigt, wo noch Pinien, wo Oliven stehen – gesäumt von Feigenbäumen und Kakteen beginnt hier Tag um Tag das Paradies ..." So schwelgerisch beginnt der guatemaltekische Schriftsteller und Literatur-Nobelpreisträger Miguel Àngel Asturias (1899–1974) sein Gedicht über „Das Meer der Balearen". Und fürwahr, die Gegend um Andratx entspricht dieser urtypischen mallorquinischen Bilderbuchlandschaft wie kaum eine andere auf der Insel. Fast bis zum Meer erstreckt sich die äußerst fruchtbare Ebene mit ihren üppig blühenden Gärten, mit Orangenhainen und Mandelbaumplantagen, mit knorrigen Olivenbäumen und den charakteristischen Pinien. Mallorca, wie es die wahren Fans schätzen und lieben, voller natürlichem Zauber, Nährboden für unendliche Urlaubsträume. Und seit November 2000 naturgegebene Kulisse für ein Hotel der Extraklasse: das Dorint Royal Golfresort & Spa Camp de Mar Mallorca.

Nur fünf Kilometer südlich von Andratx, in der hübschen Bucht von Camp de Mar, hat Dorint die optimale Location für das erste Sonnenhotel der Gruppe gefunden. Ein Haus der Extravaganz, das Urlaubsträume und mallorquinische Tradition auf höchstem Niveau vereint. Strenge Planungsvorgaben haben dafür gesorgt, dass Hotel und Landschaft vorzüglich miteinander harmonieren. Kein Wunder, konnten doch die beiden Architektur-Instanzen Pedro Otzoup und Guillermo Reynes für dieses herausfordernde Projekt gewonnen werden. Entstanden ist dabei ein Resort im Stil eines traditionellen, inseltypischen Herrenhauses, wie man es im Inselinneren auch heute noch findet. Ein Haus, das zu verschmelzen scheint mit der warmen Sonne des Mittelmeers, den facettenreichen Terracotta-Tönen der Erde und der geduckten Silhouette der Vegetation. Bestechend transparent und von erlesenem Geschmack präsentiert sich das neue Urlaubsdomizil von innen. Für die Gestaltung der Interieurs zeichnen einige der berühmtesten Dekorateure Spaniens verantwortlich. Ihrem feinen Gespür für Form und Design ist es zu verdanken, dass jeder einzelne Raum der Anlage auf seine Weise mediterranes Ambiente und mallorquinische Eleganz ausstrahlt. Natürlich auch die 162 Superior-Deluxe-Zimmer sowie die zwei Präsidenten-Suiten mit ihren geschmackvollen Arrangements aus stilvollem Mobiliar, edlen Stoffen und hochwertigen Accessoires. Je nach Lage der Zimmer blickt man von den herrlich großen Balkonen auf das sattblaue Meer oder die gepflegten Greens des Golf de Andratx, der das Dorint Royal Golfresort & Spa umschließt. Selbstverständlich sind alle Zimmer vollklimatisiert und mit allem ausgestattet, was man in einem Haus dieser Klasse erwarten kann – beispielsweise Telefon- und Faxanschluss, Safe, Radio, Sat-TV und Pay-TV. Auf einem Spaziergang durch das Resort fallen immer wieder die lauschigen Patios mit ihren Wasserspielen und die luftigen Arkadengänge ins Auge, architektonische Elemente, die den Alltag in weite Ferne rücken.

Das ist auch das Ziel der wundervollen, vom Schweizer Wellness-Spezialisten Joachim G. Hallwachs gestalteten, holistischen Spa-Landschaft. Vitalis – The World of Royal Spa, ist eine einzigartige Symbiose aus den Lehren des Feng Shui und modernem mediterranem Design. 1400 Quadratmeter im Zeichen von ganzheitlicher Erholung und Entspannung, basierend auf

vagant place, it manages to unite holiday dreams and Majorcan traditions to perfection. Built to strict planning regulations, the hotel merges harmoniously with its environment, and no wonder. The architects commissioned for this challenging project were Pedro Otzoup and Guillermo Reynes who have created a mansion-type residence similar to those which still exist on the island. The house blends in with the warm Mediterranean sun and the terracotta tones of the earth, its low architecture merging with the height of the surrounding vegetation.

The most notable features of the hotel's interiors are their transparency and good taste, indeed some of the most celebrated interior designers in Spain are responsible for the interior décor. Thanks to their fine sense of form and design, every room at the resort has its own Mediterranean ambience and Majorcan elegance.

Clearly this is also true of the 162 Superior de Luxe rooms and the two Presidential Suites which are tastefully furnished with high class furniture and fabrics. Depending on where the room is located, the wonderfully spacious balconies afford views of the deep blue sea

Die ganze Anlage spiegelt den Stil mallorquinischer Herrenhäuser wider.
The whole installation reflects the style of Majorcan mansions.

Die großzügige Lobby gibt sich als Spiegel für die ungewöhnliche Architektur des Luxushotels.
The spacious lobby is a reflection for the unusual architecture of this luxury hotel.

Das Resort besticht nicht nur beim Interieur durch die große Liebe zum Detail.
The resort impresses not only at the interieur with its harmony in every detail.

or the beautifully kept greens of the Golf de Andratx which surrounds the Dorint Royal Golf Resort & Spa. It goes without saying that all rooms are air-conditioned throughout and equipped with all the mod cons one has come to expect in a hotel of this class – telephone and fax, safe, radio, Sat-TV and Pay-TV. Strolling through the resort one is struck by the secluded patios and their fountains and the airy arcade walkways – architectural elements which make everyday life seem a million miles away. It is precisely this which the Swiss wellness specialist, Joachim G. Hallwachs, wanted to achieve with his design for the

68 HIDEAWAYS

fünf Säulen: 1. Die Aktiv-Area für Cardio- und Powerfitness; 2. Die Welt des Bades – von Sauna bis zum klassischen Pflegebad; 3. Die Indoor-Pool-Area mit Ruhe- und Mentalzone; 4. Health-Bar und Kommunikationszone; 5. Die Treatment-Area für Beauty- und Körperbehandlungen sowie ambulante ästhetisch-chirurgische OPs. Diesem Bereich kommt eine ganz besondere Bedeutung zu, steht er doch unter der Ägide von Dr. med. Erich Schulte, der internationalen Koryphäe für ästhetische Medizin. Die von ihm entwickelte Produktpalette QMS – zur natürlichen Regeneration und Zellverjüngung der Haut – wird neben anderen Top-Produkten in der Beautyfarm angewandt und vertrieben. Schultes Tochter Quirina, eine herausragende Spezialistin für die Anwendung dieser einzigartigen Lifting- und Beautybehandlungen, obliegt die Leitung der Farm.

holistic spa area. Vitalis – The World of Royal Spa, is a remarkable symbiosis of the principles of Feng Shui and modern Mediterranean design. Over 15,000 sq. feet of space has been devoted to the five pillars of holistic regeneration and relaxation: 1. The activity area for cardiac health and physical fitness; 2. The World of Baths – from saunas to traditional medicinal baths; 3. Indoor pool area with rest area and mind zone; 4. Health bar and communication zone; 5. Treatment area for beauty and body treatments as well as outpatient cosmetic surgery. The patron of this particularly important zone is Dr. Erich Schulte, the international expert in aesthetic

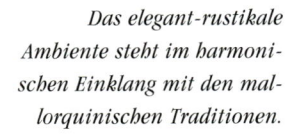

Geschmackvolle Arrangements, edle Stoffe und modernster Komfort prägen die Atmosphäre der 162 Superior-Deluxe-Zimmer.
Tastefull arrangements, nobless fabrics and most modern comfort influence the atmosphere of the 162 superiour-deluxe-rooms.

Das elegant-rustikale Ambiente steht im harmonischen Einklang mit den mallorquinischen Traditionen.
The elegant-rustical ambiance is in harmonious reconcile to the Majorcan tradition.

medicine. The QMS range of products he has developed to promote natural regeneration and rejuvenation of skin cells are applied alongside other top products at the beauty farm. Dr. Schulte's daughter, Quirina, an outstanding specialist in the application of this unique lifting and beauty treatment runs the farm. Each month Dr. Schulte himself is at the resort to carry out outpatient cosmetic surgery. An outstanding feature of the new Dorint Royal Golf Resort & Spa Camp de Mar is the fantastic 18-hole golf course – Golf de Andratx – which surrounds the hotel. Without doubt, its exacting narrow fairways, its water hazards and little stone walls which are typical of Majorca, present passionate golfers with one of the most challenging courses in the Mediterranean. In the background are the wooded slopes of the Serra Garrafa and their sun-bleached rocks. Ahead is the flag and the ever-changing blue of the sea. Obviously, house guests have priority for tee times, then its out on to the course, which springs many a surprise on the golfer including the names of the holes. Number one hole for instance is called "Heaven help me". Having got over the first shock, in actual fact this par 4, 328 yards turns out to be of medium difficulty. One then goes on to "Casa Claudia", a narrow par 4 with an obstacle on one side which is more of a mental obstacle than anything else, and is certainly just as tricky. But if your gaze does stray upwards to the house of Germany's top model, don't forget the green. The "Green Monster" is enough to send you scatty. Its 666 yards make it Spain's longest hole. It isn't only because of its distance that it's the most difficult on the course, its second and the third strokes are uphill. What is more, you have to negotiate bunkers on both sides then a water hazard on the left to reach the green. The average round takes about four and a half hours by which time you will have played such comical holes as "Birdie Time", "Damned Torrent", "Hello Mrs. Robinson", "Prince Zourab" and "Blame Herbert".

The 18th hole par 5 is dedicated to Dr. Herbert Ebertz, the course's Vice President. Golfers who have not yet achieved their handicap, women 35, men 28, can be coached by a

Dr. Schulte persönlich ist monatlich zu bestimmten Terminen im Resort, um ambulante ästhetisch-chirurgische Eingriffe durchzuführen. Herausragendes Feature des neuen Dorint Royal Golfresort & Spa Camp de Mar ist die traumhafte 18-Loch-Anlage Golf de Andratx, die das Hotel weitläufig umgibt. Mit anspruchsvollen schmalen Fairways, insgesamt sieben Teichen und Seen und den für Mallorca eigentümlichen Natursteinmäuerchen zählt der Club zweifellos zu einer der schönsten Herausforderungen für passionierte Golfer im gesamten Mittelmeerraum. Im Rücken die Hänge der Serra Garrafa, auf denen sich grüne Wälder und sonnengebleichter Fels abwechseln. Voraus der Blick auf die Fahne und das niemals gleich bleibende Blau des Meeres. Hausgäste erhalten selbstverständlich bevorzugte Abschlagzeiten, und dann geht es hinaus auf einen Parcours, der mit so mancher Überraschung und wirklich kreativen Benamsungen der einzelnen Löcher aufwartet. Bezeichnenderweise nennt sich Loch 1 gleich „Heaven help me". Nach dem ersten Schreck erweist sich das Par 4 von rund 300 Metern jedoch als mittelschwer. Als nächstes kommt man zu „Casa Claudia". Das enge Par 4 mit einem mentalen Hindernis auf der linken Seite hat seine Tücken. Wer eben mal schnell zum Haus von Deutschlands Top-Modell heraufblickt, sollte darüber nicht das Grün vergessen. Regelrecht zur

Verzweiflung bringen kann einen „Green Monster", mit 609 Metern Spaniens längstes Loch. Mit dem Stroke Index 1 ist es nicht nur wegen der Länge das schwerste auf dem Platz. Der zweite und dritte Schlag gehen bergauf, wobei der Schlag auf das Grün von Bunkern auf beiden Seiten sowie Wasser auf der linken Seite gefährdet wird. Rund vier Stunden dreißig Minuten dauert ein durchschnittliches Spiel, das zu weiteren klangvollen Löchern wie „Birdie Time", „Damned Torrent", „Hello Mrs. Robinson" oder „Prince Zourab" führt, bis schließlich „Blame Herbert" erreicht ist. Loch 18, dem Vizepräsidenten der Anlage Dr. Herbert Ebertz gewidmet, ist ein anspruchsvolles Par 5 als End- und Höhepunkt. Wer das Handicap von 35 für Damen und 28 für Herren noch nicht erreicht hat, trainiert auf der Driving-Range unter Anleitung eines erfahrenen Pros. Doch auch Nicht-Golfer finden in und um Camp de Mar alles, was das Herz begehrt: ideale Wassersport- und Tauchmöglichkeiten im nur 300 Meter vom Hotel entfernten Meer, Mountainbikes, Tennisanlagen, Reitmöglichkeiten sowie ein umfangreiches Wanderwegenetz. Familien mit Kindern steht übrigens ein animierendes Kinderprogramm zur Verfügung. Wenn die Eltern mal nur für sich sein möchten, werden die Kleinen fachgerecht betreut und unterhalten.

Das Dorint Royal Golfresort & Spa Camp de Mar steht für Urlaubsträume jenseits des Üblichen. Das gilt für alle Einrichtungen und insbesondere natürlich auch für die Qualität der Gastronomie. Schon das Frühstücksbuffet auf der Sonnenterrasse „Sa Plaza" ist ein Fest für die Sinne. Und das setzt sich in der eleganten Ambiance des A-la-carte-Restaurants „Mediterranea" fort. Dort lässt man sich internationale Zubereitungen der Extraklasse munden. Wer lieber die Geheimnisse mallorquinischer Kochkunst entdecken möchte, kommt im „El Mallorquin" auf seine kulinarischen Kosten. Dazu trägt nicht ohne Absicht die offene Showküche einen wesentlichen Teil bei. Nach dem Dinner trifft man sich zum Digestif im edlen Ambiente der Lobby-Bar oder lässt den Abend in der gemütlichen Piano-Bar ausklingen. So gedeihen Träume ohne die Tradition zu bedrängen.

professional at the driving range. However, visitors who are not golfers will also find their own needs are fully catered for at Camp de Mar. The sea, only 330 yards from the hotel, is ideal for water sports and skin diving, but there are also tennis courts, mountain biking, riding and a network of walks. For families with children, there's an entertainment programme, and if parents want to have some time on their own, they can leave their children in the capable hands of trained child-carers. The Dorint Royal Golf Resort & Spa Camp de Mar really is out of the ordinary when it comes to fulfilling hopes for a dream holiday. It has every facility you could wish for, and a quality cuisine to match. The breakfast buffet in the sun terrace Sa Plaza is a feast for all the senses. The same applies to the elegant Mediterranea à la carte restaurant which serves an excellent international cuisine. Those who want to sample the secrets of genuine Majorcan cooking are well catered for at the El Mallorquin restaurant where an open kitchen is part of the attraction. Guests meet up for after-dinner drinks in the sophisticated lobby bar or spend the rest of the evening in the piano bar. This is a place where dreams can thrive.

Vom eigenen Balkon blickt man wahlweise aufs Meer oder auf die eindrucksvollen Greens.
From the own balconies you can enjoy chooseable the view to the ocean or to the impressive golf green.

Wellness-Paradies auf Mallorca: der Royal Spa.
Wellness-paradise at Majorca: the Royal Spa.

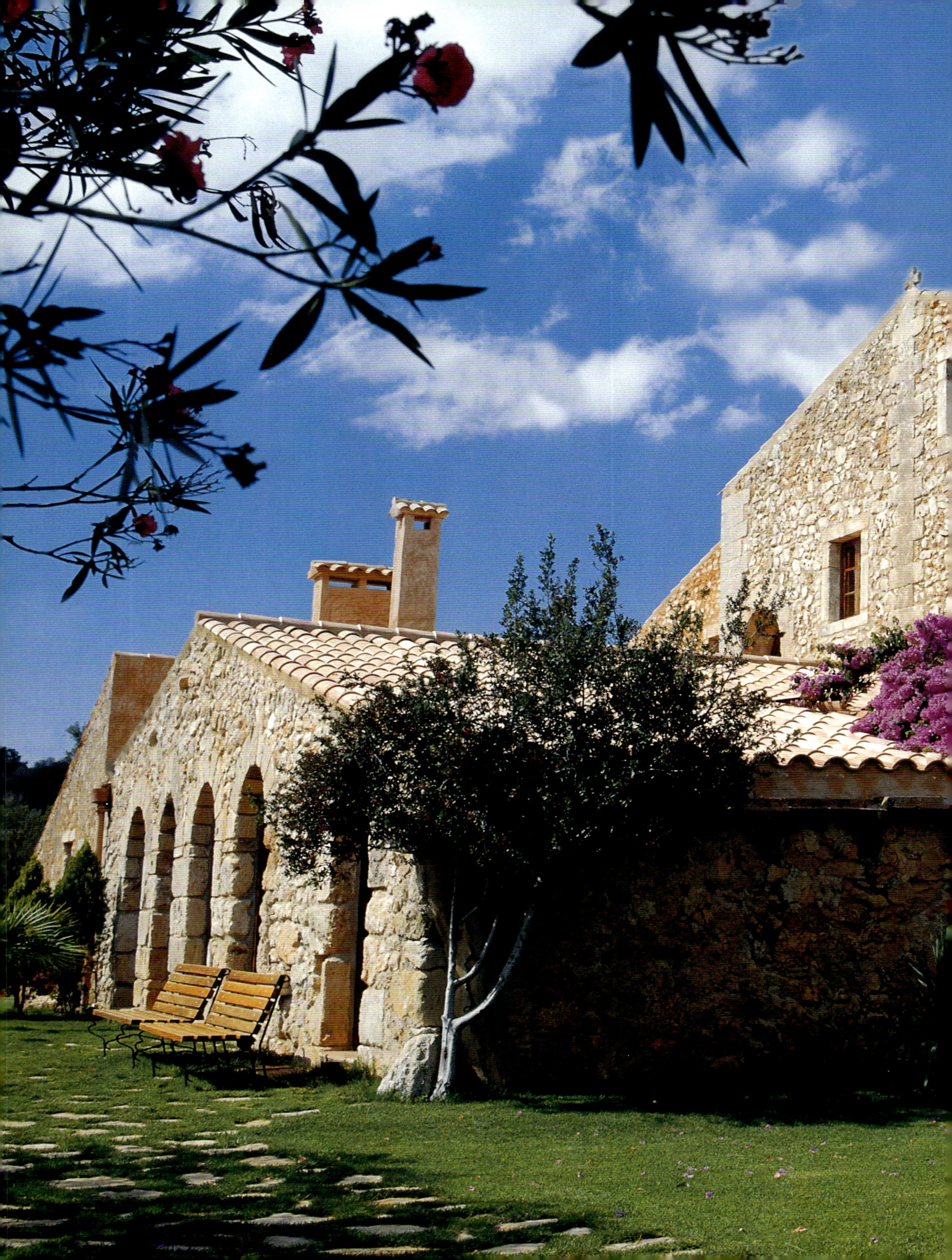

LAND- UND GOLF-IDYLLE
IM OSTEN MALLORCAS

La Reserva Rotana

IDYLLIC COUNTRYSIDE AND IDEAL GOLF
IN THE EAST OF MAJORCA

Mallorca wandelt sein Image. Die größte der Baleareninseln gilt reisenden Individualisten längst wieder als Hort geheimnisvoller Schönheiten fern vom besinnungslosen Lärm der Südküste. Idyllisch vor Manacor gelegen, der zweitgrößten Stadt des Mittelmeer-Eilands, lockt La Reserva Rotana mit authentischem Finca-Flair und exklusiven Faszilitäten für Golfer.

Majorca's image is changing. Once more and indeed for some time now the largest of the Balearic Islands has been regarded by individualistic travellers as a refuge of mysterious beauty, far from the babel of the south coast. Located at an idyllic spot near Manacor, the second largest town of this Mediterranean island, the attraction of La Reserva Rotana lies in the authentic flair of this Spanish country estate and its exclusive golfing facilities.

Text: Günter Ned · Fotos: Klaus Lorke

Der hauseigene 9-Loch-Golfplatz, exklusiv für Hotelgäste.
The own 9-hole-Golf-course is reserved exclusively for hotel guests.

Finca-Flair bis ins Detail.
Finca flair of the last detail.

The much quoted "other" Majorca has many patrons among German-speaking friends of the Balearic islands. They take no part in the leisure activities and building excesses of certain beaches and bays. Some settled here a long time ago, in love with the simplicity of the island and its variety, and contribute to the conservation of its beauty and its history.

Swiss Juan Ramón Theler and his German wife, Loretta, Princess zu Sayn-Wittgenstein Hohenstein, came to the east coast hinterland 30 years ago. They purchased an old Majorcan manor house mentioned in the chronicles of 1242 as "La Rotana". The property had previously been part of the estates of the Marquis Vilallonga Mir i Muntaner, ancient nobility of Majorca. Initially the newcomers to the island farmed their large estate – La Rotana has nearly five hundred acres. Then its landlord developed another passion, the conservation and reconstruction of original Majorcan buildings. Today more than a few old manor houses on the island have been restored to their former beauty by Don Juan, as the locals call him.

The most beautiful property is clearly the one standing on his own land. The buildings which came into the possession of this descendant of an eminent Swiss insurance dynasty date back to the 17th century. Paco and Francisca, the family who in the meantime have been farming the land and seeing to the livestock, occupied the manor house right up to the 1990s. They then moved and today where Paco and Francisca once lived, where there had been cattle sheds and storage barns, there is one of the finest country hotels in Majorca.

Exclusive rooms and suites delightfully and individually designed so as to comply with regulations govern-

D as vielzitierte „andere" Mallorca hat unter deutschsprachigen Liebhabern der Baleareninsel viele Stützen. Sie beteiligen sich nicht an den Freizeit- und Bauexzessen mancher Strände und Buchten. Sie sind zum Teil schon lange im Land, lieben die Ursprünglichkeit des Eilands mit den vielen Gesichtern, tragen bei, seine Schönheit, seine Geschichte zu bewahren.

Der Schweizer Juan Ramón Theler und seine deutsche Frau Loretta Prinzessin zu Sayn-Wittgenstein Hohenstein kamen vor 30 Jahren ins Hinterland der Ostküste. Sie erwarben einen alten mallorquinischen Herrensitz, der unter dem Namen *La Rotana* schon in Chroniken aus dem Jahr 1242 geführt wird. Zuvor gehörte der Grundbesitz zu den Ländereien des Marques Vilallonga Mir i Muntaner und damit einer alten Adelsfamilie Mallorcas.

Die Neuinsulaner trieben auf ihrem weiten Land – La Rotana ist 200 Hektar groß – zunächst Landwirtschaft. Dann entwickelte der Patron eine andere Passion, die Erhaltung und Rekonstruktion originaler mallorquinischer Bausubstanz. Heute zeigen sich auf der Insel nicht wenige alte Herrensitze in neuer Schönheit, restauriert von Don Juan, wie ihn die Einheimischen nennen.

Die schönste Finca steht wohl auf seinem eigenen Grund und Boden. Die Gebäude, die der Spross einer renommierten Schweizer Versicherungsdynastie vorfand, stammen aus dem 17. Jahrhundert. Im Herrenhaus wohnten bis in die neunziger Jahre Paco und Francisca, die Bauernfamilie, die inzwischen die Feld- und Viehwirtschaft führt. Dann zogen die Landwirte um, und heute präsentiert sich dort, wo Paco und Francisca wohnten, wo Ställe Vieh und Scheunen Vorräte bargen, eines der feinsten Finca-Hotels Mallorcas.

Exklusive Zimmer und Suiten, reizvoll individuell geschnitten aufgrund der Denkmalschutzauflagen, ein Restaurant mit Patio, ein Außen- und ein Indoor-Pool (unterm Brunnen in der ehemaligen Zisterne) empfangen Gäste, die stilvolle Ländlichkeit mit luxuriösem Komfort lieben.

Grüne Höfe und blühende Gärten umgeben „La Reserva Rotana". Man spaziert unter Pinien, Palmen und Platanen, vielfarbige Bougainvilleen wachsen über ockerfarbene Steinfassaden hinauf zu Terrakottadächern. Mit mehr Stilgefühl und größerer Liebe zum ursprünglichen Gesicht Mallorcas kann man eine Finca nicht restaurieren.

Im Herrenhaus mischen eine Suite, sieben Juniorsuiten, fünf Doppel- und ein Einzelzimmer mallorquinische Landhaus-Eleganz mit behaglicher Wohnlichkeit. Überall scheint der bauliche Charme der alten Finca durch. Zwischen venezianischem Stuck sind in den Wohnräumen Feldsteinmauern freigelegt, Bögen aus Santanyí-Stein, Wände aus sonnenfarbenem Marés fügen sich in exquisite mediterrane Interieurs. Alte Mauerhaken sind erhalten, an denen früher Sobrasadas hingen und neben Melonen und Pa-amb-oli-Tomaten überwinterten. Zimmer Nr. 12 bewahrt steinerne Futterkrippen, und die Badezimmer zählen zu den Perlen der Ambiance. In den warmen Farben der Insel gehalten, sind sie behaglich wie Wohnräume und mit ihren Wanneneinfassungen aus Travertin schmuckvoll wie die Eingangshalle mit ihren neuen Fresken.

Juan Ramón Theler kultivierte über die Jahrzehnte, die er mit seiner Familie nun schon auf Mallorca lebt, noch eine weitere Leidenschaft, das Sammeln schöner Gegenstände aus

ing the protection of ancient monuments, a restaurant with a patio, an outdoor and indoor pool (beneath a fountain where the underground cistern used to be), all this greets the guest who values sophisticated country style with luxurious comfort.
Verdant farms and flowering gardens surround "La Reserva Rotana".

Ein himmlisches Vergnügen: Frühstück mit Blick auf den Golfplatz.
A divine pleasure: breakfast with a view at the golf-course.

Das Interieur der Bar stammt aus Ramón Thelers afrikanischer Vergangenheit.
The bar interieur is from Ramón Theler's Africain past.

Überall blieb das alte Mallorca lebendig
Old Majorca remains alive everywhere.

One can stroll beneath pines, palms and plain trees. Multi-coloured bougainvillaea grows against ochre stone façades right up to the terracotta roofs. It would be impossible to restore a property with a greater sense of style or attention to its original Majorcan character.

In the manor house itself Majorcan country house elegance is combined with homely comfort in the suite, the seven junior suites, the five double rooms and the single room. The architectural charm of the original country house shines through everywhere. In the living areas natural stone walls have been exposed between the Venetian stucco work. Arches of Santanyi stone and walls built of sun-coloured marés are an integral part of the exquisite Mediterranean interiors. Old wall hooks have been retained on which in earlier time pork sausages hung to overwinter alongside melons and pa-amb-oli tomatoes. There are stone cattle troughs in Room 12, but it is the bathrooms which count among the gems of the whole ambience. Decorated in the warm colours of the island they are as comfortable as living

vergangenen Zeiten. So stand ihm ein nahezu unerschöpflicher Fundus zu Gebot, als er daranging, das Fluidum der alten Finca mit raren Antiquitäten zu schmücken. Hübsch so ein Detail wie das Luftgitter aus einer alten Abtei, in den Terrakottaboden eingelassen. Mit stilsicherem Geschmack ausgesucht und platziert Rari-

Im Restaurant genießen Gäste wie überall in der Finca das Flair des alten mallorquinischen Herrensitzes.

In the restaurant as in all parts of this country house, guest can relish the atmosphere and style of an old Majorcan manor.

---

täten wie die Waschbecken aus dem ehemaligen Grand Hotel Palmas, Kostbarkeiten wie die marokkanische Truhe in einer Juniorsuite oder in der Halle die geschnitzte Decke aus einem Kloster in Cordoba. Originell dazu das Interieur der Bar. Ihr afrikanischer Stil und die dekorativen Trophäen stammen aus einer Zeit, in der der Hausherr noch regelmäßig den Büros des väterlichen Unternehmens entfloh, um auf dem schwarzen Kontinent Großwild zu jagen. (Heute schießt er nicht einmal mehr Karnickel, sondern zieht Zicklein mit der Flasche groß.) Viele Wohnensembles haben Terrassen, ebenso die sieben Doppelzimmer und Juniorsuiten um den Außenpool.

Direktorin María Rodríguez Bécares hat ihre Kindheit im Sauerland verbracht. Angenehm fürs Publikum deutscher Zunge: sie spricht die Sprache ihres einstigen Gastlandes perfekt. Die charmante Festlands-Spanierin ist mit einem Mallorquiner verheiratet und hat sichtlich ihr Herz an La Reserva Rotana gehängt. Sie führt das Domizil drei Kilometer vor Manacor als attraktiven Stützpunkt für entspan-

rooms, and the baths bordered with travertine are as decorative as the entrance hall with its new frescoes. Over the many years Juan Ramón Theler has been living with his family on Majorca he has cultivated a further passion – collecting beautiful artefacts from past times. So, when he set about enhancing the atmosphere of the old house by adorning it with rare antiques, he had at his disposal a truly inexhaustible collection. A charming detail would be the ventilation grille from an old abbey set into the terracotta floor.

Rarities have been selected and positioned with unerring taste, such as the washbasin from the old Grand Hotel in Palma de Mallorca, treasures such as the Moroccan chest in one of the junior suites or the carved ceiling from a convent in Cordova in the hall.

The interior of the bar is yet another original feature. Its African style and the decorative trophies go back to a time when the head of the household would regularly escape from the office of his father's company to go big game hunting in Africa. (Nowadays he doesn't even shoot rabbits, preferring to bottle-feed goat kids.) Many of the units have terraces as do the seven double rooms and the junior suites around the open air pool.

María Rodríguez Bécares, the Manager, spent her childhood in Sauerland, most agreeable for German-speaking visitors. She speaks the language of her former host country perfectly. This charming woman from the Spanish mainland is married to a Majorcan and has clearly lost her heart to La Reserva Rotana. She runs the residence three kilometres from Manacor as an attrac-

María Rodríguez Bécares hat ihre Kindheit im Sauerland verbracht und spricht perfekt deutsch.

María Rodriguez Bécares, the Gerneral Manager, spent her childhood in Sauerland. She speaks German perfectly.

Landhaus-Eleganz mit Antiquitäten aus der Sammlung des Hausherrn.
Country house elegance with antiques from the owner's private collection.

tive base from which to pursue relaxing activities. In half an hour one can be rambling in the nature reserve and the most beautiful bays of the east coast are only 20 minutes away. For golfers though La Rotana is a veritable jewel of a place. The estate has a tricky nine-hole golf course which was initially laid out by Don Juan for his personal use. Nowadays only his own guests have access to the greens and fairway. There is no admission to the public. His own pro, David McGinnes (handicap 0) will willingly coach beginners. In addition there are five 18-hole golf courses nearby from Vall d'Or

nende Aktivitäten. Eine halbe Stunde spaziert man ins Naturschutzgebiet, 20 Minuten fährt man zu den schönsten Buchten der Ostküste. Als wahres Kleinod aber präsentiert sich La Rotana den Golfern. Zur Finca gehört ein trickreicher 9-Loch-Kurs, den Don Juan zunächst für sich selbst gebaut hat. Heute lädt er seine Gäste auf die Greens und Fairways, und zwar exklusiv: Es gibt keinen öffentlichen Zugang. Der eigene Pro, David McGinnes (Handikap 0), unterrichtet auch gerne Anfänger. Zusätzlich finden sich fünf 18-Loch-Plätze in der nächsten Umgebung von Vall d'Or Porto Colom über Pula Golf, Golf Costa de los Pinos und Golf Canyamel bis Golf Roca Viva.

Eingefasst ist der Rotana-Golf-Parcours von den Hügeln und Wäldern, Flüsschen und Feldern, die sich über die zweihundert Hektar Grundbesitz ziehen. Hier blüht die Landwirtschaft der Finca nach wie vor. Allein sechshun-

Behaglich wie Wohnräume: die Badezimmer.
The bathrooms: as comfortable as living rooms.

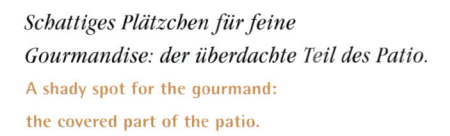

Schattiges Plätzchen für feine Gourmandise: der überdachte Teil des Patio.
A shady spot for the gourmand: the covered part of the patio.

dert Mutterschafe sprenkeln das Grün der Weiden, die oben auf der Anhöhe ins Naturschutzgebiet übergehen. Paco und Francisca führen das Gut nun von der Dependance Maiolet aus und bewirten dort auch Urlauber mit einfacheren Ansprüchen. 12 Doppelzimmer, in schlichtem mallorqinischen Stil eingerichtet, erwarten Besucher, die die rustikale Atmosphäre und die günstigen Preise schätzen.

Phantasievolle Desserts sind eine besondere Spezialität des Küchenchefs.
Imaginative desserts are the chef's speciality.

Porto Colom to Pula Golf, Golf Costa de los Pinos and Golf Canyamel to Golf Roca Viva. The Rotana golf course is encircled by hills, woods, brooks and fields which stretch across the whole of the five hundred acre estate where agriculture still continues to thrive as in the past. Six hundred ewes are scattered across the green of the fields which merge into the nature reserve up on the hill. Nowadays Paco and Francisca run the farm from Maiolet, the hotel annexe, and cater for visitors with more modest needs. 12 double rooms furnished in simple Majorcan style await visitors who prefer a rustic atmosphere and more favourable prices.

Eine delikate Vorspeisen-Kreation: Salat von Gemüsen und Langostinos.
A delicious hors d'œuvre: crayfish and vegetable salad.

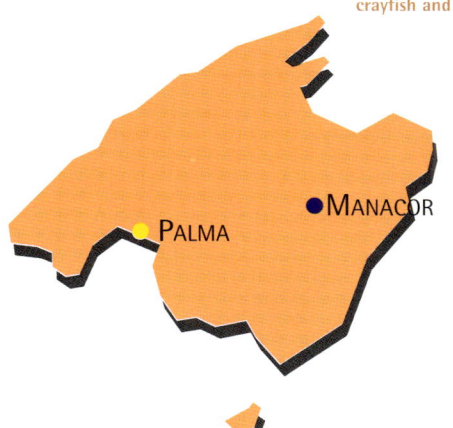

PALMA • MANACOR

HIDEAWAYS 79

PORTUGALS
GOLFKÜSTE
DER SUPERLATIVE

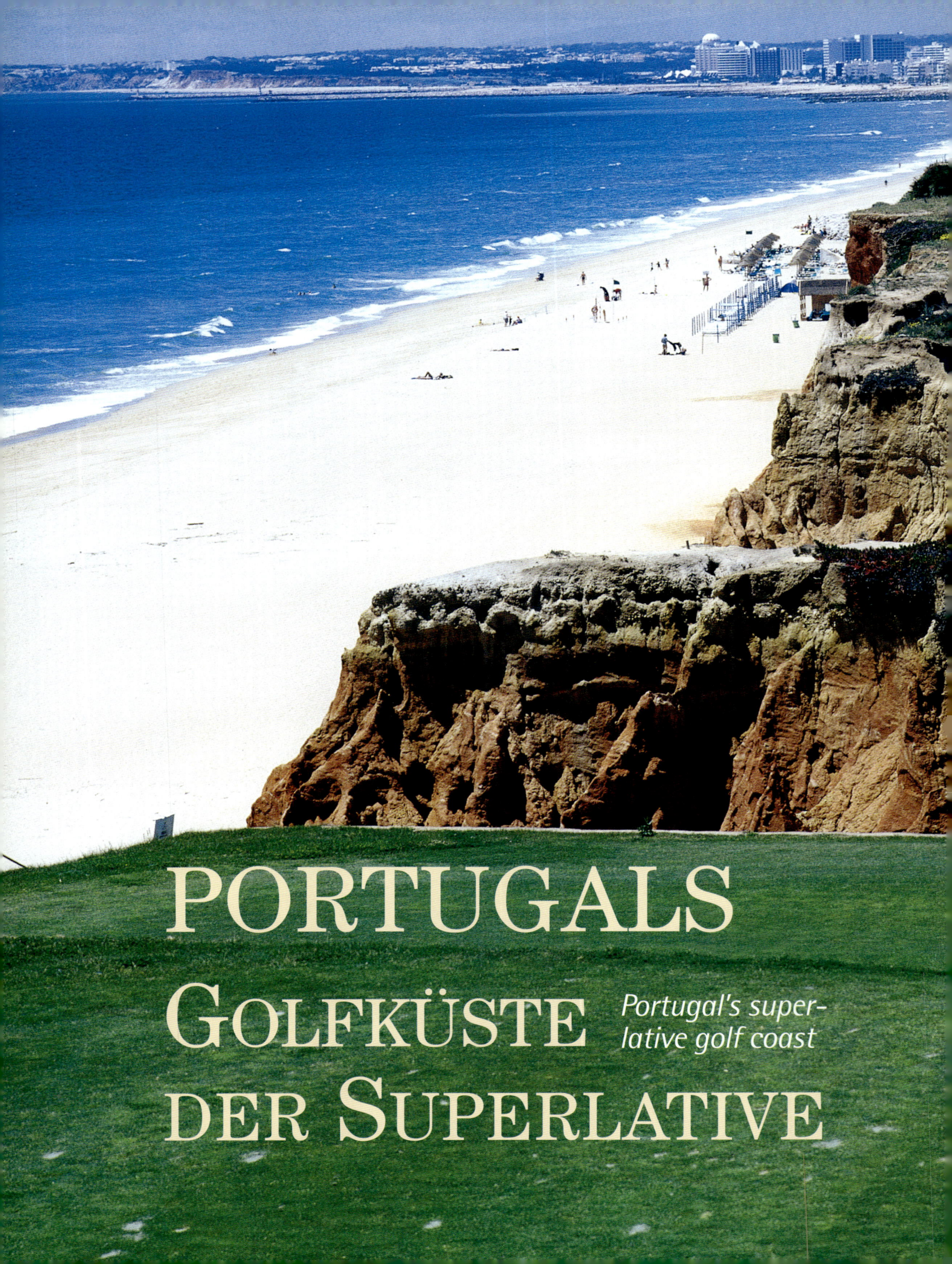

Portugal's superlative golf coast

GOLF AN DER ALGARVE

Mit 3000 Sonnenstunden pro Jahr und angenehmen Temperaturen selbst im Winter zählt Portugals Algarve seit geraumer Zeit zu den bevorzugten europäischen Zielen für passionierte Golfer. Rund 20 exklusive Clubs zwischen Sagres und Faro stehen einer begeisterten internationalen Klientel zur Verfügung. Anfänger wie Könner finden dort erstklassige Bedingungen auf den wohl schönsten Parcours des Landes — und das 365 Tage im Jahr. Zu den extravagantesten und landschaftlich reizvollsten Anlagen gehört Quinta do Lago mit gleich drei Golfplätzen, hervorragenden Freizeiteinrichtungen, exquisiten Villenurbanisationen und einem eleganten First-Class-Hotel. Dazu die wild-bizarre Küstenlandschaft, endlose Strände, romantische Buchten und die bezaubernde Natur des Nationalparks Ria Formosa.

Three thousand hours of sun a year and an agreeable climate even in winter has meant that Portugal has been a popular European destination for passionate golfers for some considerable time. About 20 exclusive clubs between Sagres and Faro are at the disposal of an enthusiastic international clientele. Both beginners and experts find that the most beautiful courses in the country are in first class condition 365 days a year. Among the most extravagant and attractive are the 3 golf courses belonging to Quinta do Lago which has superb leisure facilities, a very select residential area with little groups of villas and an elegant first class hotel. In addition, there are bizarre coastlines, endless beaches, romantic bays and the delightful nature of the conservation area of Ria Formosa.

Text: Gundula Luig · Fotos: Ulrich Helweg

Quinta do Lago

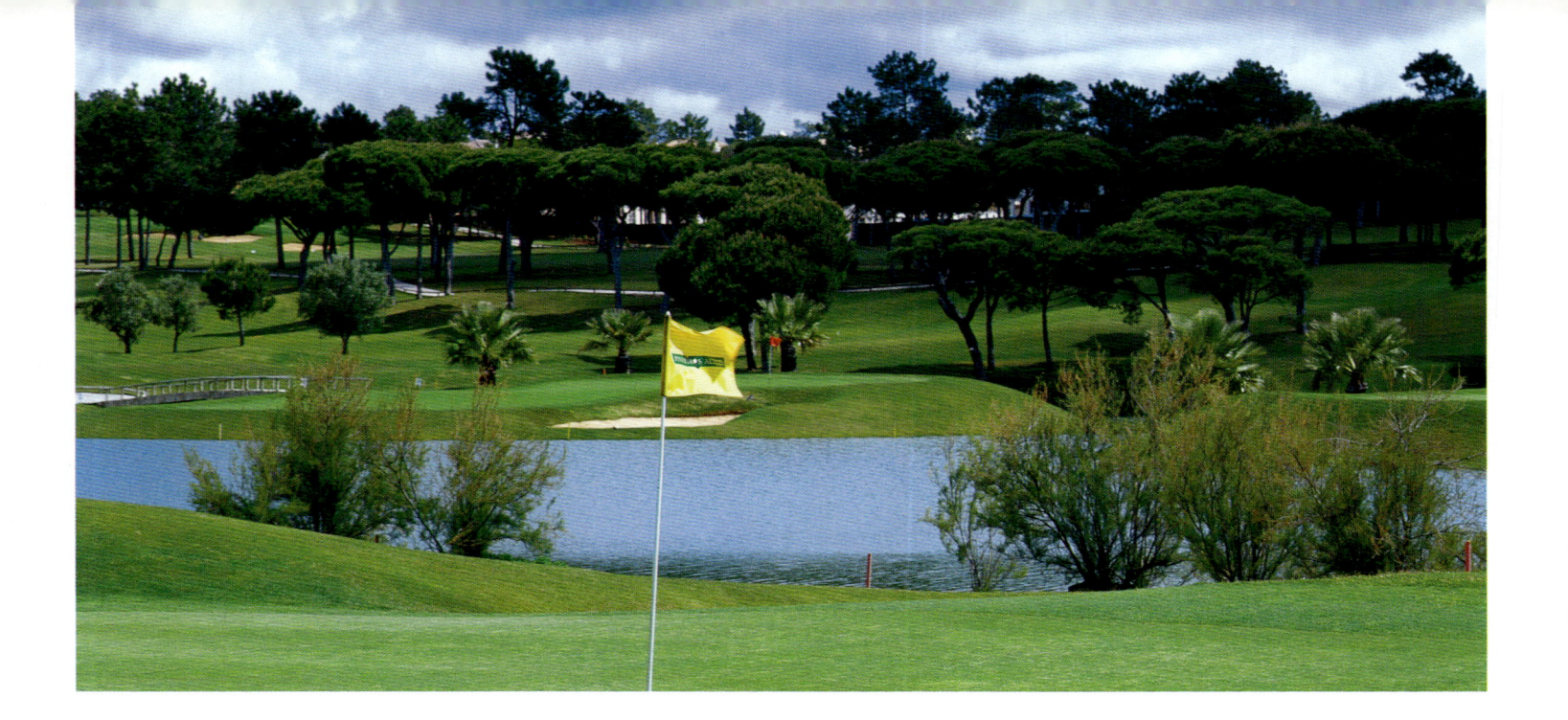

Half an hour from Faro Airport a genuine paradise awaits golf enthusiasts. The grounds of Quinta do Lago extend over an area of nearly 2000 acres across which lie three fantastically designed golf courses, Pinheiros Altos, Ria Formosa and Quinta do Lago. Two of the courses were designed by the American architect, William Mitchell, and figure among the best courses in Europe. The 18-hole Quinta do Lago course is the largest (7,759 yards par 72) and has been the venue for the Portuguese Open five times. Its second half inclines down a valley towards a lake. Unusually the 15th hole is par 3. It is played over a 208 yard stretch of water on to a well appointed green. A real challenge for every golfer is the Ria Formosa course (6,561 yards, par 72 which combines two 9-hole courses). The most recent course at the Quinta do Lago is the Pinheiros Altos course (6,735 yards, 18-hole, par 72) designed by Ronald Fream which combines holes in two totally different surroundings. The first nine, "The Pines", lead through pinewoods and the other nine, "The Lakes", are on flatter ground and are set in a lakeland landscape which requires very precise strokes. A luxury hotel of the same name is part of the Quinta do Lago complex.

Eine halbe Stunde vom Flughafen Faro entfernt eröffnet sich Freunden des grünen Sports ein wahres Paradies: die 800 Hektar umfassende Quinta-do-Lago-Anlage mit ihren drei phantastisch angelegten Golfplätzen Pinheiros Altos, Ria Formosa und Quinta do Lago. Zwei der Golfparcours wurden von dem amerikanischen Architekten William Mitchell entworfen und zählen zu den besten Anlagen Europas. Der Quinta-do-Lago-Kurs ist mit 6488 Metern, 18 Loch Par 72 der größte Platz. Siebenmal wurden dort bereits die Portuguese Open ausgetragen. Die Anlage ist in eine sanfte Hügellandschaft inmitten eines Pinienwaldes eingebettet. Ihre zweite Hälfte schmiegt sich talwärts an einen See. Außergewöhnlich ist das 15. Loch Par 3. Es wird 190 Meter über dem Wasser auf ein gut angelegtes Green gespielt. Eine echte Herausforderung für jeden Golfer stellt der Ria-Formosa-Kurs (6000 Meter, Par 72, zwei kombinierte 9-Loch-Kurse) dar. Für die vier Par 5 Löcher wird ein äußerst präzises Augenmaß benötigt. Die Bunker sind strategisch so angelegt, dass jeder Fehlschlag von ihnen aufgefangen wird. Der neueste Platz in der Quinta-do-Lago-Destination ist der von Ronald Fream designte Pinheiros-Altos-Kurs (6159 Meter, 18 Loch Par 72). Hier harmonieren zwei unterschiedliche Charaktere von Löchern miteinander. Die ersten neun, „The Pines", führen durch einen Pinienwald, die anderen neun, „The Lakes", sind sehr viel flacher und werden von einer Seenlandschaft begleitet, die ein präzises Spiel mit den Eisen verlangt. Zum Quinta-do-Lago-Komplex gehören außerdem das gleichnamige Luxus-Hotel, ein Reitzentrum, Restaurants, eleganter Shoppingbereich und exklusive private Villenurbanisationen.

Greenfee auf den Plätzen Quinta do Lago und Ria Formosa 49,88 Euro; Pinheiros Altos 52,37 Euro. Abschlagzeiten und Platzwunsch sollten wegen großer Nachfrage so früh wie möglich über die Golfinformation des Hotels Quinta do Lago gebucht werden.
Telefon: + 3 51 / 2 89 / 35 03 50
Telefax: + 3 51 / 2 89 / 39 63 93
Handicapnachweis: Herren 28, Damen 36. Bezüglich Kleider- und Softspikevorschriften sollte man sich ebenfalls im Voraus informieren.

Green fee for the Quinta do Lago course and Ria Formosa, 49.88 Euro; Pinheiros Altos, 52.37 Euro. Owing to heavy demand Tee times and choice of course should be booked as early as possible at the Golf Information desk of Hotel Quinta do Lago.
Telephone: +3 51 / 2 89 / 35 03 50
Telefax: +3 51 / 2 89 / 39 63 93
Evidence of Handicap required: men 28, ladies 36. It is recommended that golfers inform themselves in advance about clothing and regulations covering soft spikes.

Vale do Lobo

Von der Quinta-do-Lago-Anlage benötigt es nur wenige Fahrminuten, bis sich die parkartige Landschaft von Vale do Lobo ausbreitet. Die luxuriöse Ferien- und Freizeitdestination mit ihren eleganten Villen, individuellen Häusern und großzügig geschnittenen Wohnungen – alles in landestypischer, maurischer Architektur – hat es besonders vielen prominenten Zeitgenossen angetan. Nicht zuletzt aufgrund der erstklassigen, weltbekannten Golfkurse, die einst vom legendären Sir Henry Cotton entworfen und durch Rocky Roquemore eine zeitgemäße Aufwertung (Royal Course) erfuhren. Die gepflegten Fairways und anspruchsvollen Greens ziehen sich durch Schatten spendende Pinienwäldchen bis zu den breiten Stränden des Atlantik. Der berühmte „The Ocean Course" wurde trotz vieler Verbesserungen in den letzten Jahren im Originalzustand belassen. Er liegt übrigens nur zehn Minuten vom Hotel Quinta do Lago entfernt. Das 6. Loch ist entlang des Strandes platziert, eine besondere Attraktion für jeden Golfer. Der exklusive „The Royal Course" verbindet neun neu angelegte („Blue"-Course) mit den neun alten „Yellow"-Course-Löchern zu einem sehr angenehmen und zugleich herausfordernden Spiel. Das weltberühmte 16. Loch liegt hoch über den Klippen und dem Strand.

Es gehört zu den meist fotografierten Löchern Europas. Neben Golf bietet Vale do Lobo die Möglichkeit zu mehr als 25 anderen Sportarten an, darunter Tennis, Squash, Windsurfen oder Kricket. Das quirlige urbane Zentrum direkt am Strand setzt mit einer bunten Mischung aus Geschäften, Restaurants, Bars und Nachtclub weitere Akzente in diesem außergewöhnlich gelungenen Konzept.

Only a few minutes drive away from the Quinto do Lago estate, the park-like landscape of Vale do Lobo broadens out. The luxurious holiday destination with its elegant villas, detached houses and spacious apartments – all in typical Moorish architecture – appeal to many of today's eminent visitors. This is not least due to its first class, world famous golf course originally designed by the legendary Sir Henry Cotton and brought up to date by Rocky Roquemore (Royal Course). The well tended fairways and demanding greens run through shady pinewoods right down to the broad Atlantic beaches. The famous Ocean Course was left in its original state despite all the improvements made in the last few years. Incidentally, it's only ten minutes away from the Hotel Quinta do Lago. The 6th hole is beside the beach, a particular attraction for every golfer. The exclusive Royal Course links the nine holes of the recently put down Blue Course with the nine old Yellow Course holes to make a very pleasant if challenging game. The world famous 16th hole is high above the cliffs and the beach and is one of the most frequently photographed holes in Europe. As well as golf the Vale do Lobo provides facilities for 25 other kinds of sports.

Greenfee für Vale do Lobo „The Royal Course" 67,34 Euro, für Vale do Lobo „The Ocean Course" 57,36 Euro. Abschlagzeiten und Platzwunsch sollten wegen großer Nachfrage so früh wie möglich gebucht werden. Telefon: + 3 51 / 2 89 / 39 39 39, Fax: + 3 51 / 2 89 / 39 47 13. Buchungen sind auch über die Golfinformation des Hotels Quinta do Lago möglich, Tel.: + 3 51 / 2 89 / 35 03 50, Fax: + 3 51 / 2 89 / 39 63 93. Handicapnachweis: Herren 28, Damen 36. Bezüglich Kleider- und Softspikevorschriften sollte man sich ebenfalls im Voraus informieren.

Green fee for Vale do Lobo, the Royal Course, 67.34 Euro; for Vale do Lobo's Ocean Course, 57.36 Euro. Tee times and choice of course should be booked as early as possible owing to heavy demand. Phone: + 3 51 / 2 89 / 39 39 39, Fax: – 39 47 13 Booking can also be made at the Golf Information desk at the Hotel Quinta do Lago. Phone: + 3 51 / 2 89 / 35 03 50, Fax: – 39 63 93 Evidence of Handicap required: men 28, ladies 36. t is recommended that golfers inform themselves in advance about clothing and regulations covering soft spikes.

Der berühmte Golfplatz Quinta do Lago war bereits siebenmal Austragungsort der „Portuguese Open".
The famous Quinta do Lago Course has been the venue for the "Portuguese Open" seven times.

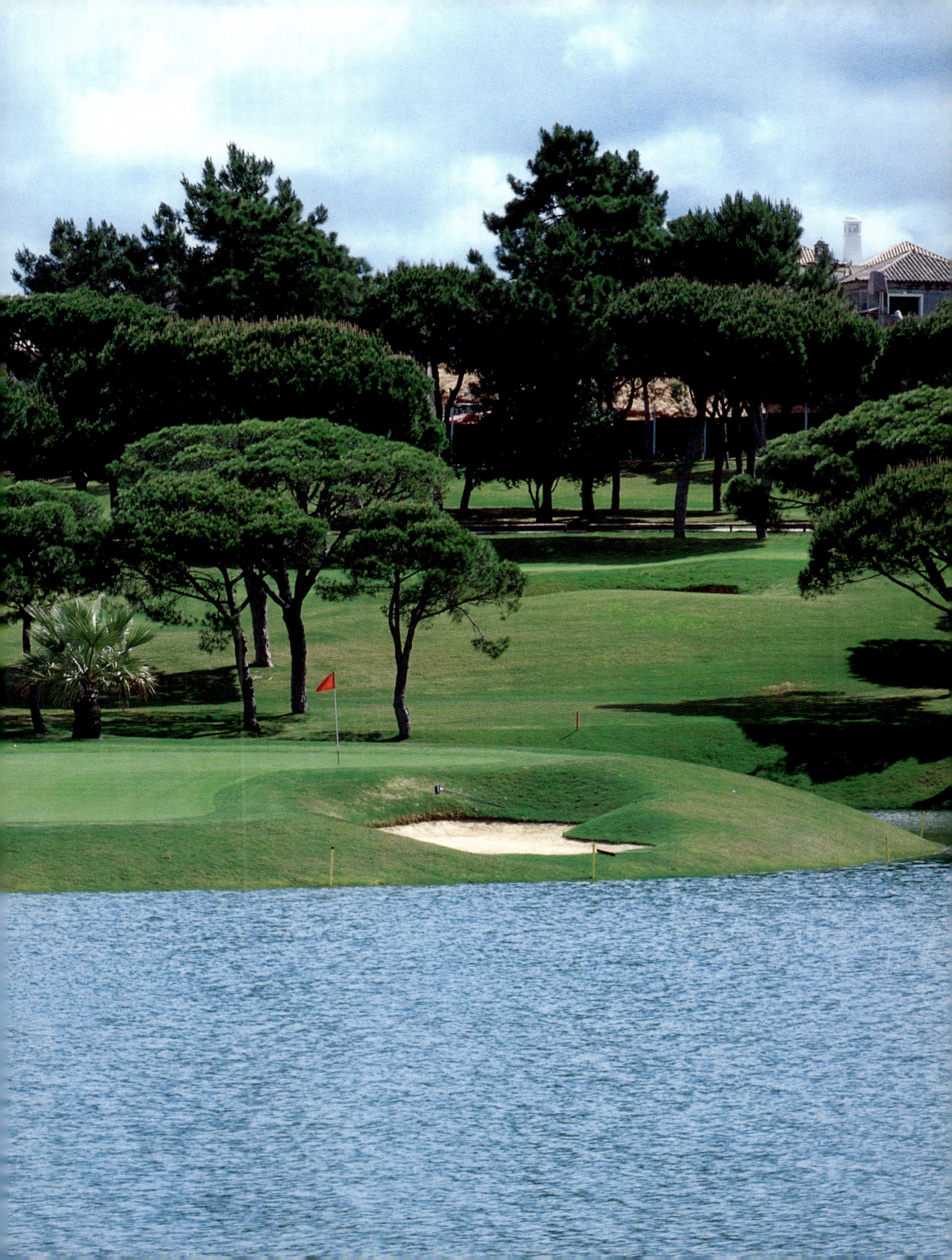

Hotel Quinta do Lago

Umgeben von einer traumhaften Landschaft mit sanften Hügeln und Pinienhainen auf der Landseite und dem idyllischen Naturschutzgebiet der Ria Formosa auf der Meerseite liegt das Hotel Quinta do Lago in der gleichnamigen Golfdestination ruhig und abgeschieden. Wer das luxuriöse Domizil, das seit drei Jahren zu den berühmten Orient-Express-Hotels gehört, besucht, spielt in der Regel Golf. Denn die Golfplätze der Quinta-do-Lago-Anlage sowie die in nächster Umgebung zählen zum Besten, was die Algarve zu bieten hat.

In a quiet and secluded spot in the golf area of the same name, the Hotel Quinta do Lago is surrounded by a fantastic landscape of undulating hills and pine groves on the land side and the idyllic coastal conservation area of the Ria Formosa. Those who stay at this luxurious residence which has been part of the renowned Orient-Express Hotel group for three years now, usually come for the golf because the courses at the Quinta do Lago and those in the vicinity are among the best the Algarve has to offer.

Text: Gundula Luig · Fotos: Ulrich Helweg

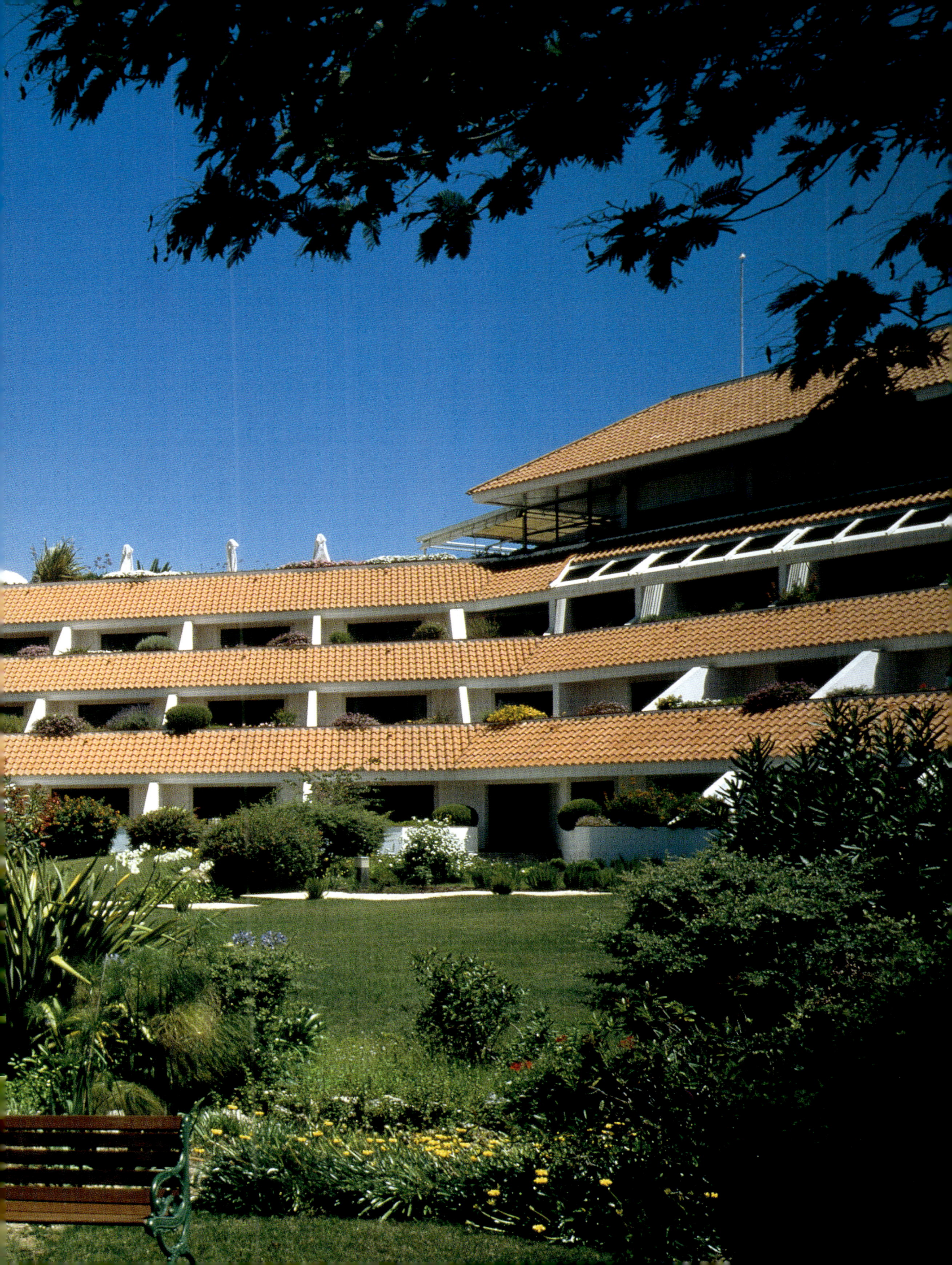

Eine gepflegte Parkanlage heißt den Gast schon beim Eintreffen willkommen.
The well-kept park makes guests feel welcome on arrival.

Elegante Villenurbanisationen grenzen direkt an die Golfanlagen wie hier an den Quinta-do-Lago-Platz.
Elegant groups of villas border the golf courses as seen here beside the Quinta do Lago course.

Kenny Fairbairn has been the PGA professional for five years at the Hotel Quinta do Lago. The smart Englishman shares his international experience enthusiastically with the keen golf clientele at the popular luxury hideaway. Beginners and advanced golfers alike are all eager to accept his advice. The three ladies faithfully following his instructions are just completing a five-day course at the Gold Academy at Quinta do Lago. However, this exclusive coaching package is suitable for every level and is available to individuals or groups. Gently undulating countryside, rustling pine

Kenny Fairbairn ist seit fünf Jahren PGA Golf Professional im Hotel Quinta do Lago. Der smarte Engländer gibt seine internationale Erfahrung engagiert und mitreißend an die Golf begeisterte Klientel der beliebten Luxusherberge weiter. Und sowohl Anfänger als auch weit fortgeschrittene Spieler nehmen gern seine Ratschläge entgegen. Die drei Ladies, die aufmerksam seinen Anweisungen Folge leisten, absolvieren gerade fünf Tage Golfakademie auf dem Quinta-do-Lago-Platz. Dieses exklusive Package-Angebot eignet sich übrigens für jede Ausbildungsstufe und wird einzeln oder in kleinen Gruppen durchgeführt. Sanfte Hügellandschaften, lauschige Pinienhaine und ein lieblicher See bilden das Szenario für die vom Designer William Mitchel phantastisch angelegten Fairways und Greens. Eine Herausforderung besonders für „junge" Golfer, aber gleichermaßen ein Genuss für Könner. Bemerkenswert ist das 15. Loch Par 3. Es wird 190 Meter über dem Wasser auf ein vorzüglich angelegtes Green gespielt. Kenny Fairbairn macht's vor, die Ladies sind beeindruckt.

Quinta do Lago gehört neben Vilamoura und Vale do Lobo zur Trilogie der Spitzen-Golfdestinationen an der südlichen Algarve. Hier blieb nichts dem Zufall überlassen, haben die besten Architekten und Designer ihr ganzes Können umgesetzt, in einer Anlage, die eine Freude für jeden Betrachter ist. Drei meisterschaftstaugliche Golf-Parcours – Pinheiros Altos, Ria Formosa und Quinta do Lago – fügen sich in eine harmonisch und aufwendig kultivierte Natur, geprägt von mediterraner Vegetation und beschaulichen Seenlandschaften. Rund eine halbe Stunde braucht man vom internationalen Flughafen in Faro bis zum Hotel Quinta do Lago, das ganz am Ende der Rua André Jordan liegt, der sich friedlich dahinziehenden Hauptverbindungsader des Sport betonten Ferienkomplexes. Sechs üppig mit Pflanzen geschmückte kleine Kreisverkehre verteilen die Besucher auf die unterschiedlichen Golfanlagen, das Reitzentrum, die großzügig im Gelände platzierten eleganten privaten Villenurbanisationen, die noble Shoppingarena und natürlich das luxuriöse und einzige Hotel vor Ort. Gediegene Eleganz mischt sich dort gekonnt mit der Leichtigkeit eines portugiesischen Sommers, mit den fröhlichen Farben südlicher Sphären. Und es sind nicht ausschließlich die Golfer Europas, die sich von dieser Atmosphäre angezogen fühlen.

Auch Gourmets, Tennisspieler, Reiter, Naturfreunde, Wassersportfans und andere Sportenthusiasten fühlen sich im Quinta do Lago bestens umsorgt. Das im Stil eines Terrassenhauses konzipierte Gebäude öffnet sich weit zum schmucken, gepflegten Garten, der bis zur Lagune des Nationalparks Ria Formosa hinunterreicht. Und von fast jedem der 141 Zimmer und Suiten genießt man diesen herrlichen Ausblick, der über die Lagune, über die vorgelagerten weißen Sanddünen bis zu den Fluten des an endlos scheinende Strände brandenden Atlantiks reicht.

groves and a lovely lake provide the backdrop for the fantastically laid out fairways and greens of designer William Mitchel. It poses a real challenge especially for golfers new to the game, yet it also provides real enjoyment for the experts. The 15th hole par 3 is unusual. It is played across an expanse of water 208 yards wide on to a superbly laid out green. Kenny Fairbairn demonstrates. The ladies are impressed. Quinta do Lago, Vilamoura and Vale do Lobo form a trio of top golf resorts in the south of the Algarve. Nothing has been left to chance. The best designers and architects

Von fast allen Zimmern genießt man diesen traumhaften Ausblick auf Garten, Lagune und Atlantik.

Nearly all the rooms have this fantastic view of the garden, the lagoon and the Atlantic.

Die Sonne der Algarve fangen viele Gäste am liebsten rund um den herrlichen Pool ein.
Many guests congregate around the wonderful pool to catch the Algarve sun.

Statt Obstkorb begrüßt das Quinta do Lago seine Gäste mit einer edlen Karaffe Portwein.
Instead of the usual fruit basket Quinta do Lago welcomes its guests with a carafe of port.

have drawn on their entire expertise to produce grounds which are a joy to behold. Three championship courses, Pinheiros Altos, Ria Formosa and Quinta do Lago, have been created to blend harmoniously into luxuriant, well-kept natural surroundings characterized by Mediterranean vegetation and a tranquil seascapes. One needs about half an hour to get to the Hotel Quinta do Lago from Faro Airport which is situated at the end of the Rua André Jordan, the connecting road which runs peacefully through this sports-orientated holiday complex. Six little roundabouts with luxuriant flower beds channel the visitors to the various golf courses, the riding centre, the spaciously set out groups of villas, the stylish shopping precinct and of course to the luxurious, indeed the only hotel in the vicinity. Inside taste and elegance merge quite naturally with the light atmosphere of a Portuguese summer and the bright colours of southern climes. It isn't only the golfers of Europe who are attracted to this atmosphere. Also gourmets, tennis players, riders, nature lovers, water sports fans and other sports' enthusiasts are utterly satisfied with the facilities at Quinta do Lago.

Zur Begrüßung findet der Gast auf seinem Zimmer nicht den obligatorischen Obstkorb vor, sondern eine hübsche Kristallkaraffe, befüllt mit rotem Port. Eine Bonbonniere enthält köstliche Nougatpralinés, die nicht nur als Betthupferl munden und jeden Tag aufgefüllt werden. Überhaupt sind es die Kleinigkeiten, die den besonderen Charme des

Das portugiesische Fischbuffet, begleitet von traditionellem Fadogesang, ist ein Highlight der Navegadores-Küche.

A Portuguese fish buffet accompanied by Fado singing is one of the highlights at the Navegadores.

Hier trifft man sich zum Tagesausklang und lässt die aufregenden Geschehnisse des Tages noch einmal Revue passieren: die Laguna Bar.

The Laguna Bar: a place to meet at the end of the day and chat about the day's exciting events.

The building set on a terraced slope opens out on to a neat, well-tended garden which extends down to the lagoon of the Ria Formosa National Park. Nearly every one of the 141 rooms and suites affords a view of this wonderful scene, across the lagoon to the offshore white sand dunes beyond, right through to the waters of the seemingly endless beaches of the surging Atlantic. The guest doesn't find the usual welcoming fruit basket in his room but a lovely crystal carafe filled with red port. A confectionery box which is refilled every day contains delicious nougat pralines which don't only taste good as late-night munches. In fact, it is the detail which defines the special charm of Quinta do Lago. The delicately perfumed body series in the bathroom, the many fresh flowers in the rooms and the attentive room service. All guest accommodation has a sun terrace or a balcony with an abundance of potted plants flowers. Cheeky sparrows love to pay regular visits and no piece of bread or little nuts or biscuits are safe from these cheerful feathered creatures.
One never experiences boredom in Quinta do Lago. Sports of course have pride of place in the leisure plans of most guests. Those who aren't on the greens may be on the hotel's own tennis court or in the superbly equipped fitness centre which looks out on to the heated indoor swimming pool and the

Quinta do Lago ausmachen. Die wohlduftende, englische Bodyserie im Bad, die vielen frischen Blumen im Zimmer, der aufmerksame Roomservice. Jedes Gästelogis verfügt außerdem über eine sehr große Sonnenterrasse oder einen ebensolchen Balkon mit reich blühender Bepflanzung. Gern statten die frechen Spatzen aus der Umgebung dort regelmäßige Besuche ab. Vor den lustigen gefiederten Gesellen sind dann kein Stück Brot und ebenso wenig Nüsschen oder Kekse sicher.

Der Langenweile wird man im Quinta do Lago nicht begegnen. Sportliche Aktivitäten stehen natürlich an erster Stelle auf den Freizeitplänen der meisten Gäste. Wer nicht gerade auf den Greens zugange ist, vergnügt sich vielleicht auf dem hauseigenen Tenniscourt, im bestens ausgerüsteten Fitnesscenter mit Blick ins beheizte Hallenbad und weiter auf den verschwenderisch großen Außenpool mit seinen gemütlichen Sonnenliegen. Da lässt es sich aushalten! Wer lieber im Atlantik badet, kann die hoteleigene Strandbasis mit

Allerfeinste venezianische Gourmetküche tischt das Restaurant Cá d'Oro auf.

The Cá d'Oro Restaurant serves the very finest Venetian gourmet cuisine.

Frisches Weiß zu original portugiesischen Azulejo-Fliesen an den Wänden. Ein schöner Kontrast, der das Restaurant Navegadores zu einem beliebten Treffpunkt zu allen Mahlzeiten macht.

Fresh white together with original Portuguese Azulejo tiles on the walls. A wonderful contrast which makes the Navegadores Restaurant a popular rendezvous at all mealtimes.

HIDEAWAYS 91

Mediterranes Flair und Romantik verbinden sich in den Zimmern zu einem optimalen Ambiente.
The rooms combine Mediterranean style and romance to produce an optimal ambience.

Original portugiesische Fliesen und hübsche bunte Keramikutensilien bringen Lokalkolorit ins Spiel.
Original Portuguese tiles and bright and attractive pottery utensils add a touch of local colour.

weiteren Liegen und strohgedeckten Sonnenpilzen in wenigen Gehminuten über die schöne Holzbrücke erreichen, die die Lagune überspannt. Reiter finden ihr Glück im Quinta-do-Lago-Pferdesportzentrum und auf langen Ausritten in idyllischer Natur. Die lässt sich auch per Leihfahrrad oder zu Fuß bequem erkunden. Und wessen Element das Wasser ist, wird auf der Lagune oder dem See beim Surfen, Segeln, Kanu oder Wasserski fahren sportliche Highlights erleben. Und damit nach so viel Einsatz die Muskeln auch schön locker bleiben, sollte man sich eine wohltuende Massage im Health Club des Hotels genehmigen und danach vielleicht noch in die Sauna gehen. Zum Zeitvertreib zwischendurch lockt eine Partie Tischtennis oder Poolbillard.

Wie es sich für ein Mitglied der Orient-Express-Hotels geziemt, offeriert die Küche Großartiges. Die Gäste haben die Qual der Wahl – zwei Restaurants locken mit hervorragenden Zubereitungen. Allen voran das Gourmetrestaurant „Cá d'Oro" mit seiner authentischen venezianischen Cucina. Eine Hommage an das Hotel Cipriani in Venedig, dessen klassischen Spezialitäten wie dem unnachahmlichen Carpaccio oder dem Risotto Primavera eine ganze Seite der Speisenkarte gewidmet ist. Während der umsichtige, äußerst charmante Restaurantmanager Octavio da Silva scheinbar mühelos das perfekte Gelingen der abendlichen Dinnerzeremonie organisiert können sich die Gäste bereits von der zauberhaften Atmosphäre des „Cá d'Oro" gefangen nehmen lassen. Kaminfeuer, Kerzenschein, venezianische Masken und Spiegel an den Wänden setzen den stimmungsvollen Rahmen für Frikassee vom Hummer in Malvasia-Wein oder das große Fischravioli an einer leichten Tomaten-Basilikum-Sauce mit frischem Spinat. Absolute Gaumenverzückung verheißt der warme Schokoladen-Wein-Kuchen an Vanille-Zimt-Sauce zum Dessert. Nicht weniger köstlich, dafür mehr international, aber auch sehr portugiesisch hat der italienische Küchenchef Vincenzo Perez die Karte des „Navegadores"-Restau-

outsize outside pool with its comfortable sunbeds. Not bad at all! Those who prefer to swim in the Atlantic can use the hotel's own stretch of beach only a few minutes walk away which has further sunbeds and straw roofed sun shades and is reached across the lovely wooden bridge spanning the lagoon. Riders can pursue their own brand of happiness at Quinta do Lago's Riding Centre and on long rides through idyllic countryside which can also be discovered by bike or on foot. Visitors whose element is water can get their highs from such sports as surfing, sailing, canoeing and water skiing on the lagoon or in the sea. Then to keep the muscles in trim after so much strain one should treat oneself to a soothing massage at the Hotel's Health Club followed perhaps by a visit to the sauna. To kill time meanwhile there is table tennis or pool. As is fitting for a member of the Orient Express Hotels, the catering is wonderful. Guests have the hard choice – two restaurants tempt the visitor with their superb dishes. The best is the gourmet restaurant Cá d'Oro which serves authentic classic Venetian cuisine. A whole page of the menu

Großzügig und elegant gibt sich die Halle vor der Rezeption.
The entrance hall infront thereception area is spacious and elegant.

Bei Marcia Cristina Teixeira Branco buchen die Gäste individuelle Golfarrangements und Abschlagzeiten direkt im Hotel.
Guests can make individual arrangements for golf and book tee times with Marcia Cristina Teixeira Branco in the hotel itself.

rants gestaltet. Hier erlebt man den romantischen Sonnenuntergang am eindrucksvollsten und genießt ganz rustikal eine Auswahl portugiesischer Wurst- und Schinkenspezialitäten oder samstags das phänomenale Fischbuffet untermalt von original Fadogesang. Der Grill an der Poolterrasse serviert außerdem schmackhafte Fleisch- und Fischgerichte in ungezwungenem Ambiente. Und anschließend lässt man den Abend bei einem leckeren Cocktail in der „Laguna"-Bar ausklingen und freut sich über das just verbesserte Handicap. Vielleicht schaut auch Kenny Fairbairn noch vorbei, von dem die Ladies noch am Abend schwärmerisch plaudern.

is a tribute to the Hotel Cipriani in Venice and features classic specialities such as its inimitable carpaccio or its Risotto Primavera.
While Octavio da Silva, the observant and utterly charming restaurant manager, seems to be effortlessly organizing evening dinner to perfection, guests can succumb to the magical atmosphere of the Cá d'Oro. An open fire, candlelight, Venetian masks and mirrors on the walls create a fitting atmosphere and milieu for lobster fricassee in Malvasia wine, or the large fish ravioli on a light tomato and basil sauce with fresh spinach. Pure rapture for the palate is the warm chocolate wine pudding with a vanilla cinnamon sauce as dessert. No less delicious but more international in nature is the menu created by Vincenzo Perez, the Italian chef at the Navegadores Restaurant, yet it remains very Portuguese. It is here that one gets the most impressive view of the romantic sunset while enjoying a selection country food including Portuguese sausage and ham or, on Saturdays, a phenomenal fish buffet to the sound of original Fado songs. In addition the grill on the pool terrace also serves tasty meat and fish dishes in informal surroundings.
Finally one can end the evening with a tasty cocktail in the Laguna Bar and happily contemplate one's improved handicap. Perhaps Kenny Fairbairn will look by and delight the infatuated ladies still chatting about him in the evening.

Der meistfotografierte Abschlag der Algarve. Das berühmte 16. Loch des Vale-do-Lobo-Parcours liegt hoch über den Klippen.
The most photographed tee in the Algarve. The famous 16th hole of the Vale do Lobo course high above the cliffs.

HIDEAWAYS 93

Golf & Sterne-Küche
Vila Joya

„Warum in die Ferne schweifen", auch Europa bietet Golfern höchst attraktive Landschaften für ihren herausfordernden Sport. In den letzten Jahren konnte Portugals Algarve zwischen Sagres und Faro dank optimaler Flugverbindungen, entsprechenden Klimas und mehr als zwanzig anspruchsvollen Clubs zum gefragten Golfparadies Europas aufsteigen. Die beeindruckende Atlantikküste sowie exklusive Urlaubsdomizile wie die Vila Joya tun ein Übriges, um der neuen Golfregion Vorschub zu leisten.

"Why swan about in far off lands…" Europe offers golfers highly attractive country venues for their challenging sport. In recent years the Algarve in Portugal, between Sagres and Faro, has established itself as a popular golfing paradise in Europe, thanks to optimal climatic conditions, easy access and more than twenty superb golf courses. Its impressive Atlantic coast and exclusive holiday residences such as the Vila Joya, are making their own contribution to fostering this new golfing region.

Text: Jürgen Gutowski, Gundula Luig
Fotos: Jürgen Gutowski, Bärbel Miebach

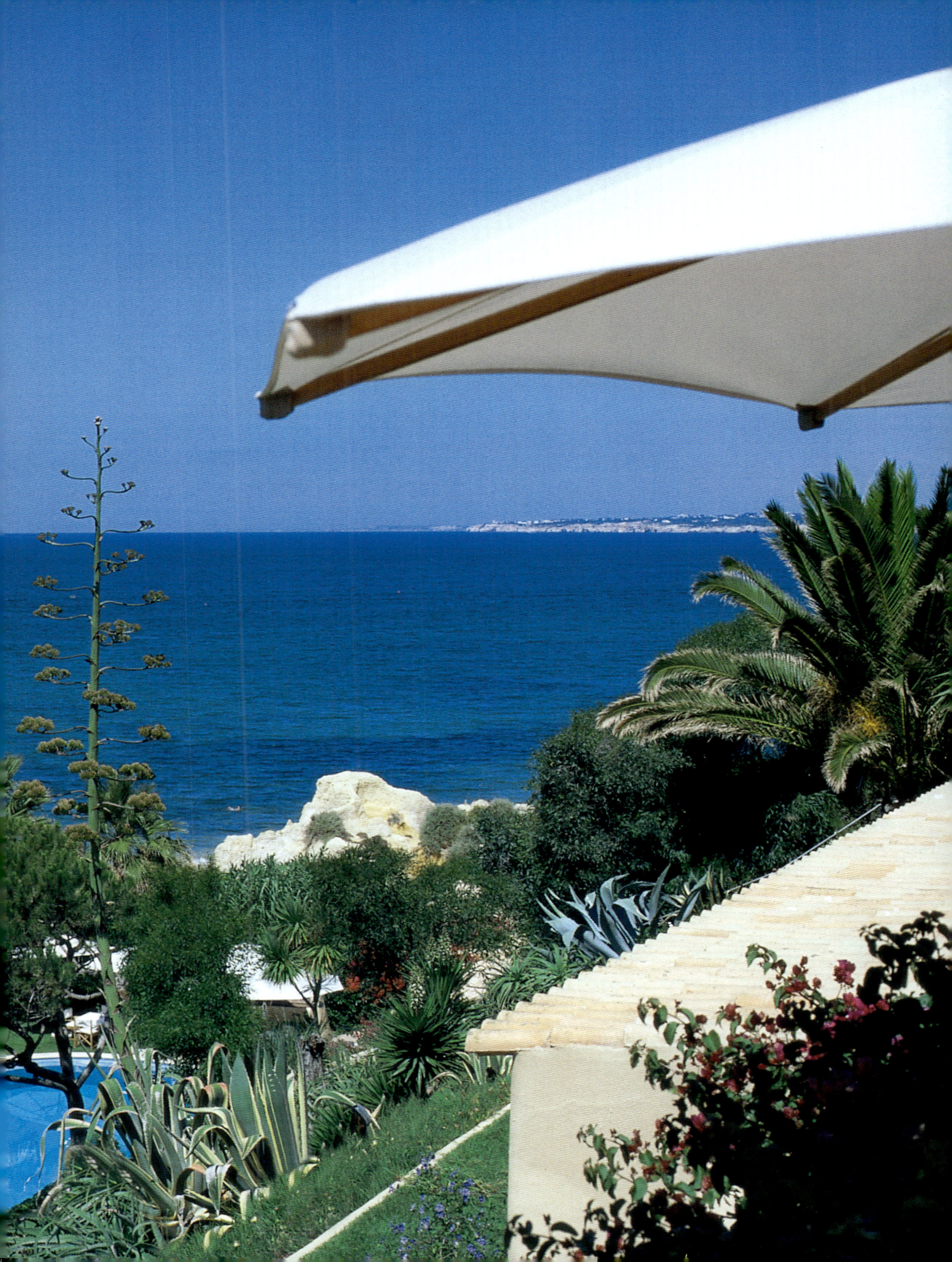

Vila Joya: das Haus des Glücks.
Vila Joya: the house of joy.

Die Vila Joya ist ein Fünf-Sterne-Haus an der wunderschönen Algarveküste.
Vila Joya is a five star house at the charming coast of Algarve.

The Portuguese Algarve: waves break on massive sandstone cliffs and fig trees nestle into the hilly landscape of the country at Europe's most southerly point. Clusters of whitewashed houses, narrow, crooked lanes and tiny baroque churches are typical of the villages where time seems to stand still. No wonder these windswept foothills that reach into the Atlantic were once called "Fim do Mundo" (the end of the world). It was here that in the 15th century Henry the Mariner collected the men around him who planned those famous voyages of discovery which were to make Portugal great. The Portuguese gave up being a seafaring nation long ago, but in recent years this little country has been at the heart of another craze and is now a sporting paradise for golfers. The Algarve has the right conditions for a golf season all the year round. Even in winter with temperatures at around 15° centigrade light clothing can be worn. What is more, the pro-

Die portugiesische Algarve: Wellen klatschen an gewaltige Sandsteinklippen, Feigenbäume schmiegen sich eng an das bergige Land am südwestlichsten Punkt Europas. Eng aneinandergedrängte, weiß gekalkte Häuser, schmale, winklige Gassen und barocke Kirchlein prägen die Dörfer, in denen die Zeit still zu stehen scheint. Kein Wunder, dass dieses windumtoste Vorgebirge, das in den Atlantik ragt, einst „Fim do Mundo" (Ende der Welt) genannt wurde. In dieser Gegend versammelte Heinrich der Seefahrer im 15. Jahrhundert einst seine Mannen, die jene großen Entdeckungsreisen vorbereiteten, die Portugal groß machen sollten. Als Seefahrernation mussten die Portugiesen schon lange abdanken, aber in den letzten Jahren macht das kleine Land in einer anderen Disziplin Furore: Als Sportparadies für Golfer. Die Algarve bietet alle Voraussetzungen für eine ganzjährige Saison, sogar im Winter lassen die Durchschnittstemperaturen um 15 °C luftige Kleidung zu. Und die Projekte der Golfmanager werden immer Aufsehen erregender. Doch dazu später. Eine halbe Autostunde westlich, kurz vor Albufeira, haben sich Wind und Wellen beruhigt. Hier, inmitten von Pinienwäldern, Orangengärten und Mandelbaumplantagen, scheint die Welt, sonnendurchflutet an 300 Tagen des Jahres, noch in Ordnung zu sein. Weit entfernt von den Betonsilos von Portimão öffnet sich hinter einem schmiedeeisernen Portal eine nach Rosen, Bougainvilleen und Atlantik duftende Einfahrt zu einem Haus, das es wahrlich in sich hat. Die Vila Joya im maurischen Baustil erinnert an einen kleinen orientalischen Palazzo, und tatsächlich tritt plötzlich ein arabischer Sultan aus der Tür. Bei der Begrüßung stellt sich jedoch heraus, dass Senhor João Dias im wallenden weißen Gewand der „Maître de plaisir" ist, und spätestens beim Handkuss für die Dame ist klar: Der Maître beherrscht die Kunst der Gastfreundschaft tatsächlich par excellence.

Die lichte, antik möblierte Halle mit einem Deckengewölbe aus kunstvoll verlegten braunen Tonklinkern umfängt den Gast mit einer Atmosphäre zwangloser Eleganz und gibt den Blick frei auf den schimmernden, unendlich scheinenden Atlantik. Von hier erreicht man mit wenigen Schritten die Panoramaterrasse des Hotels. Von dort oben streift der Blick ungehindert über den großen subtropischen Hotelpark mit Palmen, Zypressen, Pfefferminzbäumen und Agaven, mittendrin der geschwungene 180 Quadratmeter große beheizte Pool, dahinter die hellen Dünen und Klippen der Algarveküste und der Ozean. Sechs Kilometer lang ist der Strand, der an dieser Stelle selbst in der Hochsaison nie überlaufen ist.

Über die geschwungene Freitreppe gelangen die Gäste zu den Gemächern der Vila. Gerade einmal zwölf Doppelzimmer und fünf Suiten stehen zur Verfügung, angefangen vom einfachen, aber komfortablen Doppelzimmer bis hin zum Traum aus Tausendundeiner Nacht in der gleichnamigen atemberaubenden Suite „1001" in goldenen Farbtönen und Samt und Seide. Der Beweis, dass plüschene Opulenz eine gelungene Symbiose mit High-End-Komfort eingehen kann, wurde hier erbracht. Luxus der Extraklasse auch in der namentlich verwandten, aber optisch doch völlig anders konfigurierten Royal Suite 2001 mit ihrem futuristisch anmutenden Bad. Auch ist hier nichts unmöglich, wenn der Gast besondere Vorlieben hat. Insgesamt bleibt festzuhalten, dass die Zimmer keine Wünsche offen lassen, alle haben Meerblick, Telefon, Minibar,

jects of golf managers are becoming ever more sensational, but more of that later.

Half and hour's drive eastwards, just before you get to Albufeira, the wind and the waves have settled. Here, in the middle of pine forests, orange groves and plantations of almond trees, one has the impression that all's right with the world for 300 sundrenched days a year. Far away from the concrete silos of Portimão, behind a wrought iron gate is a driveway heavy with the scent of roses, bougainvillaea and the Atlantic which leads to a truly special house. Vila Joya built in Moorish style is reminiscent of a small oriental palace. Suddenly an Arab Sultan steps out of the door but as we greet one another it transpires that Senhor João Dias swathed in his white robes is the "Maître de plaisir". At latest as he kisses the lady's hand, it is clear that the Maître is a past master of hospitality.

The guest enters a light hall with a

domed ceiling built of artistically laid brown clay bricks and furnished with antiques, and is immediately enveloped by an atmosphere of informal elegance. The hall affords a view of the seemingly infinite, shimmering Atlantic. Just a few steps away is a panorama terrace from where one has a clear view across the hotel's big sub-tropical park with palms, cypresses, peppermint trees and agaves. In the middle is a big curved heated pool of 180 square metres and beyond it are the light dunes and cliffs of the Algarve coast and the ocean. The six kilometre-long beach is never crowded at this point, even in the high season.

Guests reach their rooms up a sweeping flight of steps. There are only 12 double rooms and five suites, starting with simple but comfortable double rooms to a dream from A Thousand and One Nights. The breathtaking suite of the same name "1001", furnished in golden tones, velvet and silk, is evidence indeed that opulent luxury and the highest level of comfort can be successfully combined. There is also exceptional luxury in the similarly named but optically totally different Royal Suite 2001 which has a bathroom with a futuristic design. Here too, nothing is spared for the guest who has special preferences. All in all it has to be stated that the rooms leave nothing to be desired, since all have sea views, telephone, Radio, Fön, Safe und Bademäntel. Ein besonders erfreuliches Bonbon für Musikfreunde: Jedes Zimmer ist mit einem CD-Spieler ausgerüstet, mehr als hundert Klassik-CDs stehen zur Verfügung. Außerdem spannende Bettlektüre in vielen Sprachen.

Herrlich, wenn man diesen Komfort mit dem Lieblingssport verbinden kann. Gleich auf vier der umliegenden Golfplätze erhalten Gäste der Vila Joya attraktive Greenfee-Ermäßigungen bis zu 35 Prozent. Auch übernimmt das Hotel die Buchungen von Startzeiten. Nur 2,5 Kilometer entfernt, im Vale da Perra, fordert der Salgados Golf Club mit unüberschaubaren Wasserhindernissen heraus. Die hat schon so mancher unterschätzt, denn das Terrain ist ansonsten recht flach. Ebenfalls nicht weit, bei Quarteira, lockt eine Golfoase der Superlative: Vilamoura. Gleich mehrere Plätze offerieren hier alles, was das Herz eines Golfers höher schlagen lässt. Mit dem vor wenigen Jahren sanierten Vilamoura I, dem heutigen „The Old Course", verfügt die Anlage über einen der Top-Plätze Europas. Und auf Vilamoura II und III können Spieler jeglichen Ausbildungsstandes individuell und je nach Können ihr jeweiliges Handicap verbessern. Wenn es nach einem spannungs- und sonnenreichen Spieltag Abend wird in der Vila

Eine Treppe führt direkt zum Strand.
The staircase leads directly to the beach.

Joya, liegt Musik in der atlantischen Luft, die sich sanft mit entferntem Wellengeplänkel mischt. Während des Sonnenunterganges legt die alte, ewig junge Sandsteinküste der Algarve noch ein bisschen abendliches Rouge auf ihr sprödes Antlitz. Die Kerzen flackern auf den festlich gedeckten Tischen auf der Terrasse. Hier, oberhalb des weiten Strandes „Praia de Galè", ist die Ruhe jetzt mit Händen zu greifen, die hibiskus- und oleanderduftende Stille mit jedem Atemzug zu inhalieren.

minibar, radio, hairdryer, a safe and bathrobes. A real treat for music lovers is that every room has a CD-player and more than 100 classic CDs are available for guests. In addition there are thrillers in many languages for bedtime reading. Such comfort is wonderful when combined with one's favourite sport. Guests enjoy green fee reductions of up to 35 % on four of the surrounding golf courses and the hotel can book tee times. Only 2.5 kilometres away, at Vale da Perra, the Salgados Golf Club with water hazards impossible to detect, poses a real challenge to golfers. Many have underestimated it because the terrain if fairly flat. Also not very far away, near Quarteira, is Vilmoura, a superlative golfing oasis. Several courses pro-

HIDEAWAYS 99

vide the golfer with everything the heart desires. The redeveloped Vilamoura I, now called the "Old Course", is today one of the top-ranked courses in Europe. But on Vilamoura II and III golfers of all ability levels can improve their individual handicaps. In the evening following an exciting sunny day of golf, music is in the Atlantic air at Vila Joya, merging gently with the distant sound of the surf. As the sun sets, the old, eternally youthful sandstone coast of the Algarve adds a little evening rouge to its rough countenance. Candles flicker on the beautifully laid tables on the terrace. Here, above the broad beach of Praia de Galè, the peace is a palpable; the tranquillity perfumed with hibiscus and oleander is inhaled with every

Urlaubsleben jenseits von Handy und Terminkalender. Ein leichter Wind streicht über die Terrasse des maurischen Palazzos, dessen Name korrekt übersetzt eigentlich „Schmuckkästchen" bedeutet. Und es zeigt sich auch beim Dinieren: Die Vila Joya ist wirklich mit einer wertvollen kleinen Schatulle voller Pretiosen zu vergleichen. Dass jeder Gourmet hier voll auf seine Kosten kommt, ist zuallererst das Verdienst des österreichischen Sternekochs Dieter Koschina, der das Restaurant der Vila Joya innerhalb weniger Jahre zur besten Adresse Portugals avancieren ließ. Persönlich inspiziert er regelmäßig die Märkte der Algarve, immer auf der Suche nach Lebensmitteln erster Güte. Er kauft den Atlantischen Hummer, Languste und Steinbutt von einheimischen Fischern, Trüffel, Gänseleber und Kaviar bezieht er von den besten Märkten Europas. Das Resultat: Chef Koschina und seine acht Köche präsentieren seit 1991 ein unschlagbares Qualitätsniveau von stets gleich bleibender

Güte. Die frische Leichtigkeit der erstklassigen internationalen Küche genossen denn auch schon eine ganze Reihe prominenter Persönlichkeiten, die sich von den Zubereitungen genauso begeistert zeigten wie die gestrengen Michelin-Tester: Koschinas Vila-Joya-Restaurant wurde kürzlich mit einem zweiten Stern geadelt – ohne Beispiel in Portugal.

breath. This is indeed vacation beyond the world of the mobile phone and the appointments diary. A light breeze plays on the terrace of the Moorish palace whose name correctly translated means "jewellery box", certainly true of dining at Vila Joya which really can be compared to a casket full of valuables. The fact that every gourmet delights in coming here is to the credit of top Austrian chef Dieter Koschina, who, within a few years, has promoted the restaurant at Vila Joya to the best address in Portugal. He personally visits the markets of the Algarve in his tireless search for top quality ingredients. He buys Atlantic lobster, crayfish and turbot from local fishermen and truffles, pâté de foie gras and caviar from the best markets in Europe. The result is that since 1991 Chef Koschina and his eight cooks have been producing unbeatable and consistent quality. The freshness and lightness of the first class international cuisine has been savoured by a large number of VIPs who have expressed as much enthusiasm for the dishes as the demanding Michelin inspectors. Koschina's Vila Joya Restaurant was recently bestowed with a second star – unprecedented in Portugal.

HIDEAWAYS 101

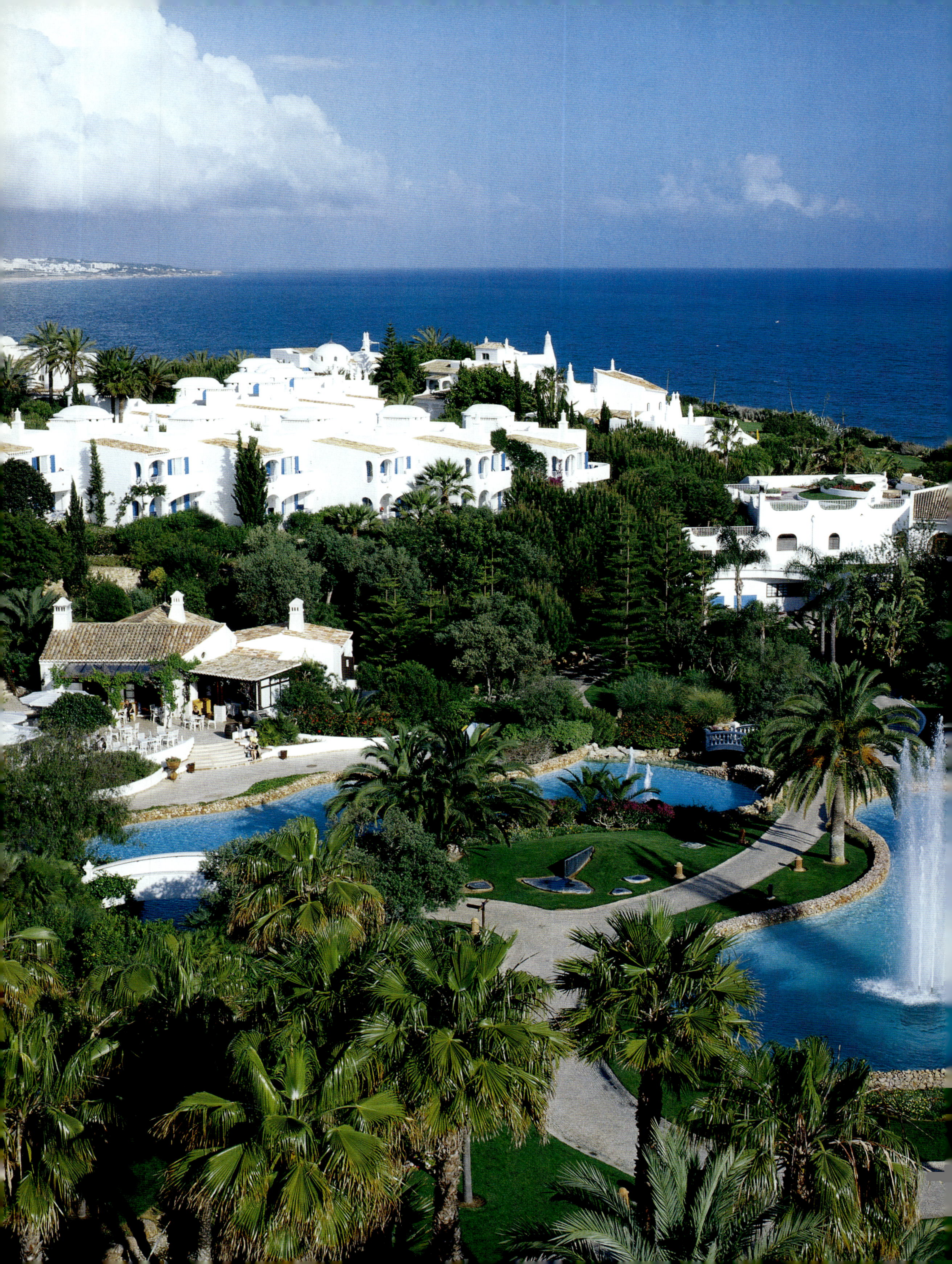

Grüne Insel auf dem Festland

Vila Vita Parc

A green island on the mainland

Urlaub unter Palmen, mit Sonne satt, Strand und Meer – ein Traum, für den man nicht unbedingt um die halbe Welt reisen muss. Ganz nah, nur knapp drei Flugstunden von Deutschland entfernt, an Portugals Algarve, wird er wahr. Denn dieser sonnenverwöhnte Landstrich gehört zu den wetterbeständigsten Regionen der Erde. Hier laden traumhafte Strände an einer abwechslungsreichen Küstenlandschaft zum Sonne tanken ein und Vila Vita Parc zu Ferien und Entspannung auf höchstem Niveau.

A holiday beneath palms saturated with sun, sand and sea – a dream for which one needn't necessarily have to journey round half the world. In fact it's very close, in Portugal's Algarve, just under three hours flying time from Germany. This sun-drenched area is one of the best regions in the world for constantly good weather. Its fantastic beaches and varied coastline are an inviting prospect for those wishing to tank up on sunshine. A vacation at Vila Vita Parc means relaxation at the highest possible standard.

Text: Gundula Luig · Fotos: Ulrich Helweg / Hélio Ramos

Das Vila Vita Parc Hotel fügt sich in beschwingter Architektur in die faszinierende Landschaftsgestaltung. Vom Aussichtsturm hat man den besten Rundumblick.
The vibrant architecture of Vila Vita Parc Hotel merges into fascinating landscaped grounds. The best all round view can be had from the look-out tower.

Wo man hinschaut Palmen und ein Meer von Blüten.
Everywhere one looks there are palms and a sea of flowers.

The white houses with their light red tiles look like a Moorish village blending aesthetically into the fabulous fifty acre site. A sea of lavish blooms ripples in the gentle Atlantic breeze. Colours range from deep magenta and brilliant orange to pale pastel tones of pink and light blue. Winding through them is a network of connecting paths intersecting neat English lawns and overlooked by an impressive variety of vegetation. Over 200 different kinds of palms, olive trees, pines, flowering hedges and bushes as well as numerous herbs unite into a symphony of the senses, a heavenly setting for the ponds, water features, fountains and lawns. Circling above this scene are the gulls, searching for vantage points here and there on the Moorish turrets and

Wie ein maurisches Dorf muten die weißen Häuser mit den blassroten Ziegeldächern an, fügen sich ästhetisch ein in den 20 Hektar messenden Paradepark. Ein Meer von verschwenderisch blühenden Blumen wiegt seine Blüten im sanften Atlantikwind. Von tiefem Magenta über leuchtend Orange bis zu blassen Pastelltönen in Rosé und Bleu reicht die Farbenpracht. Dazwischen schlängelt sich ein Netz von verbindenden Gehwegen, eingebettet in exakt gemähten Englischen Rasen, überragt von einer beeindruckenden Vegetationsvielfalt. Mehr als 200 verschiedene Arten Palmen, Olivenbäume, Pinien, Blühhecken und -sträucher sowie zahlreiche Gewürzpflanzen vereinen sich zu einer Symphonie der Sinne, geben Teichen und Wasserspielen, Brunnen und Grünflächen einen paradiesischen Rahmen. Über allem kreisen die Möven, suchen sich hier und da ein Aussichtsplätzchen auf den maurischen Türmchen und Kuppeln, deren strahlendes Weiß sich plastisch vom satten Blau des Himmels abhebt. Mit diesem ersten tiefen Eindruck bezaubert Vila Vita Parc seine ankommenden Gäste und für die Dauer ihres Aufenthalts wird der Reigen aus schönen Erlebnissen für Körper, Seele und Geist niemals abreißen.

Auch wer sich in Vila Vita Parc spontan wie im Garten Eden fühlt, möchte beherbergt werden. Und da verfügt das Resort gleich über eine Auswahl mehrerer anspruchsvoller Logismöglichkeiten. Im harmonisch mit der Landschaft verschlungenen Hotelgebäude mit seinem alles andere überragenden Aussichtsturm lassen 65 Zim-

Kuppeln und Türmchen, fließende Formen und strahlendes Weiß – die Architektur des Oasis Parc dokumentiert das arabische Kulturerbe Portugals.
Domes and turrets, flowing forms and brilliant white – the architecture of the Oasis Parc is evidence of Portugal's Arabic cultural heritage.

Wer in der Residence logiert, wird vom Rauschen des Atlantiks, in den Schlaf gewiegt.
Guests staying at the residence fall asleep to the sound of the Atlantic.

mer und acht Suiten von großzügigen Balkonen und Terrassen aus den Blick über die Gartenanlage bis hin zum Meer schweifen. Die Interieurs dieses einzigartigen Privathotels, das zu Recht den The Leading Hotels of the World angehört, wurden von feinfühlender Hand ausgewählt. Stilsicher orientiert an Land und Landschaft, ergänzt durch traditionelle Keramik, kostbare Teppiche und originale Kunstwerke. Ein Ambiente, das mit Behaglichkeit besticht. Wer das sanfte Rauschen des Meeres beim Einschlafen hören möchte, sollte sich in der „Residence" einquartieren. Das stilvolle Gebäude mit Herrenhauscharakter liegt nahe der Steilküste und verfügt über 26 elegante Zimmer sowie zwei Maisonette-Suiten und eine Suite. Im Haus befindet sich auch die beliebte „Ocean Bar", auf deren Terrasse man die traumhaftesten Sonnenaufgänge erleben kann. Wer gerne in einer Junior-Suite logieren möchte oder mit den Kindern eine Familien-Suite für vier Personen bevorzugt, fühlt sich im „Oasis Parc" wohl. Von seinen Dachterrassen aus lässt sich das mannigfaltige Farbspiel der Sonne über den Tag beobachten. Die Appartements des „Vista Parc" liegen etwas außerhalb des Vila-Vita-Areals, sind aber mit wenigen Schritten bequem zu erreichen. Sie bieten Raum für bis zu sechs Personen. Wer es noch ein wenig exklusiver möchte, entscheidet sich für die „Vila Praia" oder „Vila Trevo". Die beiden Luxusvillen auf den Klippen über dem Atlantik sind das *Nonplusultra* des

domes, their gleaming white standing out against the deep blue sky. Guests arriving at Vila Vita Parc are all profoundly affected by this first impression, and for the whole duration of their stay the round of experiences for body, soul and spirit never ceases.
But those at Vila Vita Parc who immediately feel they have arrived in the Garden of Eden need somewhere to stay, and the resort provides a whole range of high class accommodation. The hotel building whose campanile towers over everything, harmoniously blends into the landscape. It has sixty-five rooms and eight suites with spacious balconies and terraces which afford a view over the gardens to the sea beyond. The interiors of this unique private hotel which justifiably belongs to The Leading Hotels of the World were chosen with great sensitivity. The sound sense of style influenced by the land and the landscape is embellished with traditional ceramics, exquisite carpets and original works of art creating an ambience characterized by cosiness and comfort. Anyone wanting to be lulled to sleep by the gentle sound of the sea is well advised to stay at the "Residence". The stylish mansion-like building is close to high cliffs and has twenty-six elegant rooms, two maisonettes and one suite. The building also houses the popular Ocean Bar which has a terrace from which one can view the most fantastic sunrises. Guests who would rather stay in a Junior Suite or with their children in a family suite for four, are best accommodated in the Oasis Parc. From their roof terraces one can watch the play of colours in the

Portugals Fliesen-Tradition ist an den Wänden wie auf dem Boden sichtbar. Die Azulejo-Kacheln sind von Hand bemalt.
Portugal's tile tradition can be seen on walls and floors. The Azulejo tiles are hand-painted.

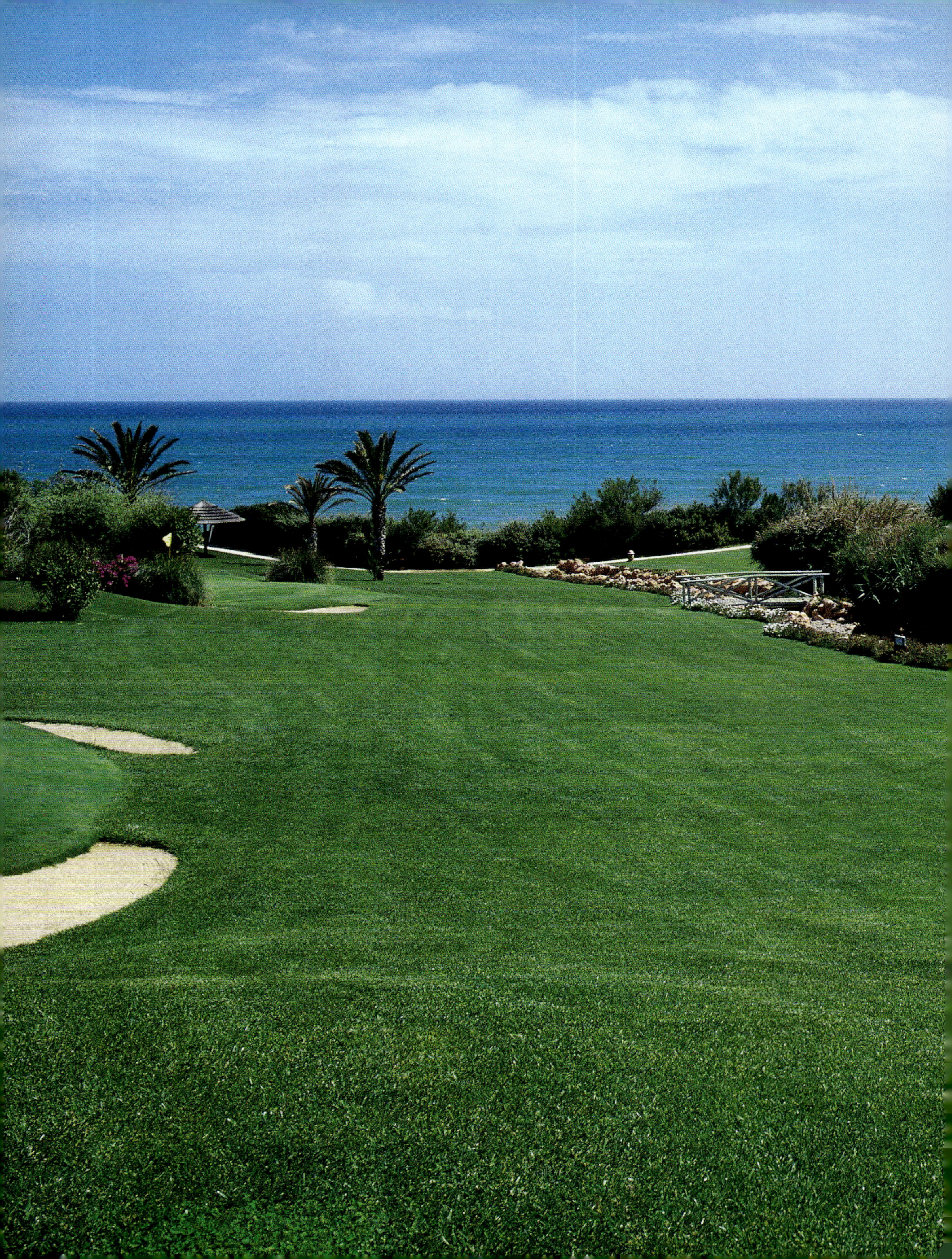

Der hoteleigene 9-Loch-Golfplatz verfügt auch über ein 18-Loch-Putting-Green.
The hotel's own 9-hole golf course also has a 18-hole putting green.

In der Bäderabteilung entführen romantische Wandmalereien schnell in eine andere Welt.

The romantic murals in the baths area transport you into another world.

sunlight throughout the day. The Vista Parc apartments are just outside the actual Vila Vita site but can be easily reached on foot. They have enough space for up to six persons. Those preferring something slightly more exclusive choose the "Vila Praia" or the "Vila Trevo". These two luxury villas with four suites each on the cliffs overlooking the Atlantic are the very best the Vila Vita Parc has to offer, and also have a garden with a private pool. Strolling through the subtropical garden one inevitably meets up on the idyllic little Piazetta. The "village square" in the centre of the grounds is the social centre for grownups and children alike. One can have an espresso at the Adega restaurant or indulge in such Portuguese specialities as cataplana. The boutique next door sells useful

Vila Vita Parc und verfügen jeweils über einen Garten mit privatem Pool.

Bei einem Spaziergang durch den subtropischen Garten trifft man unweigerlich auf die idyllische Piazetta. Der „Dorfplatz" im Herzen der Anlage ist geselliger Mittelpunkt für große und kleine Gäste. Hier trinkt man in der „Adega Bar" gemütlich seinen Vinho Verde oder lässt sich von portugiesischen Spezialitäten wie der Cataplana verführen. Die Boutique nebenan verkauft nützliche Kleinigkeiten für den Alltag sowie aktuelle Mode, landestypische Souvenirs, Sport- und Freizeitaccessoires. Verlässt man die Piazetta linker Hand, führt der Weg über Treppen und Treppchen am „Oasis Parc" vorbei direkt zum hoteleigenen Golfplatz. Die landschaftlich schöne 9-Loch-Pitch-&-Putt-Anlage verfügt über eine kurze Driving Range und ein 18-Loch-Putting-Green. Erfahrene PGA Pros betreuen die Spieler in der Golfakademie. Überhaupt kommen sportlich veranlagte Gäste im Vila Vita Parc voll auf ihre Kosten. Tennis, Squash, Tauchen und Windsurfen stehen ebenso auf dem Programm wie Wassergymnastik,

Step-Aerobics, Petanque, Strand-Jogging, Callenetics, Yoga und spezielle tibetanische Übungen zur Harmonisierung von Körper und Geist. Wer mit dem Motto „No Sports!" anreist, wird vom Angebot des neuen Vila Vita Vital Centers begeistert sein. Rosemarie Bodamer und ihre hervorragenden Mitarbeiter sind bestens auf Gäste vorbereitet, die Stress abbauen und Vitalität auftanken möchten. Mit einer großen Bandbreite von Bädern, Spezialmassagen, Aromatherapien und kosmetischen Behandlungen lässt der Erfolg nicht lange auf sich warten. Nicht zuletzt tragen sicherlich die einzigartigen Ambiancen der im Stil römischer Bäder konzipierten Wellness-Einrichtung dazu bei. Begleitet von sphärischer Musik wirken die von Säulen und Bögen geprägte Architektur, die wunderschönen Deckenfresken, die antiken Bäder sowie altertümliche Dekore auf den Betrachter stimulierend ein.

Sonnenanbeter aalen sich auf komfortablen Liegen am breiten Atlantikstrand des Resorts. Mit Hilfe Tausender Tonnen Sand, die dem Meeresboden an anderer Stelle entnommen wurden, konnte der Strandabschnitt unterhalb

1001 Nacht lässt grüßen: Beim Aladin-Grill stimmen Küche und Ambiente.
Welcome to 1001 Nights. At the Aladin Grill cuisine and atmosphere go well together.

Links: Erst vor einem Jahr eröffnet: das phantastische Vila Vita Vital Center.
Left: Opened only a year ago – the fantastic Vila Vita Vital Centre.

Links: 8 000 Flaschen lagern im acht Meter unter der Erde liegenden Cave de Vinhos. Dort eine Weinprobe zu nehmen ist ein Muss.
Left: 8.000 bottles are stored 26 feet below ground in the Cave de Vinhos. A wine tasting here is an absolute must.

Italienischen Charme versprüht das Restaurant Bela Vita. Die Gourmetküche ist exzellent.
The Bela Vita restaurant sparkles with Italian charm. The gourmet cuisine is excellent.

Das Clubhouse zur Poolside: Hier befinden sich die meisten Restaurants und Bars des Resorts.
The poolside Clubhouse where most of the resort's restaurants and bars are located.

little items for daily use as well as the latest fashions, typical Portuguese souvenirs and sports and leisure accessories.

If you leave the Piazetta on the left, the path leads over flights of steps and little steps, pass the "Oasis Parc" straight to the hotel's own golf course. The scenically beautiful golf facilities has a 9-hole course, a short driving range and a 18-hole putting green. Experienced PGA pros are in charge of players at the Golf Academy, in fact guests fond of sport are extremely well catered for at Vila Vita Parc. Tennis, squash, diving and windsurfing are as much part of the programme as water gymnastics, step aerobics, pètanque, beach jogging, callistheniscs, yoga and special Tibetan exercises to induce physical and spiritual harmony. Anyone coming here fearing there may be no sports will

HIDEAWAYS 109

Auf der Piazetta ist immer Betrieb, wie in einem richtigen Dorf. Dahinter der maurisch inspirierte Oasis Parc.

The little Piazetta is always busy, just like a real village. Behind it is the Moorish inspired Oasis Parc.

Unten: Der Strand wurde unter großem Aufwand um das Fünffache verbreitert.

Above: The beach was made five times bigger at great cost.

be absolutely thrilled with the range on offer at the new Vila Vita Vital Center. Rosemarie Bodamer and her outstanding colleagues are superbly equipped for guests who want to reduce stress and increase their vitality. They won't need to wait long here with the wide range of baths, special massages, aroma therapy and cosmetic treatments on offer. Yet the unique ambience of the wellness facility built in the style of Roman baths must also surely play its part. To the sound of celestial music the architecture dominated by pillars and arches, the wonderful murals on the ceiling, the ancient baths and old world décor have a stimulating effect on the beholder.

Sun worshippers stretch out on comfortable loungers on the broad Atlantic beach. Using thousands of tons of sand taken from the sea bed at another spot, the section of beach at the foot of the cliffs it was possible to make five times wider. Shielded from the breakers, children can

der Klippen um das Fünffache verbreitert werden. Geschützt von Wellenbrechern baden nun auch Kinder sicher. In besonderem Maße lobenswert ist die Familienfreundlichkeit dieses unvergleichlichen Urlaubsparadieses. Im Gegensatz zu vielen anderen Fünf-Sterne-Häusern sind Kinder und Jugendliche herzlich willkommen – und werden mit Sicherheit eine Superzeit verbringen. Etwa in Annabella's Kids Park, wo Spaß, Abenteuer und Unterhaltung ganztags unter fachkundiger Betreuung stattfinden. Teenager bis 17 Jahre haben ihren eigenen Club mit

vollem Freizeit- und Sportprogramm, und die Kleinsten von sechs Monaten bis zu vier Jahren fühlen sich in der Kinderkrippe wohl.

Wenn sich die Abendstimmung über der Urlaubsdestination breit macht, ist Dinnertime. Dann hat man die Qual der Wahl zwischen sechs Restaurants. Feinschmecker werden von der unvergleichlichen Vielfalt der Gerichte und Weine, die auf den Menükarten zu finden sind, begeistert sein. Eine betörende Woge der Aromen, die von den berühmten frischen Meeresfrüchten der Algarve über die traditionell portugiesische

Links: Komfortable Junior-Suite im Oasis Parc.
Left: Comfortable Junior Suite in the Oasis Parc.

Privatsphäre garantiert: Luxussuite in der Vila Praia.
Privacy guaranteed. Luxury suite in the Vila Praia.

Küche bis hin zu den besten italienischen und französischen Kreationen reicht. Liebhaber der Haute Cuisine werden im Bela Vita Restaurant und auf dessen romantischer Terrasse mit den kulinarischen Köstlichkeiten Italiens verwöhnt. Der extravagante Aladin-Grill entführt in exotisch-orientalische Gefilde. Fangfrische Fische, Krusten- und Schalentiere sowie Steaks werden in der runden Showküche im Zentrum des Restaurants vor den Augen der Gäste zubereitet. Das Atlantico setzt auf Cuisine française, inklusive fantastischem Meeresblick. Eine Aussichtsterrasse und Themenbuffets machen das helle und freundliche „The Whale" zum beliebten Familientreffpunkt. Und richtig portugiesisch rustikal, bei Fadogesang und herzhafter Küche, geht es im O Prato de Porches zu. Zum vier Kilometer entfernten Restaurant besteht ein kostenloser Shuttle-Servive. Eine besondere Attraktion und in seiner Art einzigartig an der Algarve ist der Cave de Vinhos. Das gotische Gewölbe des acht Meter unter der Erde liegenden Kellers wurde aus antiken Steinen errichtet, die eigens dafür aus Ägypten, Griechenland und Österreich importiert wurden. Hier unten lagert eine eindrucksvolle Sammlung von rund 8 000 Weinflaschen aus aller Welt. Eine Weinprobe wird da zum unvergesslichen Erlebnis.

bath here safely too. The family-friendly atmosphere of this matchless holiday paradise is highly commendable. In contrast to many other five star resorts, children and young people are most welcome, and without a doubt they have a super time. At Annabella's Kids' Parc for instance, they can have fun, adventure and entertainment the whole day long under professional supervision. Teenagers up to seventeen years old have their own club which offers a complete programme of leisure activities and sports. Nursery age children from six months to four years old are quite happy in the crèche. When duskfalls on this holiday destination it is dinner time. One then has the difficulty of choosing between six restaurants. Bon vivants will be delighted with the exceptional variety of dishes and wines on the menu. Beguiling aromas lie on the air, from the famously fresh seafood of the Algarve and traditional Portuguese cuisine to the best Italian and French culinary creations. Lovers of haute cuisine can indulge in the culinary delights of Italy at the Bela Vita Restaurant and on its romantic terrace. The extravagant Aladin Grill lures you into an exotic, oriental realm of delights. Freshly caught fish, crustaceans and steaks are cooked in full view of diners in the circular show kitchen at the centre of the restaurant. French cuisine is served at the Atlantico which also has fantastic ocean views. The Whale, a light and friendly place with an observation terrace and themed buffets, is a popular rendezvous for families. Genuine Portuguese country fare can be had at O Prato de Porches to the sound of fado singing. There is a free shuttle service to the restaurant two and a half miles away. A particular attraction, unique of its kind in the Algarve, is the Cave de Vinhos. The gothic vaults of the cellars 26 feet below ground are built of ancient stones specially imported from Egypt, Greece and Austria. An impressive collection of 8.000 bottles from all over the world is stored here. A wine tasting is an unforgettable experience.

Ein vorausschauender Zeitgenosse: General Manager Luís de Camões.
A forward looking contemporary: General Manager Luís de Camões.

Atlantischer Ozean

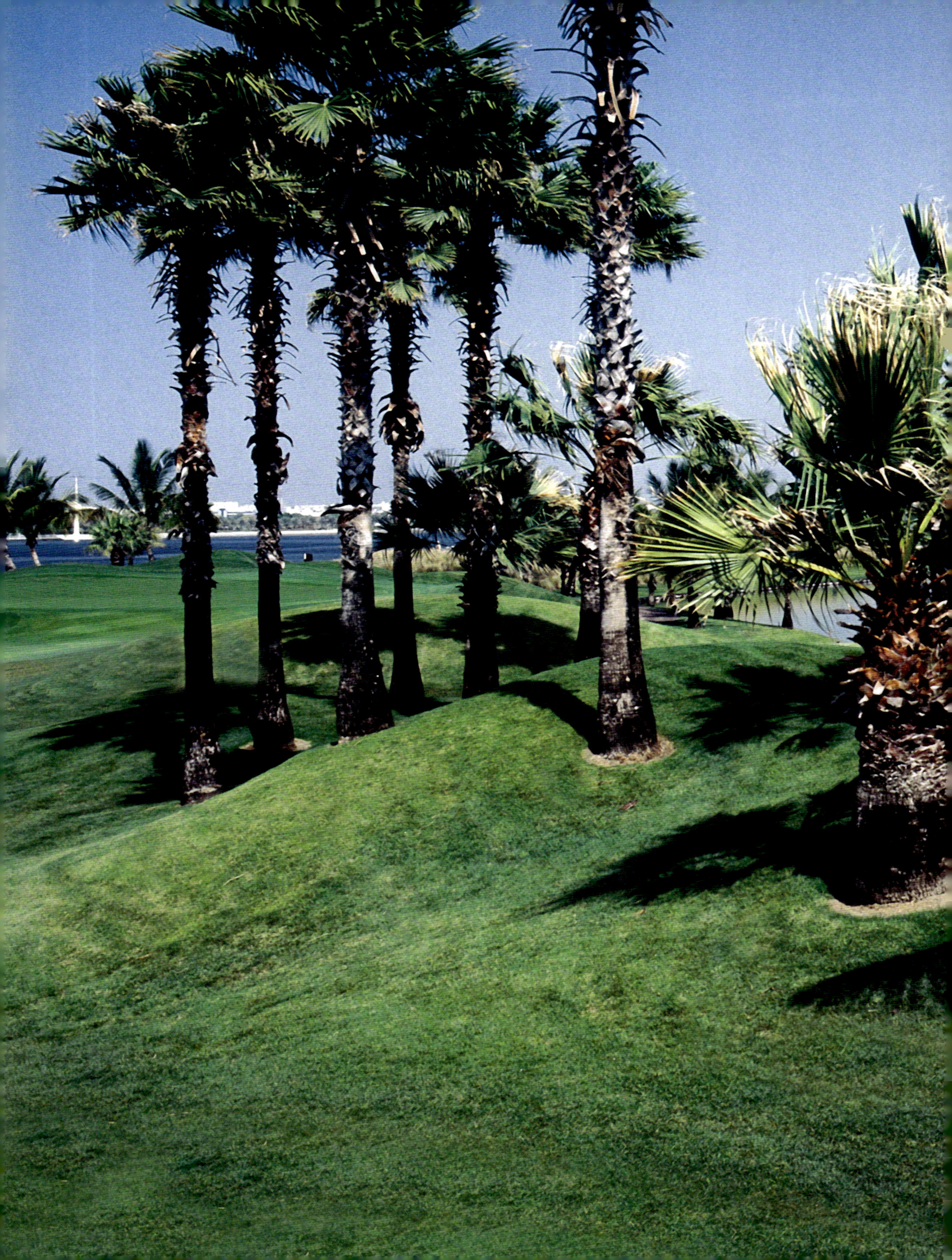

DIE WÜSTE LEBT

The desert is alive

GOLF IN DUBAI

Weltoffen, sicher, ein Hort traditioneller Gastfreundschaft und zugleich ein Musterbeispiel des modernen Lifestyles am Arabischen Golf – so stieg Dubai vom Geheimtipp zum international attraktiven Zentrum für Business, Tourismus und Sport im Mittleren Osten auf. Golfer schätzen das Scheichtum, eines der sieben Mitglieder der Vereinigten Arabischen Emirate, längst als eine der reizvollsten Destinationen weltweit. Der Emirates Golf Club und der Dubai Creek Golf & Yacht Club bieten Freizeitgolfern und Professionals erstklassige Herausforderungen und spektakuläres Design.

Cosmopolitan, confident, a centre of traditional hospitality yet at the same time a prime example of modernity on the Arabian Gulf, all these factors account for the rise of Dubai from being a personal tip to its present status as an attractive international centre in the Middle East for business, tourism and sport. Golfers value this sheikhdom, one of the seven members of the United Arab Emirates, long established as one of the most enticing destinations worldwide. The Emirates Golf Club and the Dubai Creek Golf & Yacht Club provide first class conditions and spectacular landscape design to amateur golfers and professionals alike.

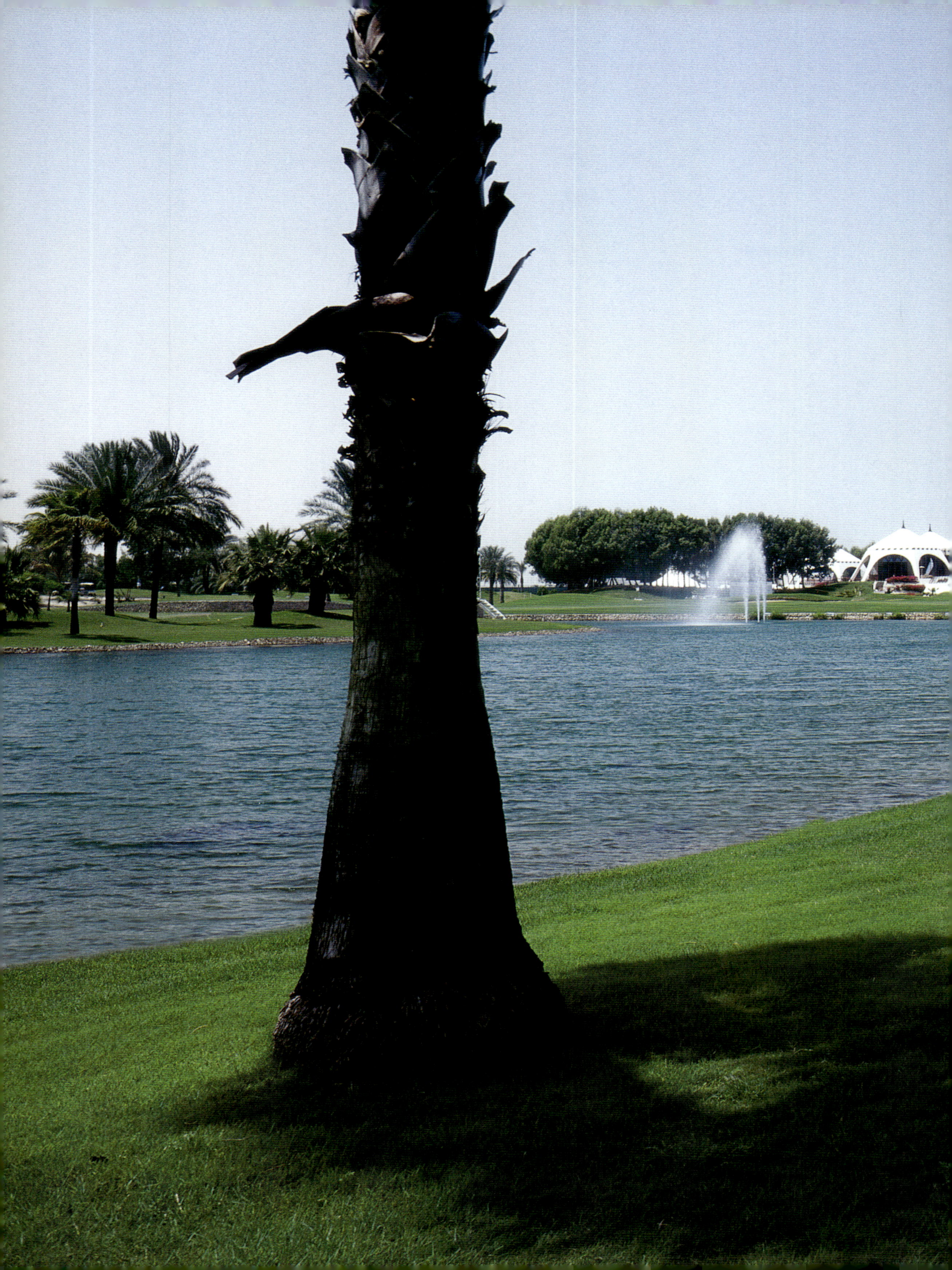

Der Doppelkurs des Emirates Golf Clubs war bei seiner Eröffnung im Jahre 1988 der erste Grasplatz im Mittleren Osten.
When the course of the Emirates Golf Club was opened in 1988, the double course was the very first grass course in the Middle East.

Dubai Creek
Golf & Yacht Club

The city of Dubai is divided by Dubai Creek, an arm of the sea which penetrates far into the desert. It was and still is the traditional anchorage for dhows, Arabian wooden ships with distinctive three-cornered sails rigged on a diagonal mast. Dubai Creek Golf & Yacht Club is directly located on the banks of the place which gave it its name. The 18-hole championship golf course (6,839 yards, par 72, venue for the Dubai Desert Classic in 1999 and 2000) attracts top golfers into the Emirate from all over the world. Date and coconut palms line the well-tended fairways and everywhere one has a view of the Creek and the skyline of Dubai. PGA professionals not only coach beginners but also willingly coach experienced golfers. The Golf Academy offers video swing analysis, and a floodlit 9-hole par 3 course without a handicap, three practice holes, driving range and putting green. The Club's heavenly swimming pools, bars and restaurants make the club very attractive for non-golfers too. A wonderful place for superb food which has a panoramic view is the „Boardwalk", the rare wood terrace of the Yacht Club's restaurant next to the marina, built like the deck of ship over the Creek.

Die Stadt Dubai wird vom Dubai Creek geteilt, einem Meeresarm, der wie ein Fluss weit in die Wüste hinein dringt. Er war und ist der traditionelle Ankerplatz für die Dhaus, die arabischen Holzschiffe mit den typischen Dreieckssegeln am schräg gestellten Mast. Der Dubai Creek Golf & Yacht Club liegt unmittelbar am Ufer seines Namensgebers, sein Clubhaus ist in spektakulärer Architektur der Form der Dhau-Segel nachgebildet. Der 18-Loch-Championship-Course (6,839 Yards, Par 72, Austragungsort des Dubai Desert Classic in 1999 und 2000) lockt Spitzenspieler aus aller Welt ins Emirat. Der Kurs ist harmonisch gewellt, seine Seen spiegeln als attraktive Hindernisse das Wasser des Creek. Dattel- und Kokospalmen säumen die gepflegten Fairways, überall hat man den Blick auf den Creek und die Skyline von Dubai. PGA-Professionals trainieren nicht nur Anfänger, sondern gerne auch erfahrene Spieler. Die Golf-Akademie bietet Videoanalysen, einen 9-Loch-Par-3-Kurs ohne Handicap, drei Übungslöcher, Driving Range und Putting Green, alles unter Flutlicht.

Der Club ist mit seinen herrlichen Swimmingpools, Bars, Restaurants auch für Nichtgolfer attraktiv. Ein besonderer Ort für feine Speisen mit Panoramablick: der „Boardwalk", die Edelholzterrasse des Restaurants im Yachtclub. Sie ist gleich neben der Marina wie ein Schiffsdeck über den Creek gebaut.

Greenfee je nach Wochentag von 345 bis 395 Dirham (1 US-$ = 3,50 Dh.), 9-Loch-Par-3-Kurs: 30 Dh., Abschlagzeiten können bis zu einem Jahr im Voraus gebucht werden (Telefon: + 9 71 / 4 / 3 47 52 05, Fax: + 9 71 / 4 / 3 47 53 77, E-Mail: booking@dubaigolf.com). Die schriftlich zu buchenden Abschlagzeiten werden je nach Verfügbarkeit sofort bestätigt. Vorausgesetztes Handicap: 28 (Herren), 45 (Damen). Kein Handicap für den 9-Loch-Par-3-Kurs.

Green fees depending on the day of the week range from 345 to 395 Dirham (1 US $ = 3.50 Dh.), 9-hole par 3 course: 30 Dh. Tee times can be booked a year in advance, Telephone: + 9 71 / 4 / 3 47 52 05, Fax: + 9 71 / 4 / 3 47 53 77, E-mail: booking@dubai.golf.com.
Reservations are confirmed immediately upon receipt of a request in writing depending on the availability of tee times. Handicap requirements: Men 28, Ladies 45. No handicap for the 9-hole par 3 course.

The Emirates Golf Club

Zum Emirates Golf Club fährt man von der Innenstadt Dubais etwa 20 Kilometer in Richtung Abu Dhabi.

Bei seiner Eröffnung 1988 konnte sich der Doppelkurs als erster Grasplatz des Mittleren Ostens präsentieren. Zwei 18-Loch-Championship-Kurse locken mit reizvollem Design und sind echte Tests für Profis und Hobbyspieler. Beide Anlagen integrieren das natürliche Hügel-und-Tal-Profil des Wüstengrundes. Das Design spielt mit den Motiven Wüstensand und Oasengrün.

Der Majlis-Course (7,101 Yards, Par 72) zeigt großzügige Fairways und weite Grüns. Besonders attraktiv beim Wadi Course (7,100 Yards Par 72): vorzüglich eingesetzte Wasserhindernisse und Roughs, wie die Wüste sie bietet.

Der Emirates Golf Club war neunmal Austragungsort des Dubai-Desert-Classic-Turniers auf der europäischen PGA-Tour. Die Architektur des Clubhauses – es ist wie ein Dorf aus Beduinenzelten gestaltet – erregte dabei nicht weniger Aufsehen als das Design der Plätze.

Umfassend ausgerichtete Golf-Akademie mit Video-Schwung-Analyse, Driving Range und Putting Green unter Flutlicht. PGA-Pros bieten individuell geschneiderte Unterrichtsprogramme, auch auf Deutsch. Cuisinier François Porte machte das Restaurant Le Classique zum Feinschmeckertreff.

To get to the Emirates Golf Club one drives for about 20 kilometres from Dubai city centre in the direction of Abu Dhabi. When it was opened in 1988, the double course was the very first grass course in the Middle East. The two beautifully designed 18-hole championship courses are enticing and pose stiff tests for professionals and amateurs alike. Both courses integrate the undulating contours of the original desert terrain. The design is around the theme of desert sand and oasis green. The Majlis Course (7,101 yards, par 72) has broad fairways and large greens. Particularly attractive features of the Wadi Course (7,100 yards, par 72) are the exceptionally placed water hazards and desert rough.

The Emirates Golf Club has been the venue for the European PGA Tour Dubai Desert Classic tournament nine times. The architecture of the clubhouse – designed like a Bedouin tent village – is no less a sensation than the design of the golf courses. There is a superbly equipped golfing academy with video swing analysis and floodlit driving range and putting green. PGA professionals offer tuition programmes tailored to your individual requirements, in German too.

Greenfee je nach Course und Wochentag von 330 bis 425 Dirham (1 US-$ = 3,50 Dh.), Abschlagzeiten können bis zu einem Jahr im Voraus gebucht werden (Telefon: + 9 71 / 4 / 3 47 52 05, Fax: + 9 71 / 4 / 3 47 53 77, E-Mail: booking@dubaigolf.com).
Die schriftlich zu buchenden Abschlagzeiten werden je nach Verfügbarkeit sofort bestätigt. Vorausgesetztes Handicap: 28 (Herren), 45 (Damen).

Green fees, depending on the course and the day of the week from 330 to 425 Dirham (1 US $ = 3.50 Dh.). Tee times can be booked up to a year in advance.
Telephone: + 9 71 / 4 / 3 47 52 05
Telefax: + 9 71 / 4 / 3 47 53 77
E-mail: booking@dubaigolf.com
Reservations are confirmed immediately depending on the availability of tee times upon receipt of a request in writing. Handicap requirements: Men 28, Ladies 45.

Die Hotelsensation von Dubai

Burj Al Arab

Sensational hotel in Dubai

Golfer, an finessenreiche und auch ästhetisch reizvolle Kurse gewöhnt, haben in der Regel ein ausgeprägtes Gespür für Design. Wer in Dubai von Abschlag zu Abschlag zieht, kann seit Dezember vergangenen Jahres in der zur Zeit wohl spektakulärsten Hotelarchitektur der Welt einchecken und zugleich in der höchsten: Burj Al Arab heißt das Luxusdomizil. Es ragt von der Küste hoch in den Himmel und ist zum neuen Wahrzeichen des boomenden Emirats am Arabischen Golf geworden.

Golfers familiar with aesthetically pleasing if tricky golf courses usually have a strong sense of design. Since last December those dragging their clubs from tee to green in Dubai have been able to check into what must be the most spectacular hotel in the world architecturally, it is certainly the highest. This luxury establishment is called the Burj Al Arab. Located beside the sea it rises up hundreds of metres into the sky and has become the new icon for this booming Emirate in the Arabian Gulf.

Text: Günter Ned · Fotos: Ydo Sol, Jürgen Gutowski

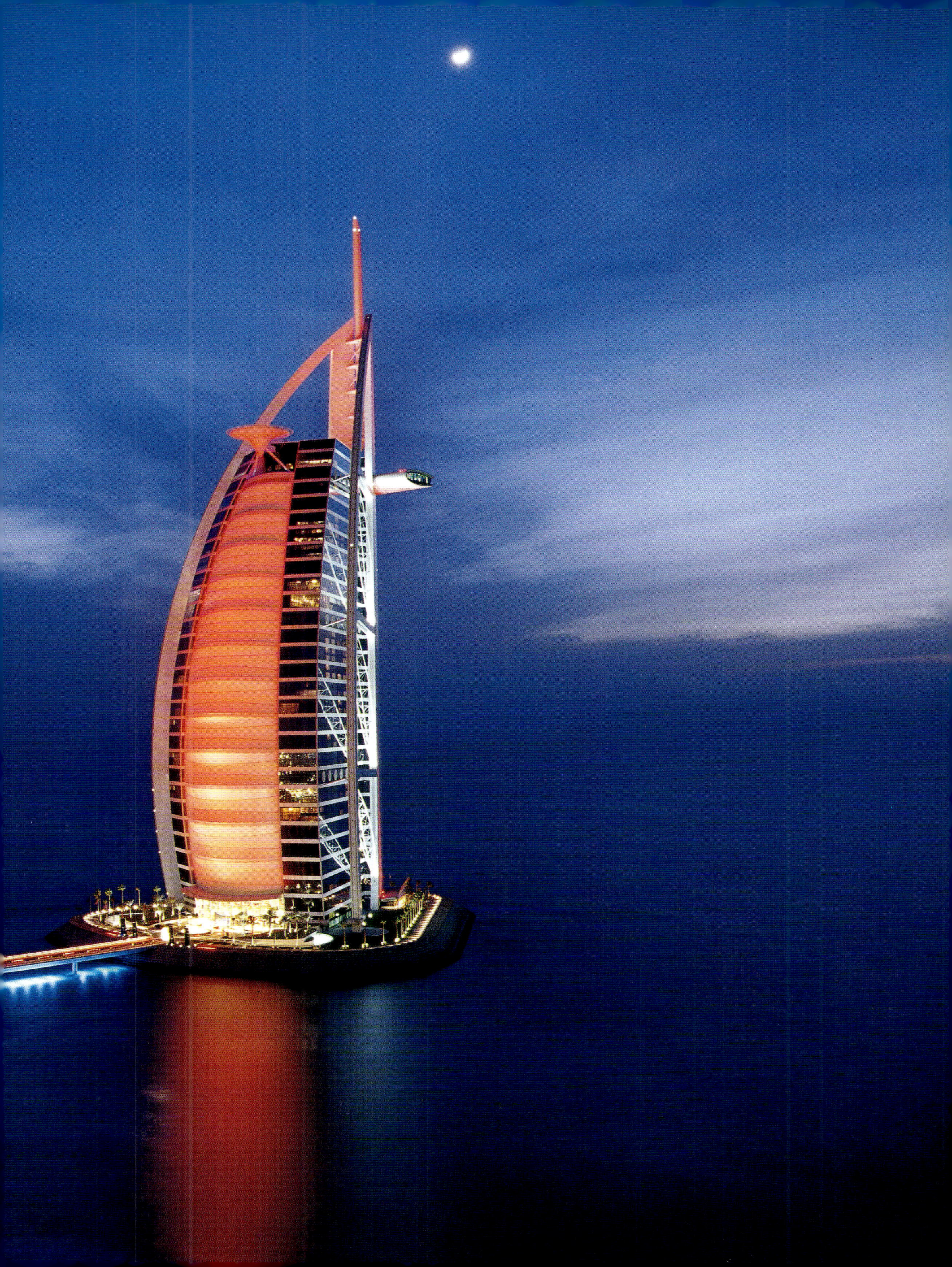

Das Atrium der Sahn-Eddar-Lounge steigt an der Innenseite des Segels einhundertachtzig Meter hinauf.

The Atrium rises one hundred and eighty metres on the inside of the sail.

Like a yacht with sails billowing, the Burj Al Arab appears to be sailing towards the coast as well as into the 21st century. As is fitting for an architectural message for the future, it enters into a new dimension. Dubai's new sensational hotel is 321 metres high from ground level to the top of the mast, so is even higher than the Eiffel Tower and only 60 metres less than the height of the Empire State Building in New York. Construction began in 1994. It took two whole years for the foundations to be laid and for the artificial island to be created on which the Burj Al Arab is built. 3,500 designers, engineers and construction workers and 300,000 cubic metres of concrete were needed to lay the foundations in the

Wie eine Yacht mit himmelhohem, geblähten Segel scheint das Burj Al Arab vor Dubais Küste einzulaufen und mit ihm das 21. Jahrhundert. Wie es sich für eine architektonische Botschaft aus der Zukunft gehört, stößt sie in neue Dimensionen vor. Dubais jüngste Hotelsensation misst vom Boden bis zur Mastspitze 321 Meter, ist damit höher als der Eiffelturm und nur 60 Meter niedriger als das Empire State Building in New York. Der Bau begann 1994. Es dauerte allein zwei Jahre, bis das Fundament und die künstliche Insel fertiggestellt waren, auf der Burj Al Arab steht. 3500 Designer, Ingenieure und Bauarbeiter waren nötig, dazu 300 000 Kubikmeter Beton, um die Basis in die See zu setzen. Man verarbeitete mehr als 9000 Tonnen Stahl und trieb 250 Grundpfeiler 40 Meter tief in den Meeresboden.

Das Segel, das die Frontfassade bildet, ein doppellagiger, weißer Schirm, gewoben aus teflonbeschichteter Glasfaser, schwingt sich zweihundert Meter hoch bis zum Helikopterlandeplatz, der wie ein Krähennest oben am Mast sitzt. Von hier ragt noch einmal hundert Meter die Struktur der Mastspitze auf, wie ein Triumphbogen des dritten Jahrtausends.

Zwei Rolltreppen verbinden den Eingangsbereich mit Sahn Eddar, der großen Atrium-Lounge. Zwischen den Treppenbändern eine breite Kaskade mit Licht- und

Sahn Eddar, die Atrium-Lounge, lässt die Gäste mit breiten Kaskaden mit Licht- und Wasserspielen in eine magische Märchenwelt eintauchen.

The wide cascades of water and light in the Sahn Eddar Atrium Lounge immerse guests in a magical fairytale world.

Wasserspielen, zu beiden Seiten Glaswände, dahinter lebendige Unterwasserwelten mit Korallenlandschaften und exotischen Fischen. Das Atrium über der Sahn-Eddar-Lounge steigt hundertachtzig Meter hinauf. Zehn, zwanzig, ja an die dreißig „Logenränge" flüchten nach oben, irgendwann hört man auf zu zählen, bevor sie sich ganz oben in der blauen Dreieckskuppel verlieren.

Bis zum dritten Rang ragen goldene Säulen auf wie Fackeln mit riesigen goldenen Flammen. Genauso hoch schießt die Fontäne aus dem Wasserspiel des Brunnens. Alles, was wie Gold aussieht im Burj Al Arab, ist wirklich Gold. 2000 Quadratmeter Blattgold von 22 Karat wurden aufgetragen, es lässt die Concierge-Muscheln auf der Eingangsebene ebenso leuchten wie die Türstöcke der Lifts, die Rahmen der Großbildschirme in den Wohnbereichen, das Treppengeländer der Royal Suiten oder die Fassaden der Boutiquen, die die Sahn-Eddar-Lounge säumen. Allein in der Kuppel des Ballsaales wurden 20 000 verschiedene Goldblätter aufgelegt.

Es gibt nur Suiten im Burj Al Arab, 202 sind es im Ganzen, jede geht über zwei Etagen, schon die „einfacheren" mit 170 Quadratmetern Fläche sind eingerichtet wie Träume aus arabischen Nächten. Der Wohnbereich unten hat eine Arbeitsnische mit Laptop, Fax, Kopiergerät, eine Bar, einen Essbereich und eine üppige Polsterlandschaft und wie der Schlafbereich im Obergeschoss ein Panoramafenster, das vom Boden bis zur Decke einen wunderbaren Blick auf das Meer und die Küste von Dubai zeigt. Die Suiten sind in den Farben gestaltet, die im ganzen Haus dominieren, Blau, Gold und Rot, die Farben der See, der Sonne und des Sonnenuntergangs, und wie im ganzen Haus lebt man umgeben von kostbarsten Materialien, farbenfrohen, handgewebten Teppichen aus Südafrika, Indien und England, Marmor aus Carrara, brasilianischem Granit, Mosaiken mit Glas aus Norditalien, Stoffen aus Irland. Alles, auch die Bilder und Skulpturen, die phantasievoll

sea. 9,000 tonnes of steel were used and 250 foundation piles had to be sunk 40 metres down into the seabed.

The sail which forms the façade at the front of the building, a double-layered white umbrella woven of teflon-coated fibreglass, curves upwards for two hundred metres to the helipad which sits on the mast like a crow's nest. From here the mast structure rises another hundred metres, like a triumphal arch of the third millennium. Two escalators link the entrance hall with Sahn Eddar, the large atrium lounge.

Einzigartiges Interieur-Design setzt in der Atrium-Lounge die Akzente.

In the Atrium Lounge the accent is on unique interior design.

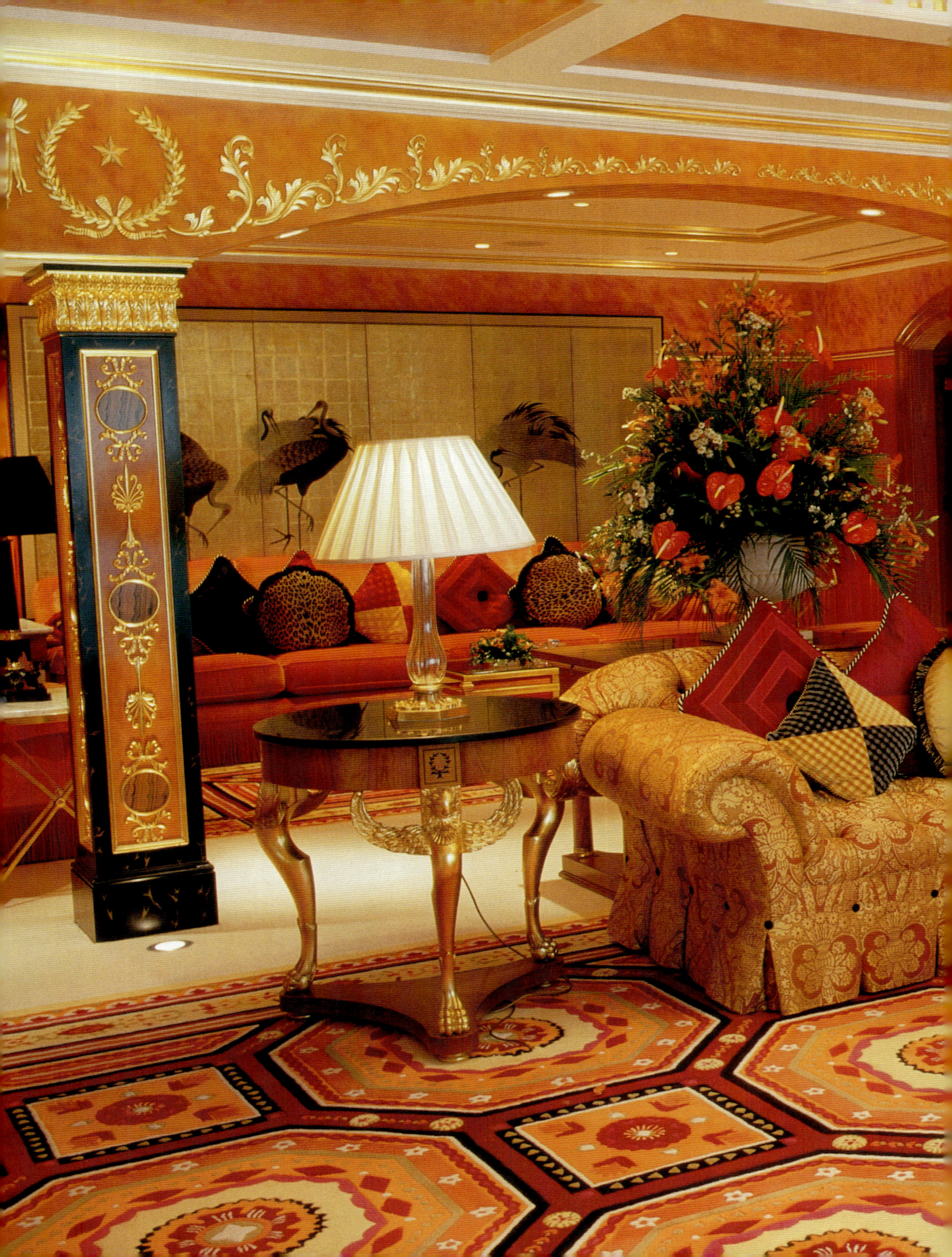

Wohn-Träume aus Tausendundeiner Nacht: die Royal Suiten.
Dream living straight out a Thousand and One Nights: the Royal Suites.

Between the escalators is a wide cascade of light and fountains with glass walls on either side. Behind is an underwater world complete with colonies of coral and exotic fish. The Atrium Lounge rises one hundred and eighty metres on the inside of the sail. Ten, perhaps twenty or even thirty circles of boxes rise upwards, in the end one has to stop counting as they disappear into the blue triangular dome. Golden pillars soar up to level three like torches with giant golden flames. The fountain springs just as high out of the water down below. Everything that looks like gold in Burj Al Arab really is gold. 2,000 square metres of 22 carat gold leaf has been applied putting as much

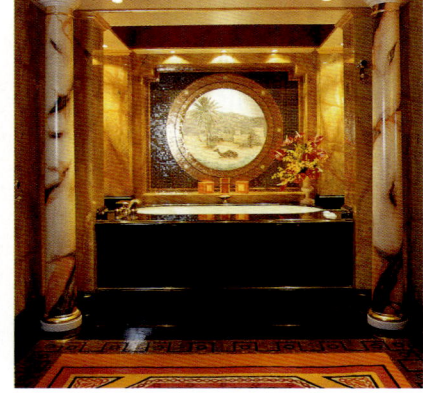

arabische Themen variieren, sind speziell für Burj Al Arab angefertigt. Exzeptionell die elektronische Ausstattung. Mit einer Fernbedienung öffnet man Vorhänge, wählt bis zu 100 TV-Kanäle (wer an der Tür läutet, erscheint ebenfalls auf dem Bildschirm), lässt Besucher ein. Mit 10 Telefonen ist bereits eine One-Bedroom-Suite ausgestattet, vom Schreibtisch bis zum Whirlpool oben im Bad. Von je 25 Apparaten telefoniert man in den beiden Royal Suiten auf der 25. Etage. Sie bieten das Ultimative an Luxus, das im Burj Al Arab zu haben ist: privates Kino, eigenen Lift, zwei Schlafsalons (bei einem dreht sich auf Wunsch das Bett um die eigene Achse), Räume für jede Gelegenheit auf 780 Quadratmetern Fläche, und überall Panoramablick und Pracht wie im Palast eines Scheichs. Einen der besonders bleibenden Eindrücke

Wohn-Träume aus Tausendundeiner Nacht: die Royal Suiten.

Dream living straight out a Thousand and One Nights.

hinterlässt die perfekte Symbiose von modernster Technik mit märchenhafter Szenerie und grenzenloser, traditionell arabischer Gastfreundschaft. Was die 1200 Mitarbeiter (wohlgemerkt: für 202 Suiten, ein einzigartiges Verhältnis) an Service bieten, ist nicht zu schlagen. Jede Suite hat ihren persönlichen Butler, jede Etage ihre eigene Rezeption (Check-in und Checkout im eigenen Zimmer). Erstaunlich schon, wie das Burj Al Arab seine Gäste zwischen Himmel und Meeresgrund kulinarisch verwöhnt. Al Muntaha (arabisch für: das

Höchste) ragt vom Mast des Segels weg nach hinten in den freien Himmel, 200 Meter hoch. (Es ist direkt mit dem gläsernen Außenlift zu erreichen.) Entsprechend spektakulär ist das Panorama aufs Meer und auf Dubai, nicht weniger das futuristische Interieur. Im Al Muntaha serviert man ausgezeichnete mediterrane Küche, hier trifft sich das glamouröseste Publikum. Feinste libanesische Cusine, aber auch internationale Klassiker hat das Al Iwan, das arabische Restaurant neben der Sahn-Eddar-Lounge, auf der Karte, dazu ein Dekor in Rot, Gold und Schwarz, ganz so, wie es die arabischen Könige des Mittelalters liebten, und es hat Kellner, die bedienen, als wären diese Könige ihre Gäste (kommen sie zweimal hintereinander, weiß man nicht nur ihren Namen, sondern auch ihre Speisen von gestern und schlägt neue Delikatessen vor).

shine on the concierge shells at the entrance as on the door posts of the lifts. It is also on the big TV frames in the living rooms, the handrails of the Royal Suites and the façades of the boutiques around the Sahn Eddar Lounge. Even the domed ceiling of the ballroom has been faced with 20,000 separate sheets of gold leaf.

The Burj Al Arab only has suites, 202 in all, each of them with 2 storeys. Even the smaller ones have 170 square metres of space and are furnished like a dream straight out of One Thousand and One Nights. The living area below has a work alcove with a laptop, fax, copier, bar, dining area and plush sofas and chairs in front of the picture window. As on the floor above, the window reaches from floor to ceiling and affords a wonderful view of the gulf and the coast of Dubai.

The furnishings of the suites echo the colour scheme throughout the whole hotel, blue, gold and red, the colours of the sea, the sun and the sunset. In the suites as in the whole building one is surrounded by the costliest of materials, bright hand-woven carpets from South Africa, India and England, marble from Carrara, Brazilian granite, glass mosaics from Italy and fabrics from Ireland. Everything, including the pictures and sculptures depicting highly imaginative Arab themes, have all been especially crafted for the Burj Al Arab.

The electronic equipment is exceptional. The curtains may be drawn by remote control which can also be used to switch on up to 100 TV channels. Anyone ringing the doorbell also appears on screen. A one-bedroom suite is equipped with 14 telephones placed anywhere from the desk to the whirlpool in the bathroom upstairs. Each of the two Royal Suites on the 25th floor has 27 phones and provides the ultimate in luxury that the Burj Al Arab has to offer: private cinema, own lift, two bedrooms (the bed in one can be made to turn on its own axis) and rooms for every requirement covering an area of 780 square metres. Everywhere there are panoramic views and splendour as in a Sheikh's palace.

One particularly strong impression among others is left by the perfect symbiosis of the latest technology, the legendary landscape and the limitless traditional Arab hospitality. The service offered by the 1,200 staff (please note – a unique ratio

Links: Das Restaurant Al Mahara liegt unter dem Meeresspiegel, man nimmt Platz vor der Unterwasserwelt des Arabischen Golfes.
Left: The Al Mahara Restaurant is below sea level. Seating is in front of the underwater world of the Arabian Gulf.

Im Al Iwan, dem arabischen Restaurant, wird feinste libanesische Cuisine serviert.
Al Iwan, the Arabian Restaurant, serves the finest Lebanese cuisine.

Im Al Mutaha liegt den Gästen das Panorama Dubais zu Füßen. Hier genießt man eine erlesene mediterrane Küche.
In Al Muntaha guests have the panorama of Dubai at their feet. Here one can enjoy exquisite Mediterranean cuisine.

for 202 suites) is unsurpassed. Every suite has its own butler and every floor has its own Reception (check-in and checkout in the same room). It is quite amazing how well the Burj Al Arab spoils it's guests on the culinary front with a cuisine not bettered anywhere in the world. Viewed from outside, Al Muntaha (Arabic for the highest) juts out from the main mast like the tail fin of a giant fish rising 200 metres into the sky, and is reached by an exterior glass lift. The panoramic views of the sea and Dubai are no less spectacular than its unique interior. Al Muntaha serves excellent Mediterranean cuisine and is a meeting place for the most glamorous clientele.

The finest Lebanese dishes and international classics are on the menu at the Al Iwan, the Arab restaurant beside the Sahn Eddar Lounge. Its décor is in red, gold and black, colours favoured by Arab rulers of the Middle Ages and its waiters treat their guests as if

Bab Al Yam ist ein lockeres Café-Restaurant am Außenpool auf Meeresebene. Allein ein Sojasprossensalat mit Zitronengras und kurzgebratenem frischen Thunfisch ist eine lukullische Finesse.

Das sensationellste Ambiente hat zweifelsohne Al Mahara (die Muschel). Es liegt tief unter dem Meeresspiegel, man nähert sich durch einen langen goldenen Muschelgang und nimmt dann Platz vor der Unterwasserwelt des Arabischen Golfs (mit 500 verschiedenen Spezies von Fischen). Die Küchenrichtung versteht sich von selbst: erlesen zubereitetes Seafood. Die Restaurants sind nur ein Ausschnitt des Märchenlandes Burj Al Arab. Das Erlebnis des Assawan Spa & Health Clubs (er geht über zwei Etagen und ist nach dem Muster traditioneller arabischer Bäder designt), der Sonnenuntergang, genossen in der intimen Bar-Lounge Juna (Sonnenauge), eine After-Dinner-Stunde im Sahn Eddar, während vier festlich gekleidete Damen Kammermusik spielen und Scheichs, gekleidet in weiße Dishdashas, auf roten Diwans plaudern, wären alle eigene Geschichten wert, nicht weniger die 15-minütige Luftreise vom Flug mit dem Helikopter über Dubai, die Anfahrt in einer

Limousine der weißen Rolls-Royce-Silver-Seraph-Flotte (wer mit seiner Yacht kommt, macht nebenan in der Marina fest) oder die allabendliche Lightshow. Man sieht sie am besten von der 280 Meter langen Brücke, die das Burj Al Arab mit dem Festland verbindet, oder vom wohlbewachten Privatstrand des Hotels, wo sich am Abend die Palmen in Lichterperlen kleiden. 142 Iridium-Fluter zaubern ein Lichtspektakel in allen Regenbogenfarben auf die himmelhohe Segelfassade, der „Vulkan" vorm Eingang jagt dazu Wasserfontänen hoch und aus vier schwarzen Säulen schießen Feuerflammen empor.

Das Burj Al Arab, am 1. Dezember 1999 eröffnet, ist mit Recht zum neuen Wahrzeichen Dubais geworden, einer Destination im Mittleren Osten, die längst internationales Format gewann und wirtschaftlich, touristisch, sportlich durchstartet in eine rasante Zukunft. Die Zeichen sind unübersehbar, vom soeben fertiggestellten Emirates-Tower über den neuen Flughafen bis zu Design-Spektakeln wie dem Dubai Creek Golf & Yacht Club oder eben dem Segler aus dem neuen Jahrtausend, dem Burj Al Arab.

they were these rulers. By their second visit guests are not only known by name but the waiters even remember the dishes they ordered the time before and are able to suggest new delicacies. The Bab Al Yam is an informal café-restaurant at sea level beside the open-air pool. One can sit inside or out (during the mild winter) to enjoy a soya bean sprout salad with lemon grass and quick-fried tuna fish, an epicurean delight. The Al Mahara (the shell) below sea level has the most sensational ambience. One goes down a long golden tunnel of shells and takes a seat in front of the underwater world of the Arabian Gulf which has 500 species of fish. The restaurants are only a detail of the Burj Al Arabs wonderland, experiencing the Assawan & Health Club (on two floors and based on the design of traditional Arab baths) or viewing the sunset from the intimate lounge of the Juna Bar (eye of the sun), or the hour after dinner in the Sahn Eddar Lounge where four female musicians in evening dress play European chamber music and sheikhs clad in their white robes are seated on red divans deep in conversation, these are all tales worth telling.

No less an experience is the 15 minute helicopter flight over Dubai, the drive in a white limousine of the Rolls Royce Silver Seraph fleet (guests arriving in yachts moor them in the adjoining marina), and the evening "son et lumière". The best view of the show can be had from the 280 metre long causeway which connects the Burj Al Arab with the mainland, or from the hotel's well guarded private beach where palm trees twinkle with illuminations in the evenings. 142 iridium projectors create a spectacle of light in all the colours of the rainbow on the surface of the sail which rises high into the sky. In front of the entrance a "volcano" sends up fountains, and four black towers shoot out balls of fire. The Burj Al Arab, opened on 1st December 1999, has become the new symbol of Dubai, and rightly so. It is a Middle Eastern destination which is enjoying international status in the world of commerce, tourism and sport. The signs are there for all to see, from the recently completed Emirates Tower to the new airport, design sensations of the Dubai Creek Golf & Yacht Club and the vessel of the new millennium, the Burj Al Arab.

Der international renommierte Hotelier Wolfgang Nitschke, ein gebürtiger Berliner, leitet das Burj Al Arab mit großer Kompetenz.
The internationally renowned hotelier Wolfgang Nitschke, a native of Berlin, runs the Burj Al Arab with total competence.

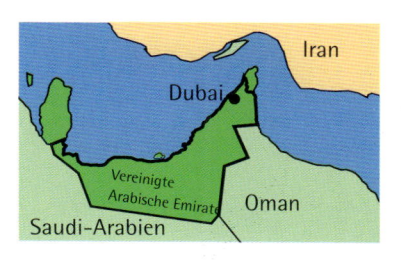

Der Assawan Spa & Health Club erstreckt sich über zwei Etagen nach dem Muster traditioneller arabischer Bäder.
Based on the traditional Arabian baths the Assawan Spa & Health Club is accommodated on two floors.

HIDEAWAYS 127

GOLF IN SÜDAFRIKA

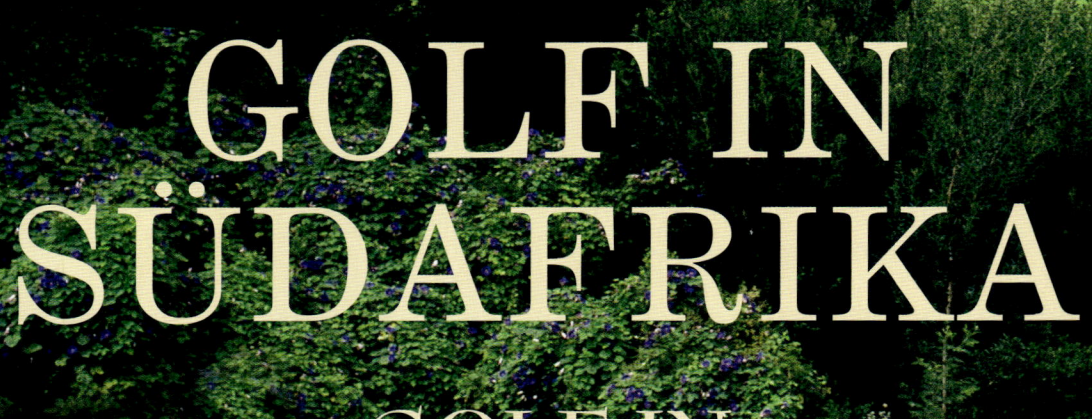

GOLF IN SOUTH AFRICA

Nicht nur das ganzjährig milde Klima ist der Grund dafür, dass Südafrika zu einer der begehrtesten Destinationen für Golfer gehört. Auch die günstigen Greenfees und Landschaftsbilder, die einfach nur als sensationell bezeichnet werden können, tragen hierzu bei. Der aufregendste Golfplatz ist zweifellos der von Gary Player designte Fancourt Course an der malerischen Garden Route. Hier wird im Jahr 2002 erstmals auf afrikanischem Boden der weltberühmte „Presidents Cup" ausgetragen, bei dem die zwölf besten US-Golfer gegen die zwölf besten Spieler aus dem Rest der Welt antreten.

It is not only the all-year-round mild climate that makes South Africa one of the most sought after destinations for golfers. Other contributing factors are its favourable green fees and surrounding countryside, which has frequently been described as sensational. The most exiting golf course is without doubt the Fancourt Course designed by Gary Player and located on the picturesque Garden Route. In 2002 for the first time on African soil, it will be the venue of the world famous "President's Cup" tournament, in which the 12 best American golfers compete against the 12 best of the rest of the world.

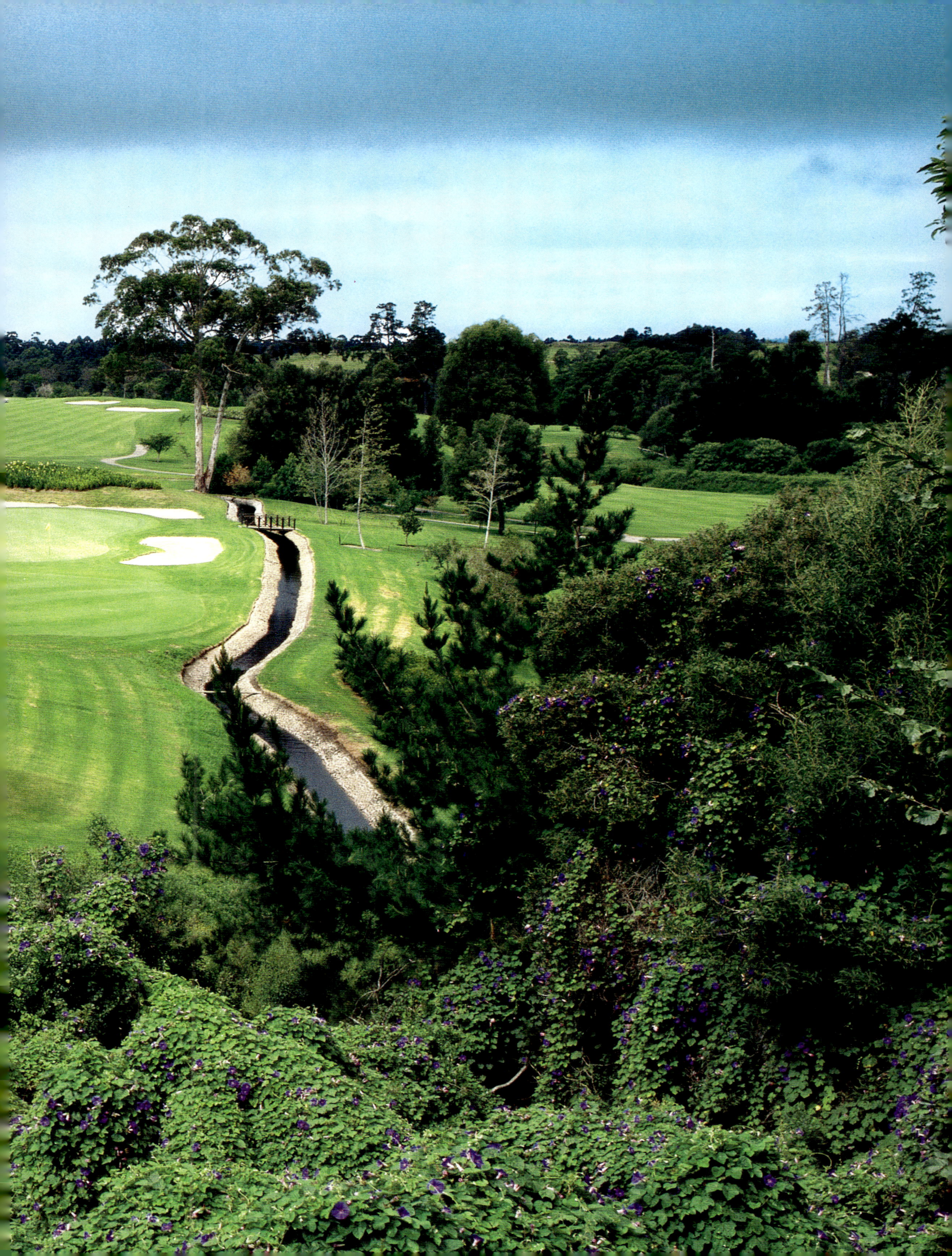

Austragungsort des Presidents Cup 2002
FANCOURT HOTEL &
Das Top-Golf-Resort an der südafrikanischen „Garden-Route"

Golf venue for the President's Cup 2002

Country Club Estate

The top Golf Resort on South Africa's Garden Route

Text & Fotos: Jürgen Gutowski

Den Fancourt-Gästen stehen außergewöhnliche Luxusunterkünfte zur Verfügung. Und drumherum ein Golfplatz der Superlative.
Fancourt guests are accommodated in absolute luxury surrounded by superb golf links.

When Nelson Mandela gives his wife, Graca Machel, a birthday present, you can be sure it is a very special gift indeed, because South Africa never had such an imaginative President before. On his wife's fifty-fifth birthday the eighty-year old Mandela presented her with a long weekend at the Fancourt Golf Resort, and threw a brilliant tea party with 200 schoolchildren between the tees. We don't know why Mandela chose Fancourt, but having been guests ourselves at Fancourt on more than one occasion, we can at least speculate about the reason. It could be because of the countryside around the little town of George. To the

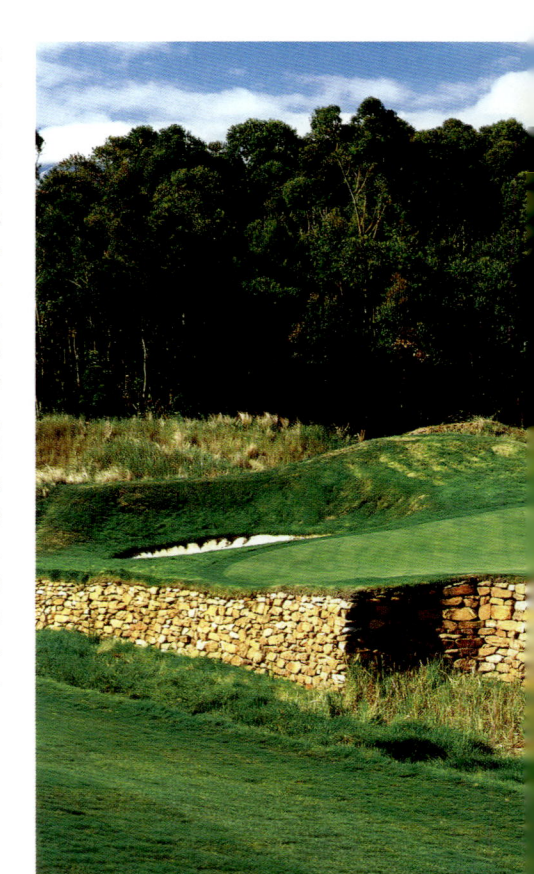

Wenn Nelson Mandela seiner Frau Graca Machel etwas zum Geburtstag schenkt, dann kann man wohl davon ausgehen, dass es sich bestimmt um ein ganz besonderes Geschenk handelt, denn einen kreativeren Präsidenten hatte Südafrika sicherlich noch nie. Also schenkte der achtzigjährige Nelson seiner Graca zum Fünfundfünfzigsten ein verlängertes Wochenende im Fancourt Golf Resort und feierte mit ihr und 200 Schulkindern eine rauschende Teeparty zwischen den Tees. Wir wissen nicht, warum, aber nachdem wir nun zum wiederholten Mal selber im Fancourt zu Gast waren, können wir es uns zumindest denken. Da ist zunächst die Gegend um die kleine Stadt George herum. Schauen wir nach links, erblicken wir die berühmte Garden-Route, die ihrem blumigen Namen alle Ehre macht und sich an den warmen Gewässern des Indischen Ozeans entlang schlängelt. Wenden wir den Blick nach rechts, so sehen wir das mächtige „Outeniqua"-Gebirge, zu Deutsch „Land des Honigs". Eine treffende Beschreibung dieser fruchtbaren und sonnenverwöhnten Landschaft, in der eigentlich immer Sommer angesagt ist, wo mehrmals jährlich geerntet wird, und – wo man rund ums Jahr unter beneidenswerten Bedingungen Golf spielen kann.

Das dachte sich wohl auch Gary Player, der ungekrönte König aller Golfspieler, als er zum ersten Mal durch das saftige Weideland des Fancourt-Anwesens stapfte, damals noch eine Milchfarm, und er sagte zum Besitzer des Grundstücks: „Dieser Platz ist für Golfer gemacht, er ist viel zu gut für Kühe!" Der Champion entwarf die Pläne und gestaltete das Gelände rund um das historische „Fancourt Manor House" zum aufregendsten Golfplatz Südafrikas.

left is the famous Garden Route which certainly lives up to its flowery name as it meanders beside the warm waters of the Indian Ocean. To the right are the mighty Outeniqua Mountains – translated the "Land of Honey" – a fitting description of this sun-blessed landscape which yields several harvests a year where the sun shines constantly. Golf is played here throughout the year in wonderful conditions. Gary Player, the uncrowned king of golfers, had this thought as he plodded across the lush pastures of the Fancourt estate when it was still a dairy farm. He told the estate's owner, "this place is made for golfers, it's far too good for cows". The champion then drew up plans for a golf course around the historic Fancourt Manor House which was to become the most exciting in the whole of South Africa.

When you stand on the raised ground of the first tee, the view is of immaculately mowed fairways and perfectly raked bunkers, a stretch of green hills and valleys criss-crossed by sparkling brooks which flow into pools where ducks swim between

Unten: Zum Gesundheits- und Beautysalon gehört ein traumhafter Pool.
Below: the Health and Beauty area houses a fantastic pool.

HIDEAWAYS 133

Dutzende „Rasenkosmetiker" pflegen das herrliche Terrain.
Dozens of hands keep the lawns immaculate.

the water lilies. Even the old trees were easy to transplant. They now thrive on the 1,300 acre estate and lend an historic aura to the course. Golf professional Larry Gould, a South African by choice, considers the greens of the Cape to be "world class". The famous Compleat Golfer Magazine which subjects golf courses to the most rigorous tests describes Fancourt as "the best kept golf course in South Africa". The Montagu Course now voted No. 1 in South Africa. No wonder then that Fancourt is the venue for several national and international golf championships, including the renowned Bell's Cup. It was the vision of the german estate owners, Hasso and Sabine Plattner, to raise the standards and facilities to one of the best in the world. And they really made it: the world famous President's Cup which pitches the twelve best US golfers against the twelve best golfers from the rest of the world will take place for the very first time on African soil in November 2002 on the newly laid down Links at Fancourt. Over three hundred million TV viewers worldwide will watch the contest after its Honorary Chairman, President Thabo Mbeki, opens this spectacular world-class event. Fancourt is well prepared for the President's Cup because Gary Player and his designer, Phil Jacobs have once again done a splendid job. They turned the old airfield of George into a links-style golf landscape unique to South Africa. Its superbly maintained undulating dune-like terrain,

Steht man an der erhöhten Abschlagstelle des ersten Tees, schweift der Blick über makellos gemähte Spielbahnen und tadellos geharkte „Bunker", über eine grüne Berg-und-Tal-Bahn, von sprudelnden Wasserläufen durchzogen, die in seerosenverwöhnten und entenbewohnten Teichen und Gewässern münden. Selbst alte Bäume, die dem Golf Ground eine geradezu historische Aura verleihen, ließen sich willig hierher verpflanzen und wachsen und gedeihen prächtig auf dem mehr als 500 Hektar großen Anwesen. Golfprofi Larry Gould, Wahlsüdafrikaner wegen der Top-Plätze im Land am Kap, meint denn auch: „Die Greens sind Weltklasse!" Und das renommierte „Compleat Golfer Magazine", das Golfplätze gnadenlos und anonym testet, stellt fest: „Fancourt ist der bestgepflegte Golfplatz Südafrikas!" Der Montague Course wurde jetzt zur Nr. 1 in Südafrika gewählt. Kein Wunder, dass die Fancourt-Greens Schauplatz

mehrerer nationaler und internationaler Golfmeisterschaften waren, darunter auch der berühmte „Bell's Cup". Das Anwesen gehört den Deutschen Hasso und Sabine Plattner. Damit wurde ihre Vision Wirklichkeit, das Fancourt Hotel zu einem der besten Golf Resorts der Welt zu machen. Aber es kommt noch besser: Der weltberühmte „Presidents Cup", bei dem die zwölf besten US-Golfer gegen die zwölf besten Spieler aus dem Rest der Welt antreten, wird im November 2002 erstmals auf afrikanischem Boden ausgetragen, und zwar genau hier auf den neu angelegten Links von Fancourt. Rund dreihundert Millionen Fernsehzuschauer werden weltweit an den Bildschirmen verfolgen, wenn der Ehrenvorsitzende des spektakulären Auftritts, Staatspräsident Thabo Mbeki, das triumphale Großereignis eröffnen wird. Fancourt ist gut vorbereitet auf den Presidents Cup, denn Gary Player und sein Designer Phil Jacobs haben erneut ganze Arbeit geleistet: Aus dem alten Flugplatz von George hat er eine in Südafrika einzigartige „Link-Style" Golflandschaft modelliert, aus der beinahe unvorstellbaren Menge von 700 000 Kubikmetern Erde ein grünes, topgepflegtes welliges Dünen-Terrain entstehen lassen. Rolling Greens vom Meister für Meister und ihre Meisterschaften.

Mit meinem Elektro-Golf-Cart fahre ich wie auf einer Berg-und-Tal-Bahn durch die grüne weite Fancourtlandschaft. Allenthalben begegnen mir eifrig scherende Rasenkosmetiker, deren oberstes Ziel es ist, die höchsten Standards in der Pflege des Geländes zu setzen, ständig auf der Suche nach neuen Wegen, die Bespielbarkeit und Ästhetik weiter zu perfektionieren. Links eine Allee mit zwei Dutzend Privatlodges mit direktem Zugang zu den Greens, rechts ein Teich mit blühenden Wasserrosen, dazwischen führt der Weg über eine kleine Brücke zum spektakulären Clubhaus mit seiner eleganten weißen Fassade und hölzernen Verzierungen, perfekt positioniert vor der noch spektakuläreren Kulisse der Outeniqua-Berge. Vor dem Haus, wo an diesem Wochenende fast 200 Caddies auf Kundschaft warten, parke ich meinen „Golf" und schlendere durch den Flur des Clubhauses, scherzhaft „Hall of fame" (Halle des Ruhms) genannt, weil an den Wänden die Konterfeis der berühmtesten Golf-Cracks der Welt zu bestaunen sind. Eine alte Golfregel besagt: „Erst relaxen, dann spielen!" Kein Problem durch den Gesundheits- und Schönheitssalon des Golf Resorts. Alle Wünsche des gesundheitsbewussten Gastes werden in fünf perfekt eingerichteten Behandlungsräumen erfüllt, im Angebot sind u. a. spezielle Massagetherapien, inkl. Sportmassage, und unzählige Schönheitsbehandlungen. Im Untergeschoss befinden sich zwei Saunen, zwei Dampfbäder, ein gekühltes Tauchbecken und vier Räume für (Aroma-)Bäder und Wasserbehandlungen, nebenan das „Römische Bad" samt Jacuzzi wie auch der Kraftraum mit elektronisch gesteuerten Geräten der neuesten Generation. Ein erfahrener Trainer ist ständig anwesend.

Das Herz des Fancourt-Hotels bildet das historische, denkmalgeschützte „Manor House", im 19. Jahrhundert gebaut von Sir Henry Fancourt und mit Millionenaufwand durch die Besitzer Hasso und Sabine Plattner wieder hergerichtet. Eine Atmosphäre von Tradition und Luxus durchweht die altehrwürdigen Räume mit ihren dunklen Holzböden und lichten Suiten.

rolling greens designed by a master for champions and their championships, has been created from an unimaginable volume of 700,000 cubic metres of earth.

My electro golf buggy takes me along a road over the hills and through the valleys of the green Fancourt landscape. On all sides, there are people trimming the grass whose sole purpose is to maintain the highest possible standards for the grounds and who are constantly looking for ways of perfecting the playing areas and the aesthetics of the place. To the left is an avenue of two dozen private lodges with direct access to the greens. On the right is a pool with flowering water lilies, and leading past it a path which goes over a little bridge to the spectacular clubhouse with an elegant white façade and wooden embellishments. It is perfectly situated against the even more spectacular backdrop of the Outeniqua Mountains. I park my golf cart in front of the house where, this weekend over 200 caddies are waiting for business, and stroll through the hall of the clubhouse, jokingly called the "Hall of Fame" because displayed on the walls are portraits of the most famous golfers in the world. There's an old golf saying, "first relax then play". This poses no problem at this resort because of all the beauty and health facilities available. Every desire of the health-conscious visitor can be fulfilled in five perfectly equipped treatment rooms. On offer are specialized massage therapies including sports massage and innumerable kinds of beauty treatment. In the basement are the saunas, two steam baths, a cool diving pool and four rooms dedicated to aroma-therapy and hydro-treatment. Next door is the Roman Bath and jacuzzi as well as the body-building studio with the very latest electronic equipment. A professional coach is in constant attendance. The heart of the Fancourt Hotel is the historic 19th century Manor House, now classified as an historical monument and under a preservation order. The present owners Hasso and Sabine Plattner spent millions on its restoration. An atmosphere of tradition and luxury pervades the time-honoured rooms with their dark wooden floors and light-filled suites. Antiques are placed throughout the 30 guest rooms and suites as well as is the Garden Lounge of the Manor House which is still heated by an open fire. The values of the past are stylishly combined with every conceivable luxurious mod con of today. The 45 Garden Suites

Antikes Mobiliar findet sich sowohl in den 30 Gästezimmern und Suiten wie in der kaminbeheizten Gardenlounge des Manor-Hauses: Die Werte der Vergangenheit gehen eine stilvolle Liaison mit den Annehmlichkeiten jedes nur denkbaren modernen Luxus' ein.

Nicht minder luxuriös sieht es in den 45 Gartensuiten am Rande des Golfplatzes aus. Zur Verfügung stehen Einraumstudios und Suiten mit einem, zwei oder drei Schlafzimmern. Praktisch: eine voll eingerichtete Kitchenette mit Kühlschrank, Tiefkühltruhe, Kaffeemaschine, Mikrowelle und allem, was anspruchsvolle Hausfrauen und -männer enthusiastisch werden lässt. Atmosphärisch: voll funktionsfähige offene Kamine. Romantisch: Schlafzimmer mit kleinen Erkern und Winkeln. Sauber: Top-Badezimmer mit edlen Kacheln in dezent-eleganten Farben. Bequem: 24-Stunden-Room-Service.

So international wie die Golf spielende Klientel ist auch das kulinarische Angebot des Hotels. In fünf feinen Restaurants spiegeln sich die Geschmäcker dieser Welt, zum einen in einem der renommiertesten A-la-carte-Restaurants Südafrikas: Das „Montagu", ein traulich-behagliches Gourmetsanktuar, bietet südafrikanische und internationale Gerichte. Bis zu 40 Gäste können sich hier bei klassischer Musik und flackerndem Kaminfeuer von einer perfekten Küchencrew und einem außergewöhnlich freundlichen und zuvorkommenden Bedienungspersonal topkulinarisch verwöhnen las-

Die Aromen der Welt begeistern in der „Bramble Lodge."
Guests can delight in the aromas of the world at the "Bramble Lodge".

sen! Unbedingt empfehlenswert: Geräuchertes Krokodilfilet in exotischer Curry-Orangen-Sauce mit roten und grünen Paprikaschoten, serviert mit wildem Reis. — Im Fischrestaurant „Le Pecheur" bereitet Chef Maurice van Gaart aus Holland die berühmten kleinen Austern aus Knysna mit dem typisch nussigen Geschmack zu, er serviert sie auf Eis, alternativ als Gratin mit — natürlich — holländischer Sauce oder auch mal mit Spinat und einem Hauch Pernod. Fish & Chips finden sich auf der „Pecheur"-Karte genauso wie asiatisches Seafood-Curry oder südafrikanische Forellen, und Fischasketen können zwischen verschiedenen Fleisch- und vegetarischen Gerichten wählen. — In der eleganten „Bramble-Lodge" verbindet der Chef Frédéric Robichon die Aromen, Kräuter und Gewürze der Welt, um alle Geschmackssinne zu begeistern: Schwarze Tigergarnelen mit süß-saurer Soße aus Thailand gibt es hier, außerdem gefüllte Wachteln mit wildem Reis und Feigensoße, als Dessert steht beispielsweise ein Orangen-Mascarpone mit karamellisiertem Orangensirup auf dem Programm. — In der italienischen „Cantina" kann man in einer ungezwungenen Atmosphäre aus einer Riesenauswahl an Pizza und Pasta wählen, die Minestrone schmeckt wirklich wie auf der Piazza von Genua, und hier ist die inkarnierte Sünde unter den Nachspeisen zu finden: Doppelte Schokoladeneiskrem mit Sahne und heißer Schokoladensoße! — „A touch of Asia" durchweht das durchgehend geöffnete „Morning Glory", wo man zu jeder Tageszeit *hot & sour chinese soup*, malaysisches Lamm-Curry oder knusprige Hühnerspießchen mit Chillies und Erdnusssoße ordern kann. Da all diese Hochgenüsse unmöglich an einem verlängerten Wochenende zu bewältigen sind, wird — glaubt man den unbestätigten Gerüchten, die im Hotel kursieren — Altpräsident Nelson Mandela schon bald seine charmante Gattin erneut ins Fancourt entführen.

bordering the golf course are no less luxurious. There are one-room studios and suites with one, two or three bedrooms. A practical aspect is the fully equipped kitchenette with fridge, deep-freeze, coffee machine, microwave, and everything else to delight the sophisticated housewife or house man. There is also a real fireplace for atmosphere, and romance can be found in the bedroom with its tiny oriels and little corners. The super bathroom has good quality tiles in tasteful, muted colours and the 24-hour room service is very convenient indeed. The culinary side of the hotel is as international as the golfers themselves. The tastes of this world are reflected in five beautiful restaurants, one of them, the Montagu, is the best A-la-carte restaurant in South Africa. Up to forty gourmet guests can be accommodated in this cosy sanctuary serving a South African and international cuisine. To the strains of classical music guests sit in the flickering firelight and are pampered by a superb kitchen team and remarkably friendly and obliging staff. The smoked crocodile filet in an exotic orange-curry sauce served with red and green peppers and wild rice can be highly recommended. In Le Pecheur, the fish restaurant, the Dutch chef, Maurice van Gaart, prepares little oysters from Knysna which have a typical nutty taste to be served on ice. Alternatively he serves them au gratin and, of course, with a Hollandaise sauce or with spinach and a drop of Pernod. Fish & chips are just as much part of the Pecheur menu as Asian seafood curry or South African trout. Those who eschew fish have a choice of various meat and vegetarian dishes. In the elegant Bramble Lodge chef Frédéric Robichon combines the aromas, herbs and spices of this world to delight the taste buds. Black tiger prawns in a sweet-and-sour sauce from Thailand is on the menu and stuffed quail with rice and a fig sauce. For dessert, for instance, you could have the orange mascarpone with caramelized orange syrup. The informal Italian Cantina serves an enormous range of pizza and pasta. The minestrone really does taste the same as it does on the piazza at Genoa, and you'll find sin incarnate among the puddings – double chocolate ice cream with cream and a hot chocolate sauce. A touch of Asia pervades Morning Glory where you can order hot and sour Chinese soup, Malaysian lamb curry and crispy spit-roasted chicken with chillies and peanut sauce at any time of day. A long weekend is far too short to indulge in all these delights. There are unconfirmed rumours circulating in the hotel that the elderly President Mandela will soon bring his charming wife back to the Fancourt on a return visit.

Maurice van Gaart, kreativer Chef des Fischrestaurants Le Pecheur.
Maurice van Gaart, the creative chef of the fish restaurant Le Pecheur.

WO SICH DIE MEERE MISCHEN

Where oceans come together

GOLF IN MEXICO

Los Cabos, die Kap-Region der Baja California, der 1300 km langen Halbinsel zwischen der Cortez-See und dem Pazifischen Ozean, hat sich in den letzten Jahren zu einer der führenden Golf-Domänen Mexikos entwickelt. Sämtliche Plätze sind 18-Loch-Anlagen und Par-72-Kurse — sportliche Hochgenüsse für Profis wie für Anfänger, und das übers ganze Jahr. Die Küstenlandschaft bietet dazu faszinierende Naturschauspiele.

Los Cabos, in the cape region of the Baja California, is a 800 miles peninsula set between the Cortez Sea and the Pacific Ocean. Over recent years it has developed into one of Mexico's leading golf locations. Every golf course is 18 hole and Par-72 — an all year round sporting delight for professionals and amateurs alike. In addition the coastal landscape offers any golfer one of nature's great spectacles.

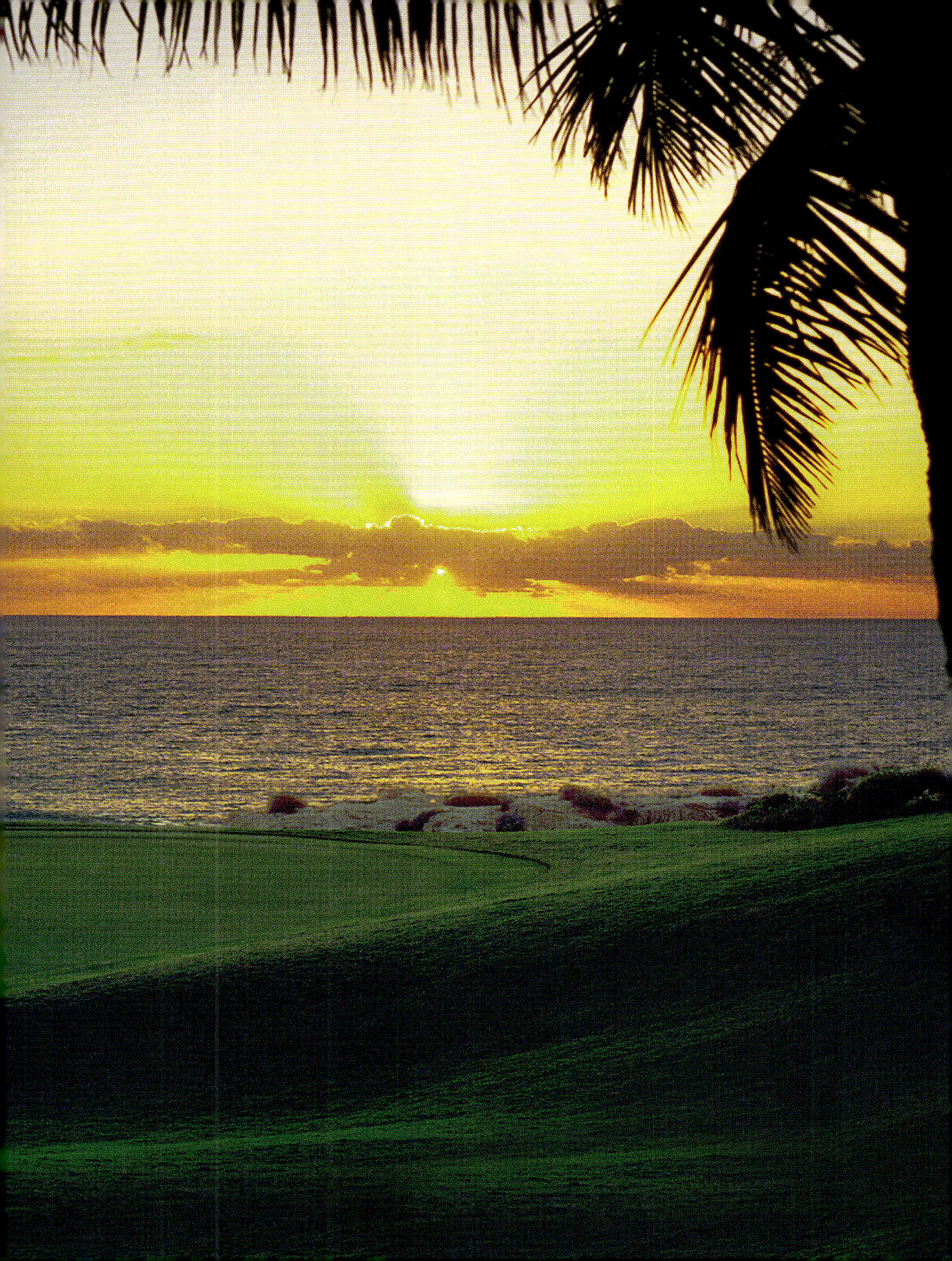

Fünf Meisterschaftskurse am Garten Eden

Las Ventanas al Paraiso

Five championship courses in the Garden of Eden

Am Kap von Mexiko zeigt die Schöpfung unvergessliche Schönheiten. Hier führt die Natur mit Wind und Sonne, mit Wüste und Meer Schauspiele auf, als wären die ersten Menschen ihr Publikum. Ein Szenario, wie geschaffen für fünf der spektakulärsten Golf-Parcours dieser Küste und ein zauberhaftes Hotel, das hier die Fenster zum Paradies öffnet.

The scenic beauty of the Mexican cape is unforgettable. The desert and ocean, the wind and sun stage a drama as if playing to the very first human audience. The scene appears to have been specially created for five of the most spectacular golf courses on this coast and the charming hotel whose windows open out on to paradise.

Text: Günter Ned · Fotos: Klaus Lorke/Las Ventanas

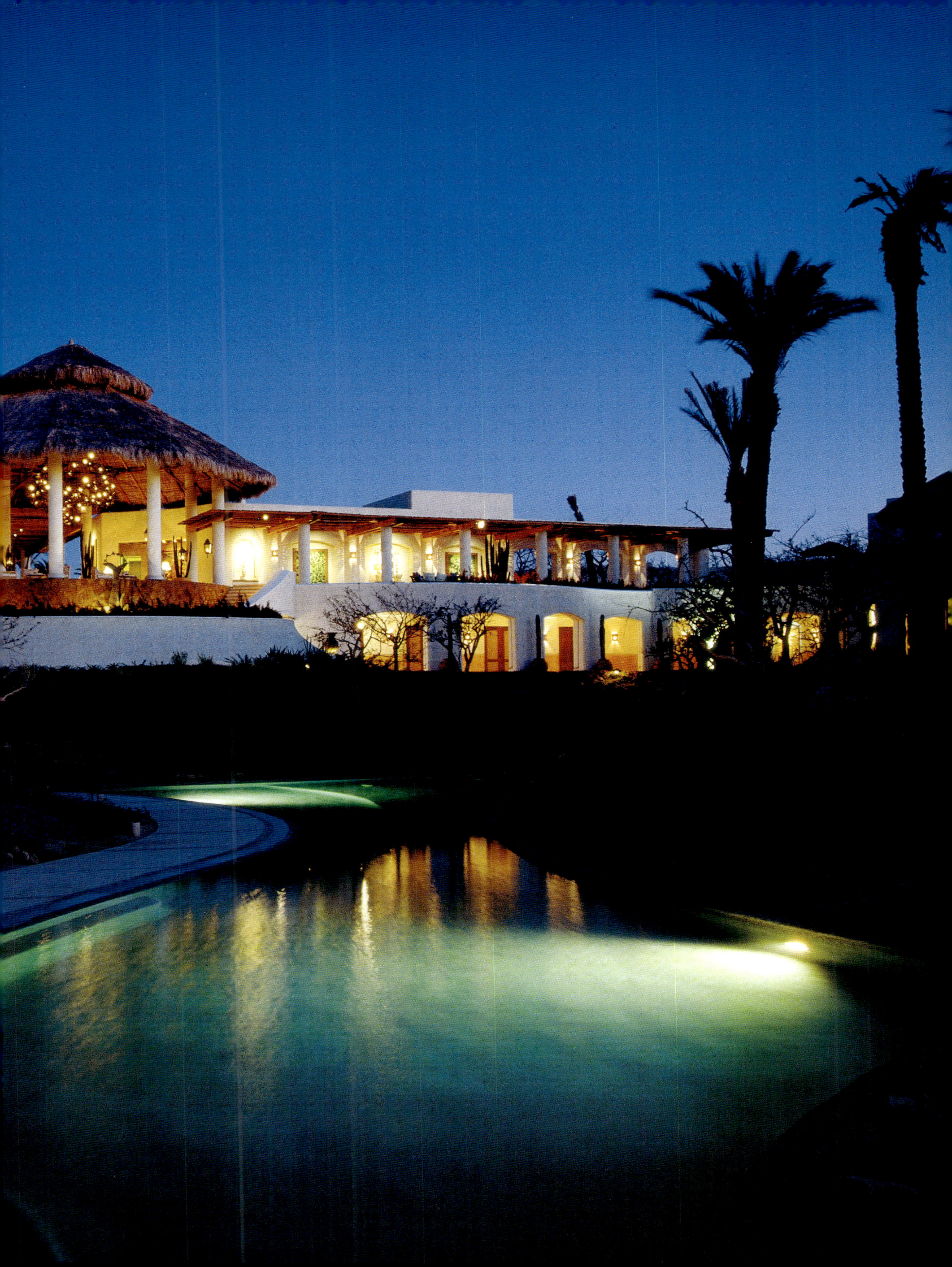

Das Las Ventanas präsentiert sich nicht wie ein Hotel, sondern als eleganter Pueblo, als ein märchenhaftes Dorf.
Las Ventanas looks more like an elegant pueblo than an hotel, a fairytale village.

South of the Mexican border, California separates from the continent and continues for 807 miles between two seas right down to the Tropic of Cancer. This peninsula is called Baja California - Lower California - and is between 25 and 136 miles wide. Endless sandy beaches and turquoise blue lagoons lie along its coastline from above, the landscape inland is a chain of deserts and mountains, rusty brown and radiantly gold in the perpetual

Südlich der mexikanischen Grenze löst sich Kalifornien vom Kontinent und reicht zwischen zwei Meeren 1300 Kilometer weit hinab bis zum Wendekreis des Krebses. Die Landzunge heißt Baja California, Niederkalifornien, ist zwischen 40 und 220 Kilometer breit. Endlose Sandstrände und türkisblaue Lagunen säumen ihre Ränder, das Innere zeigt sich dem Blick vom Himmel als Kette von Wüsten und Wüstengebirgen, rostbraun und golden leuchtend in der ewigen Sonne. An der Westküste brechen sich die Wogen des Pazifiks, an der Südspitze, dort wo die Cortez-See und der Stille Ozean ineinanderfließen, ist die Welt zu Ende, hier beginnt das Paradies.

So jedenfalls mag es Besuchern eines Hotels erscheinen, das so gar nicht als Hotel erscheint, eher als eleganter Pueblo, als ein märchenhaftes Dorf aus schlanken, weißen, verwinkelten Häusern, unterschiedlich hoch mit schmalen Fenstern, freien Treppen, Dachterrassen, Kaminen wie Zinnen. Traditionelle mexikanische Architektur klingt an, auch der mediterrane Stil nordafrikanischer Bauweisen. Wer hier umherblickt, sieht Traumbilder. Zwischen den Villen blüht Wüste auf zu zauberhaften Gärten.

In den Villen mischen sich eleganter Pueblo-Stil und nordafrikanische Architektur.
Villas combine elegant pueblo style and North African architecture.

142 HIDEAWAYS

sunlight. The surf of the Pacific breaks on the western coast and on the southern tip where the Sea of Cortez and the Pacific flow into one another. Here, where the world comes to an end, is the beginning of Paradise.

At least, that is how it appears to visitors. The hotel looks more like an elegant pueblo than an hotel - a fairytale village with narrow, white houses of varying heights with many corners, narrow windows, flights of steps, roof terraces and turret-like chimneys. It's all very reminiscent of traditional Mexican architecture, but also the Mediterranean-style buildings in North Africa. Gazing at this scene is like having a vision.

Between the villas the desert has flourished into enchanting gardens. A symphony of blue tones has been painted on to nature's backcloth, from meandering watercourses flowing down to the open sea, to the blue of cloudless sky. Two by two, pelicans dive into the waves for fish, and whales leap on the horizon. When the sun sets, the crest of the Chileno headland glows, and the moon rises from the sea like an orange-red fireball. It's as if all the windows open on to paradise. Indeed, the name of the hotel is Las Ventanas al Paraiso.

Its success is a measure of just how popular the area has become. The 61 suites have been in constant demand since the resort opened in October 1997. The attraction of the resort is not least due to the fact that the architects of Las Ventanas wanted to create something quite unique. What they have produced is a work of art for the exclusive luxury end of the hotel business. It begins with the landscaping but certainly doesn't end with the interior design. A basic principle was to create harmony with the locality and incorporate the characteristic features of the region. These guiding principles have led to an interesting consequence for flora. Desert plants were planted. Those familiar with

Überall finden sich Ruheplätze zum Verweilen mit faszinierenden Ausblicken.
There are a lot of resting places with fascinating views.

Eine Symphonie aus Blautönen ist in die Natur gemalt von meandernden Wasserläufen zur weiten See bis hinauf in den wolkenlosen Himmel. Fischende Pelikane stürzen sich paarweise in die Wellen, am Horizont springen Wale. Wenn die Sonne sinkt, glüht der Kamm der Landspitze Chileno, der Mond steigt aus dem Meer als orangeroter Feuerball, überall, scheint es, öffnen sich Fenster zum Paradies. Und so heißt auch das Hotel: Las Ventanas al Paraiso.

Wie sehr das gelungen ist, zeigt der Erfolg. Die 61 Suiten erfreuen sich seit der Eröffnung im Oktober '97 ungebrochener Nachfrage. Die Attraktivität des Resorts dürfte nicht zuletzt darin liegen, dass die Architekten von Las Ventanas al Paraiso auf eine Kreation aus waren. Sie schufen ein Gesamtkunstwerk exklusivster Luxushotellerie. Das beginnt beim Landschaftsdesign und endet bei der Gestaltung der Interieurs noch lange nicht. Grundprinzip war die Harmonie mit dem Ort, mit der Charakteristik der Region. Die Maxime hatte eine originelle Konsequenz für die Flora: Man pflanzte Wüstenvegetation. Dass damit nicht Ödnis Einzug hielt,

HIDEAWAYS 143

Originale Materialien und einheimische Handwerkskunst schaffen in den Zimmern und Suiten authentische Wohnszenerien.

Original materials and local craftmanship have created authentic living spaces in the rooms and suites.

Das Entrée im Schimmer der Gaslaternen.

The entrée in the glimmer of gas lamps.

the Baja California know that this doesn't necessarily hasten the advance of aridity. On the few days of the year when it does rain, the desert suddenly bursts into bud and begins to flower. Since the earth of Las Ventanas is being watered all the year round, visitors stroll through ever-flowering desert gardens on their way from their suites to the beauty & spa, or from the restaurants to the gift boutique.

The 15th hole of Robert Trent-Jones-II's golf course, the Cabo Real, rolls imperceptibly into the floral scenery – which brings me to our theme, the spectacular golf courses around the Garden of Eden. In recent years Los Cabos, the cape region between San José del Cabo in the east and Cabo San Lucas in the west, has developed into one of the leading golf regions of Mexico. All the courses are 18-hole and par 72. The five world class courses provide professionals as well as beginners with a top quality golfing experience, in short, golf surrounded by spectacular scenery where desert and ocean meet. For top golf course designers, Jack Nicklaus, who designed the El Dorado, the Cabo del Sol and the Palmilla courses, Robert Trent-Jones II (Cabo Real) and Roy & Pete Dye (Cabo San Lucas Country Club), the task posed a huge challenge. While the surroundings appeared to be competing with their own creativity, they had to provide real challenges to golfers' skill and technique. However, everyone can be highly satis-

ist Kennern der Baja California geläufig. Hier beginnt die Wüste an den wenigen Tagen im Jahr, wo Regen fällt, schlagartig zu grünen und zu knospen, und da die Erde von Las Ventanas übers ganze Jahr bewässert wird, spazieren Besucher auf ihren Wegen von der Suite zur Beautyfarm, von den Restaurants zur Geschenkeboutique durch einen immer blühenden, malerischen Wüstengarten. Das 15. Loch des Robert-Trent-Jones-II-Golfkurses von Cabo Real fügt sich dabei wie gewachsen in die florale Landschaft. Womit wir beim Thema wären, den spektakulären Golfplätzen rund um den Garten Eden.

Los Cabos, die Kap-Region zwischen San José del Cabo im Osten und Cabo San Lucas im Westen, hat sich in den letzten Jahren zu einer

Gäste der Luxussuiten schwimmen im privaten Pool.

Luxury suite guests can swim in their private pools.

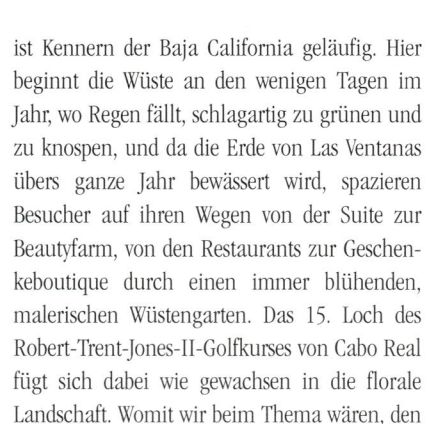

der führenden Golf-Domänen Mexikos entwickelt. Sämtliche Plätze dort sind 18-Loch-Anlagen und Par-72-Kurse. Profis wie Anfängern bieten die fünf Weltklassekurse ganzjährig sportlichen Hochgenuss – in einem Atemzug zu nennen mit dem großartigen Naturschauspiel einer Landschaft, bei dem die Wüste sich mit dem Ozean vermählt. Für die hochkarätigen Golfplatz-Designer Jack Nicklaus (nach seinen Entwürfen wurden drei Anlagen gestaltet: El Dorado, Cabo del Sol und Palmilla), Robert Trent Jones II (Cabo Real) sowie Roy & Pete Dye (Cabo San Lucas Country Club) eine gewaltige Herausforderung. Die natürliche Umgebung als Konkurrenz zur eigenen Kreativität und spieltechnischen Notwendigkeiten. Mit dem Ergebnis können alle höchst zufrieden sein. Kreateure, Spieler und last but not least die Natur. Cabo Real ist der Klassiker unter den Parcours. Der Austragungsort des PGA Senior Slam Tournament 1999 misst über 7000 Yards. Drei seiner Löcher liegen in direkter Ozeannähe. Seinem Namen alle Ehre macht El Dorado, jüngstes Mitglied im Quintett. Der 7050-Yards-Kurs besticht durch sechs unmittelbar am Meer gelegene Löcher, wo die Wellen nur wenige Schritte vom Grün auf den Strand schlagen. Die übrigen 12 Löcher sind wie wundervolle Cañons in die Wüste gemeißelt. Von interessanter Architektur mit neun wasserseitigen und neun bergseitigen Löchern ist der 6939 Yards umfassende Palmilla Kurs. Fast von jedem Standort aus bietet sich Golfern ein traumhafter Panoramablick auf die Cortez-See. Vom Wasser geküsst, zieht sich der so genannte Ocean Course des Cabo del Sol über eine Meile am Strand von Playa Barco Varado entlang. Seine Attraktion sind die dort platzierten spektakulären drei Endlöcher. Gesamtlänge 7037 Yards. Charakteristisch für den Cabo San Lucas Country Club sind die verschwenderisch angelegten Bunker, ein Markenzeichen seiner

fied with the result, golfers and wild life alike. The Cabo Real is the true classic among the golf courses. The venue of the PGA Senior Slam Tournament 1999, it is 7,000 yards long. Three of the holes are very close to the sea. The El Dorado, the most recent of the quintet, is true to its name. The 7,050 yard course is special

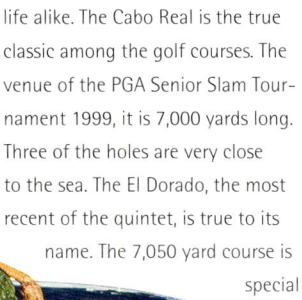

Im eleganten Restaurant wird eine kreative mexikanisch-mediterrane Küche serviert, unterm Palmdach beim Spa wartet die Ceviche- und Tequila-Bar mit Urmexikanischem auf.
The elegant restaurant serves creative Mexican cuisine, under the palm roof of the Sea grill beneath the Spa guests enjoy genuine Mexican fare.

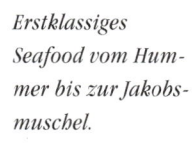

Erstklassiges Seafood vom Hummer bis zur Jakobsmuschel.
Excellent seafood from lobster to scallop shells.

HIDEAWAYS 145

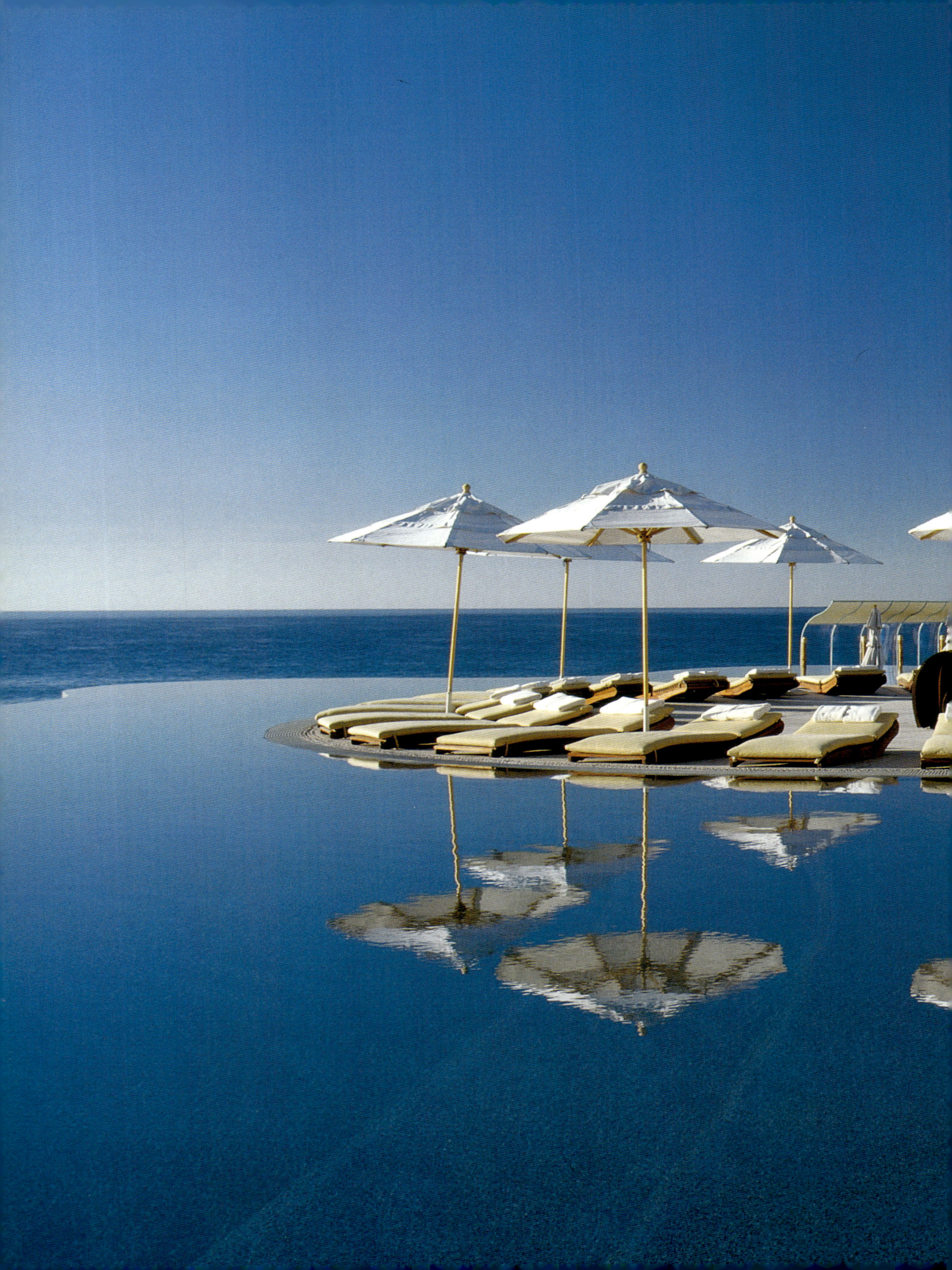

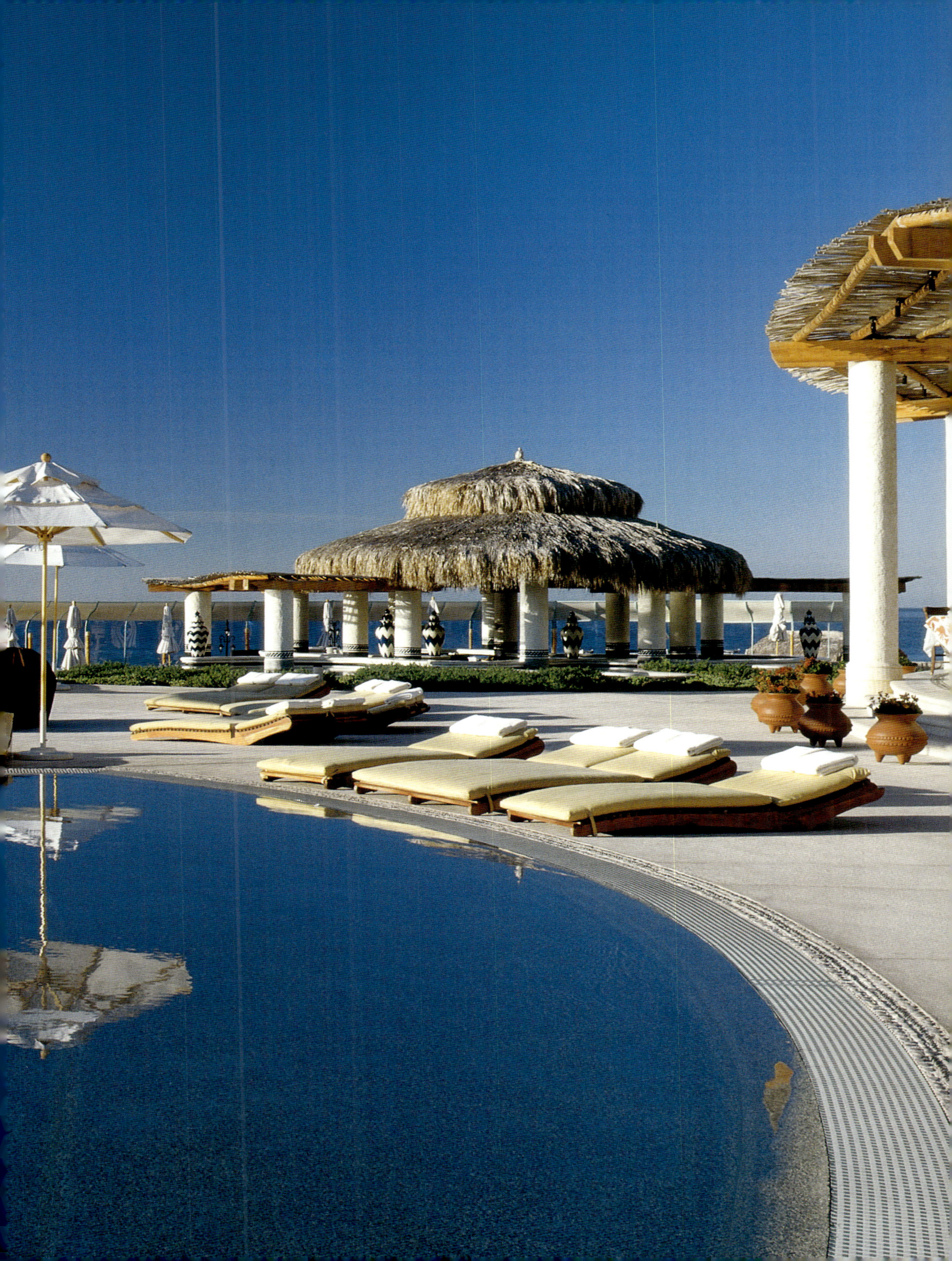

Relaxen im Pool oder Abschlag am Meeresufer – im Las Ventanas ist beides möglich.
Relaxen in the pool or tee-off at the coastline – at Las Ventanas both is possible.

Sonnenuntergang in einem naturbelassenen Stück Paradies.
Sunset in an unspoilt corner of paradise.

because of its links section – six holes are right beside the seashore where waves break only a few feet away from the green. The remaining twelve holes are like wonderful canyons carved into the desert. The architecture of the 6,939 yard Palmilla course is interesting owing to the fact that nine holes are located beside water and nine bordered by mountain terrain. From wherever the golfer is standing there are spectacular panoramic views over the Sea of Cortez. Over a mile of Cabo del Sol's Ocean Course (7,037 yards) lies beside the shore of Playa Barco Varado. Its chief attraction are the sensational three final holes. The most striking feature of the Cabo San Lucas Country Club course (7,270 yards) are its extravagant bunkers, a trademark of its designer. The seventh hole beside a long, deep blue lake, is particularly tricky. Yet, however enjoyable a day of golf spent at the gates to the Garden of Eden, all golfers return gladly. Some like to refresh themselves in the cleverly laid out chain of swimming pools which wind their way through the gardens of Las Ventanas. Originating beneath the mermaid in the hotel lobby, it flows under a footbridge, curves around the sun terrace between the restaurant and the Sea Grill and its water bar, tempting the residents of the Ocean View and Roof Terrace suites to take a dip, and ends at the luxury suites at the edge of the resort, which have their own intimate, private swimming pools. The most spectacular pool view however, is from the semi-circular restaurant which has an open interior and roofed terrace where pool and ocean meet. The pool looks like the surge of the sea splashing right up to the tables, and the round palm roof of the Sea Grill and its sunshades situated nearer the beach, rise up as if from the dip of a wave. The harmonious atmosphere of the place and its Mexican style can also be enjoyed by window-gazers-on-to-paradise while they are eating. In the Sea Grill there is a relaxed atmosphere, and freshly caught sea creatures are laid out on the grill. In the elegant restaurant, sophisticated palates can delight in the creative Baja Mediterranean cuisine. Beneath the palm roof of the Spa, the Ceviche and Tequila Bar serves genuine Mexican fare. Ceviche is the term used by the locals for a wide range of seafood from lobster to mussels marinated in the juices of citrus fruits. The gallery of famous agave brandies behind the bar mustbe the biggest tequila collection in the whole region. What is more, the personal service at the pool, on the beach and in the intimate atmosphere of the suites is simply excellent. Finally, the harmony with the locality and the atmosphere of the country radiate from all the interiors where spaciousness and luxury merge with style. Original materials and local

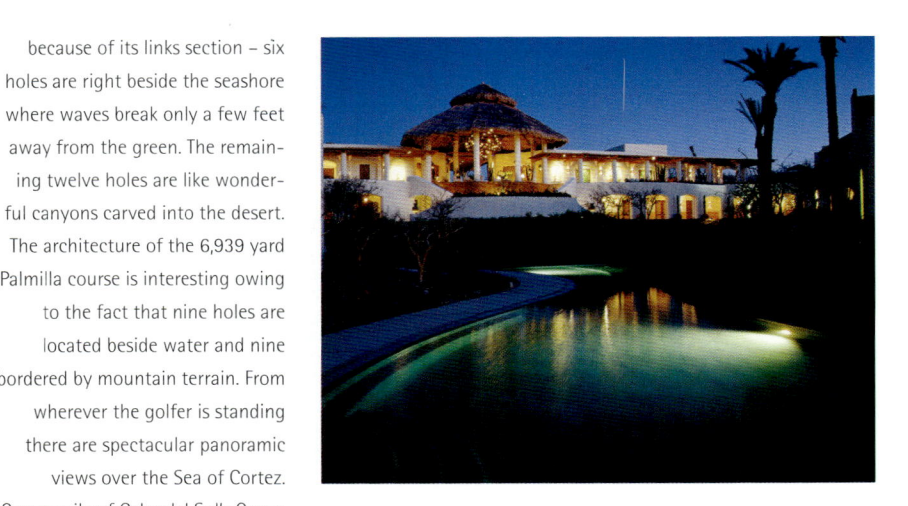

Designer. Als besonders tückisch erweist sich Loch sieben an einem tiefblauen, langen See. Parcourslänge 7270 Yards. Doch so schön es vor den Toren des Garten Eden auch sein mag, nach einem sportlich geprägten Tag kommen alle mit Freude wieder zurück. Beispielsweise, um sich in den Wasserläufen des Las Ventanas zu erfrischen, die sich durch die Gärten schlängeln und nichts anderes sind als eine raffiniert angelegte Kette von Swimmingpools. Sie beginnt unter der Meerjungfrau an der Lobby, unterläuft eine Fußgängerbrücke, umschlingt die Sonnenterrasse zwischen dem Restaurant und dem Sea Grill mit seiner Wasserbar, lockt Bewohner der Ocean-View- und Dachterrassen-Suiten zum Schwimmen und endet an den Grenzen des Resorts vor den Luxussuiten mit ihren intimen, privaten Badebecken. Den spektakulärsten Poolblick hat man wohl vom Restaurant, einem Halbrondell mit offenem Innenraum und überdachter Terrasse. Hier werden Pool und Meer eins, ja der Pool erscheint als eine Woge der See, die bis an die Tische plätschert, und das runde Palmdach des Sea Grills, der tiefer zum Strand hin liegt, seine Sonnenschirme, ragen auf wie aus einem Wellental. Die Harmonie mit dem Ort, mit der Eigenart Mexikos genießen die Fenstergucker am Paradies natürlich auch beim Speisen. Im Seagrill liegt bei lockerer Badeatmosphäre frisch gefangenes Meeresgetier auf dem Rost. Im eleganten Restaurant werden feine Gaumen mit kreativer Baja-mediterraner Küche verwöhnt. Und unterm Palmdach beim Spa wartet die Ceviche- und Tequila-Bar mit Urmexikanischem auf. Ceviche nennen die Einheimischen variantenreiches Seafood vom Hummer bis zur Jakobsmuschel, das in Zitrussäften gegart und eingelegt wurde. Die Galerie des berühmten Agavenbrandes hinterm Tresen ist wohl die umfangreichste Tequilakollektion der Region. Exquisit auch der Speisenservice am Pool, am Strand und in der privaten Atmosphäre der Suiten.

Und schließlich strahlt die Harmonie mit dem Fluidum des Landes aus allen Interieurs. Großzügigkeit und Luxus präsentieren sich mit Stil. Originale Materialien und einheimische Handwerkskunst schaffen authentische Wohnszenen. Beispielhaft die Phantasien in Stein. In allen Innenräumen, auf allen Terrassen geht man über Böden aus Conchuela, einer Steinart aus Yucatan, der die Natur fossile Seemuscheln eingepresst hat, und überall wird das Auge gefangen von der reichen Ornamentik des Pebble Work, der traditionellen Kunst, Kieselsteine dekorativ und malerisch in Zement einzulegen.

Wo Gott so verschwenderisch mit Meer und Lagunen, mit Wüstengold und Feuerbällen malt, kann der Mensch nicht zurückstehen. Kostbare Bilder und Plastiken, unaufdringlich über das Resort verstreut, manche exklusiv dafür geschaffen, heben die Aura Mexikos, die Schönheit von Las Ventanas ins Reich der Poesie. Besucher genießen die Schöpfung, die himmlische und die irdische, auf vielerlei Weise. Die einen sammeln Muscheln und Kiesel in der Brandung; manche fliegen aus zu den Sehenswürdigkeiten der Region, kommen aber meistens bald zurück; andere fahren aufs Meer, um Wale zu streicheln, die hier im Winter zusammenfinden und sich vermehren. Romantische Paare lassen sich auf Dachterrassen im Schimmer der Gaslaternen von vier Händen massieren, die mondbeschienene See im Blick und die beiden steinernen Fackeltürme, die überm Strand Signal geben vom Ende der Welt. Es ist ein guter Ort, um loszulassen, zu schmunzeln vielleicht über die Endlichkeit unseres Tuns, ein Ort auch, neue Kraft zu schöpfen.

craftsmanship have created authentic living spaces. For example the fantastic stonework. Inside all the rooms and on all the terraces, one walks on conchuela floors, a kind of stone from Yucatán impressed by nature with fossilized sea shells. Everywhere the rich ornamentation of the pebble work catches the eye, the traditional craft of laying pebbles artistically and decoratively into cement. Here, where God has been so extravagant with the sea and lagoons, with desert gold and fireballs, it would be impossible for man to remain in the background. Dispersed unobtrusively throughout the resort are precious paintings and sculptures, some of which have been exclusively created for the resort. They raise the atmosphere of Mexico and the beauty of Las Ventanas into the realm of poetry. Visitors to Las Ventanas can savour creation, both heavenly and earthly, in many ways. Some collect shells and pebbles in the surf, some go on air excursions to see the sights of the region but often return early. Others go out to sea to stroke the whales which gather here in winter to procreate. Romantic couples can be massaged by two pairs of hands on the roof terraces in the glow of glass lanterns, while gazing out across the moonlit sea towards the two stone lighthouses which emit signals at the end of the world. This is a good place to let go and smile about the finite nature of human affairs, a place to draw new strength.

Üppige Natur umgibt das Hoteldorf.
Opulent nature is surrounding the pueblo-style hotel.

Pool und Meer werden eins.
Where the pool and sea merge.

HIDEAWAYS 149

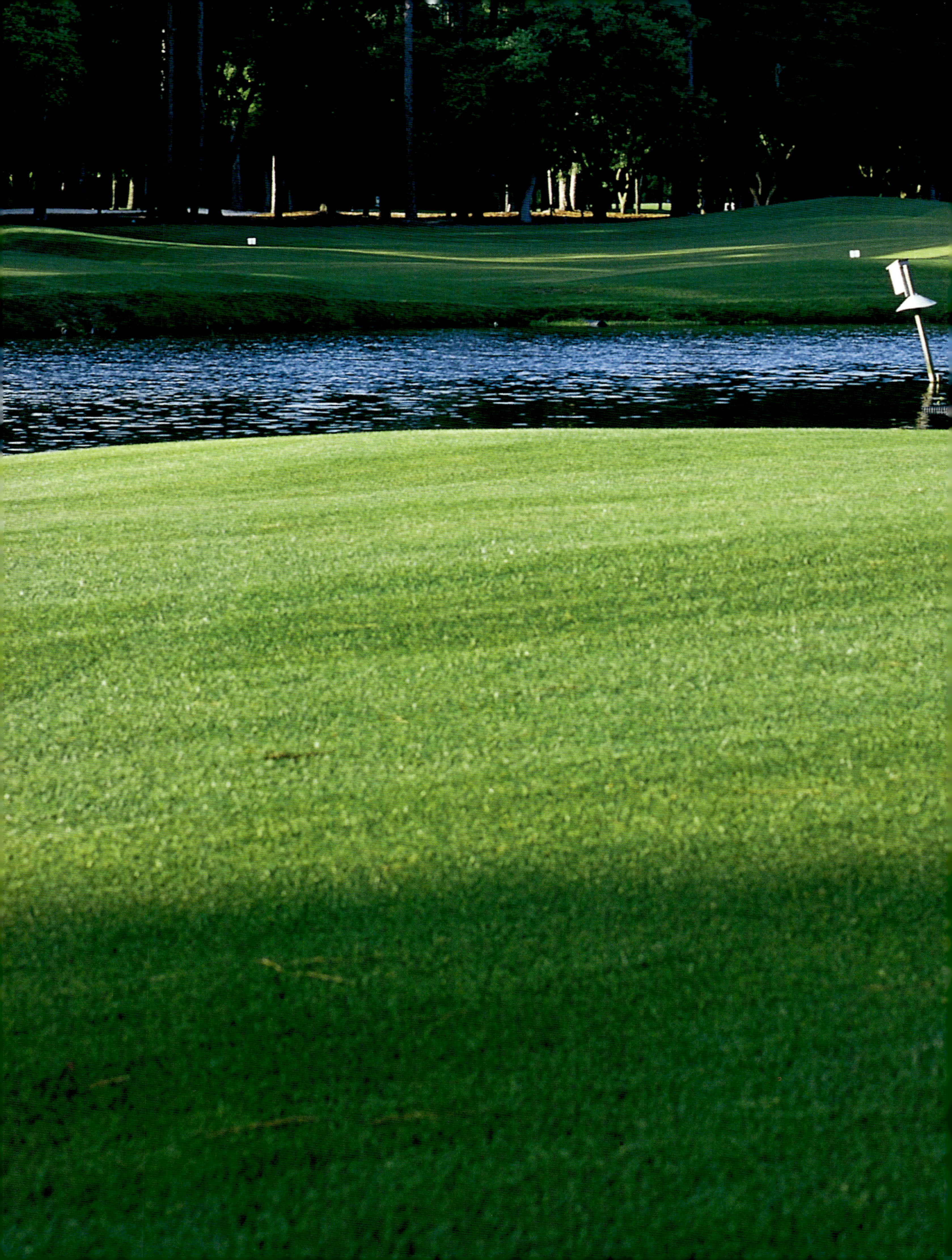

GOLFEN AUF PFLANZER-GRUND

Golf in plantation country

GOLF IN SOUTH CAROLINA

Zur Sklavenzeit schöpften South Carolinas Pflanzer aus der Plantagenwirtschaft ihren Wohlstand. Dabei kultivierten sie den eleganten Lebensstil der Südstaaten-Aristokratie. Heute ist dort, wo einst Indigo und Reis gewonnen wurden, ein Golfparadies entstanden. Wohnen kann man auf historischen Plantagen immer noch, umgeben vom Charme des alten Südens.

When slavery was still in existence South Carolina's planters grew wealthy from their estates. As the aristocracy of the Southern States' they were able to cultivate an elegant lifestyle. Where once indigo and rice were harvested is today a golf paradise where one still lives on historic plantations enveloped by the charm of the old South.

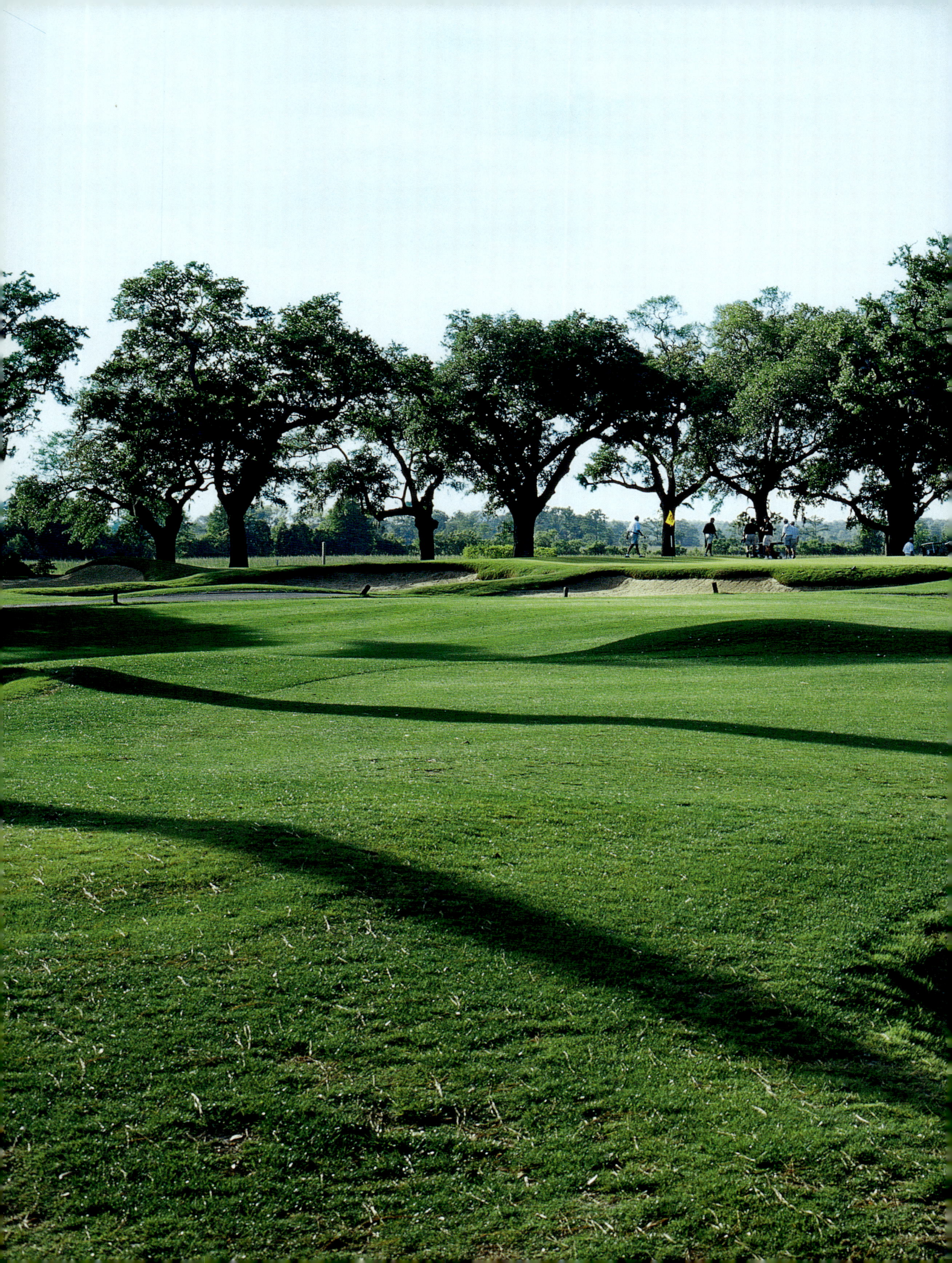

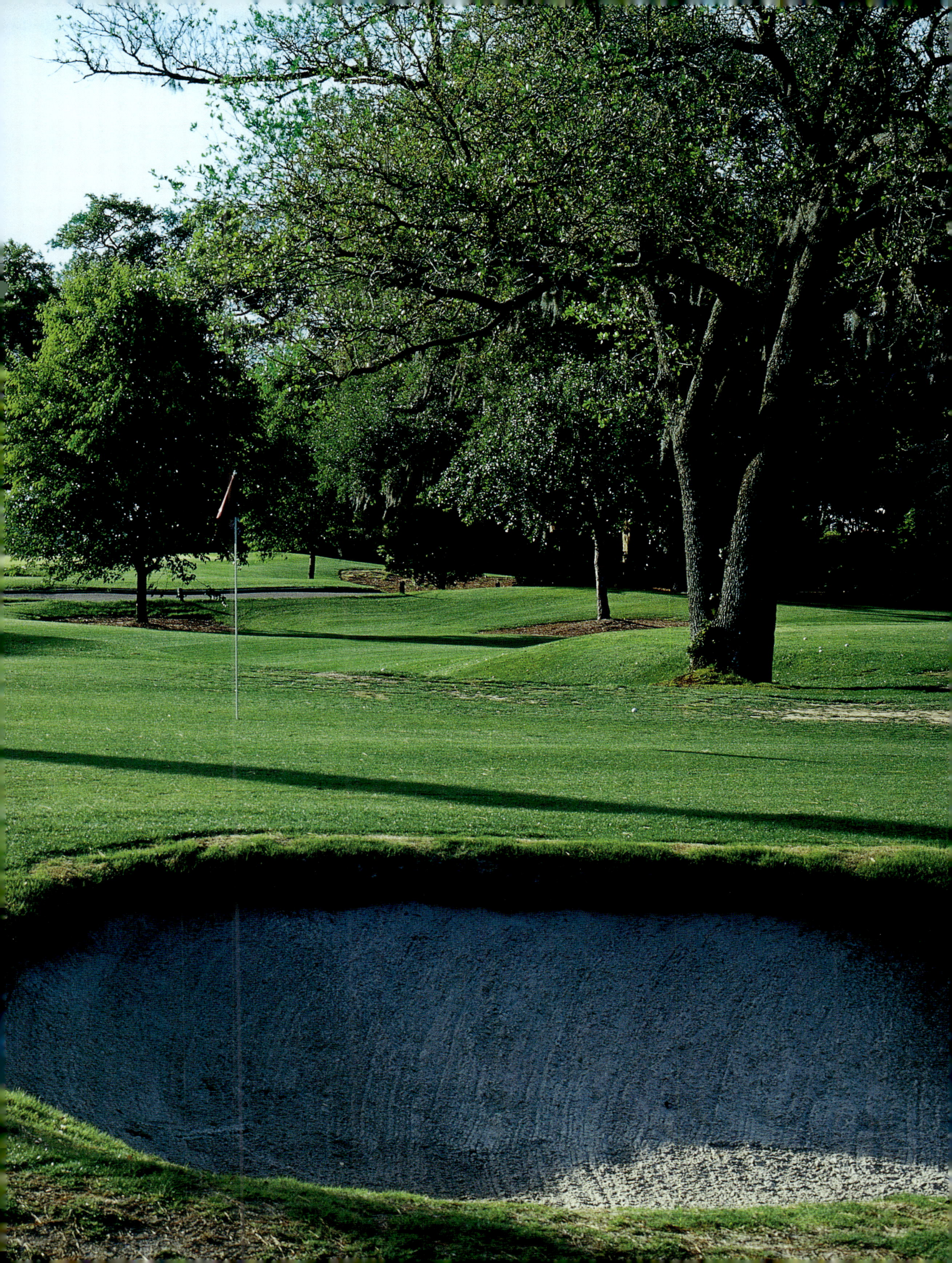

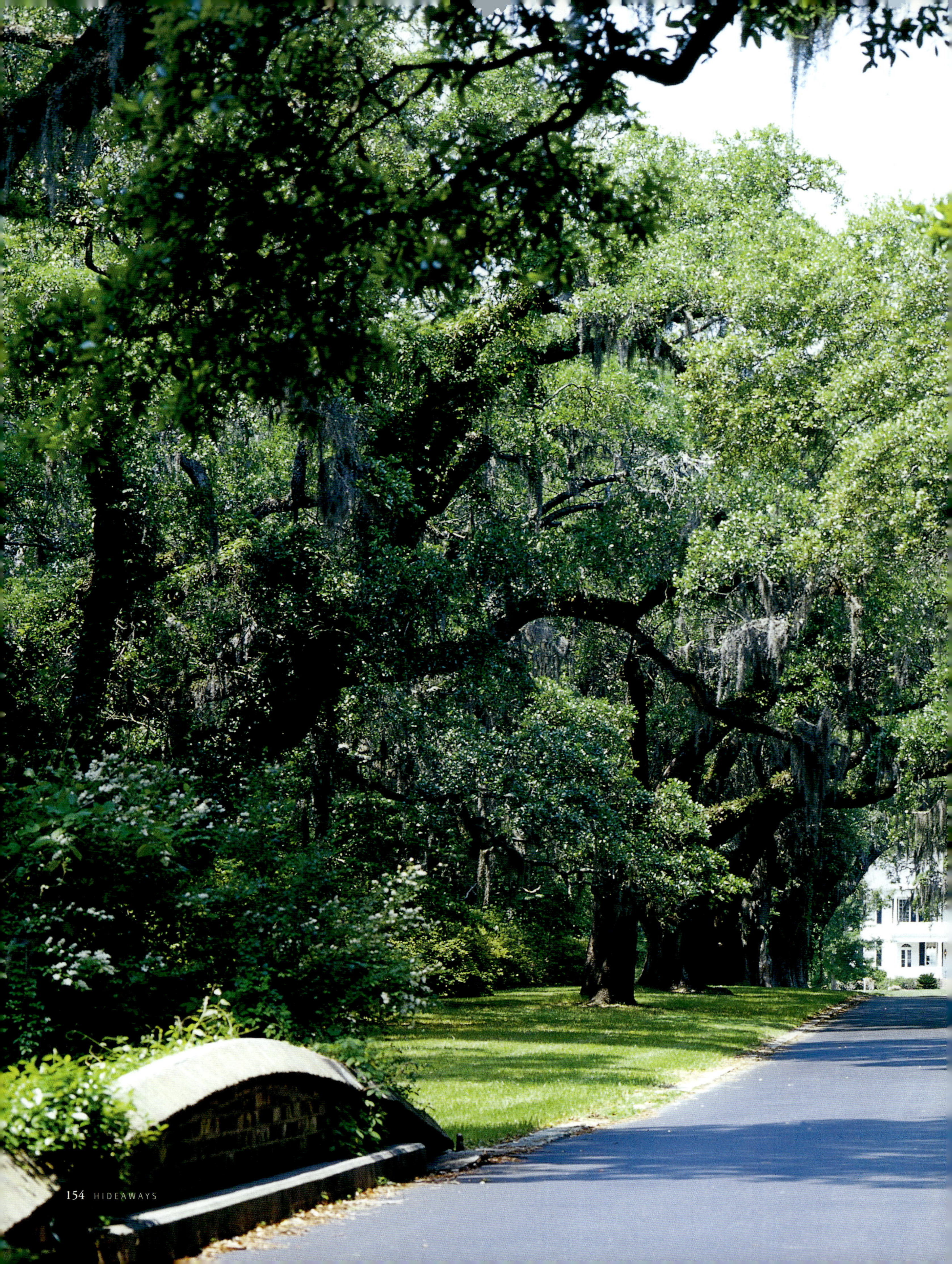

Umgeben vom Flair der Südstaaten

Litchfield Plantation

Golf in plantation country Southern States

Der "Grand Strand" von South Carolina reicht von North Myrtle Beach bis nach Georgetown und ist etwa hundert Kilometer lang. Die flussreiche Gegend am Atlantik ist ein einziges Golf-Paradies. Litchfield Plantation bietet dazu die unberührte Natur einer historischen Reisplantage und die Wohnkultur des tiefen, aristokratischen Südens.

The Grand Strand of South Carolina which stretches from Myrtle Beach to beyond Georgetown is nearly 63 miles long. This region lying along the Atlantic coast has many rivers and is a unique golfers' paradise. What is more, Litchfield Plantation offers the unspoilt scenery of an historic rice plantation and the lifestyle of the deep South.

Text: Günter Ned · Fotos: Freddy Peterburs

Rechts: Das Plantagenhaus – es birgt heute vier Suiten – stand schon um 1740.
Right: The Plantation House – today with four suites – was already standing on this spot in 1740.

Versteckt hinter moosbehangenen alten Bäumen: der Carriage House Club mit dem Fine-Dining-Restaurant. Unten: Alligator im Reisfeld.
Hidden behind old trees draped in spidery moss: the Carriage House Club and its Fine Dining Restaurant. Below: alligator in a rice field.

Flying upwards from the old rice fields into the morning sky is a pair of grey herons. "Live Oaks" border the avenue leading to the plantation house. It is a quarter of a mile long. The "Live Oaks" are so called because they don't shed their leaves in winter. Down the centuries their treetops have grown sturdy and now incline towards one another, their branches interweaving to form a living cathedral. "Spanish Moss", webs of fine silver needles hangs from their branches. They look like oversized versions of the goatees traditionally worn by Spaniards at the time of their overseas' conquests. The Spanish Moss is no para-

Aus den alten Reisfeldern schwingt sich ein graues Reiherpaar in den Morgenhimmel. „Live Oaks" säumen zu beiden Seiten die Avenue, die zum Plantagenhaus führt. Sie ist eine Viertelmeile lang. Die „Lebenseichen" heißen so, weil sie im Winter ihre Blätter behalten. Durch die Jahrhunderte sind ihre Kronen mächtig geworden und haben sich einander zugeneigt. Sie sind über der Avenue ineinandergewachsen und bilden nun gemeinsam einen lebendigen Dom. Von ihren Ästen hängt „Spanisches Moos". Das sind Gespinste aus feinen silbernen Nadelblättern. Sie sehen aus wie übergroße Ausgaben jener Spitzbärte, die zur Tracht der Spanier während der Zeit ihrer überseeischen Eroberungen gehörten. Spanisches Moos ist kein Schmarotzer. Es nutzt die Bäume nur als Halt, ernährt sich von der Feuchtigkeit der Luft und vom Wasser, das über die Äste rinnt. Es gibt vielerlei Symbiosen auf der Litchfield Plantation.

Die fruchtbarste für Golfer ist der Austausch, den das Luxusresort mit dem paradiesischen Patchwork an Golfkursen in der Umgebung pflegt. „Wir haben im Umkreis von achtzig Kilometern über hundert Golfplätze", kann Karl W. Friedrich, Direktor von Litchfield Plantation, versichern. Zehn davon sind mit dem Auto in wenigen Minuten zu erreichen, darunter die attraktivsten der Gegend, im Blick auf die ästhetischen Qualitäten der Anlage wie hinsichtlich ihrer Ansprüche ans Können.

In unmittelbarer Nachbarschaft locken Willbrook (6704 Yards, Par 72, Architekt: Dan

Gäste wohnen in Villen, die über die ganze Plantage verstreut sind.

Guests stay in villas scattered across the whole estate.

Maples, weite Fairways, interessante Bunker, die so groß sind, dass man mit dem Cart hineinfahren kann), The River Club (6677 Yards, Par 72, Architekt: Tom Jackson, sehr viel Raum nach den Abschlägen, aber die Annäherungsschläge müssen sehr genau kommen, das Kernstück ist das letzte Loch, außerdem gibt es zwei Fairways, die übers Wasser gehen) und der Litchfield Country Club (6752 Yards, Par 72, Architekt: Willard Byrd, ein typischer Willard-Byrd-Kurs zwischen uralte Lebenseichen und Pinien gesetzt).

Unwesentlich weiter fährt man zur schönsten Anlage weit und breit hier im Küstengebiet von South Carolina, zwischen Myrtle Beach und Georgetown, dem Caledonia Golf & Fish Club (6526 Yards, Par 70, Architekt: Mike Strantz). Der Kurs sammelt förmlich Auszeichnungen, liegt auf einer ehemaligen Reisplantage, absolut malerisch, mit Blumen an den Tees, entzückenden kleinen Seen auf den Fairways. Zum Clubhaus führt eine Eichenallee, einen Creek entlang, auf dem die Clubmitglieder auch zum Fischen fahren. Traditionell trifft man sich am Dienstag, um den frischen Fang zu braten. Mike Strantz designte auch den anspruchsvollsten Kurs dieses faszinierenden Golfplatzreigens, den True Blue (6451 Yards, Par 72). Spannend, ihn zu spielen. „Er ist der schwierigste Kurs, und er ist dabei ganz neu, erst zweieinhalb Jahre alt", charakterisiert ihn Karl Friedrich. „Das Angebot ist wirklich toll. Kürzlich war eine Gruppe aus Deutschland bei uns, sechs Freunde. Sie blieben eineinhalb Wochen und haben jeden Tag einen anderen Kurs gespielt."

site. It only uses the trees to cling to but feeds off the moisture in the air and from the water which runs down the branches. There are many such symbioses on the Litchfield Plantation.

The most rewarding experience for golfers is the contact cultivated by the luxury resort with the golf courses in the surrounding area. "We have over one hundred golf courses within a fifty mile area", Karl W. Friedrich, General Manager of the Litchfield Plantation, assures us. Ten of them are only a few minutes drive away, among them the most attractive in the whole area, that is from the point of view of the aesthetic

Er hat die schönsten Holes im Golfer-Paradies: der Caledonia Golf & Fish Club.

The most beautiful holes in this golfers' paradise are at the Caledonia Golf and Fish Club.

Außenposten auf den Dünen: das Strandhaus der Litchfield Plantation.
Advance post on the dunes: the Litchfield Plantation's beach house.

qualities of the course as well as the level of skill required.

In the immediate vicinity there is Willbrook (6,704 yards, par 72, architect Dan Marples) which has broad fairways and interesting bunkers which are so big you can go in them with the cart. The River Club (6,667 yards, par 72, architect Tom Jackson) has plenty of space after the tees but the approach strokes have to be very accurate. The crucial point is the last hole but there are also two fairways which go over water. Then there is the Litchfield Country Club (6,752 yards, par 72, architect Willard Byrd) a typical Willard Byrd course between age old Live Oaks and pine trees.

Da kann, bei der ständigen Konzentration auf Entfernungen, Annäherungen, Hindernisse, die landschaftliche Schönheit schon mal aus dem Blick geraten. Gut, wenn man dann in einem Resort wohnt, das alle Reize der traditionsreichen Plantagenszenerie South Carolinas versammelt. Litchfield Plantation hat sie in klassischer Ausgabe (neben geheiztem Swimmingpool, eigenen Tennisplätzen etc.). Das Plantagenhaus stand schon um 1740. Damals wurde Litchfield Plantation von der Simon-Familie gegründet. Die berühmtesten und wohlhabendsten Reisanbauer auf Litchfield waren später die Tuckers. Einer von ihnen, Dr. Henry Messingberd Tucker, war zugleich Arzt, und so rief man ihn oft auch nachts zu Krankenbesuchen. Bei seiner Rückkehr stieg er am Pförtnerhaus nicht vom Pferd, sondern klingelte mit dem Griff seiner Reitpeitsche. Im Haus hatte er für sich eine separate Treppe bauen lassen, die ihn, ohne dass er jemanden stören oder sehen musste, in sein Zimmer brachte. Nach Dr. Tuckers Tod soll es noch lange am Tor geklingelt haben. Schließlich ließ ein Nachbesitzer den Knopf abbauen. Danach wurde es zwar leiser, aber Dr. Tucker wird, so heißt es, bis heute noch nachts auf seiner ehemaligen Plantage und auf seiner Privattreppe gesehen. Während unserer Visite muss er leider Urlaub genommen haben.

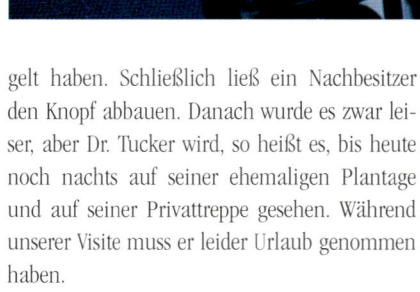

Natürlich hat sich die Einrichtung seit Tuckers Zeiten etwas verändert. Sie ist frisch, der Komfort richtet sich nach unseren heutigen Maßstäben. Doch die Eleganz, der Lebensstil der

Heitere Eleganz im Restaurant. Auf dem Teller: Thunfisch in der Sesamkruste.
Brightness and elegance in the restaurant. Dish: tuna fish in a sesame crust.

Südstaaten-Aristokratie ist nach wie vor zu spüren, hier wie auf der ganzen Litchfield Plantation. Es gibt vier Suiten im Plantation House. Dazu schöne Salons und Veranden. Die letzteren, gesellschaftlichen Räume teilen die Gäste miteinander, ob es nun Freunde und Familien oder Fremde sind, die hier nach Art der Country Inns zusammenfinden. Die Privatsphäre der Suiten bleibt dabei unangetastet. So ist die Unterbringung auf der ganzen Plantage geregelt.

Man blickt vom Plantagenhaus entweder nach vorne zur Allee der Lebenseichen oder nach hinten auf die weiten historischen Reisfelder. Litchfield Plantation umfasst heute 250 Hektar trockenes Gebiet, dazu kommen noch einmal 100 Hektar Reisland. Es reicht bis zum Waccamaw River hinüber, der hier sein Delta hat und zum „Intercoastal Waterway" gehört. Von der Marina aus führt ein Creek direkt zum Fluss. So sieht man immer wieder am Horizont Boote vorüberziehen, als führen sie durch die Reisfelder. Die werden natürlich längst nicht mehr bestellt – Sklaven, die das früher taten, gibt es nicht mehr, ein paar Gräber sind an Dickichtstellen des Parks von ihnen geblieben. Heute sind die von Wasserläufen durchzogenen Felder und das Parkland an seinen Ufern ein

If one drives on a little farther one comes to by far and away the most beautiful course on the coast of South Carolina, the Caledonia Golf & Fish Club (6,526 yards, par 70, architect Mike Strantz). The course positively collects awards. It lies across what used to be a rice plantation and is absolutely beautiful, with flowers at the tees and charming little lakes on the fairways. An avenue of oaks leading to the clubhouse runs along a creek where members can also go fishing. Traditionally members meet on Tuesdays when the fresh catch is fried.

Mike Strantz also designed the most demanding of the courses of the group, the True Blue (6,451 yards, par 72) – exciting golf. Karl Friedrich describes it as "the most difficult even though it's really new, only two and a half years old." "What we offer is quite fantastic. Just recently we had a group from Germany, six friends. They stayed one and a half weeks and played on a different course every single day."

It is of course possible that while one is constantly concentrating on the distances, the approach and the hazards of a course one loses sight of the scenic beauty of the place. So, its good if one can stay at a resort which brings together all the

HIDEAWAYS 159

charm and appeal of the traditional plantation scenery of South Carolina. Litchfield Plantation is a classic example of such a place (as well as having a heated swimming pool, its own tennis courts etc.). The house dates back to 1740, the time the Litchfield Plantation was established by the Simon family. Later on the most famous and certainly the richest rice planters on Litchfield were the Tuckers, one of whom was a GP, Dr. Henry Messingberd Tucker, who was often called out at night to attend the sick. On his return he didn't dismount at the gatekeeper's house but used to ring the bell with the handle of his riding whip. In the house he had a separate staircase built so that he could get to his room without disturbing anyone. It is said that the ringing went on long after Dr. Tucker's death. In the end a later owner dismantled the bell, and the ringing did get quieter! But Dr. Tucker is still seen at night on his old plantation and on his private stairs. He must have been on holiday when we were there. It goes without saying the décor is now somewhat different from that of Tucker's time. It is new and comes up to present day standards, yet the elegance and lifestyle of the southern aristocracy is still to be felt here, indeed on the whole of the Litchfield Plantation, just as it used to be. There are four suites in the

einzigartiges Biotop für die artenreiche Fauna des Südens. Man beobachtet Reiher, Enten, wilde Schildkröten, Alligatoren (keine Angst, sie sind sehr scheu), Rehe, Opossums, Eichhörnchen mit Augenringen wie Waschbären oder den Cardinal, einen hier heimischen, leuchtend roten Vogel, der aussieht wie ein Papagei.

Die anderen 34 Zimmer und Suiten finden sich in Villen, die idyllisch über die ganze Plantage verstreut und versteckt sind, im Guest House zum Beispiel. Sein früherer Besitzer, der deutsche Unternehmer Willy Korf, spielte eine bedeutende Rolle in der Industriegeschichte der Region. Er gründete 1967 die Stahlmühle im nahen Georgetown (15 Minuten Weg mit dem Auto). Das Guest House birgt die repräsentativste, die Executive Suite. Ihr Salon zeigt noch Korfs originalen Schreibtisch. Die Villen am Simons Lane haben einen malerischen Blick auf einen kleinen See, die am Chapel Creek auf einen romantisch umwaldeten, träge dahinfließenden Flusslauf.

An der Stelle, wo Dr. Tucker seine Remise und seine Ställe hatte (davon ist kein Stein mehr übrig), steht heute der Carriage House Club. Clubmanager Jay Rowe lädt hier in attraktive kulinarische Räume, in die Bar mit der Bibliothek etwa, oder in die drei Zimmer des Restaurants. Was Küchenchef Orobosa Uwagbai aus Nigeria da zaubert, ist ein Genuss für jeden Feinschmecker und eine Symbiose ganz eigener Art. Man lässt sich eine Oliven-Tomaten-Suppe schmecken, deren Rezept Orobosa schon als Junge in seinem Heimatdorf Ishan Ewohimi von der Mutter lernte, daneben typische, aber raffiniert verfeinerte Low-Country-Cuisine, also

Ambiancen mit dem Charme des alten Südens.
Ambience with the charm of the old south.

die Küche des Tieflands, des Südens. Signifikant etwa die Kombination von Fisch und Fleisch: köstlich so eine Hummer-Estragon-Sauce zum Lamm-Carré, und ein Gedicht immer Orobosas eigene Fine-Dining-Kreationen von der She-Crab-Soup (mit dem Rogen des Taschenkrebs-Weibchens) bis zum kurz gebratenen frischen Thunfisch in der Sesamkruste mit Ingwer-Dressing. Kein Wunder, dass Litchfield Plantation, und nicht nur wegen der

Die Executive Suite im Guest House ist die repräsentativste des Resorts. Hier das Schlafzimmer.
The Executive Suite in the Guest House is the resort's most imposing accommodation. Shown here, the bedroom.

romantischen Szenerie, ein Paradies für Hochzeiten geworden ist.

Natürlich auch ein Stützpunkt für Ausflüge zu den Sehenswürdigkeiten des alten Südens, aber auch in die Entertainment-Szene von Myrtle-Beach oder an den zehn Minuten entfernten Atlantikstrand von Pawleys Island – dort, auf den Dünen, wartet das Strandhaus der Plantage –, es sei denn, man zieht vor, wie schon angesprochen, jeden Tag einen neuen südcarolinischen Golfkurs zu bespielen. Direktor Karl W. Friedrich kümmert sich gerne um die Abschlagzeiten.

Plantation House and lovely drawing rooms and verandahs. The sitting rooms are shared by all the guests, whether friends and families or strangers who happen to find themselves thrown together in the same way as they might be in a country inn. However, this doesn't affect the privacy of the suites. Accommodation on the whole plantation is arranged in this way. The view from the front of the planter's house is of the avenue of Live Oaks and from the rear the land where the rice fields used to be. Litchfield Plantation today has nearly 620 acres of dry land and in addition nearly 250 acres of rice fields, an area which stretches to the delta of the Waccamaw river which belongs to the Intercoastal Waterway. From the marina a creek leads straight to the river so one always sees boats passing on the horizon, as if they were sailing on the rice fields. Naturally there are no more slaves to do the work. A few of their graves remain beside thickets in the park. Today the fields criss-crossed by watercourses and the parkland on its banks form a unique biotope for the large number of species of Southern fauna. One sees herons, ducks, wild tortoises, alligators (not to worry, they are very tame), deer, opossums, squirrels with rings round their eyes like racoons, and the cardinal bird with bright red feathers resembling a parrot which is native to the region. The other 34 rooms and suites are in villas scattered across the whole plantation and often hidden from view, like the Guest House. Its former owner, the German entrepreneur, Willy Korf, played a significant part in the industrial development of the region. In 1967 he founded the steel mill near Georgetown (15 minutes away by car). The Guest House has the most imposing suite, the Executive Suite. In its drawing room is Korf's own writing desk. The villas on Simon's Lane have a wonderful view of a little lake and the ones at Chapel Creek look out over romantic woods beside a river flowing lazily by. On the spot where Dr. Tucker had his outbuildings and stables (not a stone remains) is the Carriage House. Here Jay Rowe, the Club Manager, invites the guest into attractive culinary surroundings, the bar with the library for instance, or the three rooms of the restaurant. The dishes conjured up by Orobosa Uwagbai, the Chef from Nigeria, delight every gourmet and are a unique symbiosis of a very special kind. He serves an olive-tomato soup whose recipe he learnt as a boy from his mother in his home village of Ishan Ewohimi but also typical cleverly refined Low Country cuisine, that is, the food of the Southern lowlands. Significantly it combines fish and meat. A lobster-tarragon sauce is delicious with slices of lamb, so is Orobosa's own Fine Dining creation, a "she-crab soup" (with the roe of the female crab) is sheer poetry, and also the quick-fried thuna fish in a sesame crust with a ginger dressing. No wonder the Litchfield Plantation has become a paradise for weddings, and not only because of the scenery. Of course it can also be a base for excursions to the sights of the old South and for the entertainment scene of Myrtle Beach. It is also only twenty minutes away from the Atlantic beach of Pawley's Island. There on the dunes is the Plantation's beach house, that is if one doesn't want to play golf on a different course in South Carolina every day. General Manager Karl W. Friedrich willingly assists with booking tee times.

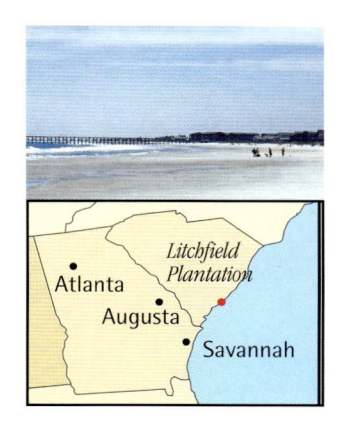

Von der Marina führt ein Flusslauf zum Waccamaw River. Der Atlantikstrand ist zehn Autominuten entfernt.
A stream runs from the marina to the Waccamaw River. The Atlantic beach is only 10 minutes away by car.

Die Gastgeber der Litchfield Plantation: Küchenchef Orobosa Uwagbai mit Clubmanager Jay Rowe. Unten: Direktor Karl W. Friedrich.
The hosts of the Litchfield Plantation: the chef Orobosa Uwagbai seen here with Club Manager Jay Rowe. Below: General Manager Karl W. Friedrich.

HIDEAWAYS 161

Das Hotel Cambridge Beaches auf den Bermudas

Pretty in Pink

Bermuda ist das nördlichste Korallenatoll unter den Britischen Übersee-Territorien. Tausend Kilometer von North Carolina und nur sieben Flugstunden von Europa entfernt. Ein Traum für Sonnenanbeter, Strandläufer, Naturliebhaber und vor allem für Anhänger des grünen Sports. Acht landschaftlich beeindruckende Kurse teilen sich 57 Quadratkilometer Fläche. Damit hat Bermuda die größte Golfplatzdichte der Erde. Und wer Gelegenheit hat, während seiner Golferferien im legendären Cambridge Beaches Hotel zu logieren, erlebt das Reich der Fairways dazu noch von seiner exklusivsten Art.

Bermuda is the most northerly coral atoll of the British Overseas Territories. A thousand kilometres from North Carolina and only a seven hour flight from Europe it is a dream for sun worshippers, bathing beauties, nature lovers but above all for golf fans. Eight scenically stunning courses are spread across an area of 57 square kilometres giving Bermuda a greater density of golf courses than anywhere else in the world. Anyone on a golfing holiday who has the opportunity of staying at the legendary Cambridge Beaches Hotel, experiences the realm of the fairways at its most exclusive.

Text: Jürgen Gutowski / Gundula Luig · Fotos: Martina und Jürgen Gutowski

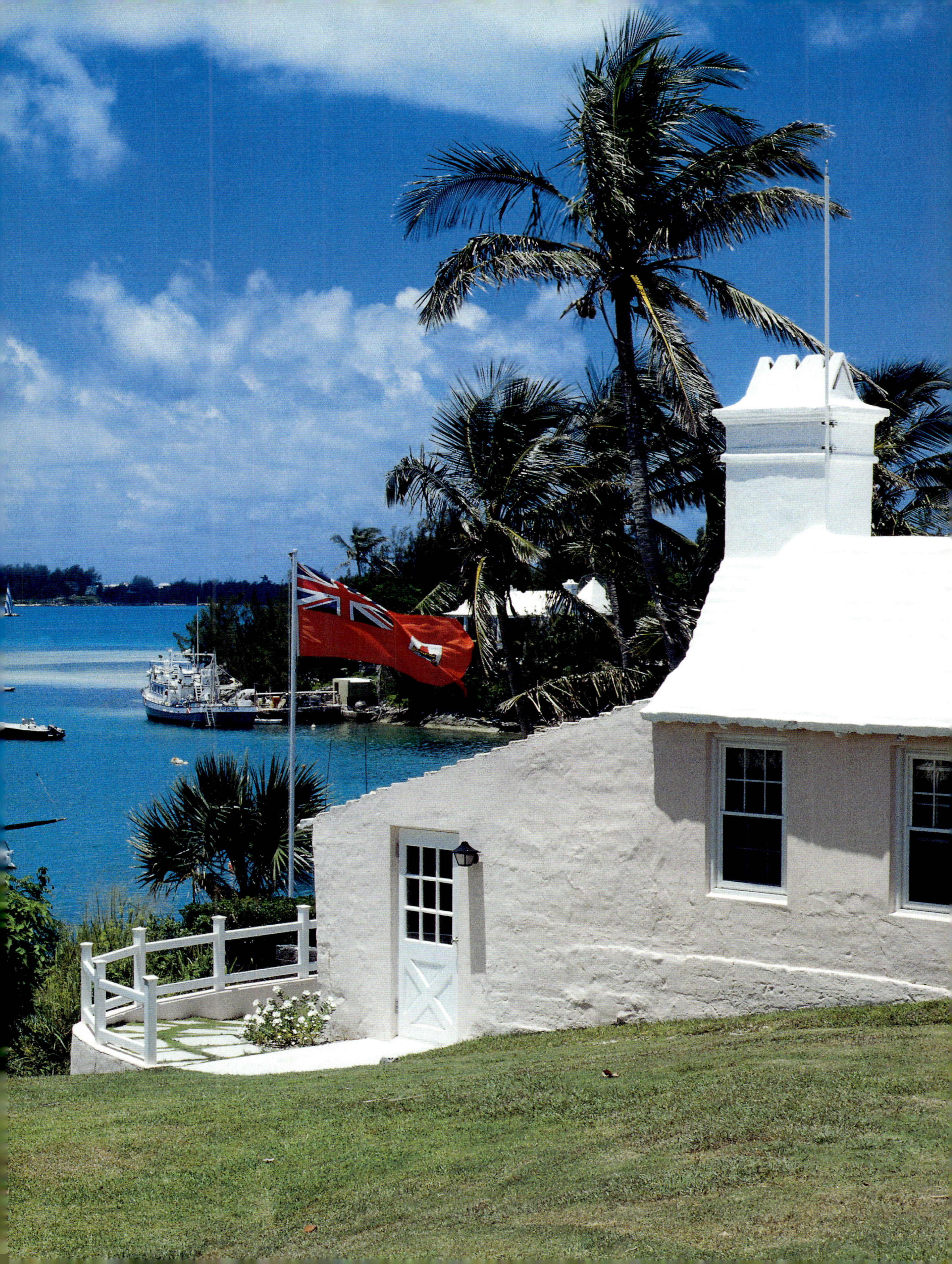

Golf in Bermuda is a genuine pleasure all the year round because the thermometer never drops below 15° centigrade. Golfers from around the world, professionals and amateurs, come here to indulge in their passion on the seven immaculately tended 18-hole courses or on the 9-hole course. Hardly surprising. Combined, the variety of the courses, the imagination of the golf architects and the spectacular landscape – which isn't just scenery, warm breezes off the turquoise sea have put many a golfer to the ultimate test – explain the big attrac-

Golfen auf den Bermudas ist das ganze Jahr über ein wahres Vergnügen, denn das Quecksilber sinkt nie unter 15°C. Golfsportler aus aller Welt kommen deshalb hierher, um auf den vorbildlich gepflegten sieben 18-Loch-Plätzen oder der 9-Loch-Anlage ihrer Passion entweder als Profi oder Hobbyist zu frönen. Kein Wunder, die Vielfalt der Kurse, die Phantasie der Golf-Architekten, dazu eine spektakuläre Landschaft nicht nur als Kulisse (tückische Böen vom türkisblauen Meer haben schon so manchem Spieler das Äußerste abverlangt) – all das zusammengenommen erklärt die große Anziehungskraft der sieben mit Brücken verknüpften „Golf"-Inseln des Bermudaatolls,

The Hon. Michael J. Winfield, Präsident des Hotels Cambridge Beaches, im klassischen Bermuda-Look.

The Hon. Michael J. Winfield, President of the Hotel Cambridge Beaches, in the classic Bermuda-look.

die insgesamt nur fünfunddreißig Kilometer lang und höchstens drei Kilometer breit sind. Alles ist nah.

Auch das legendärste unter Bermudas Spitzenhotels. Es liegt ganz im Westen auf einer eigenen Halbinsel, wo schon die Namen der Region die menschlichen Glückshormone in Wallung bringen: Die zarten Wellen des „Mangrove Bay" zum Beispiel spülen sachte auf einen der fünf Strände, die das Cambridge Beaches Hotel umgeben. Der kleine Ort mit dem weißen Kirchlein und ein paar Kramläden nebenan heißt „Somerset". Die Luft ist klar, die Abendsonne freut sich strahlend über die rosafarbenen Häuschen des hügeligen Anwesens. Zum niedrigen Haupthaus mit der umrankten Eingangstür geht's vorbei am Krocketplatz und dem gepflegten Putting-Green, begleitet vom mäkelnden Gequake der für die meisten Reisenden unsichtbar bleibenden Baumfrösche. Innen umfängt die hölzern-rustikale Atmosphäre eines englisch anmutenden Landhauses, im Jahr 1740 errichtet, ausgestattet mit britischen und bermudianischen Antiquitäten. Im Winter, der deutschen Frühlingstemperaturen entspricht, knistert in der Lounge der Kamin, ganzjährig kredenzt man hier den Nachmittagstee. Durch die großen Fenster hindurch schweift der Blick auf den spiegelglatt daliegenden „Bay",

tion of the seven "golf islands" linked by bridges of the Bermuda atoll, which is only 35 kilometres long and at most 3 kilometres wide. Everything is close at hand.
This is also true of the most renowned amongst Bermuda's top hotels.

Die Räumlichkeiten des Cambridge Beaches, wie hier die North Rock Suite, sind stilvoll mit britischen und bermudianischen Antiquitäten eingerichtet.

The spaciality of Cambridge Beaches, like the North Rock Suite pictured here, are stylishly furnished with British and Bermudan antiques.

It stands at the most westerly point on its own peninsula where even the name of the region releases a surge of human happy hormones. The gentle waves of the Mangrove Bay for instance lap softly on to one of the five beaches which surround the Cambrige Beaches Hotel. This tiny place with its little white church and a couple of gift-shops nearby is Somerset. The air is clear and the evening sun beams down upon the little pink houses of this hilly estate.

Making our way to take out the low main building, its front door adorned by a bower of creeper, we pass the croquet lawn and the well-kept putting green to the accompaniment of the musical croaking tree frogs which remain invisible to most visitors. Inside, one is enveloped by the atmospheric rustic wood interior of a charming English country house built in 1740 and furnished with British and Bermudan antiques. In winter which has German springtime temperatures, a fire crackles in the lounge fireplace and afternoon tea is served all the year round. From the big windows one's eyes range across the glass-like surface of the bay. The white beach of

in weitem Halbrund schwingt sich der weiße Strand der Mangrove Bay hinüber zum Bootshaus, wo ein paar Cambridge-Gäste die hoteleigenen Surfbretter testen. Eine Handvoll Angelfreunde besteigt eines der Motorboote, eine Familie fährt mit dem kostenlosen Wassershuttle zum Einkaufen in die Hauptstadt Hamilton. Und drei sportlich trainierte Golffans lassen sich zum nahe gelegenen Port Royal Golf Course bringen. Die in Regierungsbesitz befindliche Anlage gehört zu den schönsten im Lande, ein vor dreißig Jahren vom Golfarchitekten-Genie Robert Trent Jones gestaltetes Terrain mit atemberaubendem Ocean-View. Der rund 6000 Meter und Par 71 umfassende Kurs wartet mit einigen sehr spektakulären Löchern auf. Par 3 auf dem 16. Green gehört zu den berüchtigsten auf Bermudas Golfplätzen. Wer hier seinen Ball verschlägt, platziert ihn nicht selten im Atlantischen Ozean. Wie es sich für einen Golf-Club dieses Niveaus geziemt, begegnet dem Spieler im eleganten Clubhaus eine kultivierte Atmosphäre. Neben bestausgestatteten Umkleidebereichen sorgen die gediegene Bar und das stilvolle Restaurant für Frühstück, Lunch sowie den Snack zwischendurch für gesellige Abwechslung. Natürlich ist auch auf den anderen Plätzen der Insel genügend Platz für einen meisterhaften Putt – und Golf-Hopping stellt auf den Bermudas nun wirklich kein Problem dar. Bei all dem sportlichen Ehrgeiz sollte man aber den Vorzügen des Cambridge

Beaches Hotels seine Aufmerksamkeit ebenso schenken. Denn 25 Hektar Idylle warten nur darauf, erkundet zu werden. Verstreut über das weitläufige Gelände schwimmen die Dächer der pastellfarbenen Cambridge-Cottages mit ihren 82 Wohneinheiten durch Palmen und Kasuarinenbäume. Fast jede Veranda, möbliert mit Sonnenliegen und Essecke, ist ein Ausguck über den vielfarbigen Atlantik. In der Ferne teilt ein Kreuzfahrtschiff den Horizont, ganz nah gleitet ein Glasbodenboot über die üppigen Korallengärten. Ein zweiter weiter Strand öffnet sich unter Kokospalmen, in das friedliche Bild hineingesprenkelt sind ein paar himmelblaue Sonnenschirme, unter denen gerade ein Champagnerpicknick zelebriert wird. Dicht daneben die kleine Strandbar mit internationalen Durstlöschern jeder Art. Zwei weitere menschenleere winzige Buchten lassen Robinson-Stimmung aufflackern. Wer noch nicht romantisch ist, wird

Mangrove Bay curves round in a wide half-circle to the boathouse where a couple of Cambridge guests are testing the hotel's own surfboards.

A few anglers board a motor boat, a family goes shopping to the capital, Hamilton, on the free water shuttle and three athletic golf fans are taken to the nearby Port Royal Golf course.

The estate which is government property is amongst the most beautiful in the country. Planned and designed over thirty years ago by the genius golf architect Robert Trent Jones, the grounds have a breathtaking ocean view. The 71 par course over about 6000 metres has its own spectacular holes. Par 3 on the 16th green is one of the most in Bermuda's golf courses. A wrong stroke here can often drive the ball straight into the Atlantic. As is fitting for a golf club of this class, the golfer encounters a refined atmosphere in the elegant Clubhouse. Beside superbly equipped changing rooms, the bar and a stylish restaurant provide breakfast, lunch and snacks between meals and ensure congenial company. Naturally other courses on the island have enough space for master strokes, and golf hopping between Bermuda courses poses no problem at all.

Even with all this sporting ambition one should pay some attention to the advantages of the Cambridge Beaches Hotel. After all there are nearly 30 idyllic acres waiting to be explored. Scattered across the extensive grounds between the palms and casuarina trees, are the roofs of the pastel-washed Cambridge cottages with their 82 accommodation units. Nearly every veranda, furnished with sunbeds and a table corner, is a lookout over the multicoloured Atlantic. In the distance a cruise ship parts the horizon and much closer a glass-bottomed boat glides over the dense coral gardens.

A second broad beach opens up beneath coconut palms, a peaceful scene sprinkled with a few pale blue

Auf den Bermudas herrscht Ordnung: Gauner und Diebe wurden früher auf dem Dorfplatz von Hamilton öffentlich an den Pranger gestellt.

In the Bermudas, order reigns: In former times crooks and thieves were publicly put in the pillory in Hamilton's village square.

Rosa-weiße Traumstrände, oftmals von Palmen eingefasst, laden auf den Bermudas zu karibischen Badefreuden ein.

Pink-white dream beaches, often bordered by palm trees, invite you to enjoy a Caribbean swim on the Bermudas.

sunshades spread over a champagne picnic celebration. Next to it is a little beach bar with every sort of international thirst-quencher. Two more tiny little bays, both deserted, put one in Robinson Crusoe mood. The unromantic become romantic here for sure a reason why so many "just-marrieds" and alderly couples choose the Cambridge. President, Michael J. Winfield, is always thinking up something new especially for them. They like it. In fact it is thanks to Winfield's élan that the Cambridge Beaches Hotel figures among the Top Ten Resort Hotels worldwide. Guests express their gratitude by coming again and again, recorded on an impressive plaque beside the bar. Immortalized on it are hundreds of guests who have returned to the Cambridge, ten times, twenty times, indeed fifty times. Many come back because they can experience a piece of traditional hotel life, something rarely found any more in the neighbouring Caribbean. One doesn't just grab a bite here. On certain designated evenings in the week guests partake of dinners in the Tamarisk Restaurant. For the last fifteen years, the multi-prize-winning cuisine has been the creation of five-star chef, Jean-Claude Garzia. His forte is classic French cuisine with elements of Italian and local dishes. Members of the English and Saudi royal houses have heaped praise on his "finely chopped Italian ham with figs, and melon and grated Parmesan", and now as in the past one can still feast on a "mussels lasagne with Chinese shiitake mushrooms and fish soup with saffron ribbons".

The day closes with a sundowner in the Residents' Bar. Then, anyone watching a shooting star in the quiet of the night can make a wish and dream his way contentedly into the new day.

es hier ganz sicher. Ein Grund dafür, warum so viele frisch vermählte junge und ältere Pärchen das Cambridge wählen. Gerade für die lässt sich Manager Michael J. Winfield immer wieder etwas Neues einfallen. Und das kommt an. Winfields Elan ist es zu verdanken, dass er das Cambridge Beaches Hotel unter die Top-Ten-Resort-Hotels weltweit geführt hat. Der Dank der Gäste: sie kommen immer wieder, davon legt eine Wandtafel neben der Bar eindrucksvoll Zeugnis ab. Hunderte von Gästen sind dort verewigt, die schon zehnmal, zwanzigmal, ja sogar fünfzigmal im Cambridge abgestiegen sind. Viele kommen, weil sie hier ein Stück traditionelles Hotelleben erfahren, das man zum Beispiel in der benachbarten

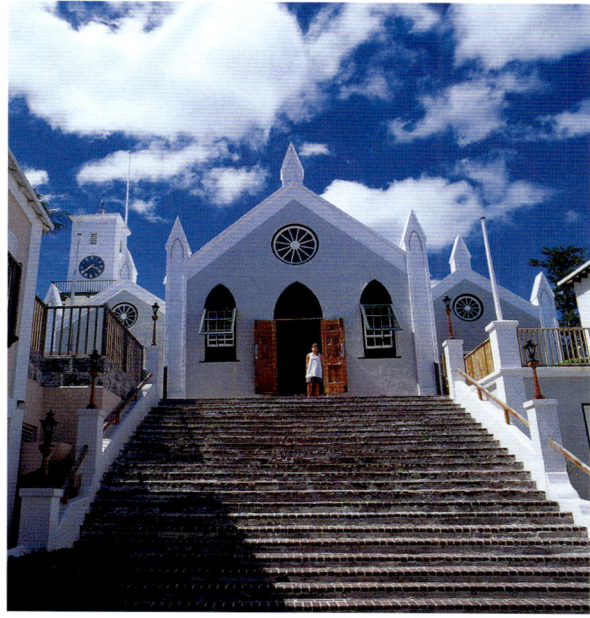

Karibik kaum noch findet. Man geht nicht „mal eben was essen", sondern man begibt sich an einigen, besonders ausgewiesenen Abenden der Woche zum festlichen Dinner ins Tamarisk-Restaurant. Das vielfach preisgekrönte Restaurantangebot wird seit fünfzehn Jahren vom Fünfsterne-Chef Jean-Claude Garzia komponiert. Sein Thema ist die klassische französische Küche mit italienischen und lokalen Anleihen. Mitglieder der englischen und saudi-arabischen Königshäuser waren voll des Lobes über „Feingeschnittenen italienischen Schinken mit Feigen, Melonen mit geriebenem Parmesan", und man labte sich damals wie heute an einer Muschel-Lasagne mit chinesischen Shiitakepilzen und einer Fischsuppe mit Safranfäden. Und zum Tagesabschluss noch einen Sundowner in der Residents-Bar. Wer sich dann in der Stille der Nacht beim Sternschnuppenschauen noch was wünscht, kann zufrieden in den neuen Tag träumen.

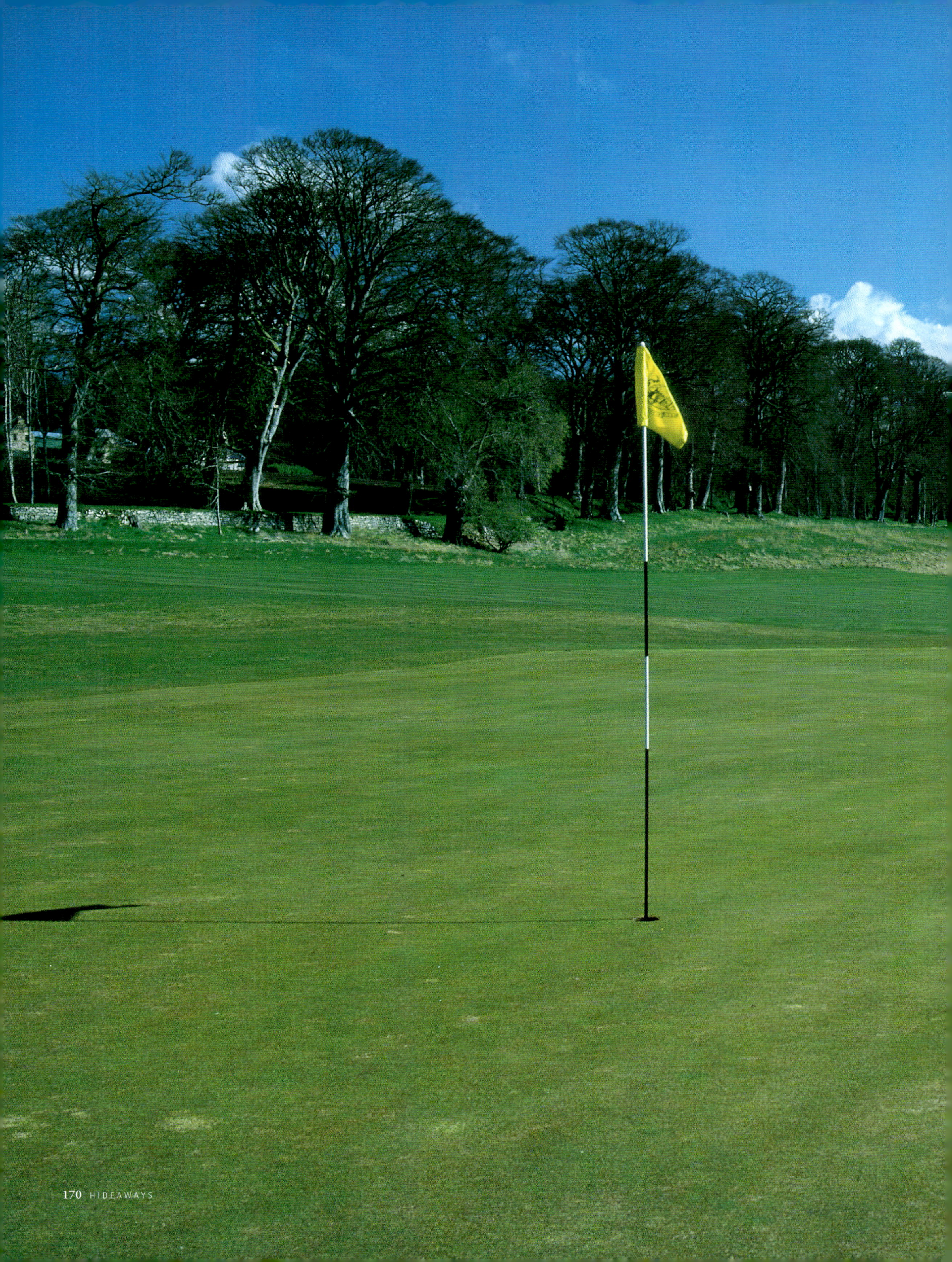

WO DAS SPIEL BEGANN

Where the game began

GOLF IN SCHOTTLAND

Text: Günter Ned · Fotos: Ydo Sol

Als die Schotten das Golfen erfanden, steckte ihr Land noch im tiefsten Mittelalter. Spätere Könige verboten das faszinierende Spiel mit dem kleinen Ball entweder (James II. im Jahr 1457) oder sie förderten es wie James VI., der gleichzeitig König von England war. Man erzählt sich, dass selbst das Damen-Golfen nicht nur schottischen, sondern auch königlichen Ursprungs ist. Die schöne Mary, Queen of Scots, soll für den ersten weiblichen Abschlag der Geschichte gesorgt haben. Heute gibt es um Schottlands Lochs und Firths an die 500 Golfplätze. Darunter sind Clubs, die man zu den exklusivsten des Vereinigten Königreiches, ja der Welt zählt.

When the Scots came up with the game of golf their country was still deep in the Middle Ages. Later kings either prohibited the fascinating game with the little ball (James II in 1457) or they promoted it, as did James VI of Scotland (James I of England). It is said that ladies' golf is not only a Scottish game but also of royal origin. The fair Mary Queen of Scots is supposed to have been the first woman in history to tee off. Today there are up to 500 golf courses around Scotland's lochs and firths, among them clubs which rank among the most exclusive in the United Kingdom, indeed in the world.

Die Heimat des Golfs
OLD COURSE HOTEL ST. ANDREWS
The Home of Golf

St. Andrews ist das Mekka für Golfer. Mindestens einmal im Leben muss jeder Golfer auf dem Old Course von St. Andrews, dem ältesten Golfplatz der Welt, die Schläger geschwungen haben. Auf diesem Links Course wird seit über 600 Jahren Golf gespielt, jeder Golfchampion hat auf den wohl berühmtesten 18 Löchern im Kingdom of Fife an der Ostküste von Schottland die Schläger geschwungen. Tiger Woods komplettierte im Sommer 2000 auf diesem Traditionsplatz mit dem Sieg der British Open den Karriere-Grand-Slam. Woods logierte wie alle Stars im Old Course Hotel Golf Resort & Spa und genoss die schönste Aussicht im Golf: Aus fast allen Zimmern der Luxusherberge schaut man auf den Old Course und das alte schottische Universitätsstädtchen. Direkt vor dem Hotel liegt das berüchtigte 17. Loch, das Road Hole.

St. Andrews is certainly a golfer's dream. Every golfer is longing to play the Old Course of St. Andrews, the oldest golf course in the world, at least once in a lifetime. Golf is played here for more than 600 years and every golf champion has walked the fairways of the most famous 18 holes of golf in the Kingdom of Fife on the Eastern coast of Scotland. In summer 2000 Tiger Woods completed his career grand slam on this traditional course by winning the British Open. Like all the other big names in golf, he also stayed at the Old Course Hotel Golf Resort & Spa and enjoyed the best view in golf. Almost all rooms and suites of this luxury hotel offer a terrific view of the Old Course and the medieval university town of St. Andrews. Directly in front of the hotel is the infamous 17th hole, the Road Hole.

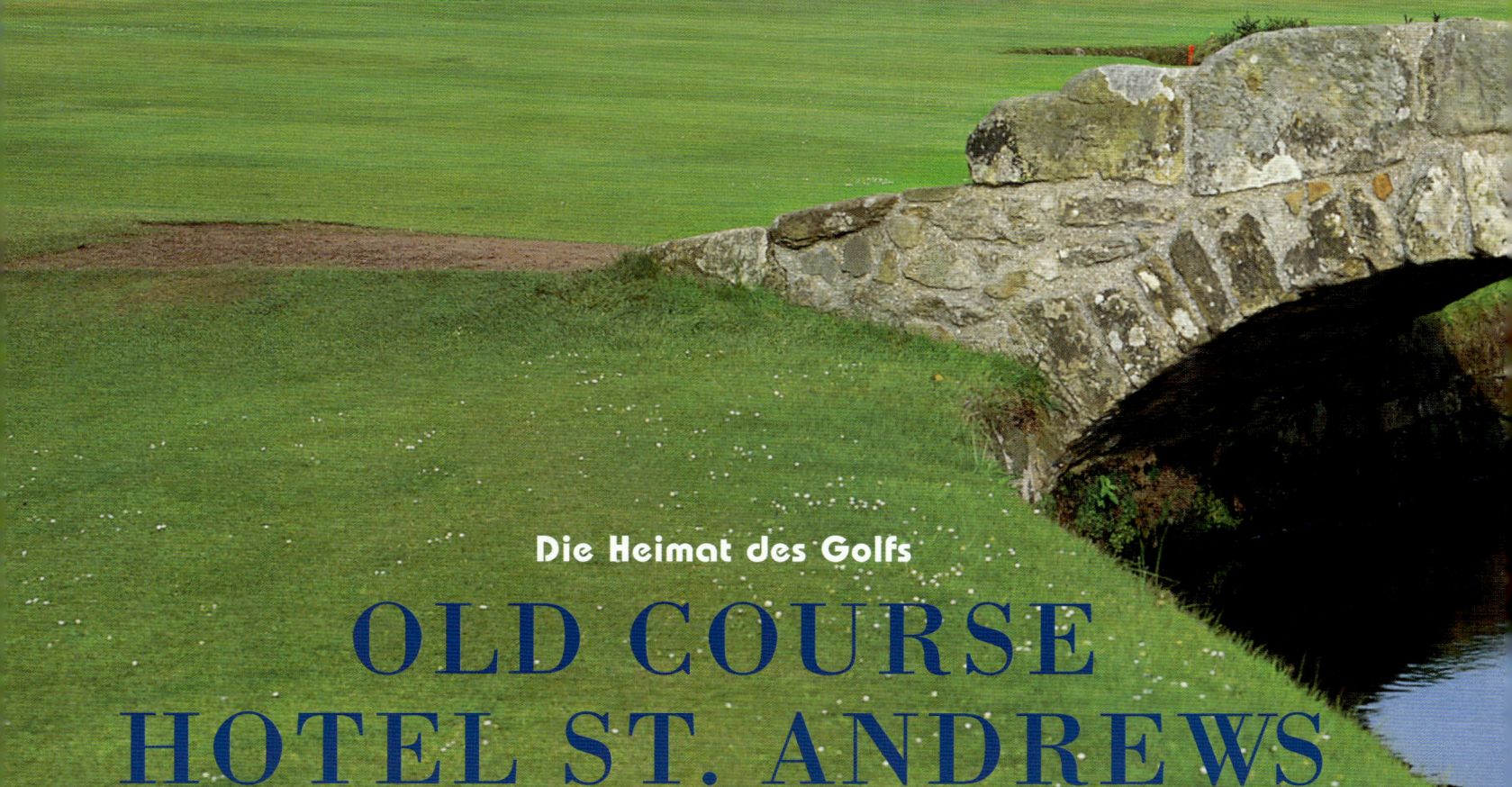

Text: Günter Ned • Fotos: Klaus Lorke, Old Course Hotel

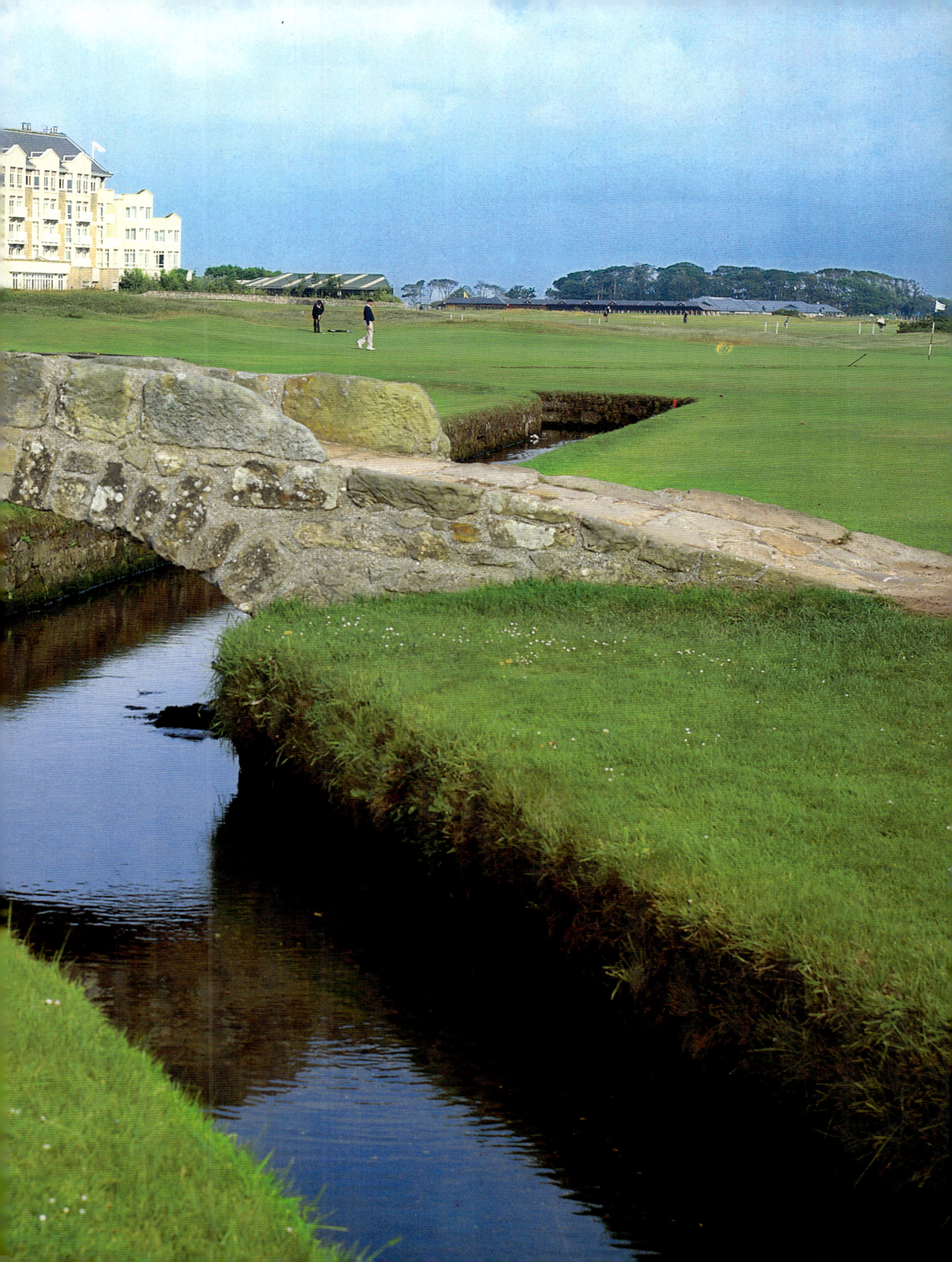

"I often say to my staff that here we're in the business of dreams. For many of our guests, a visit to St. Andrews and a round on the Old Course is right at the top of the list of things they want to achieve in life. The fact that we are part of this experience is something very special." You can count on it because General Manager Andrew Phelan and his staff contribute to all that makes an experience in a Leading Hotel of the World quite unique. Even the location of this 5-star hotel at St. Andrews makes it hard to beat. The Old Course – the most renowned course in the world – is literally at the foot of the Old Course Hotel. When a good player

Blick vom Old Course Hotel über den Old Course auf St. Andrews.
View across the Old Course at St. Andrews from the Old Course Hotel.

Ich sage meinen Mitarbeitern oft: Unser Thema hier sind Träume. Für viele unserer Gäste steht ein Besuch in St. Andrews, und dort eine Runde auf dem Old Course ganz oben auf der Liste mit den Dingen, die sie im Leben einmal erreichen wollen. Dass wir im Old Course Hotel Teil dieser Erfahrung sind, ist etwas ganz Besonderes." Man kann darauf rechnen: Direktor Andrew Phelan und seine Crew tragen bei, was man von einem Leading Hotel of the World erwarten kann, um das Erlebnis einzigartig zu machen.

Schon wegen seiner Lage ist das einzige 5-Sterne-Domizil von St. Andrews schwer zu schlagen. Der Old Course, der legendärste Golfplatz der Welt, liegt dem Old Course Hotel buchstäblich zu Füßen. Wenn ein guter Spieler am Tee des 17. Lochs, des berühmten Road Holes, abschlägt, jagt er den Drive über einen Teil des Hauses. Unmittelbar hinter dem Old Course liegt der New Course, dahinter der Jubilee, dann kommt der breite Sandstrand und dann zieht sich die blaue Nordsee bis zum Horizont.

Damit nicht genug. Verfolgt man die Old-Course-Spieler auf ihrem Weg zum 18. Grün, bleibt der Blick direkt am Haus des traditionsreichen Royal and Ancient Golf Club of St. Andrews hängen. Der „R & A" legt weltweit, mit Ausnahme der USA und Mexikos, die Golfregeln sowie das Amateurstatut fest und ist außerdem Veranstalter der British Open. Weiter am rechten Rand des Panoramas: die malerische Skyline von St. Andrews, der Stadt mit der ältesten Universität Schottlands. Die Gelehrtenschmiede wurde im Jahr 1457 gegründet. Prominentester Kommilitone heute ist Prinz William. 1862 durfte sich der erste weibliche Student Großbritanniens hier einschreiben. Für Golfer ist St. Andrews wegen einer anderen Premiere legendär. Auf den begrünten Dünen der St. Andrews Bay wurde vor 600 Jahren der erste Golfball der

Welt abgeschlagen. Schauplatz: der Old Course. Er wurde über die Jahrhunderte in seiner ursprünglichen Form erhalten. Kein Mensch ist für das Design verantwortlich. In St. Andrews sagt man: „Gott war der Architekt."

Mehr als die Hälfte der 114 Zimmer und 32 Suiten haben dieses spektakuläre Panorama, ebenso im vierten Stock die Road Hole Bar, das Fine-Dining-Restaurant Road Hole Grill und auf ebener Erde die Terrasse des Jigger Inn. Wer zur anderen Seite wohnt, schaut auf zwei weitere der fünf öffentlichen Golfplätze von St. Andrews: Strathtyrum und Balgove. Allesamt sind sie Links-Courses.

Ideale Lage also zu den Abschlägen der Traditions-Parcours. Doch damit begnügte sich das Old Course Hotel nicht. 1995 schenkte es St. Andrews einen sechsten Golfplatz, den Duke's Course. Er war der einzige Neubau im vergangenen wie im gerade begonnenen Jahrhundert. Wer auf ihm spielen will, lässt sich vom kostenlosen Hotelshuttle drei Kilometer von der Küste ins Hinterland chauffieren, in den Craigtoun Park oberhalb von St. Andrews. Entsprechend kontrastreich zu den Links-Courses auf den Dünen präsentiert er sich zunächst auch: als

tees off at the 17th hole – the famous Road Hole – his drive goes over part of the house. Directly behind the Old Course is the New Course, and behind that the Jubilee. Then comes a wide sandy beach and the blue of the North Sea to the horizon, but that's not all. Golfers on the Old Course on their way to the 18th green, have a clear view of the Royal and Ancient Golf Club of St. Andrews. The R & A determines the rules of golf worldwide – with exception of the USA and Mexico – and lays down the requirements of amateur status. It also organizes the British Open. Farther away to the right of the panorama is the town of St. Andrews which has the oldest university in Scotland. A seat of learning founded in 1457. Prince William is currently its most famous undergraduate. The very first woman in the British Isles to study at a university was admitted to

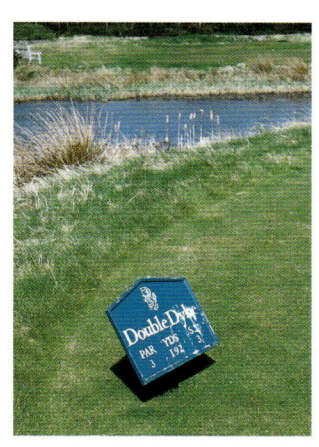

Links: Feuchtbiotop am Duke's Course. Unten rechts: Clubhaus des Duke's Course.
Left: Damp biotope on the Duke's Course. Below right: The Duke's Course clubhouse.

HIDEAWAYS 175

Oben: Restaurant Sands. Suiten im neuen Flügel. Fine Dining Restaurant Road Hole Grill.

Sands Restaurant. Suites in the new wing. Fine Dining Restaurant Road Hole Grill.

St. Andrews in 1862. For golfers, St. Andrews is legendary for quite a different reason. It was on the grassy dunes of St. Andrews Bay that the very first golf ball was hit 600 years ago. The site became known as the Old Course which has been preserved in its original form for hundreds of years. The person who created it is not known, at St. Andrews they say God was its architect. Over half of the 114 rooms and 32 suites have spectacular panoramic views, as do the Road Hole Bar, the Fine Dining Restaurant Road Hole Grill on the fourth floor, and the terrace of the Jigger Inn at ground level. Guests who occupy rooms on the other side of the house look at two of the five other public courses in St. Andrews: the Strathtyrum and the Balgove, all of them links courses. The location of the traditional course is ideal, but this was not enough for the Old Course Hotel. In 1995 it gave St. Andrews a sixth golf course, the Duke's Course, the only new one for over a century. Golfers who want a game there take the free chauffeur-driven hotel shuttle two miles inland up to Craigtoun Park overlooking St. Andrews. In contrast to the links courses on the dunes, it is a classic Scottish inland course. The Duke's Course has proved to be an ecological asset, winning several ecology prizes, mainly because over

klassischer schottischer Binnenland-Parcours. Die Anlage erwies sich dabei für die Natur als Erholungsmaßnahme. Der Duke's Course gewann bereits mehrere Umweltpreise, unter anderem deshalb, weil sich hier die Landschaft seit fünf Jahren so regenerieren darf, wie sie war, bevor das Terrain zu Bauernland wurde. Duke's-Course-Sekretär Stephen Toon gibt Beispiele: „Der Weiher am 12. Loch, einem langen Par 3, war bereits da. Wir haben ihn zu einem Feuchtbiotop gemacht. In den Bäumen sehen sie überall Nistboxen. Wir haben sie angebracht. So sind seltene Vögel zurückgekommen. Es gibt Eulen hier. In den letzten fünf Jahren haben wir 8000 Bäume gepflanzt." Ein Golfplatz mit Parklandprofil also. „Trotzdem", fährt Stephen fort, „gibt es auch typische Merkmale der Links Courses: Wir haben kaum Wasserhindernisse, viele Grüns sind vorne offen, der Ball kann ins Grün rollen, er muss keine Wasser- oder andere Hindernisse überwinden, wir haben tiefe Topfbunker, keine flachen Fairwaybunker wie etwa auf amerikanischen Plätzen." Dazu Neil Paton, Head Pro des Old Course Hotels: „Das liegt zum einen an Peter Thompson." Der australische Spitzengolfer, fünfmaliger British-Open-Gewinner in den 50er Jahren, war der Architekt. „Peter liebt Links-Golf, das spürt man auch in seinem Design, und zum anderen gehören Links-Course-Elemente einfach zum Flair von St. Andrews. Also haben wir auch im Duke's Course ein gewelltes Profil, Topfbunker, aber das Terrain ist ganz anders als an der Küste. Man spielt umgeben von schottischen Pinien, Heidekraut, hohen Buchen, ganz so wie es sich für einen Binnenland-Platz gehört."

Der 18-Loch-Championship-Kurs ist mit 6649 Metern (gemessen von den Professional

Oben: Die Lounge, englische Behaglichkeit rund um den Kamin.
Above: The lounge – fireside comfort.

Großzügigkeit und Stil prägen die Interieurs der Zimmer und Suiten.
Rooms and suites are spacious and stylish.

the last five years the countryside here has been able to regenerate and has now returned to the natural state it was in prior to it becoming agricultural land. Stephen Toon, the Secretary of the Duke's Course, cites examples. "The pond at the 12th – a long Par 3 – was already here so we turned it into a damp biotope. We've put nesting boxes all over the place in the trees up here, and now rare birds have returned. Even owls are back. In the last five years, we've planted 8,000 trees."

Neil Paton, Head Pro at the Old Course Hotel, adds, "it's primarily due to Peter Thompson". The champion Australian golfer, British Open winner five times in the 1950s, was the architect. "Peter just loves links golf, you notice that from his design. The flair of links is an integral element of St. Andrews. The Duke's Course has a hilly character too, and bunkers, but the terrain is completely different from the coast. Golfers are surrounded by Scottish pines, heather and tall beeches, as is only fitting for an inland course". The 18-hole championship course is 7271 yards from the back tees, and the longest inland course in Scotland. It is the only private course in

Die Road Hole Bar: Jede schottische Destillerie ist vertreten.
The Road Hole Bar: every Scottish distille is represented.

Head Pro Neil Paton am Grün des berühmten Road Hole. Die Links Courses von St. Andrews.
Head Pro Neil Paton on the green of the famous Road Hole. St. Andrews golf links.

Hat in St. Andrews sechs Golfplätze zu bieten: Old-Course-Hotel-Direktor Andrew Phelan.
Andrew Phelan, General Manager of the Old Course Hotel, has six golf courses to offer to his guests.

St. Andrews which allows golf carts. As well as granting access to paying golfers, there's an international club – incidentally the only one in the area – which grants membership to both sexes. Prince Andrew, Duke of York, hit the very first ball at the official opening of the course. From the clubhouse which is situated in ideal surroundings there are views of the whole course as well as St. Andrews, the links, and the bay. Head Pro Neil has much to offer to his guests. He and his professional golf coaches give individual and group instruction on the practice area. Neil is always willing to talk shop and golfers appreciate his hints on such matters as how best to tackle the course at the home of golf, and how today's wind might affect play? His stewards see to tee time bookings for all the courses at St. Andrews, and even when faced with a major problem, he always finds a solution. How can one get a booking for the Old Course? Because of it uniqueness, the course is one of the most sought-after in the world. Since privilege plays no part, there are only three ways to do it. You can book personally or through the hotel – for the summer season you have to book at least six months ahead to even have a

Tees) der längste Inland Course Schottlands. Der Privatplatz ist der einzige in St. Andrews, auf dem man Golf-Carts benutzen darf. Es gibt neben der Zugänglichkeit für zahlende Spieler eine internationale Clubmitgliedschaft, übrigens die einzige im Ort, die beiden Geschlechtern zugleich zugänglich ist. Den ersten Ball schlug bei der Eröffnung Prince Andrew, Duke of York, daher der Name Duke's Course. Ideal gelegen das Clubhaus. Man blickt über den ganzen Parcours, St. Andrews, die Links Courses und die Bay.

Head Pro Neil hat seinen Gästen viel zu bieten. Er und seine professionellen Golflehrer geben auf dem Übungsgelände des Duke's Course Einzelunterricht und Gruppenstunden. Neil ist immer für Fachsimpeleien zu haben, Spieler schätzen seine Tipps. Wie spielt man die Plätze in der Heimat des Golfs am geschicktesten? Welchen Einfluss hat heute der Wind? Seine Golf-Stewards kümmern sich um die

Buchung der Abschläge auf allen Courses von St. Andrews, und selbst beim größten Problem im Mekka des Golfs weiß er Rat: Wie kommt man an eine Buchung für den Old Course?

Er ist wegen seiner einzigartigen Aura einer der begehrteste Plätze der Welt. Da es keine Privilegien gibt, sind nur drei Wege offen: Man bucht selbst (oder über das Hotel), dann muss man sich für die Hochsaison im Sommer mindestens ein halbes Jahr zuvor anmelden, um eine Chance zu haben; man nimmt an der täglichen Verlosung von Abschlagzeiten teil oder man nutzt Angebote der Hotels, die Abschlagzeiten kaufen können. Neils heißer Tipp: „Man sollte im Herbst und Winter zu uns kommen. Wir haben ein Mikroklima, das uns gerade dann viel schönes Wetter und wenig Niederschläge bringt. Die ideale Zeit, um ohne Druck zu spielen und St. Andrews zu genießen." Das „Winterpass-Arrangement" bietet zwei Übernachtungen, Dinner an beiden Abenden, außerdem drei

Runden auf den berühmten Links Courses von St. Andrews, eingeschlossen (!) eine garantierte Runde auf dem Old Course. Das Package gilt von November bis März. Der Preis betrug im Winter 2000/2001 pro Person £ 263. Reizvoll für Nichtgolfer, z. B. dann, wenn sie Golfer begleiten: Wer nicht zu den Tees zieht, verbringt fürs gleiche Geld zwei Tage im schönen Spa des Old Course Hotels, mit maßgeschneiderten Winter-Entschlackungs-Anwendungen von der Algenpackung bis zur Aromatherapie, mit Schwimmen im glasüberdachten Pool, mit Sauna, Fitnesstraining und Lunch im Bademantel.

Womit wir zurück bei den Wohltaten wären, die das Haus selbst zu bieten hat. Das Old Course Hotel, Golf Resort & Spa, 1968 von British Transport an der Stelle des ehemaligen Bahnhofs von St. Andrews errichtet, hat sich nach Erweiterungen und Renovierungen in den Jahren 1990 und 2000 und nach der Übernahme durch die Kosaido-Gruppe zu einem stattlichen Komplex entlang des Road Holes entwickelt. Sehr luxuriös zum Beispiel der neue Flügel, im letzten Winter fertig gestellt mit ausgezeichneten Tagungs- und Ausstellungsräumen, dazu topkomfortablen, großzügig geschnittenen Suiten. Als Tiger Woods die British Open 2000 auf dem Old Course gewann, wohnte er hier. Ausgezeichnet auch, was Direktor Andrew Phelan kulinarisch zu bieten hat: feinste, klassische Grill-Cuisine im Road Hole Grill mit Fisch aus der Nordsee und bestem schottischen Fleisch (die Gegend ist absolut frei von allen aktuellen Beeinträchtigungen der Viehzucht), mit unkomplizierter Brasserie-Küche im modern gestylten Sands, mit einem einmaligen Whisky-Angebot in der Road-Hole-Bar (über 170 verschiedene Sorten, jede schottische Destillerie ist vertreten) und mit dem Jigger Inn. Das ist ein original schottisches Pub im Haus des ehemaligen Bahnhofsmeisters. Antoinette ist hier seit zehn Jahren Wirtin, versorgt durstige Golfer, Hotelgäste, aber auch Publikum aus dem Ort von 11 bis 11 mit Pints of Lager oder Bitter und mit typischen Pub-Snacks.

Traumhaft immer wieder der Blick, beim Frühstück (im Road Hole Grill, vierte Etage, köstlich die frisch gebratenen Zutaten zum Rührei, von Bacon bis zu original schottischem Haggis), wie am Abend nach dem Golf, wenn der Mond aufgeht über St. Andrews. Die Brandung rauscht, die Luft über der Bay ist wie Champagner, der Vollmond leuchtet warm wie tagsüber die Sonne und wie jetzt, wo es dunkel wird, die illuminierte Skyline des mittelalterlichen St. Andrews.

Antoinette ist seit zehn Jahren Wirtin im Pub Jigger Inn.
Antoinette has been the landlady of the Jigger Inn for the last ten years.

chance in the daily draw for tee times. Alternatively, you can take advantage of the opportunity offered by the hotel which can purchase tee times. Neil's advice to the visitor is "come in autumn or winter. We enjoy a micro-climate with good weather and very few showers. It's the ideal time to play golf without the hassle and enjoy St. Andrews." The Winter Package offers two nights and includes dinner on both evenings, three rounds on St. Andrews' famous links, and a guaranteed round on the Old Course. The package applies from November to March. The price in the winter 2000/2001 is £ 263 per person. For the same price the non-player e.g. if you are accompanying a golfer, you can spend two days in the beautiful spa of the Old Course Hotel, and indulge in special winter treatments ranging from algae packs to aromatherapy. There is also swimming in the indoor glass-roofed pool, sauna, fitness training and lunch in a bath robe. Which brings us back to all the good things the hotel has to offer. The Old Course Hotel, Golf Resort & Spa, built by British Transport on the site of the old St. Andrews Station, was renovated and extended in 1990 and 2000, and after being taken over by the Kosaido Group, has been developed into a splendid complex along the Road Hole. The new wings finished in winter last year for example, are very luxurious. They have excellent conference and exhibition facilities and spacious, lavishly furnished suites. Tiger Woods stayed here when he won the British Open on the Old Course in 2000. What General Manager Andrew Phelan has to offer on the culinary side is excellent too. The Road Hole Grill serves a sophisticated classic grill cuisine including fresh fish from the North Sea and the very best Scottish meat (the region's cattle is completely clear). There is plain brasserie-type cooking in the modern Sands restaurant which stocks a unique variety of over 170 Scottish whiskies representing all Scottish distilleries. The Jigger Inn is a real Scottish pub in the old stationmaster's house. Antoinette has been its landlady for 10 years, serving thirsty golfers and hotel guests as well as the locals with pints of bitter or lager and typical pub snacks from 11 a.m. to 11 p.m. The view never ceases to impress, whether at breakfast on the fourth floor in the Road Hole Grill or in the evening after golf when the moon is rising over St. Andrews. The traditional fried breakfast is delicious with one addition – haggis. At night the air in the bay is like champagne. The full moon shines as warmly as the daytime sun on to the surf, illuminating the medieval skyline of St. Andrews.

Das Spa: Der Pool ist mit Glas überdacht.
The Spa pool has a glass roof.

HIDEAWAYS 179

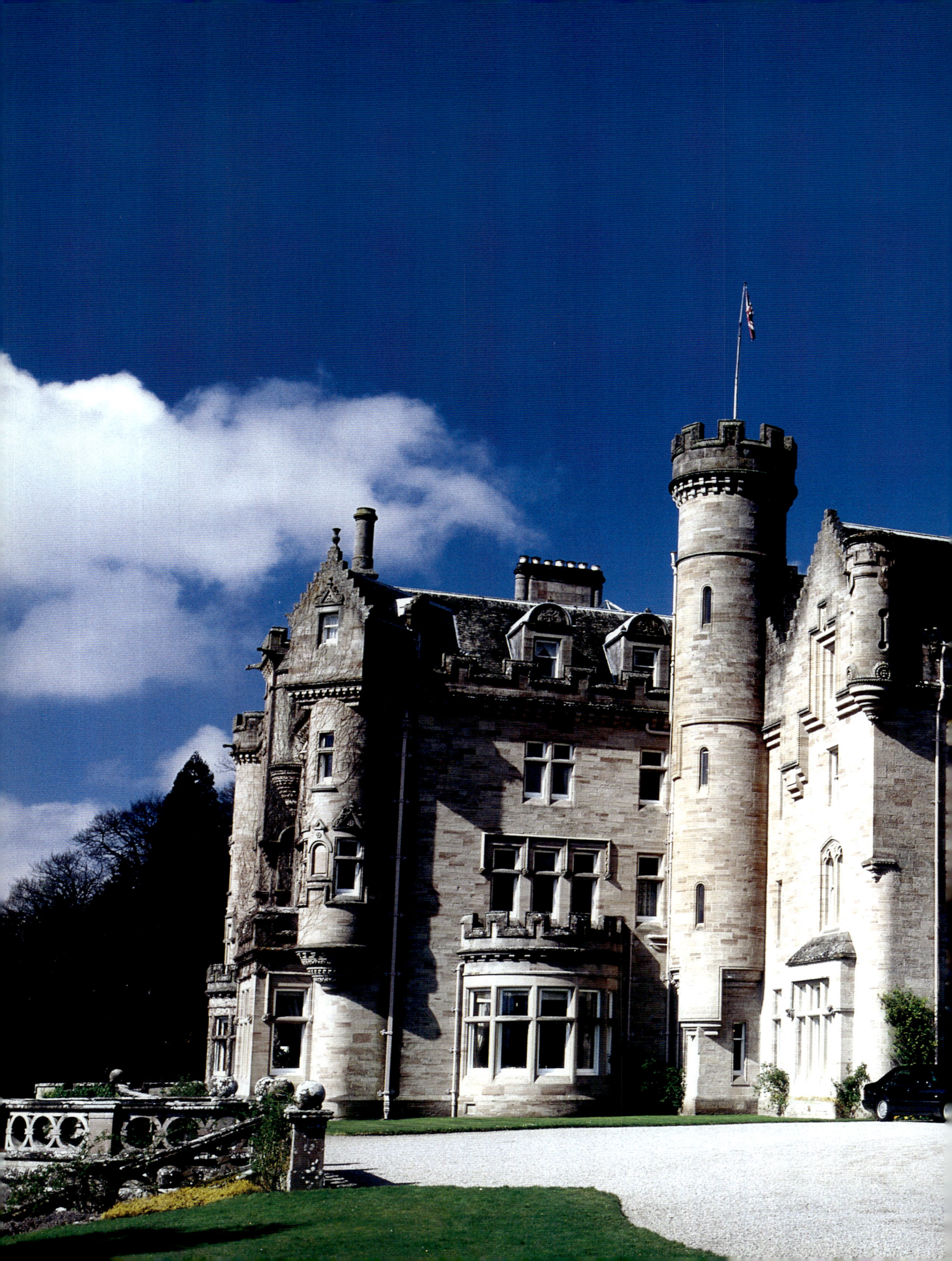

Heaven on Earth

DER CARNEGIE-CLUB ZU SKIBO CASTLE

Am Dornoch Firth, am Ostrand der nördlichen schottischen Highlands, liegt eine der Wiegen des Golfsports, der berühmte, auch historisch bedeutsame Championship-Course Royal Dornoch. Ganz in seiner Nähe wurde vor fünf Jahren eine weitere Meisterschaftsanlage eröffnet. Sie wird von Experten inzwischen zu den interessantesten Herausforderungen in Großbritannien gezählt und bietet dazu ein einzigartiges Erlebnis: Skibo Castle.

At Dornoch Firth on the eastern edge of the Highlands in the north of Scotland is one of the cradles of golf, the famous and historically important Royal Dornoch championship course. Five years ago a further championship course was opened nearby which experts now rate as one of the most interesting challenges in the British Isles – Skibo Castle. Moreover it offers a unique experience.

Text: Günter Ned · Fotos: Ydo Sol

Skibo is supposed to be derived from the Celtic word *schytherbolle* which means fairyland or place of peace. Down the centuries this idyll sustained a certain amount of wear and tear, but today it is perfect once again. The 18-hole golf course, a classic links, is in a fabulous location. Golfers are aware that links connect land with the sea. The sea beside the Skibo Castle links is actually the Dornoch Firth, an inlet penetrating deep into the Highlands at the little town of Dornoch, a dune landscape of infinite harmony.

When the tide is in, the waters of the glistening Firth lap the grass of the links, and the outgoing tide exposes a broad band of mud flats. Since Skibo Castle Championship Course lies on a promontory, the sea is on three sides. It is generally considered that Donald Steel, one of the most important links architects, created a real masterpiece here, not least because nature has been left undisturbed. Jim Achenbach of *Golf Week* commented: "The way the links look now, shepherds could have laid it out two hundred years ago." The road from the Castle to the golf house and to the first tee is just under a mile. There is of course a regular shuttle. Even the way there is delightful. One drives along the coastal road of the Firth, through a little pine forest then finally across a dam between the Firth and Lake Evelix. At the end of the dam there is a little bridge under which the lake flows into the sea and where the salmon start their swim up the salmon ridges to reach the fresh-

Golf vor der Naturkulisse der schottischen Highlands: Der Blick geht über den Dornoch Firth auf das 15. Loch und das Golfhaus.
Golf against the backdrop of the Scottish Highlands. View across the Dornoch Firth of the 15th hole and the golf house.

Skibo soll vom keltischen Wort Schytherbolle kommen, das mit Märchenland oder Ort des Friedens übersetzt wird. Die Idylle trug durch die Jahrhunderte einige Beschädigungen davon, heute ist sie wieder vollkommen. Der 18-Hole-Platz, ein klassischer Links Course, liegt sagenhaft schön. Golfern ist geläufig, dass ein Links-Course nicht deshalb so heißt, weil er sich etwa nach links krümmte oder weil er nur für Linkshänder ausgelegt wäre. Ein Links Course (das englische Wort *link* bedeutet bekanntlich Verbindung) fasst Land und Meer zusammen. Beim Platz von Skibo Castle wird die See durch den Dornoch Firth repräsentiert, einen Meeresarm, der beim Städtchen Dornoch tief in die Highlands eindringt, das Land durch eine Dünenszenerie von unendlicher Harmonie. Bei Flut spielt der glitzernde Firth direkt um die Gräser, bei Ebbe entblößt er ein breites Wattband. Da der Championship Course von Skibo Castle auf einer Landzunge liegt, umsäumt ihn das Meer an drei Seiten. Donald Steel, einer der bedeutendsten britischen Links-Course-Architekten, hat hier nach allgemeiner Einschätzung ein wahres Meisterwerk vollbracht, nicht zuletzt an Naturbelassenheit. „So wie der Kurs aussieht, konnten ihn auch Schäfer vor zweihundert Jahren angelegt haben", schrieb Jim Achenbach in *Golf Week*.

Der Weg vom Schloss bis zum Golf House und zum ersten Tee ist eine knappe Meile lang. Es gibt natürlich einen ständig abrufbaren Shuttle. Schon die Anfahrt ist ein Naturgenuss. Man fährt am Ufer des Firth entlang, durch ein Kiefernwäldchen und schließlich über einen Damm, der den Firth vom Loch Evelix trennt. Am Ende des Damms gibt es eine kleine Brücke, darunter fließt der See ab ins Meer, von dort führt eine Lachsleiter herauf ins Süßwasser. Den Damm säumen Ginster- und Johannisbeerbüsche, im Frühjahr von gelben und pinkfarbenen Blüten übersät.

Ein zweiter Kurs liegt nur wenige Schritte von Skibo Castles beeindruckender Halle entfernt, 9 Loch, Par 35, *for club members only*, The Monks Walk. (Den 18-Loch-

Championship-Platz dürfen neben Mitgliedern auch Gäste bespielen, aber nur einmal. Wollen sie nach Skibo Castle zurückkehren, müssen sie um Mitgliedschaft ansuchen). Die Clubleitung hält den Mönchs-Gang-Kurs unter anderem für geeignet, „um Appetit vorm Frühstück zu entwickeln oder im Sommer, um vielleicht das Dinner abzuarbeiten". (Wir befinden uns, nicht zu vergessen, etwa auf der nördlichen Breite von Stavanger, das bedeutet zur warmen Zeit helle Nächte.)

Seinen Namen hat The Monks Walk aus der Geschichte, aus dem 12. Jahrhundert, als Gilbert de Moravia, Bischof von Caithness, Skibo zu seiner Residenz ausbaute. In der Halle kann man ihn sehen, die bunte Bleiverglasung im Treppenhaus zeigt den Geistlichen im mittleren Fenster. Links von ihm ein Häuptling aus der Zeit, als die Wikinger in Sutherland herrschten, rechts ist der Marquis von Montrose zu sehen. Zum Tode verurteilt, verbrachte er auf Skibo Castle seine letzte Nacht. Tags darauf begab er sich nach Edinburgh, um gehängt, gestreckt und geviertelt zu werden.

Die beiden übrigen Farbglasbilder erzählen von einer Abfahrt im Segelboot und einer Wiederkehr im luxuriösen Dampfschiff. Der Reisende ist der Mann, ohne den es das exzeptionelle Erlebnis Skibo Castle nicht gäbe, Andrew Carnegie, legendärer Stahl-Tycoon, Stifter unter anderem der Carnegie Hall in New York, Sohn armer schottischer Weber, der 1848 in die Staaten auswanderte und ab 1887 als einer der reichsten Männer der Welt seine Sommermonate wieder in der alten schottischen Heimat verbrachte. 1898, nach der Geburt seiner Tochter Margaret, kaufte er Skibo Castle und baute es – Geld spielte keine Rolle – zu einem Schloss voller Schönheit und zugleich voller Modernität um. Es gab ein Installationssystem, das König Edward VII., einen häufigen Gast, neidisch werden ließ, fließend warmes und kaltes Wasser, Zentralheizung, indirekte Beleuchtung in Mrs. Carnegies Wohnzimmer, einen Lift (den ersten Otis-Elevator in einem Privathaus in Europa). Am Ufer des nahen Loch Ospisdale ließ Carnegie aus Marmor einen riesigen

water headwaters. The dam is bordered by gorse and blackcurrant bushes which blossom yellow and pink in Spring.

A second course, the 9-hole par 35 Monk's Walk, is only a few steps away from Skibo Castle's impressive hall but is for members only. (Guests as well as members have access to the 18-hole Championship links but only once. If they want to return to Skibo Castle they have to apply for membership.) The Club management regards the Monk's Walk useful "to work up an appetite before breakfast, or in the summer to work off dinner in the evening". (Bear in mind we are roughly on the same latitude as Stavanger which means light nights during the warm season.)

The name, Monk's Walk, goes back in history to the 12th century when Gilbert de Moravia, Bishop of Caithness, converted Skibo into a residence for himself. He can be seen in the hall, the priest in the centre stained glass window on the staircase. On his left a chieftain of the period when the Vikings ruled Sutherland. On his right is the Marquis of Montrose who was sentenced to death and spent his last night at Skibo Castle. The next day he was taken to Edinburgh to be hanged, drawn and quartered. The other two stained glass windows depict a departure in a sailing boat and a return in a luxury liner. The passenger is the man without whom Skibo Castle would have nothing exceptional to offer, Andrew Carnegie, legendary steel tycoon and, among other

Stahl-Tycoon Andrew Carnegie machte Ende des 19. Jahrhunderts Skibo Castle und die idyllische Umgebung zu seiner Sommerresidenz.
Steel tycoon Andrew Carnegie made Skibo Castle and its idyllic surroundings his summer residence.

HIDEAWAYS 183

things, founder of Carnegie Hall in New York. The son of a poor Scottish weaver, he emigrated to the States in 1848. By 1887 he was one of the wealthiest men in the world and used to spend the summer months back home in Scotland. In 1898, after the birth of his daughter Margaret, he bought Skibo and converted it – money no object – into a castle of great beauty which he also modernized. A plumbing system was installed which was envied by King Edward VII, a frequent guest. There was constant hot and cold water, central heating, indirect lighting in Mrs Carnegie's living room and a lift – the very first Otis elevator in Europe in a private house.

On the banks of the nearby Loch Ospisdale, Carnegie had an enormous heated swimming pool built which was roofed over with a construction of glass and iron. The private bath of the steel magnate could apparently slide along rails from the bathroom to the bedroom. The story goes that he once proudly demonstrated die Mechanik einmal voller Stolz Besuchern vorführte. Als die Wanne ankam, war sie nicht leer. Mrs. Carnegie nahm gerade ein Bad.

Der neueste Stand der Technik diente einem Komfort, den man in Ambiancen voll kostbarer Eleganz und Behaglichkeit lebte. Der Weckruf kam pünktlich um acht Uhr von einem Dudelsackpfeifer. Dann nahm man – zu den Klängen der großen Orgel in der Halle – das Frühstück im Morning Room mit Blick auf die meilenlange Buchenallee, die zum Haus führt, auf die Gärten, auf die weite Parklandschaft, Anlagen, der sich die Dame des Hauses mit Leidenschaft widmete. Tagsüber spielte Andrew Carnegie mit seinen Gästen Golf auf dem 9 Hole Course, er hatte ihn beim legendären John Sutherland in Auftrag gegeben. Der Kurs lag jenseits eines Damms, ebenfalls vom Hausherrn angelegt, der den Fluss Evelix zum Loch Evelix staute.

Man ging jagen oder fischen, und am Abend fand sich die illustre Gesellschaft nach den Cocktails an der Table d'hôte in Mr. Carnegies Dining Room zusammen. Dabei achtete der mächtig gewordene Webersssohn darauf, unter die Noblesse seiner Zeit auch immer Gäste mit einfacher Herkunft und eigenen Verdiensten zu mischen.

Und heute? Wie erleben die Gäste des Carnegie Clubs heute Skibo Castle? Einfach zu erzählen: Um 8 Uhr morgens marschiert in traditioneller Tracht der Piper über die Terrasse und weckt die Gäste mit der Musik seines Dudelsacks. Während des Frühstücks bringt der Organist in der Halle die Orgelpfeifen zum Klingen. Im Morning Room, im Wohnzimmer, in Mrs. Carnegies Living Room oder in der Bibliothek genießt man müßige Stunden in Interieurs und in einer Atmosphäre, als hätten die Carnegies Skibo Castle nie verlassen. Peter de Savary, dem heutigen Besitzer, ist es gelungen, den gastfreundlichen Ort in der Stimmung und der Gestalt zu erhalten, wie sein Gründer sie einst geschaffen hat. Etwa drei Viertel der Einrichtung sind original geblieben, von den Kaminen, die auch heute das ganze Jahr geheizt werden, über die Ledersessel mit ihrer wunderschönen Patina bis zur Eichenholztäfelung im ganzen Haus und den verblichenen Seidentapeten (der Rest wurde mit vielen Antiquitäten stilsicher ergänzt). Gäste gehen jagen, vielleicht mit Falkner Andrew McLeod, der jeden Morgen um 9.30 Uhr seine Vögel vorführt, oder sie fischen, Forellen im Loch Ospisdale, Lachs im Loch Evelix. Sie schwimmen im riesigen Pool, unter gleichem Dach warten die Fachkräfte des Spa. Sie lassen

Die Interieurs präsentieren den Stil Andrew Carnegies so, als hätte er Skibo Castle nie verlassen.
The interiors after the style of Andrew Carnegie's period make Skibo Castle feel as if he had never left.

sich auf den Zimmern und in den Lodges mit erlesener Gastfreundschaft verwöhnen, bedient von Butlers im Kilt wie seinerzeit. Sie schlafen auf hohen Himmelbetten, machen sich fein für den Abend in Badezimmern wie Boudoirs, die Whisky-Karaffe ist immer aufgefüllt. Und am Abend, an der Table d'hôte im Dining Room, ist es fast, als hätte Andrew Carnegie selbst geladen. Clubsekretärin Henriette Ferguson oder Direktor Charles P. Oak eröffnen die Tafel mit einem Toast auf ihn, den Hausherrn, und würzen das Menü (Küchenchef John MacMahon setzt die wunderbaren Produkte der Highlands gourmeterfahren in Szene) mit mancher originellen Geschichte aus originaler Zeit.

Und natürlich geht man, wie einst der Hausherr, golfen, im Monks Walk, einem typischen Parkland Course mit Weihern, Gehölzen und Marschland, der erste Anschlag liegt direkt neben dem Walled Garden des Schlosses, oder jenseits des künstlichen Damms auf dem 18-Loch-Championship-Parcours, den Donald Steel immer mit Blick auf Carnegies ursprünglichen Kurs designte. Er ist mit sei-

strated the mechanism to visitors. When the bath arrived it wasn't empty … Mrs Carnegie was in it taking a bath.

The most up-to-date technology of the period provided a level of comfort enjoyed in an ambience of refined luxury and opulent surroundings. One was woken on the dot of eight by a piper playing the bagpipes. Then, to the accompaniment of the grand organ in the hall, breakfast was taken in the morning room which looks out over the mile-long beech-lined drive leading to the house, the gardens and extensive parkland – grounds which the lady of the house looked after with great devotion.

During the day Andrew Carnegie

Golfdirektor David Thompson, erfahrener PGA-Professional, auf dem Links Course.
Golf Manager David Thompson, an experienced PGA professional, on the link.

and his guests played golf on the 9-hole course which he had commissioned the legendary John Sutherland to design. The course, also built by the master of the house, was on the other side of a dam which held back the water of the River Evelix from flowing into Loch Evelix. One went hunting or fishing and in the evening after drinks the illustrious company would gather together in Carnegie's dining room for dinner-table d'hôte. Yet this weaver's son who rose to such heights always made sure that people from humble origins who had also achieved something were invited to mingle with his aristocratic guests.

Direktor Charles P. Oak leitet Skibo Castle ganz im Geist seines Gründers.
General Manager Charles P. Oak runs Skibo Castle entirely in the spirit of its founder.

Skibo Castle, von Osten gesehen. Madonna war vom Zauber des Schlosses angetan, dass sie dort unlängst ihre Hochzeit feierte.

Skibo Castle as seen from east side. Madonna was taken with the magic of the Castle, so that she has been celebrating her wedding there.

What about now? How do today's Carnegie Club guests experience Skibo Castle? Simple. At eight o'clock guests are woken by the sound of the bagpipes played by a kilted piper striding along the terrace. During breakfast the organist plays the organ in the hall. In the morning room or the drawing room, in Mrs Carnegie's living room or in the library, one can spend leisurely hours in rooms which feel as if the Carnegies never left Skibo Castle. Peter de Savary, the present owner, has succeeded in retaining the contents and atmosphere of this hospitable place just as its founder created it. About three quarters of the furnishings and fittings are original. Fires are still kept burning in the fireplaces all the year round and there are still leather upholstered chairs with their wonderful patina, oak panelling throughout the whole house and the faded silk wallpaper (the remainder has been furnished with many matching antiques). Guests can go hunting, perhaps with Andrew McLeod, a falconer, who appears with his falcons every morning at 9.30, or trout fishing in Loch Ospisdale or salmon fishing in Loch Evelix. They can swim in the enormous pool with spa experts on

nen 6,571 Yards für heutige Verhältnisse nicht allzu lang, aber er stellt große Ansprüche ans Können selbst der Besten, vor allem bei Wind. Golfdirektor David Thomson, erfahrener PGA-Professional, ist da ein zuverlässiger Führer. Zugleich verwöhnt die Anlage Spieler mit der

Ein Originalstück aus Carnegies Zeiten: der überdachte riesige Swimmingpool.

Original feature from the time of Andrew Carnegie: the giant roofed-over swimming pool.

Der 9-Loch-Kurs The Monks Walk beginnt unmittelbar am Schloss.
The Monk's Walk, a 9-hole golf course, starts beside the Castle.

Falkner Andrew McLeod zeigt jeden Morgen um 9.30 Uhr im Schloss seine Vögel.
Falconer Andrew McLeod shows his birds at the Castle at 9.30 each morning.

unglaublichen Schönheit der schottischen Landschaft, mit einer Fülle naturgeschützter Fauna und Flora. So gibt es allen Grund – nehmen wir als Beispiel das 18. Loch, ein Dogleg – nicht nur zu entscheiden, wie weit der Teeshot über das Watt gehen soll (wenn man nicht den schwersten Abschlag, von jenseits des Firths, wählt) oder wie nahe am Meer man den zweiten schlägt, um günstig ans Grün zu kommen und den tückischen Topfbunker an seiner rechten Seite zu meiden. Sondern man hat auch viel Anlass, einmal aufzuschauen und den Blick schweifen zu lasssen über die 7500 Acre Land von Skibo Castle, über die Bucht Poll na Caorach – Jahr für Jahr kommen Pfeifenten und Wildgänse aus Island, um ihre Brut aufzuziehen –, über die See hinüber zum heidekrautbewachsenen Struie Hill und hinein in die Highlands. Es fällt nicht schwer, Andrew Carnegie zu verstehen, der Skibo Castle und sein Land, dieses Bild von Frieden und Stille, als *heaven on earth* erlebte. Zu Carnegies Einschätzung fand James M. Lane im *Links Magazine* einen hoffnungsfrohen Kommentar: „Und wenn der Himmel nur halb so schön ist, haben Golfer allen Grund, sich aufs Jenseits zu freuen."

hand under the same roof. They can allow themselves the indulgence of exquisite hospitality and be served by butlers in kilts, just like it used to be in Carnegie's time. They sleep in high four-poster beds, dress for dinner in boudoir-like bathrooms and the whisky decanter is always being replenished. In the evening at dinner in the dining room, it is as if the host, Andrew Carnegie, is actually present. Henrietta Ferguson the Club Secretary, or Charles P. Oak, the General Manager, opens with a toast to their patron, and add flavour to the menu (chef John MacMahon creates dishes with wonderful Highland ingredients) be telling some original tales from the olden days. Then of course one plays golf like the old master of the house used to do on Monk's Walk, a typical parkland course with ponds, thickets and marshland. The first tee is right next to the castle's walled garden or rather the other side of the artificial dam on the 18-hole championship course designed by Donald Steel within sight of Carnegie's original course. At 6,571 yards it is by today's standards not too long but it poses a real challenge even to the best golfers, especially in the wind. The Golf Manager David Thompson, an experienced PGA professional, provides reliable leadership. Golfers are spoilt by the grounds which are set in incredibly beautiful Scottish landscape with an abundance of listed flora and fauna.

However, one is faced with serious decisions. For instance at the 18th hole, a dog-leg, how far should the tee-shot go over the mud-flats (that is, if one hasn't chosen the most difficult tee-shot this side of the Firth), or how close to the sea should one drive the second to find the best way of reaching the green while avoiding the notorious bunker on its right. Yet, there is every reason to look up and allow one's gaze to roam over the 7,500 acres at Skibo Castle, across Poll na Caorach Bay where year after year ducks and geese arrive from Iceland to raise their chicks, and over the sea past the heather-clad Struie Hill into the Highlands beyond. It isn't hard to understand Andrew Carnegie for whom Skibo Castle and his own country, a picture tranquillity, were "heaven on earth". M. Lane added his own comment to Carnegie's view in *Links Magazine*: "Even if heaven is only half as beautiful, golfers will have every reason to look forward to life on the other side."

Foto: Brian Morgan

NOBLESSE OBLIGE

Loch Lomond Golf Club

Die Schotten haben ein berühmtes Lied. Es erzählt von einem Landsmann, der nach Hause reist. Die Sehnsucht treibt ihn zur Eile an, hin zu einem bestimmten Ort, obwohl er dort seine wahre Liebe nie wieder treffen wird, zu den „bonny bonny banks of Loch Lomond". An diesen „wunderschönen Ufern" hat heute einer der exklusivsten Golfclubs der Welt seine Zuflucht gefunden.

The Scots have a famous song which tells of a Scotsman coming home. Longing drives him onwards to a particular place, even though he will never meet his true love there again – the "bonny bonny banks of Loch Lomond". On these "wonderful banks" is one of the most exclusive golf clubs in the world.

Text: Günter Ned · Fotos: Ydo Sol

The stone doorway at the 18th hole is 15th century according to the drawings, but it could be even older. The high spot of the ceremony is when a kilted piper leads the winner through this gateway for the ceremonious award of the trophy. Here, at the birthplace of golf, there is always a tremendous atmosphere when the champion of the annual Standard Life Loch Lomond Golf Championship is honoured in this way.

Adjoining the stone doorway is a stone wall, but that is all that remains of Rossdhu Castle, the old seat of the Colquhoun clan, one of the oldest and most aristocratic families in Scotland. The Royals have always liked to spend time here on a peninsula of the western banks of Loch Lomond about 19 miles from Glasgow. The story goes that

Das steinerne Tor am 18. Loch stammt aus dem 15. Jahrhundert, soweit belegen es jedenfalls die Aufzeichnungen, es kann auch älter sein. Auf dem Höhepunkt der Zeremonie führt ein Dudelsackpfeifer im traditionellen Kilt den Sieger durch dieses Tor. Dann wird ihm feierlich die Trophäe überreicht – eine stimmungsvolle und, im Geburtsland des Golfsports, auch sinnige Weise, den Champion des alljährlich ausgetragenen Standard-Life-Loch-Lomond-Golf-Turniers zu ehren. Zum steinernen Tor gehört eine steinerne Mauer, und das ist schon alles, was heute von Rossdhu Castle geblieben ist, dem angestammten Sitz des Colquhoun-Clans, einer der nobelsten und ältesten Familien Schottlands. Die Royals weilten hier schon immer gerne, auf der Halbinsel am Westufer des Loch Lomond, rund 30 Kilometer nordwestlich von Glasgow. Überliefert ist, dass Maria Stuart, die schöne Königin der Schotten, in der Burg, zu der die Mauer einst gehörte, einige ihrer leidenschaftlichsten Liebesbriefe schrieb. Die Burg wurde unter anderem deshalb zur Ruine, weil sich die Colquhouns 1773 nebenan ein neues Herrenhaus bauten und dafür auch Steine des Castles verwendeten. In den 70er Jahren des 20. Jahrhunderts zog der Clan aus (das Gebäude zu erhalten, war zu teuer geworden) und überließ das Heim dem Zahn der Zeit. Inzwischen erstrahlt das georgianische Mansionhouse wieder in alter Schönheit, verwöhnt seine Gäste zugleich mit allen modernen Annehmlichkeiten. Rossdhu House präsentiert sich heute als das noble Heim des wohl exklusivsten Golfclubs Europas, vergleichbar etwa mit dem US-amerikanischen Augusta. Das britische Königshaus zählt zu den Mitgliedern, außerdem Zelebritäten auf gleichem Level aus Politik, Wirtschaft und Gesellschaft in aller Welt.

Die Mitgliedschaft im Loch Lomond Golf Club wird bewusst international gehalten, Repräsentanten aus über vierzig Ländern geben sich ein Stelldichein. Um zu verhin-

Mary Stuart, the beautiful Queen of Scots, wrote some of her most passionate letters in the Castle of which the wall was once part.

One of the reasons for the Castle becoming a ruin is because in 1773 the Colquhouns built a new mansion alongside using the stones of the Castle. In the 1970s the clan moved out (the upkeep of the building was simply too costly) and left the place to the ravages of time. Yet now the Georgian mansion house is restored to its former glory, pampering its guests with every modern amenity. Rossdhu House is now home to probably the most exclusive golf club in Europe, comparable perhaps with America's Augusta. The British Royal Family are members but also society people, celebrities, and VIPs from the realms of politics and commerce from all over the world.

Membership of the Loch Lomond Golf Club is deliberately kept international so the Club has become a rendezvous for representatives from over forty countries. To prevent one particular country upsetting the balance of this mix, a waiting list has been introduced for the United Kingdom and one is about to be introduced for the United States. The Club Management does not divulge the number of current members or their identity. However, on our visit we did hear that Prince Andrew, the brother of the heir to the throne, loves the Stuart Suite. We also learned that the number of rounds on the 18-hole course is restricted to 15,000 rounds a year (other Scottish courses reckon with about 45,000 rounds). The reason is not only to maintain the course in first class condition because Loch Lomond is quite simply not only to do with golf. The Loch Lomond Golf Club is about providing the aristocracy and social elite from around the globe a perfectly secure sanctuary of great beauty and luxury.

Members can relax here, arrange private dinner parties or hold work-

HIDEAWAYS 191

ing meetings. They can invite their guests to the Club, go on boating excursions to the islands in the lake, join pheasant shoots, hunt red deer, go fishing for trout or pike, in short they can enjoy one of the most idyllic spots in Scotland and play golf now and again.
The Club's owners, the American real estate investor Lyle Anderson, and the Investment Company DMB, also American, have spared neither trouble nor expense in restoring the Colquhoun family seat to all the glory and luxury it might have had

dern, dass ein Land die ausgewogene Mischung dominiert, führte man für das Vereinigte Königreich eine Warteliste ein, für die Vereinigten Staaten ist man kurz davor. Über die Anzahl der Mitglieder schweigt die Clubleitung ebenso wie über deren Identität. Immerhin konnten wir bei unserem Besuch erfahren, dass Prinz Andrew, der Bruder des Thronfolgers, die Stuart-Suite sehr liebt; auch, dass man die Beanspruchung des 18-Loch-Championship-Platzes auf 15 000 Runden pro Jahr beschränkt (die anderen schottischen Kurse rechnen mit etwa 45 000 Runden). Die Absicht ist nicht nur, den Platz in erstklassiger Form zu halten. Es geht im Loch Lomond Golf Club

schlicht und einfach nicht ausschließlich um Golf. Es geht auch darum, einer globalen, adeligen und bürgerlichen Crème der Gesellschaft eine perfekt geschützte Zuflucht voller Luxus und Schönheit zu bieten. Die Members relaxen, veranstalten Private Dinings, aber auch Arbeitsmeetings. Sie führen im Club ihre Gäste aus, machen Bootsausflüge zu den Seeinseln, jagen Fasane und Rotwild, fischen Hecht und Forelle, kurz, sie genießen einen der idyllischsten Flecken Schottlands, und dabei spielen sie gelegentlich auch Golf.
Der amerikanische Immobilien-Investor Lyle Anderson, Präsident und, zusammen mit der ebenfalls amerikanischen Investment-

Gesellschaft DMB, Eigentümer des Clubs, scheute kein Geld und keinen Aufwand, um das Herrenhaus der Colquhouns in all der Pracht und Behaglichkeit wiederherzustellen, die es im 18. Jahrhundert gehabt haben könnte. Dabei versuchte man erfolgreich, den viel strapazierten, leicht femininen englischen Landhausstil zu vermeiden. Die dreiundzwanzig Suiten im Mansionhouse, im Carriage House und in den Gardener Cottages am 3. Hole, das Wohnzimmer, die Bibliothek und all die anderen erlesenen Räume im Herrenhaus zeigen sich männlich schottisch, von den Farben und Stoffen bis zu den dekorativ eingesetzten Sporrans, den berühmten Täschchen, die traditionell vorne auf dem Kilt getragen werden. Im Clan Dining Room, einem der beiden Gourmet-Restaurants, sind damit sogar die Vorhänge zurückgebunden. (Man nimmt in diesen Restaurants nur das Dinner ein. Tagsüber, von 7 Uhr morgens bis zum letzten Whisky in der Nacht, stärkt man sich in der Spike Bar. Ihre Terrasse geht zum 9. Loch, günstig für ein kleines Break in der Mitte der Runde.)

Der Golf-Course, den Lyle Anderson für sein handverlesenes Publikum pflegen lässt, stieg seit der Eröffnung 1994 zügig unter die besten fünfzig Plätze der Welt auf. Harry Lauder beschwört in seinem berühmten, sehn-

in the 18th century. At the same time they tried – with successs – to avoid the rather feminine English country house style which has been flogged to death.
The 23 suites in the Mansion House, the Carriage House and the Gardeners' Cottages at the 3rd hole, the sitting room, the library and all the other exquisite rooms in this mansion are very Scottish and male in character. This is evident from the colours and materials to the sporrans (the famous pouches worn in front of the kilt) used as decorations.

Die Clubhaus-Ambiance, hier eine Suite, zeigt die Schönheit und Eleganz des 18. Jahrhunderts.

Clubhouse ambience – a suite with the beauty and elegance of the 18th century.

In fact in the Clan Dining Room, one of the two gourmet restaurants, the curtains are even tied back. (One only has dinner in this restaurant. During the day from 7 o'clock in the morning until the last whisky at night one fortifies oneself in the Spike Bar. Its terrace goes to the 9th hole, ideal for a little break in the middle of a round.) The golf course which opened in 1994 and which Lyle Anderson keeps maintained for a hand-picked clientele soon ranked among the 50 best courses in the world. In his famous, wistful song, Harry Lauder conjures up the image of the "bonny bonny banks of Loch Lomond". The 18-hole golf course, designed by champions Tom Weiskopf and Jay Morrish, possesses all the attraction and enchantment of Loch Lomond´s beautiful banks, the green, blossoming, wooded peninsula over which the course lies, the romantic scenery, hills on one side and the lake and its islands on the other. And across the water is the mountain, Ben Lomond (3,191 ft).

Tom Lehman, Loch Lomond Champion 1997, has written a description of each of the 18 holes which vividly explains why the course so fascinates even world class players. Let us take one hole, the 7th for example (400 yards par 4): "I consider this is a truly classic hole by any definition. It's a hole which makes you feel you want to cut your drive a little, but if you do that you can tangle with a tree that hangs over and seems to catch everything up. I try to hit a straight shot right over the middle of the fairway with maybe just a little cut. This generally leaves anything from a six-iron to a nine-iron to a green. (…) The seventh hole is very definitely one of my favourites. Maybe that's why I've made a lot of birdies there."

The next Standard Life Loch Lomond Golf Championship takes place in July this year. Champs like Lee Westwood, Nick Faldo and Colin Montgomery, the present title-holder, have already confirmed they'll be taking

Feudal wie ein Wohnsalon: der Gentlemen's Locker Room, der Umkleideraum für die Herren.

Like a sumptuously furnished living room: the Gentlemen's Locker Room, the men's changing room.

suchtsvollen Lied die „bonny bonny Banks of Loch Lomond". Die 18-Loch-Anlage, entworfen von den Champions Tom Weiskopf und Jay Morrish, führt alle Reize dieser wunderschönen Ufer des Loch Lomond vor, die grünende, blühende, bewaldete Halbinsel, auf der der Kurs liegt, die romantische Hügellandschaft zur einen Seite, den See und seine Inseln zur anderen und drüben am anderern Seeufer den 973 Meter hohen Berg Ben Lomond.

Von Tom Lehman, dem Loch-Lomond-Champion von 1997, gibt es eine Einzelbeschreibung aller 18 Holes, die plastisch macht, wie sehr der Kurs gerade auch Weltklassespieler fasziniert. Greifen wir nur ein Loch heraus, das siebte zum Beispiel (440 Yards, Par 4): „Ich denke, das ist nach jeder Definition ein wahrhaft klassisches Hole. Ein Hole, das Ihnen das Gefühl gibt, Sie möchten Ihren Drive gerne etwas cutten. Aber wenn Sie das tun, kann es Ihnen passieren, dass Sie sich in einem Baum verheddern, der überhängt und der den Eindruck macht, als wolle er alles abfangen. Ich versuche, einen geraden Ball rechts über die Mitte des Fairways zu schlagen, vielleicht mit einem kleinen Cut. Das lässt alle Möglichkeiten offen, zum Grün zu kommen, vom Eisen 6 bis zum Eisen 9. (…) Das siebte Loch ist entschieden eines meiner Favoriten. Vielleicht, weil ich dort schon viele Birdies gemacht habe." Das nächste Standard-Life-Loch-Lomond-Golfturnier findet im Juli dieses Jahres statt, Champs wie Lee Westwood, Nick Faldo und Titelverteidiger Colin Montgomerie haben ihre Teilnahme bestätigt. Im Oktober ist der Kurs dann Schauplatz des amerikanisch-europäischen Kräftemessens beim Solheim Cup, er ist so etwas wie der Ryder Cup für Damen. Beides Gelegenheiten auch einmal für Nichtmitglieder, sich dem solitären Erlebnis des Loch Lomond Golf Clubs hinzugeben, einer Erfahrung, die Tom Weiskopf, einer der beiden Kurs-Architekten, mit großer persönlicher Zuneigung beschreibt: „Ich denke, ich habe am Loch Lomond dem Golf ein Denkmal gesetzt, das bleiben wird. Diesen Golf-Kurs zu designen, bedeutete für Jay und mich, Ehrfurcht zu haben und einen Sinn für Verantwortung. Es ist einer der schönsten Orte der Welt. Es gibt uralte Bäume und atemberaubende Blicke, in den Steinen und in den Wassern des Sees schlummert Schottlands Geschichte. (...) Loch Lomond ist ein ganz ungewöhnlicher und wirklich einzigartiger privater Club, ein warmherziger und freundlicher Stützpunkt in dem Land, in dem das Spiel begann."

part. In October the course is the venue for the Solheim Cup, the American-European competition somewhat equivalent to the Ryder Cup for women.
Both occasions are good reason – also for non-members – to enjoy the unique experience of the Loch Lomond Golf Club, an encounter described by Tom Weiskopf, one of the two course architect, with great personal affection: "I believe I've built a monument to golf at Loch Lomond which will last. For Jay and me, designing this golf course meant having respect and a sense of responsibility. It is one of the most beautiful places in the world. There are ancient trees and breathtaking views. Scotland's history slumbers in the stones and in the waters of the lake. (...) Loch Lomond is a completely unusual and totally unique private Club, a warm-hearted and friendly base in the land where the game began."

GENUSS UND SPIEL, IMMER EIN PAAR

Pleasure and play, a good twosome

GOLF IN FRANKREICH

Golfen in Frankreich, das bedeutet immer eine charmante Verbindung von Sport und Genuss. Wo man auch aufschlägt, man freut sich nicht nur über attraktive Platz-Designs, man wird auch verwöhnt von immer neuen kulinarischen Landschaften und ihren typischen Delikatessen. Welchem Wein-Freak schlägt nicht das Herz höher, wenn etwa von Puilly und Sancerre die Rede ist. Wer im Genuss wie im Spiel die Spitze sucht, der gelangt nicht weit von diesen schönen Weinorten ans Ziel. Dort, bei den berühmten Schlössern der Loire, hat Golf à la français sein Mekka.

Golf in France always means a charming union of sport and pleasure. Wherever you tee off one not only takes pleasure in the course design but one is also spoilt by forever changing culinary landscapes and their typical delicacies. Which wine connoisseur wouldn't relish the mention of Puilly and Sancerre? Whoever seeks the best in pleasure and play will reach his destination not far from these wine regions. It is there, close to the châteaux of the Loire, where golf à la français has its Mecca.

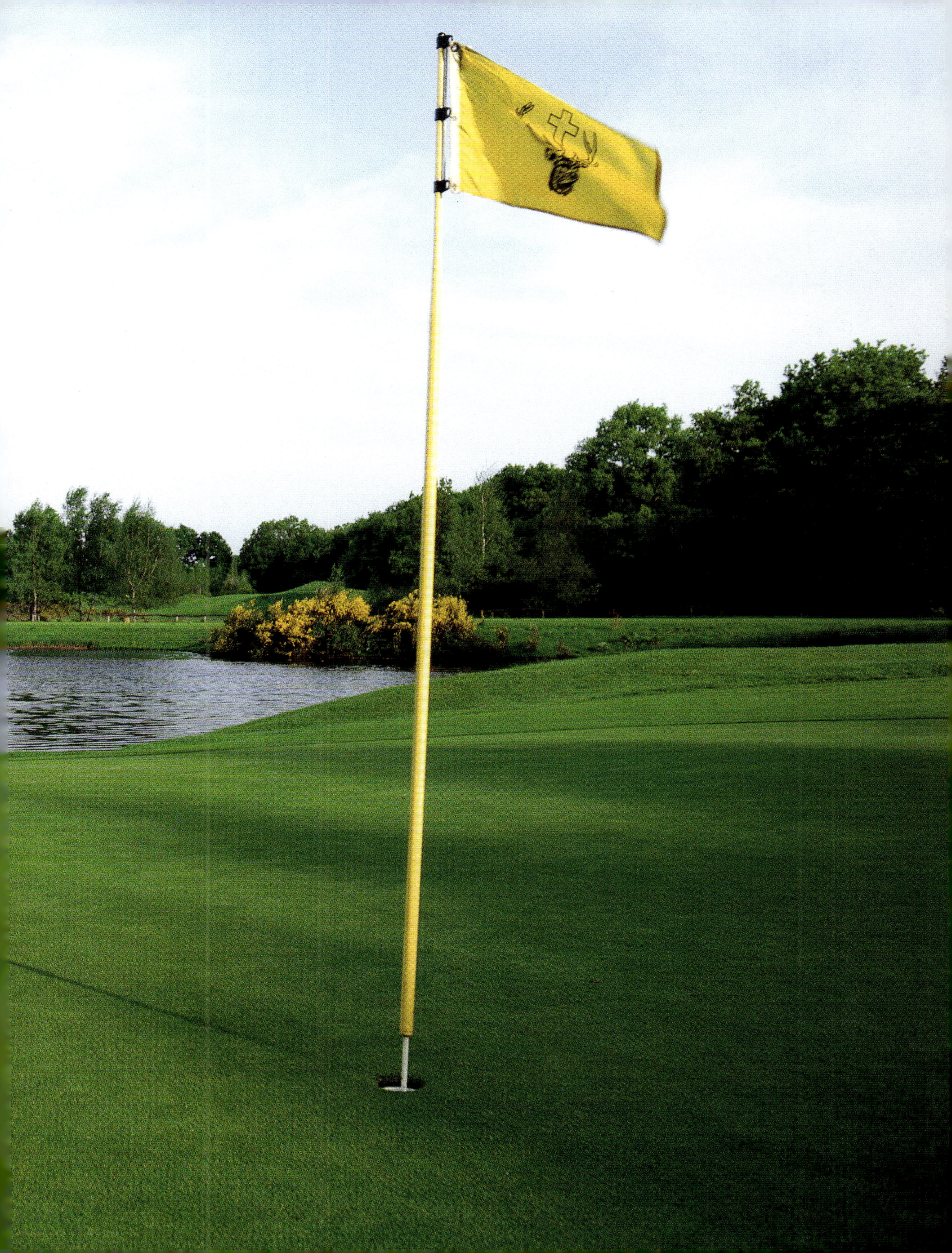

„Chez Bich" in der Sologne

Les Bordes

"Chez Bich" in the Sologne

Les Bordes gilt unumstritten als der beste Golfplatz auf dem europäischen Festland. Der „Peugeot Golf Guide", der „Michelin-Führer" für Golfer, gibt nur den Plätzen in der Nähe von Orléans und in Valderrama die Höchstnote. Der 18-Loch-Championship-Course unweit der Loire und ihrer schönen Schlösser ist eine Herausforderung für jeden Amateur, aber auch an jeden professionellen Spieler – und er ist mehr: ein Gesamterlebnis, das über ein aufregendes Platzdesign hinausgeht.

Les Bordes is undoubtedly one of the best golf courses in Europe. The "Peugeot Golf Guide", the prestigeous "Michelin Guide" for golfers, awards the highest ranking for best golf course on the European continent only to Les Bordes near Orléans and Valderrama in Spain. The 18-hole championship golf course not far from the Loire and its castles, is much more than just a challenge for both amateurs and professionals. It is the all-round experience which goes far beyond its exciting design.

Text: Günter Ned · Fotos: Klaus Lorke

Rechts: Putting Green und Clubhaus. Unten: Rodin-Statue am Putting Green. Hinter dem See das Tee des ersten Lochs. Unten rechts: Jim Shirley war der erste Direktor von Les Bordes. Er hat den Kurs mitgebaut und kennt ihn wie seine Westentasche.

Right: Putting green and clubhouse. Below: The Rodin statue on the putting green. Beyond the lake, the tee of the first hole. Below right: Jim Shirley was the first General Manager of Les Bordes. He co-designed the course and knows it like the back of his hand.

Les Bordes was born out of friendship and love – the friendship between two business partners, and the love of a Parisian for the woods of the Sologne. Baron Bich, a member of an ancient French aristocratic family, accumulated his wealth from the world famous BiC brand of cigarette-lighter, ball-point pen and disposal shaver. He left Paris as often as he could for the peace and quiet of his country residence in the Sologne. After his successful business career, he swopped the hassle with shooting game – wildfowl, deer and boar – in the wonderful flat, moist countryside of the Loire. It doesn't appear to have been the best choice because at the age of 68 he had a heart attack. Until then he didn't have a clue about golf. All that changed. Yoshiaki Sakurai, Bich's Japanese friend and business partner, an excellent golfer and busy golf course builder, suggested taking up the game. The Asian was well acquainted with the reflective side of the game. The Frenchman took up golf and fell in love with the game. Of course, Bich then wanted to have his own golf course, so he and Sakurai agreed to share the costs. The man from Japan built the course and the European opened up his country estate and provided the clubhouse and cottages. Bich's aim was to create a course which would enable French players to achieve international championship standards and this meant that the architect had to be world class. The man

Les Bordes ist aus Freundschaft und Liebe entstanden, aus der Freundschaft zweier Geschäftspartner, aus der Liebe eines Parisers zu den Wäldern der Sologne. Baron Bich, Repräsentant eines alten französischen Adelsgeschlechts, hatte seinen Reichtum mit den weltbekannten BiC-Feuerzeugen, -Kugelschreibern und -Einmalrasierern gemacht. Er verließ Paris sooft er konnte und suchte Ruhe auf seinem Landsitz in der Sologne. Dort ersetzte er die Hatz nach wirtschaftlichem Erfolg durch die Jagd nach Enten, Rehen und Wildschweinen in der flachen, feuchten, wunderschönen Landschaft des Loirebogens. Es scheint nicht der beste Ausgleich gewesen zu sein. Mit achtundsechzig kam der Herzinfarkt. Bis dahin hatte der Baron keine Ahnung von Golf.

Das sollte sich ändern. Yoshiaki Sakurai, Bichs Freund und Geschäftspartner aus Japan, ein exzellenter Golfer und eifriger Golfplatzbauer, legte ihm den Sport mit dem weißen Ball nahe. Der Asiate war mit den beschaulichen, meditativen Kräften des Spiels bestens vertraut. Anzufangen und sich in Golf zu verlieben, muss für den Freund aus Frankreich eins gewesen sein.

Nun wollte Bich seinen eigenen Golfplatz. Er und Sakurai einigten sich darauf, dass jeder die Hälfte des Werkes tragen würde. Der Japaner baute den Platz, der Europäer stellte seinen Landsitz zur Verfügung, sorgte für Cottages und Clubhaus. Bichs Anspruch an den Platz war: Er sollte französischen Spielern ermöglichen, Golf auf internationalem Turnier-Niveau zu trainieren. Das hieß: der Architekt musste Weltklasse sein. Damit stieß ein Mann aus der Neuen Welt zum europäisch-asiatischen Joint Venture: Robert van Hagge.

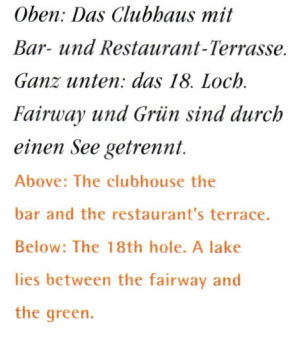

Oben: Das Clubhaus mit Bar- und Restaurant-Terrasse. Ganz unten: das 18. Loch. Fairway und Grün sind durch einen See getrennt.

Above: The clubhouse the bar and the restaurant's terrace. Below: The 18th hole. A lake lies between the fairway and the green.

Der Name des Texaners ist weltweit mit dem Design von ca. 200 Golfplätzen verbunden. Einige davon hatte er für Yoshiaki Sakurai gebaut. Er war für Bichs Ansprüche der richtige Mann, und er setzte eine weitere Forderung des Barons um: Der Platz musste in die Schönheit der Sologne-Landschaft passen. Van Hagge ging geschickt und ökonomisch vor. Zwei kleine Seen waren auf dem Areal vorhanden, er schuf zehn weitere Wasserflächen. Mit der ausgehobenen Erde formte er um die Wasser herum seinen Platz. So entstand, wie das Fachmagazin „Golf in France" formulierte, ein Stück „Florida in Frankreich". Der Kurs „hat all die typischen amerikanischen Merkmale, Wasser überall (es kommt bei 12 Löchern ins Spiel), weite Sandbunker, hohe modellierte Hügel, die Grüns sind gestufter als ein französischer Weinberg, der Drive geht lange Wege zu plateauförmigen Fairways".

Der Baron bekam also, was er sich wünschte, einen Platz mit Weltklasseformat, hineingesetzt und harmonisch verbunden mit der Natur des Landes. Heute, keine 15 Jahre nach der Eröffnung, sieht der Platz aus, als wäre er ewig hier. Selbst Jim Shirley ist erstaunt. „Verblüffend, wie sich alles entwickelt hat. Auf den künstlichen Inseln zum Beispiel ist die typische Vegetation von hier hochgeschossen."

Jim Shirley, Golfplatzkonstrukteur und -designer aus South Carolina, wurde von Bob von Hagge als Unterstützung für die letzten sechs Monate der Fertigstellung geholt. Für länger war der Aufenthalt nicht geplant. Es wurden 15 Jahre daraus. Jim war der erste Direktor von Les Bordes, er kennt den Platz, seine Geschichte und seine Geschichten wie die eigene Westentasche. „Loch 7 war Baron Bichs Favorit. Er liebte diesen Blick hier, das war für ihn die Sologne.

they chose for this European-Asian joint venture was an American, Robert van Hagge, a Texan with a world-wide reputation for building golf courses. He already had 200 courses to his name, some of them built for Yoshiaki Sakurai, so he was ideal for Bich's requirements. He was also able to realize the other stipulation of the Baron, that the course be laid down in the beautiful countryside of the Sologne.

Van Hagge undertook the task economically and with great skill. Two small lakes were already on the grounds but he created 10 further ponds and built the course around them with the soil which had been removed to create them. In this way, according to the Golf in France magazine, he created a piece of Florida in France. The course "has all the typical American features, water everywhere (it comes into play on 12 holes) vast white bunkers, huge sculptured mounds, greens with more tiers than a French vineyard, long carries to plateau fairways". The Baron got what he wanted, a world class course which merged harmoniously with its natural surroundings. Today, 15 years after it opened, the course looks as if it has been here for ever. Even Jim Shirley was amazed. "It's extraordinary how everything has developed. Even on the artificial islands, indigenous vegetation has

Baronesse Bich hat Bar und Restaurant im ländlichen Stil der Sologne gestaltet.

The rural Sologne dècor of the bar and restaurant was the creation of Baroness Bich.

shot up." Jim Shirley, golf course architect and designer from South Carolina, was brought in by Bob van Hagge to work alongside for the final last six months of the project. The six months became fifteen years. Jim was the first General Manager of Les Bordes and he knows the course, its history and its stories like the back of his hand. "Baron Bich's favourite was the 7th hole. He just loved the view from here – the lake beside it, the marshland and its low bushes and willows, the woods all around, mainly oak, chestnut and birch. The yellow flowers over there are wild irises – it epitomized the Sologne for him. The hole is a long par 5 and difficult to play because of the lake. The drive has to carry the ball on to the peninsula but not too close to the water. If you're a first class player, try using your second drive to hit the ball across the whole length of the lake straight on to the green. You then stand a chance of getting a birdie. The average golfer usually drives the ball across the width of the lake and uses his third to get to the green. He then has two putts to

Der See, daneben die Feuchtgebiete mit ihren niederen Büschen und Weiden, drumherum der Wald mit den Bäumen, die hier vorherrschen, Eichen, Kastanien, Birken, die gelben Blüten dort drüben sind wilde Iris. Das Loch ist ein langes Par 5, schwierig zu spielen durch den See. Der Drive muss bis auf die Halbinsel gehen, aber nicht zu nahe ans Wasser. Wenn Sie ein erstklassiger Spieler sind, versuchen Sie mit dem zweiten Shot über die ganze Länge des Sees direkt aufs Grün zu kommen, so haben Sie ihre Chance zum Birdie. Ein regulärer Spieler macht seinen zweiten Schlag quer übers Wasser, das ist nur die halbe Distanz, und kommt mit dem dritten zum Grün. Bleiben ihm zwei zum Putten und zum Par." Jim schmunzelt: „So ist es jedenfalls in der Theorie."

Baron Bich sind sieben Jahre geblieben, um seinen Platz zu spielen und seine Golfbegeisterung zu genießen. Brian Sparks, seit drei Jahren Direktor von Les Bordes, erzählt beim Lunch, dass das kleine Nebenzimmer des Restaurants einmal Frühstückszimmer hieß. Dort stärkten sich Bich und Sakurai immer morgens, bevor sie zu ihrer Runde aufbrachen. Beide hatten auch den Les-Bordes-Golf-Club gegründet. Solange der Baron lebte, gab es nur zwei Mitglieder: Sakurai und Bich. Die Mitgliederzahl ist exklusiv geblieben. Heute sind es fünfunddreißig.

Von Beginn an war Les Bordes offen für jeden, der hier spielen wollte, ganz unabhängig vom Club. Baron Bich hatte dafür fünf Cottages mit insgesamt 20 Zimmern an den See gebaut, der das Grün des 18. Lochs vom Fairway trennt. Die Zimmer haben nach hinten hinaus französische Fenstertüren. Dort sitzt man gemütlich auf der Rasenterrasse, beobachtet andere Spieler am Ende ihrer Runde und sieht so manchen Ball auf dem Weg zum Grün im Wasser versinken. Im vergangenen Jahr kamen noch einmal so viele Häuser und Zimmer dazu, in der zweiten Reihe parallel zu den ersten fünf Cottages. Bevor der Baron starb – das war 1994, er wurde 80 Jahre alt – verkaufte er dem Freund seinen Anteil an Les Bordes. Heute gehören zu der von Sakurai persönlich geführten Kosaido-Gruppe 25 Golfplätze in zehn Ländern auf vier Kontinenten, darunter der Duke's Course mit dem Old Course Hotel in St. Andrews, Schottland, der Kosaido International Golf Club in Düsseldorf und, in unmittelbarer Nachbarschaft von Les Bordes, der wesentlich leichter zu spielende Prieure de Ganay. Sein Architekt Jim Shirley hat im vergangenen Oktober die letzten 9 der 36 Löcher fertig gestellt.

Dass nicht nur der Golfplatz von Les Bordes, sondern auch die Zimmer und das Clubhaus zur Sologne passen, dafür sorgte die Gattin des Barons. Baronesse Bich war verantwortlich für die gesamte Inneneinrichtung und kreierte ein Ambiente im rustikal-eleganten Jagdhausstil der Gegend. Dazu gibt es jeden modernen Komfort, von Marmorbädern bis zu Satelliten-TV und Zimmerservice.

Urbehaglich das Clubhaus. Bar und Restaurant schließen aneinander an, beide Räume sind wie Scheunen gestaltet mit haushohen offenen Dachstühlen. Die Balken sind massives altes Holz, es gibt mächtige Steinkamine, große, wertvolle alte Ölgemälde, tiefe Ledersessel und -sofas in der Bar, bequeme Holzsessel um die Tische des Restaurants. Überall liegt der Charme im geschmackvoll gesetzten Detail, in phantasievoll inszenierten Antiquitäten.

Vor dem Clubhaus befindet sich eine riesige Terrasse. Man blickt zum Putting Green (mit 36 Löchern das größte Europas und wohl das einzige, das sich mit einer Statue von Rodin par." Jim smiles: "Well, that's the theory"! Baron Bich had seven years left to enjoy golf on his own course. Brian Sparks, General Manager of Les Bordes for the last three years, relates at lunch that the little room beside the restaurant used to be called the Breakfast Room where Bich and Sakurai used to fortify themselves in the morning before setting out for their round of golf. While he was still alive, there were only two members, Sakurai and Bich. Membership has remained very exclusive. Today there are only thirty-five.

From the very beginning Les Bordes has been open to anyone who wanted to play, quite apart from the club. Baron Bich built five cottages with 20 rooms for this purpose. They stand beside the lake which lies between them and the 18th green. The rear windows have French shutters. Visitors can relax on the grassy terrace and watch other golfers as they come to the end of their round – and the balls which land in the water on their flight to the green. Last year, the same number of cottages with the same number of rooms were added alongside the first five cottages.

Before the Baron died at the age of 80 in 1994, he sold his share of Les Bordes to his friend. Today, it belongs to the Kosaido Group personally headed by Sakurai which has 25 golf courses in ten countries on four continents. Among them are the Duke's Course and the Old Course Hotel at St. Andrews in Scotland, the Kosaido International Golf Club in Düsseldorf, and the Prieure de Ganay course which is very close to Les Bordes but much easier to play. Last year Jim Shirley its architect completed the last 9 of its 36 holes.

The Baron's wife, Baroness Bich, ensured that not only the Les Bordes golf course but also its clubhouse and accommodation became one with the landscape of the Sologne. It was she who was responsible for the whole of the interior design and for incorporating the regional

Locker Room und Golf-Cart-Flotte: Für Komfort auf der Runde ist gesorgt.

Locker room and golf cart fleet – the best facilities for a round of golf.

Ein Erlebnis für sich: Didier Girolets feine Küche. Köstlich sein Salade Gourmande mit Hummer und foie gras.
Fine cuisine – Didier Girolet's delicious Salade Gourmande with lobster and foie gras.

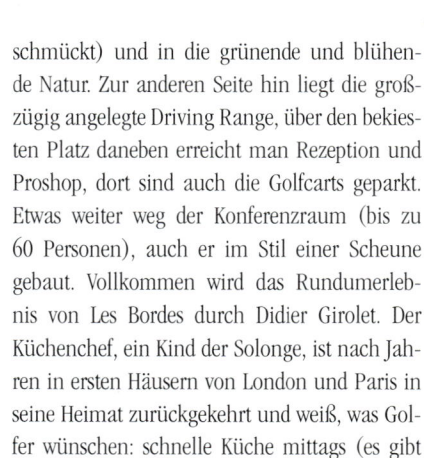

Man wohnt behaglich im Landhausstil der Loire-Region.
The hotel is like a country mansion of the Loire region.

elements which have created the ambience of a rustic hunting lodge. Yet, every conceivable comfort and luxury is provided, from the marble bathrooms to satellite TV and room service. The clubhouse is wonderfully cosy. The bar and restaurant are interconnected, and both rooms are designed like barns with house-high ceilings and roof trusses. The old cross-beams are solid wood, there are huge stone fireplaces, large valuable old oil paintings, deep leather armchairs and sofas in the bar, and comfortable wooden armchairs around the tables in the restaurant. The place has much charming detail and has been imaginatively furnished with antiques. Both the bar and the clubhouse have their own terraces which afford views of the putting green and the surrounding countryside. Not only has the putting green 36 holes making it the largest in Europe, it has a sculpture by Rodin. On the other side is the spacious

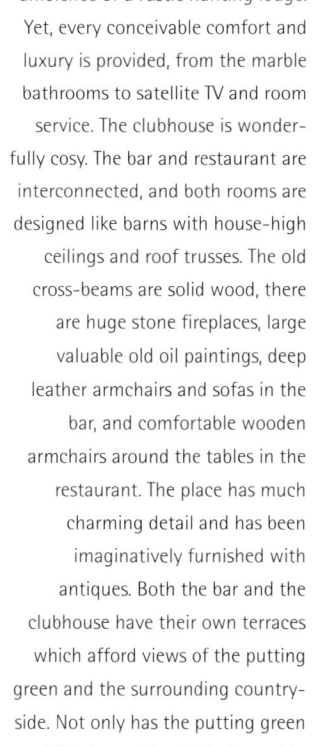

schmückt) und in die grünende und blühende Natur. Zur anderen Seite hin liegt die großzügig angelegte Driving Range, über den bekiesten Platz daneben erreicht man Rezeption und Proshop, dort sind auch die Golfcarts geparkt. Etwas weiter weg der Konferenzraum (bis zu 60 Personen), auch er im Stil einer Scheune gebaut. Vollkommen wird das Rundumerlebnis von Les Bordes durch Didier Girolet. Der Küchenchef, ein Kind der Solonge, ist nach Jahren in ersten Häusern von London und Paris in seine Heimat zurückgekehrt und weiß, was Golfer wünschen: schnelle Küche mittags (es gibt ein üppiges kaltes Buffet, dazu warme Gerichte à la carte, alles bis halbfünf Uhr nachmittags) und abends ein gepflegtes Abendessen mit mehreren Gängen zur Auswahl. Didiers exzellente französische Küche lässt mit ihren mal feinen, mal herzhaften lokalen Einflüssen keine Wünsche offen. Ausgezeichnet der Keller. Man lasse sich Entenbrust an Spargel schmecken (beides Produkte aus der Region), dazu einen St. Emilion Grand Cru aus dem privaten Château des Barons, man genieße die fast familiäre Atmosphäre, und man verstehe, warum Franzosen nicht sagen: Wir spielen Les Bordes, sondern ganz freundschaftlich: Wir spielen „chez Bich", „bei Bich".

Das Tüpfelchen auf dem i ist der Gastgeber, Direktor Brian Sparks. Brian wurde mit 16 Jahren Golfprofessional, spielte erfolgreich auf der europäischen Tour, war 15 Jahre lang Golflehrer in Frankreich und spricht französisch so fließend wie englisch (auch die Crew betreut Gäste grundsätzlich zweisprachig). Spieler sind sichtlich angetan, in ihm einen Gesprächspartner zu haben, der von Golf mindestens ebenso begeistert ist wie sie. Der große schlanke Engländer mit der Neigung zum französischen Art de vivre nimmt Spielern mit höherem Handikap gerne die Scheu vor Les Bordes: „Natürlich, der Platz ist schon für einen Professional eine Herausforderung. Er hat 18 völlig unterschiedliche Löcher, übt vom ersten Tee an den Druck auf sie aus, jeden Ball exakt zu spielen. Ein Freund sagte kürzlich: Der Platz hat Dich ständig im Griff, er lässt Dich nicht mehr los. Einem schwächeren Spieler rate ich: Kommen Sie hierher, akzeptieren Sie, dass Sie mehr Bälle verlieren, dass Ihr Score höher sein wird als sonst, bringen Sie Ihre Liebe zur Natur, zu gutem Essen und gutem Wein mit, und Sie werden bei uns eine wunderbare Zeit verbringen." Später sitzen wir auf der Terrasse, beim Kaffee nach Didiers delikater Entenbrust. Es ist still, nur die Natur spricht mit vielen Stimmen, die Dunkelheit bricht herein. Drüben hinter dem See kommen Rehe auf die Lichtung und ziehen gemächlich zum ersten Tee. Es wird kein Schuss fallen.

driving range and beside it a pebbled area which you have to cross to get to the reception area and the Pro Shop where the golf carts are parked. A little farther on is the conference room which can accommodate up to 60 people. It too is built like a barn. However, the experience of Les Bordes would not be complete with Didier Girolet, the master chef from the Sologne. After years at top establishments in London and Paris, he returned to his roots and knows exactly what golfers want – a fast meal at noon – he provides a lavish cold buffet with a warm à la carte menu until 4.30 p.m. – and in the evening a sophisticated dinner. Didier's excellent French cuisine which alternates between the exquisite and hearty local fare, leaves nothing to be desired. The wine list is excellent. What could be tastier than duck served on a bed of asparagus – both regional products – with a St. Emilion Grand Cru from the Baron's own château? Enfolded by such a homely atmosphere, one begins to understand why the French don't refer to the golf course as Les Bordes but as chez Bich. The icing on the cake is its host, General Manager Brian Sparks. Brian became a golf professional at the age of 16, enjoyed success on the European tour, then spent fifteen years as a golf coach in France. His French is as fluent as his English, and his staff are totally bilingual when it comes to looking after the guests. Golfers are clearly impressed by the fact that he is just as keen on golf as they are. The tall, slim Englishman with a penchant for the French art de vivre soon puts players at their ease who are daunted by Les Bordes. "Obviously the course is demanding, even for professionals. It has 18 holes which are all completely different and demand very accurate play from the first tee. Recently a friend said to me that the course has always got you in its grip, and never lets go. I would advise the average golfer to come here and simply accept that he will lose more balls than usual, and that his score will inevitably be higher than usual. If you come here because you love nature, good food and good wine, you'll have a marvellous time." Later on we sit on the terrace drinking coffee after Didiers exquisite breast of duck. It is very quiet, only the sounds of nature break the silence. Darkness falls. On the other side of the lake deer appear in the clearing and move in a leisurely fashion towards the first tee. Here, not a shot will be fired.

Golf-Professional und herzlicher Gastgeber: Brian Sparks, seit drei Jahren Direktor von Les Bordes.

Brian Sparks, golf professional and genial host, has been the General Manager of Les Bordes for three years.

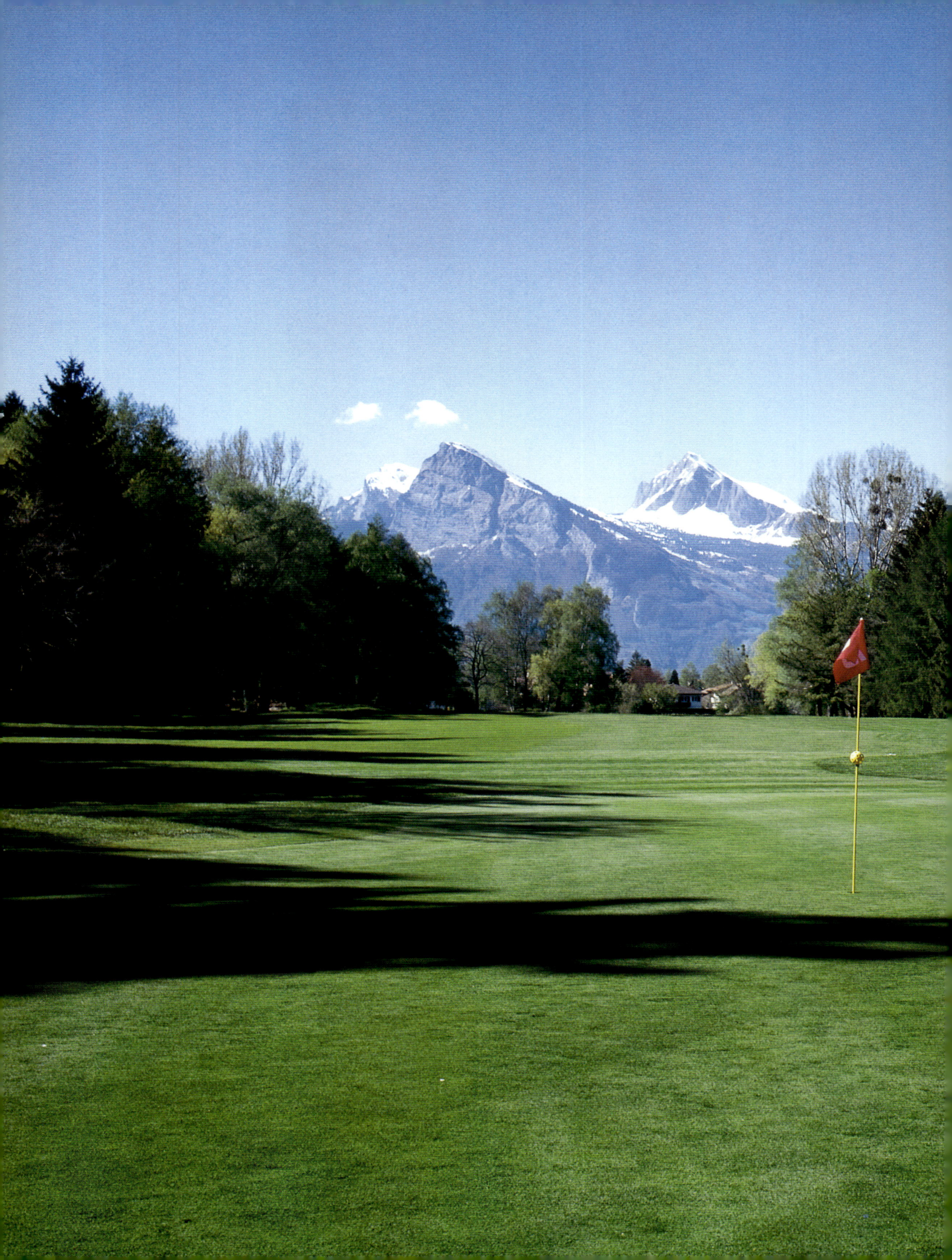

ABSCHLAG IN DEN ALPEN

Tee off the Alps

GOLF IN DER SCHWEIZ

Für Golfer sind die Naturlandschaften, die die Parcours umgeben, oftmals von ebenso großer Bedeutung wie das Design der Plätze selbst. Eine eigene Faszination übt dabei die malerische Alpenkulisse aus. Schneebedeckte Gipfel in weiter Ferne und blühende Almwiesen mit bezaubernder Pflanzenvielfalt sorgen dabei für erholsame Golftage. Vom Bergfrühling bis zum Herbst genießt man zudem eine wechselnde Farbenpracht, die dem Menschen Erholung im Einklang mit der Natur vermittelt.

For golfers, the countryside surrounding golf courses is often as important as the design of the courses themselves. Picturesque alpine scenery exerts its own fascination. Snow-capped peaks in the distance and flowery alpine pastures with their delightful array of different plants, enhance a golfing holiday. From spring to autumn in the mountains, colours which induce peace and harmony in human beings are always changing.

GrandHotels BadRagaz

Golf vitale im Health, Spa & Golf Resort

Die „GrandHotels BadRagaz" sind die einzigen Hotels der Schweiz, die über einen eigenen 18-Loch-Golfplatz verfügen. Doch es sind nicht nur die anspruchsvollen Greens und Fairways vor malerischer Voralpenkulisse, die jedes Jahr Gäste aus aller Welt in den historischen Kurort Bad Ragaz locken. Der glamouröse Zauber der beiden Luxushotels und die einzigartige Bäder- und Wellnesslandschaft des „to B. the leading HealthClubs" öffnen jedem Erholung Suchenden die Tore zur aktiven Erholung und inneren Entspannung.

The "GrandHotels BadRagaz" are the only hotels in Switzerland which have an 18-hole golf course. Yet, it isn't only the challenging greens and fairways set in the picturesque scenery of the foothills of the Alps which draw guests from all over the world into the historic spa village of Bad Ragaz. It is also the glamour and magic of both luxury hotels, and the unique pool and wellness area of the "to B. the leading HealthClub" whose doors are open to all seeking rest and relaxation and who want to take an active part in their own recuperation and ease tension.

Text: Sabine Herder · Fotos: Ulrich Helweg

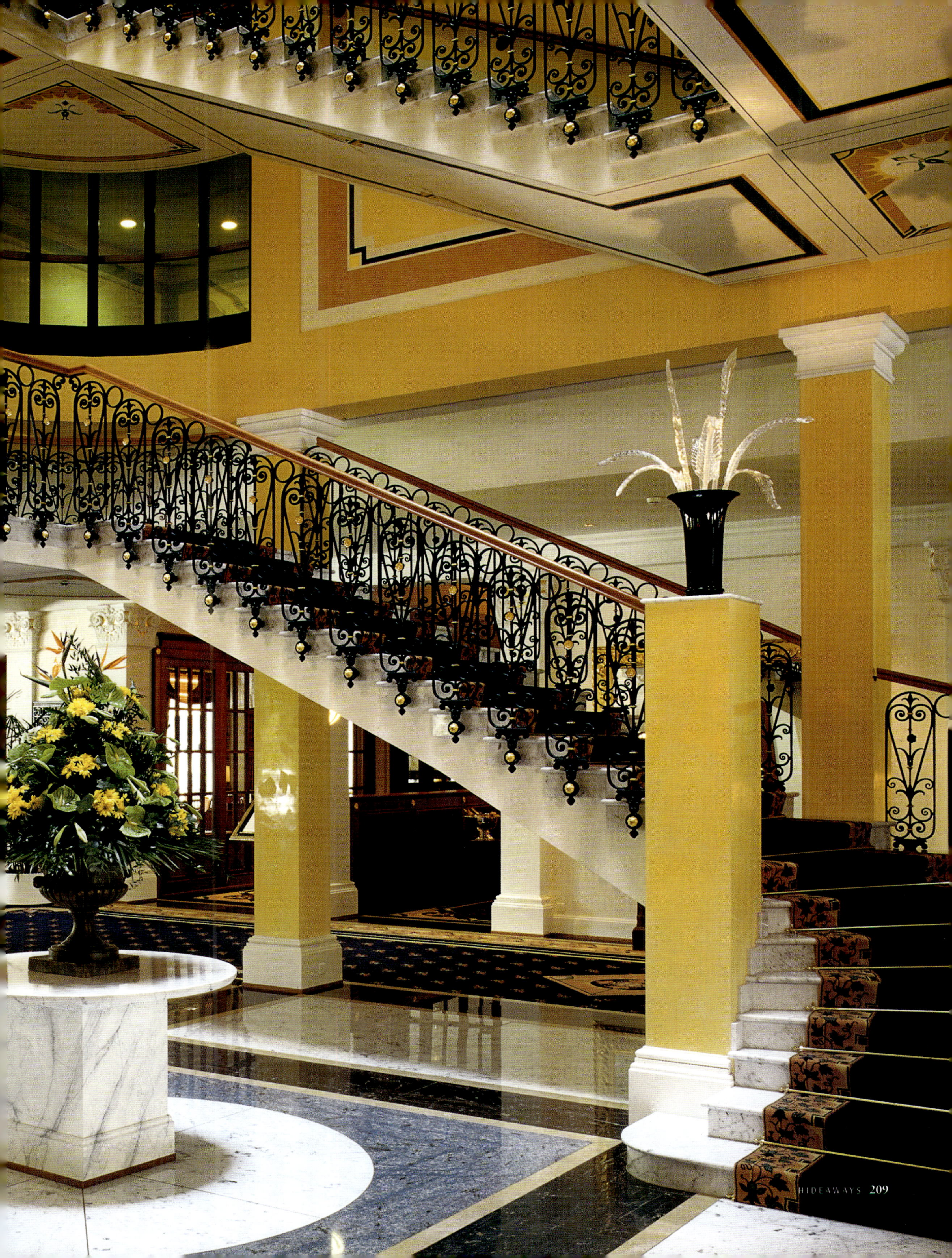

Looking on with a stern if not surly gaze from the big oil painting in the light-flooded hall of the "GrandHotel Quellenhof" is Bernhard Simon, the founder and original owner of the Ragaz-Pfäfers Baths and Spa. On the 28th March 1868 the Swiss architect who had risen to fame and fortune at the court of the Czar, purchased a concession for the use of the thermal springs which rise in the nearby Tamina gorge. Even though it had been discovered in 1038, the healing water first became famous along with Bad Ragaz after the renowned architect built the "GrandHotel Quellenhof" and the Medical Centre. News of the thermal springs abounding in more water than anywhere else in Europe spread very quickly, and the hotel, super luxurious by

Beautiful stucco work decorates the music salon in the carefully restored Palace of the prince-abbot dated 1774.

Streng, ja fast mürrisch schaut Bernhard Simon, eigentlicher Begründer und ursprünglicher Besitzer der Bad- und Kuranstalten Ragaz-Pfäfers, von dem großen Ölgemälde in der lichtdurchfluteten Halle des GrandHotels Quellenhof. Am 28. März 1868 hatte der Schweizer Architekt, der am russischen Zarenhof zu Ehren und Geld gekommen war, die Konzession für die Nutzung der Thermalquellen, die in der nahe gelegenen Taminaschlucht entspringen, erworben. Obwohl schon im Jahre 1038 entdeckt, errang das heilende Wasser und mit ihm Bad Ragaz seinen Ruhm erst, nachdem der berühmte Architekt das „GrandHotel Quellenhof" samt Kursaal und Medizinischem Zentrum errichtet hatte. Sehr rasch sprach sich die heilende Kraft der wasserreichsten Akratotherme Europas herum, und das für damalige Verhältnisse überaus luxuriöse Grandhotel entwickelte sich zum angesagten Treffpunkt gekrönter Häupter und des europäischen Geldadels. Unter ihnen zahlreiche Engländer, die auf ihrem Weg ins Engadin in

Wunderschöne Stuckarbeiten zieren den Musiksalon im liebevoll restaurierten „fürstäbtlichen Palais" aus dem Jahre 1774.

Bad Ragaz Station machten, um sich in dem gesunden Klima auf 500 Metern Höhe und in den mondänen Thermalbädern von den Strapazen ihrer Reise zu erholen. Dabei verzichteten sie nur ungern auf ihr liebstes Hobby, das Golf spielen. Und so entstand in Bad Ragaz schon vor über 100 Jahren einer der ersten Golfplätze der Schweiz. Selbstverständlich hat der heutige, resorteigene 18-Loch-Golfplatz nichts mehr mit den gemähten Wiesen von einst gemein. Doch an der malerischen Voralpenkulisse mit ihrem berauschenden Naturreichtum hat sich kaum etwas verändert: links und rechts erheben sich die zum Teil schneebedeckten Berggipfel über den blumengesprenkelten Wiesengründen des Rheintales. Die sattgrünen und stets top-gepflegten Fairways sind eingebettet in eine Parklandschaft mit altem Baumbestand, der sich in der Golfsaison von März bis November in wechselnder Farbenpracht präsentiert. Alles in allem eine Idylle, bei der das Handicap leicht zur Nebensache werden kann.

the standards of the time, developed into a rendezvous for crowned heads and the European nouveaux riches. Among them were numerous English who would stop off at "GrandHotel BadRagaz" on their way to Engadine so that they could recuperate from the stresses and strains of their journey at the chic thermal baths in the healthy climate of 500 metres above sea level. However they were unwilling to go without their favourite hobby, golf. Consequently, one of the very first golf courses in Switzerland was laid down over a hundred years ago. Obviously the hotel's present 18-hole golf course has nothing in common with the mowed lawns of those times yet little has changed in the ravishing scenery of the alpine foothills with its abundance of plant life. To the left and to the right mountains, some of them snow-capped, tower above the flowery meadows of the Rhine Valley. The luscious greens and immaculately kept fairways are set in parkland with an old stock of trees decked out in all their transient glory during the golf season from March to November. All in all, it is

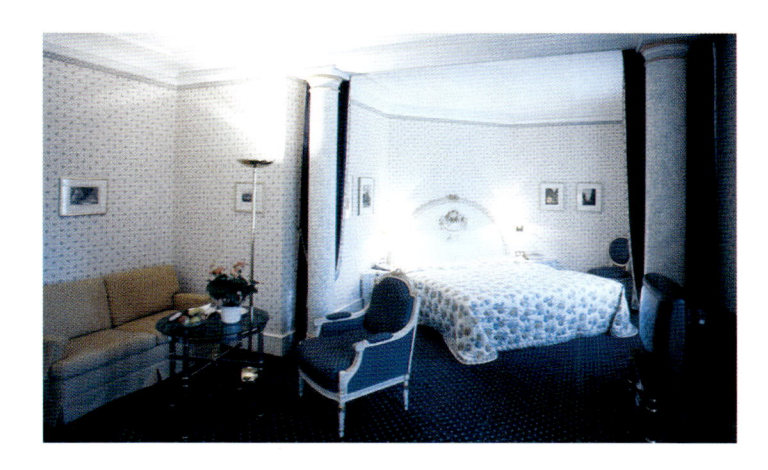

Im „GrandHotel HofRagaz" spiegeln die individuellen Zimmer im historischen Palais die alte und große Hotelkultur des Resorts wider.
At "GrandHotel HofRagaz" the individual rooms in the historic palace reflect the grand tradition of hotel culture in earlier times.

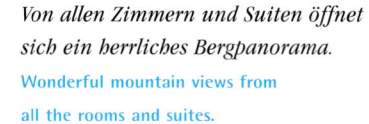

Von allen Zimmern und Suiten öffnet sich ein herrliches Bergpanorama.
Wonderful mountain views from all the rooms and suites.

Jedes der 18 Löcher bietet hohen spielerischen Reiz und wunderschöne Ausblicke.
Every single one of the 18 holes demands great skill but has wonderful views.

HIDEAWAYS 211

Schlafen, wie es einem König gebührt – in der Royal Suite.
Bedtime in surroundings befitting of a king – the Royal Suite.

Rückzugsmöglichkeit für beschauliche Mußestunden: die ruhige Halle.
A place to retreat for one's leisure hours: the peaceful hall.

Idylle auf dem hoteleigenen 18-Loch-Golfplatz.
Idyll on the hotel's own golf course.

an idyllic place where one's handicap soon becomes a minor matter. For the ordinary part of the course one doesn't have to be in the best of condition, all the same there are all manner of golfing challenges to discover. Some of the fairways are long and narrow and need a precise tee-off demanding hard concentration even from the pros when they come to the famous Bad Ragaz PGA Seniors Open in August, just one of the many matches during the season which attracts top golfers. Just as well then that in the Driving Range and Indoor Training Centre three experienced pros are available to aid ambitious golfers, an advantage which visiting golfers really appreciate. Golfers also like being able to book tee times, the 50 per cent green fee reduction and the short distances inside the resort. The golf course is only a few steps away from the "GrandHotel Quellenhof". There in the spacious hall, the stern eyes of its architect would only recognize a few details of his own because down the years the old hotel has undergone conversion and reconstruction several times but in the end could not keep pace with the ever-increasing demands of its discriminating

Für das durchgängig flache Gelände braucht man zwar nicht die beste Kondition, trotzdem gibt es jede Menge golferische Herausforderungen zu entdecken. Die teilweise langen und engen Fairways verlangen präzise Abschläge, die selbst den Profis bei dem berühmten Bad Ragaz PGA Seniors Open im August – nur eines der zahlreichen hochkarätig besetzten Turniere in der Saison – höchste Konzentration abverlangen. Nur gut, dass in der Driving Range und der Indoor-Trainingsanlage den ambitionierten Golfern drei erfahrene Golflehrer mit Rat und Tat zur Seite stehen. Vorteile, die der Golf spielende Hotelgast genauso zu schätzen weiß wie die fest reservierten Abschlagszeiten, die 50-Prozent-Greenfee-Ermäßigung und natürlich die kurzen Wege im Resort. Nur wenige Schritte trennen den Golfplatz vom „GrandHotel Quellenhof". Dort, in der beeindruckenden Halle, erblicken die gestrengen Augen des einstigen Baumeisters nur noch wenige Details, die aus seiner eigenen Ideenschmiede stammen. Denn das im Laufe der Jahrzehnte immer wieder umgebaute alte „GrandHotel Quellenhof" konnte den ständig steigenden Bedürfnissen anspruchsvoller Reisender nicht mehr Rechnung tragen, und so wurde es nach reiflicher Überlegung komplett abgetragen und von Grund auf neu gebaut. Mit der Eleganz des 19. Jahrhunderts, aber mit allen Errungenschaften modernen Komforts ausgestattet, stieg das neue „GrandHotel Quellenhof" nach aufwendigen Baumaßnahmen wie Phönix aus der Asche und präsentiert sich seit Herbst 1996 glanzvoller denn je. Und selbst Pionier

Bernhard Simon hätte seine helle Freude an der internationalen Eleganz, die heute genauso wie damals die Atmosphäre des Leading Hotels prägt. Spiegelnder Marmor, kristallene Lüster, Säulen mit vergoldeten Kapitellen, Stuckornamente, flauschige Teppiche, edle Stoffe, goldgerahmte Spiegel und große Fensterfronten, die den Blick durch das Grün der Parkanlagen auf den Kursaal, einem „Simonschen" Zeitzeugen, frei geben, bestimmen den besonderen Zauber in den öffentlichen Räumen. Über das repräsentative Treppenhaus mit seinem kunstvoll geschmiedeten Geländer, einem Originalstück aus dem 19. Jahrhundert, oder natürlich mit dem Lift gelangt man in die vier oberen Etagen, wo das „zweite Zuhause" in Form von 97 Juniorsuiten und neun Suiten auf die Gäste wartet. In allen Räumen gehen Luxus und mo-

Die Royal Suite lässt keinen Wohntraum unerfüllt.
The Royal Suite leaves no dream for luxury unfulfilled.

Die großzügigen Juniorsuiten im „GrandHotel Quellenhof" lassen keinen Komfort vermissen.
The spacious Junior Suites at "GrandHotel Quellenhof" leave no desire for comfort unfulfilled.

Die öffentlichen Bäder der berühmten Tamina Therme sind für Hotelgäste bequem durch einen überdachten Wandelgang zu erreichen.
The public baths of the well-known Tamina Therme are easy to access for hotel guests through a roofed-over connecting passage.

guests. So, after due consideration it was completely demolished and rebuilt from scratch. Refurbished with a 19th century elegance and provided with every amenity of the modern era after a costly building programme, the new "GrandHotel Quellenhof" rose phoenix-like from the ashes and since autumn 1996 it has been more radiant than ever before. Even the pioneering Bernhard Simon would have been absolutely delighted with its cosmopolitan elegance, a mark of this Leading Hotel, just like it used to be. Gleaming marble, crystal chandeliers, pillars topped by golden capitals, stucco ornamentation, soft carpets, good fabrics, gold framed mirrors and big windows which look across the green of the parkland to the Kursaal, a "Simonesque" object of its time, characterize the special

HIDEAWAYS 213

Eine Variation rund um die Gänseleber – im Frühling vielleicht gebraten mit jungem Rhabarber in Grenadine mit Kräuterheu.
A variation on goose liver – in Spring perhaps fried in Grenadine with new rhubarb and flavoured with herbs.

Gabriella Cecchellero, Küchenchefin der Äbtestube.
Gabriella Cecchellero, head-chef of the Äbtestube.

Der hausmarinierte Lachs kommt mit Sauerrahm, Kaviar und blauen Kartoffeln daher.
The home-made marinated salmon is served with sour cream, caviar and blue potatoes, a cross between potatoes and beetroot.

magic of the public rooms. The four upper storeys can be reached up the imposing 19th century stairway with very artistic wrought ironwork, or of course in the lift, where a second home from home in the shape of 97 junior suites and nine suites awaits the guest. In all rooms luxury and the most up to date amenities, space and atmosphere go hand in hand. There is a divine panoramic view from the suite's own balcony and a wonderful bathroom. But before snuggling down between the sheets one shouldn't miss the chance of visiting the unique baths and wellness area, the "to B. the leading HealthClub". Spread over 22,600 square feet this world of water, steam and fragrance turns out to be a paradise for all those who battle against the stresses and strains of daily life. Under professional management, the centre offers a multiplicity of activities and relaxation programmes second to none. Whether exclusive facials or whole body treatments in the Beauty Oasis or special relaxation massages and techniques which include fitness training – a complete list of everything available would be beyond our scope – this is a place where the doors to inner harmony seem to open automatically. If anything at all remains of daily stress, at the very latest a dip into the warm water of the Helena Bath, the hotel's own thermal bath, completely washes it away.
As well as "to B. the leading Health Club" offering its many wide variety of wellness programmes there are other attractions too. There is the picturesque scenery where a whole range of wildlife experiences and a variety of sporting and leisure activities are possible all the year round, the hotel's own golf course, the affiliated Medical Centre specializing in locomotor disorders and pain therapy and the culinary arts, also an important pillar upon which rests the philosophy of the General

Das Restaurant Bel Air bietet den stilvollen Rahmen für einen rundum gelungenen Abend.
The Restaurant Bel Air provides the stylish ambience for a thoroughly successful evening.

dernster Komfort, Geräumigkeit und Atmosphäre Hand in Hand – herrlicher Panoramablick vom eigenen Balkon und wunderschöne Bäder inklusive.

Bevor man sich jedoch gemütlich in die Laken kuschelt sollte man nicht versäumen, der einzigartigen Bäder- und Wellnesslandschaft, dem „to B. the leading HealthClub", einen Besuch abzustatten. Auf 2100 Quadratmetern entpuppt sich diese Welt aus Wasser, Dampf und Düften als Paradies für all diejenigen, die dem Stress und der Hektik des Alltages den Kampf ansagen wollen. Unter professioneller Leitung findet man dort ein vielschichtiges Aktiv- und Entspannungsangebot, das seinesgleichen erst einmal suchen muss. Von der exklusiven Gesichts- und Körperpflege in der Beautyoase über spezielle Entspannungsmassagen und -techniken bis zum Fitnesstraining — eine komplette Auflistung aller Angebote würde den Rahmen sprengen — öffnen sich hier die Tore zur inneren Entspannung fast von selbst. Und sollte trotz allem noch ein Rest Alltag übrig sein – spätestens beim Eintauchen in das warme Wasser des hoteleigenen Thermalbades, dem Helenabad, wird auch dieser vollends abgespült.

„Tatort" für so manche Gaumenschmeichelei: das Gourmetrestaurant Äbtestube.
Scene of a good many delectable meals: the Gourmetrestaurant Äbtestube.

Neben dem „to B. the leading Health-Club" mit seinen vielschichtigen Wohlfühl-Programmen, der malerischen Landschaft, die das ganze Jahr über unzählige Naturerlebnisse und ein abwechslungsreiches Sport- und Freizeitangebot bietet, neben dem eigenen Golfplatz, dem angeschlossenen Medizinischen Zentrum, das sich auf Störungen des Bewegungsapparates und die Schmerztherapie spezialisiert hat, sind die kulinarischen Künste eine wichtige Säule, auf der die Philosophie von Direktor Hans Geiger ruht.

Die Auswahl und das Niveau der kulinarischen Welt beeindrucken dabei genauso wie alle

Direktor Hans Geiger prägt zusammen mit seiner Frau Silvia seit über 13 Jahren die luxuriöse und sehr individuelle Gastlichkeit in den „GrandHotels BadRagaz".

For the last 13 years the General Manager Hans Geiger and his wife Silvia have been shaping the luxurious and very individual brand of hospitality at the "GrandHotels BadRagaz".

anderen Bereiche des Resorts. Am Abend haben die Gäste die Qual der Wahl zwischen vier ganz unterschiedlichen Lokalitäten, so dass auch in diesem Punkt keinerlei Langeweile aufkommen kann. Im eleganten Restaurant Bel Air mit seiner wunderschönen Gartenterrasse glänzt das „GrandHotel-Quellenhof"-Team Abend für Abend mit einer marktfrischen französischen Küche und modernen internationalen Spezialitäten auf höchstem Niveau. Gar fürstlich, und das sogar im wahrsten Sinne des Wortes, speist man im Gourmetrestaurant Äbtestube. Unter der mächtigen Gewölbedecke im Untergeschoss des einstigen fürstäbtlichen Palais' führt Gabriella Cecchellero das Regiment. Die junge Küchenchefin, deren Können mit 16 Gault-Millau-Punkten ausgezeichnet ist, hat viel für die Küche südlich der Alpen übrig. Der besondere Reiz ihres Konzeptes liegt jedoch in ihrer eigenen, scheinbar unerschöpflichen Kreativität, mit der sie beste Zutaten immer wieder aufs Neue komponiert. Jedes Gericht besticht durch die Liebe zum Metier und eine aromenreiche Harmonie, die jeden Bissen zum Ereignis macht. Wer den Gegensatz liebt, speist am nächsten Abend in der gemütlichen Dorfbeiz Zollstube, die gleich nebenan zu Fondue und herzhaften Schweizer Spezialitäten lädt.

Und wer bei all diesen Verführungen doch einmal über die Stränge schlägt, braucht sich keine Gedanken machen. Die 18 anspruchsvollen Greens und das einzigartige Angebot des „to B. the leading HealthClubs" hat solch verzeihlichen Sünden jede Menge entgegenzusetzen.

Manager, Hans Geiger. The selection and the standard of the culinary world are just as impressive as the other areas of the resort. In the evening guests have the difficult choice between four very different restaurants so that no boredom creeps in. At the Restaurant Bel Air, the elegant hotel restaurant which has a wonderful garden terrace, evening for evening the "GrandHotel Quellenhof" staff dazzle with their market-fresh French cuisine and international nouvelle cuisine of the highest order. One dines royally in the true sense of the word in the Gourmetrestaurant Äbtestube. Under the solid vaulted ceiling in the basement of the erstwhile prince abbot's palace, Gabriella Cecchellero is in charge. The young Chef whose skill is acknowledged by 16 Gault Millau points, has a great liking for the cuisine south of the Alps. However, her special gift appears to be her inexhaustible creativity, enabling her to continually produce new ideas for dishes made from the best ingredients. Every dish is special because of her love of her métier, an aromatic harmony which makes every mouthful an eventful experience. Those who like contrasts can eat at the cosy Dorfbeiz Zollstube next door which has a tempting menu of fondue and hearty Swiss specialities.

But if one does succumb to all these temptations and overdoes it somewhat, no need to worry. The 18 demanding greens and the unique range available at to B. the leading HealthClub includes any number of treatments to counteract such forgivable sins.

Exklusives Herzstück des „to B. the leading HealthClub" ist das wunderschöne Helenabad.

The exclusive heart of "to B. the leading HealthClub" is wonderful Helena Bath.

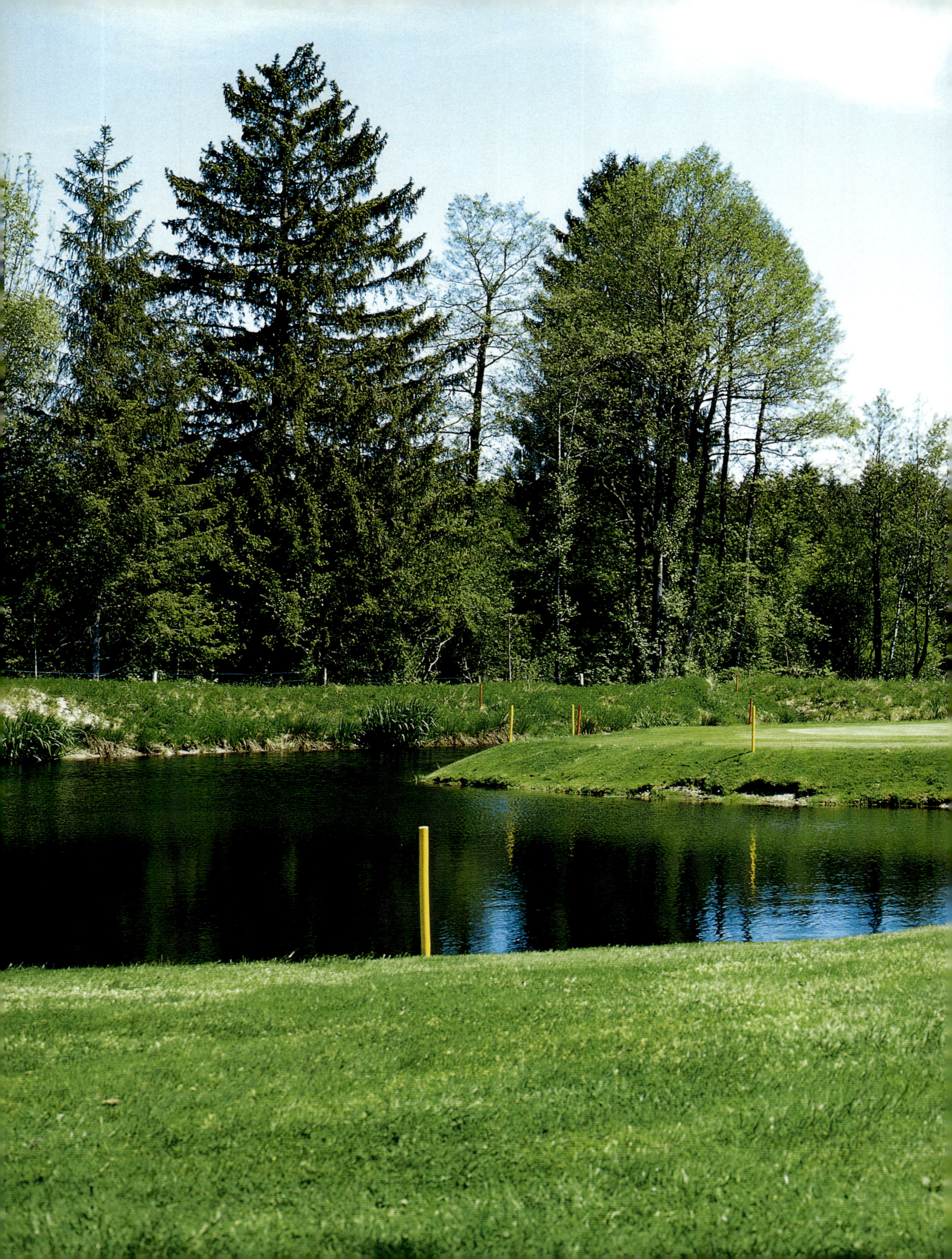

ÜBER BERG UND TAL

Over mountains and valleys

GOLF IN DEUTSCH-LAND

Der Süden bietet besondere Reize — gerade für Golfer. Viele, die in Deutschland der Leidenschaft für den kleinen weißen Ball nachgehen, lieben die Plätze in Bayern. Hier findet man nicht nur Kurse, die für alle Spielstärken ausgewogene Herausforderungen bereithalten, hier spielt natürlich auch die Landschaft ihre ganz eigene Rolle, vor allem je näher die Berge rücken. Ob man beim Spiel das Gebirge als imponierende Kulisse vor Augen hat oder ob Berg und Tal das Platzdesign ganz unmittelbar prägen, es warten spannende Erfahrungen.

Southern Germany offers unique attractions to golfers. Many who indulge in the passion surrounding the small white ball are cannot resist the golf courses of Bavaria. It naturally combines well-designed courses for all levels of play with a stunning landscape, especially nearer the mountains. Thrilling experiences await golfers who either seek a spectacular mountain backdrop for their play or who want to try a course where mountains and valleys have been incorporated in its design.

218 HIDEAWAYS

Golfidylle am Tegernsee
Der Margarethenhof
Golf idyll beside Lake Tegernsee

Im tiefen Süden Deutschlands geht's bekanntlich in die Höhe. Von München aus sieht man die Alpen, die Seelandschaften südlich der bayerischen Hauptstadt zeigen zauberhafte Naturszenerien. Wer hier seine Golftasche auspackt, dem schenkt das Land noch andere Blicke als nur die auf die Score-Karte. Einen der schönsten Plätze bietet, hoch über dem Tegernsee, der Margarethenhof Golf und Country Club.

It is a known fact that the deep south of Germany gains in altitude. The Alps can be seen from Munich and the lakeland landscape south of the Bavarian capital has some enchanting scenery. Anyone unpacking his golf bag here has something quite different to look at than just a score card. One of the most beautiful places high above Lake Tegernsee is the Margarethenhof Golf and Country Club.

Text: Günter Ned · Fotos: Freddy Peterburs

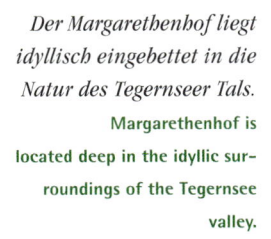

Der Margarethenhof liegt idyllisch eingebettet in die Natur des Tegernseer Tals.
Margarethenhof is located deep in the idyllic surroundings of the Tegernsee valley.

Its location is stunning. Reception, pro shop, clubhouse and hotel are right in the middle of the golf course and circling around it golfers move from tee to tee, improving their tee-off at the driving range or practising at the practice bunkers and on the chip and putting greens. Then there is the view. Wherever one goes or stands there are the most glorious panoramic views of the alpine foothills – the mountains, meadows and woods of the Tegernsee valley. From the 5th hole you can see the lake, and from the 12th as far as Munich when the Föhn wind is blowing.
The area is hilly so is the golf course. Head Pro, Achim Lehnstaedt, sketches the difficulties and the advantages. "Owing to its many slopes the place is quite challenging. There are very few spots where one is standing on level ground and choosing

Die Lage ist nicht zu schlagen. Rezeption, Pro-Shop, Clubhaus und Hotel liegen mitten im Golf-Kurs. Drumherum ziehen die Spieler von Tee zu Tee, verbessern ihren Abschlag auf der Driving Range, trainieren in den Übungsbunkern, auf den Chip- und Putting-Greens. Und dann der Blick. Wo man geht und steht, breitet sich das herrlichste Voralpenpanorama aus, die Berge, Wiesen und Wälder des Tegernseer Tals. Vom 5. Loch sieht man den Tegernsee, vom zwölften bei Föhn bis nach München.

Die Lage am Berg charakterisiert auch den Golfkurs. Head Pro Achim Lehnstaedt umreißt Schwierigkeiten und Vorzüge: „Der Platz stellt wegen seiner vielen Hanglagen natürlich bestimmte Ansprüche. Die Anpassung der Schläge an diese Grundsituation will trainiert sein. Vor allem Spieler, die vom Flachland kommen, müssen sich den Gegebenheiten schwungtechnisch oft erst anpassen. Auch etwas Kondition schadet nicht, wir bieten aber Carts an, derzeit haben wir eine Flotte von 13 Wagen, wir lassen sie auch bei Turnieren zu. Der Margarethenhof ist jedoch ein recht fairer Golfplatz. Er bietet breite Flächen, seine Konturen sind sehr großzügig gemäht. Wir mähen auch die Roughs ziemlich kurz herunter, so dass sich die Bälle ohne Mühe finden lassen. Man kann auf den meisten Bahnen ganz gut streuen und dennoch im Spiel bleiben. Die Bahnen sind nicht so extrem lang, zusammen etwas über 6000 Meter, die Spieler müssen also gar nicht so weit schlagen können, um den Platz zu bewältigen. Wir haben sehr wenige Bunker, gerade mal 34, das ist sicher ein Vorteil für Anfänger. Die Bunker sind relativ fair platziert, nie so, dass man wirklich Probleme hat, das Grün zu treffen. Es bleiben immer Möglichkeiten, den Bunker zu umspielen, man muss ihn nicht überspielen. Mit anderen Hindernissen wie Wasser oder Ausgrenzen, die sehr nahe am Fairway sind, halten wir uns auch zurück. Die Grüns sind eher etwas klein gehalten, sie liegen in der Regel leicht unter 500 Quadratmeter, lassen sich fair putten, werden nie so runtergemäht, dass es sehr schwierig wird, die Geschwindigkeiten überhaupt zu dosieren, und sie haben keine allzu starken Ondulationen. Die Vorzüge zeigen

the right club for this kind of situation certainly needs practice. Especially golfers who come from lowlands have to get used to the conditions and adjust their technique. In fact it helps to be in good shape though we do have carts available – at present we've got a fleet of 13. We also allow them be used during tournaments. The Margarethenhof course is a very fair one though. It has broad expanses and their edges are well mowed. We also cut the roughs fairly short so that balls are easy to find. One can hit the ball quite wide on most of the fairways yet still be able to stay in the game. The fairways are not too long, all in all about 6,560 yards so players don't even need to drive the ball very far to manage the course. We don't have many bunkers, only 34 actually, certainly an advantage for beginners. The bunkers are relatively

Wo man geht und steht auf dem Golfplatz des Margarethenhofs, liegt einem die faszinierende Voralpenkulisse zu Füßen.
Wherever you are on the Margarethenhof golf course, you have the fascinating landscape of the alpine foothills at your feet.

Im Margarethenhof wird eine anspruchsvolle, saisonorientierte Frischeküche serviert.
Margarethenhof serves sophisticated, seasonal dishes cooked with fresh ingredients.

fairly placed so that one never has any real problems reaching the green. It's always possible to play around a bunker, one doesn't have to play over it. We've held back on other hazards such as water or boundaries too close to the fairway. The greens have been kept quite small – about 5,380 square feet in area – and are fair for putting. They are never mown so short that it becomes too difficult to regulate speed, and there are no extreme undulations. The advantages always become apparent in the results, especially of private tournaments when golfers might be playing for the first time and are then surprised to find they've improved their handicaps. That often happens." Clearly the course provides a challenge for good players yet can give novices a sense of achievement. In fact the Golf & Country Club goes far beyond providing the usual golf service. Commenting on the appealing aspects of the place, General

sich immer wieder in den Ergebnissen, gerade auch bei Privatturnieren. Da treten Spieler zum ersten Mal an und sind dann überrascht, dass sie ihr Handicap verbessert haben. Das erleben wir oft."

Ein Kurs also, der dem guten Spieler Herausforderungen bietet, dem Anfänger die notwendigen Erfolgserlebnisse sichert. Ein Golf- und Country-Club aber auch, der weit über den puren Golf-Service hinausgeht. Direktor Günter Esterer zu den verlockenden Highlights des Konzepts: „Der Margarethenhof ist in seiner Ganzheit, glaube ich, ein bisschen einzigartig. Es gibt in Deutschland nicht so oft die Situation, dass ein Hotel mitten im Golfplatz liegt. Wenn Sie zu uns hoch fahren, müssen Sie ja fast aufpassen, dass Sie nicht von fliegenden Bällen getroffen werden. Wir sind ein kleines, aber sehr schönes Hotel mit 38 Zimmern, und die Möglichkeit, im Grunde mit den Spike-Schuhen bis vor die Haustür zu gehen oder innerhalb von einer Minute auf dem Platz zu sein, wo gibt es die noch? Das Ganze kombinieren wir mit einer hochwertigen Gastronomie, die sich nach dem Hotelcharakter richtet und sich daher natürlich von üblichen Clubgastronomien unterscheiden muss. Das beginnt schon mit der Öffnungszeit, sieben Tage von sieben Uhr morgens, also vom Frühstück an, durchgehend bis 22 Uhr. Aber auch unsere Mitglieder hier aus dem Tegernseer Tal stellen hohe Ansprüche. Sie möchten zwar nach dem Spiel ihre Kartoffelsuppe mit Debreziner Würstchen

haben, später allerdings, am Abend, wenn sie sich wieder frisch gemacht haben, dann gehen sie fein essen, ob das jetzt ein schönes Steak oder Hummer ist, sie möchten es in guter Qualität. Und natürlich immer, wie bei Golfern üblich, mit dem Blick aufs gute Preis-Leistungs-Verhältnis. Das alles haben wir zu bieten, dazu für Firmen die Möglichkeit zu ungewöhnlichen Incentives. Sie haben ideale Tagungsfaszilitäten, können heute ihr Arbeitsmeeting abhalten, morgen ein Putting-Turnier, ein Golfseminar oder Ähnliches. Die frische Luft macht den Kopf frei, der Teamgedanke wird gestärkt, und gleich daneben wohnen Sie auch noch schön."

Alles in allem also ein perfekter Ort, um die Golflust mit einem kurzen oder auch längeren Urlaub zu verbinden. Wer die Probe aufs Exempel macht, verlebt Tage im bayerischen Oberland, wie geschaffen zum Auftanken. Die Naturkulisse zeigt sich von Frühjahr bis Herbst in malerischer Üppigkeit, zu genießen nicht nur auf den Fairways, sondern auch beim Wohnen. Keine der 23 Juniorsuiten und 15 zweistöckigen Galerie-Appartements, die nicht Balkon oder Terrasse hätte. Die Wohneinheiten sind großzügig geschnitten, mit 50 bis 85 Quadratmetern Fläche, und zeigen abwechslungsreiche Gesichter. Hier präsentiert sich der Landhausstil behaglich bayerisch, dort mit leichtem englischen Touch oder auch mal mediterran. An modernem Komfort gibt es keinen Mangel vom ISDN- und Laptop-Anschluss bis zum Videorecorder.

Einen der schönsten Blicke auf das Wahrzeichen der Gegend, den 1722 Meter hohen Wallberg, und auf die anderen Tegernseer Höhen genießt man auf der Terrasse des Clubhauses, ob man gerade die bevorstehende Golfrunde bespricht (der erste Abschlag ist gleich neben der Terrasse), ob man hungrig und durstig vom achtzehnten Loch zurückkehrt oder schon Platz genommen hat zum Mittagessen. Die Terrasse gehört zugleich zum Restaurant Gut Steinberg. Es lädt innen auf zwei Ebenen zu Tisch, unten zum herzhaften Schmausen, oben zu den feinen Genüssen, und dass Gastronomiedirektor Stefan Kleins Küchencrew auf beiden Etagen zu Hause ist, das bestätigt sich bei jedem Gericht auf der Karte. Klein zeichnet seit der Eröffnung des Clubhauses im Jahr 1989 für die Bewirtung verantwortlich, vorher stand er viereinhalb Jahre im Gourmetrestaurant Leeberghof (auch hoch überm Tegernsee) am Herd. Er kocht im Margarethenhof den Linseneintopf ebenso frisch wie das Saltimbocca von Lotte und Lachs, er ist im bayerisch-österreichischen Stil genauso zu Hause (köstlich sein Tafelspitz) wie in der italienischen Küche, er sorgt bei einer leichten Kleinigkeit gerne für den gewissen Pfiff, bei einer sautierten Geflügelleber auf Rucola-Salat vielleicht für leckere Grünkernplätzchen, er beweist seine Kreativität aber natürlich auch beim exquisiten Abendmenü oder beim täglichen Lunchangebot (drei Gänge, ein Getränk, 28 Mark). Die gästefreundliche Preiskalkulierung zieht sich durchs ganze Konzept, ein Vergnügen, die kleine, aber feine Weinkarte zu lesen, oder beim Digestif festzustellen, dass man nicht auf scheinbar unverzichtbare große (und entsprechend teuere) Namen setzt, sondern auf die wunderbaren Obstbrän-

Manager Günter Esterer says, "to my mind Margarethenhof is quite unique. There aren't many places in Germany where a hotel is in the middle of a golf course. When you drive up to us you actually have to take care to avoid being hit by the balls flying about. We're a small but very beautiful hotel with 38 rooms where you can go right up to the front door in your spiked shoes or be on the course inside a minute. Where else can you have that? We combine all this with high quality gastronomy tailored to the nature of the hotel so it's obviously different from the usual club cuisine. For a start our opening hours are different, seven days a week from seven o'clock in the morning right through to ten o'clock at night, in other words from breakfast all the way through until 10 p.m. Also our local members from the Tegernsee valley have high expectations. After their game they want their potato soup with little Debrezin sausages but later on in the evening when they've changed they expect to eat in style. Whether steak or lobster they want good quality. Of course like all golfers they keep an eye on the price-benefit ratio which has to be good. We offer all that but also unusual incentives for companies. They have ideal conference facilities here. They can hold their business meetings today and tomorrow have a putting competition or a golf seminar or something like that. The fresh air clears the head, team spirit is strengthened and what is more, they have beautiful accommodation close by".

All in all a perfect place to satisfy one's craving for golf and combine it with a short or maybe a longer holiday at the same time. Anyone putting it to the test spends his/her days in the Bavarian uplands, a region created for rest and recuperation. From spring to autumn the scenic backdrop is clothed in all its luxuriant raiment, something to be enjoyed not only on the fairways but also where you stay.

Not one of the 23 junior suites and 15 two-storey galleried apartments does not have a terrace or a balcony. The units have plenty of space, from 538 to 915 square feet and each one has a different decor. One of them might be in country house style, cosily Bavarian but with a touch of the English look, another could be Mediterranean. There is no lack of up-to-date equipment, from ISDN

Rezeption, Pro-Shop, Clubhaus und Hotel liegen mitten im Golfkurs.
Reception, pro shop, clubhouse and hotel are in the middle of the golf course.

Die Zimmer und Suiten präsentieren sich im eleganten Country style, der sich mal behaglich bayrisch, mit leichtem englischen Touch oder mediterran inspiriert zeigt.

The rooms and suites either have elegant country style décor combining Bavarian comfort with an English touch, or are Mediterranean in style.

and a laptop connection to a video recorder. One of the most beautiful views is of the local landmark, the Wallberg, a mountain 5,648 feet high, and of the other mountains around Lake Tegernsee. The prospect can be seen from the Clubhouse terrace – whether one is chatting about the next round of golf (tee off is beside the terrace) or just returned hungry and thirsty from the 18th hole, or indeed already seated for lunch. The terrace belongs to the Restaurant Gut Steinberg. Inside tables are arranged on two levels; the lower one serves hearty tasty meals, the upper level fine cuisine. It's obvious from every dish on the menu that head chef Stefan Klein and his team are at home in both parts of the restaurant. Klein has been in charge of catering ever since the Clubhouse opened in 1989. For the four and a half years prior to that he was chef at the Leeberghof gourmet restaurant, also high above Lake Tegernsee. At Margarethenhof his lentil stew is just as fresh as his saltimbocca of monkfish and salmon. He is equally at home with Italian cuisine as he is with Austro-Bavarian dishes (his Tafelspitz – an Austrian speciality made of tail of beef – is delicious). He always likes to add that little extra something to a light snack, for instance the seed biscuits served with the sautéed chicken liver on Rucola lettuce. But he also demonstrates his creativity in his exquisite evening menus or in the daily lunches (3 courses and a drink 28 Marks). The moderate prices are a constant feature throughout. The small but excellent wine list is a pleasure to read but also because when it comes to brandies it doesn't depend on the big names assumed de und -wasser von Lantenhammer am nahen Schliersee, einem der interessantesten Edelbrenner im deutschsprachigen Raum. Mit seiner ausgereiften kulinarischen Philosophie hat Stefan Klein der Margarethenhof-Gastronomie zu einem vorzüglichen Ruf weit über die Region hinaus verholfen.

Golf und erlesene Cuisine, die Kombination ist eines der schönsten Highlights im Golf und Country Club, 868 Meter hoch über dem Tegernsee. Reizvoll für Hotelgäste, die keine Mitglieder sind: Sie zahlen zwar im Gegensatz zu den Mitgliedern Greenfee (70 Mark), werden aber wie sie bei der Reservierung der Abschlagzeiten mit Vorzug behandelt. Für Anfänger und Trainingswillige besonders empfehlenswert: der Frühling. Im April und Mai wird der Platz naturgemäß noch wenig bespielt, eine gute Zeit also, in Ruhe an seinen Schwachstellen zu feilen oder überhaupt die ersten Erfahrungen als Neugolfer zu machen, eine Zeit, in der man Anfängern auch ohne Platzreife erlaubt, schon mal die eine oder andere Übungsrunde zu spielen.

Aber natürlich ist es eine Überlegung wert, im Margarethenhof auch Mitglied zu werden. Nur ein Vorteil von vielen: die greenfeefreien Abschläge in über sieben assoziierten Partnerclubs in Deutschland. Gute Anlässe, zwischendurch mal auszufliegen und die Kurse von Gut Kaden, St. Leon-Rot oder Schloss Liebenstein zu spielen. Zurückgekehrt ist noch jeder gern in den schönen bayerischen Heimatclub. Wunder ist das keines, selbst Golfdirektor Achim Lehnstaedt, seit zehn Jahren Pro im Margarethenhof, kommt heute wie damals über die Landschaft ins Schwärmen: „Nehmen wir nur den Blick vom Loch 17, wir haben es im letzten Jahr neu angelegt. Da schauen Sie zum Grün und sehen hinten die neue Brücke, die über die Schlucht führt. Wenn Sie die Brücke dann ablaufen zum 18. Abschlag, da geht es erst leicht den Berg hoch und dann tut sich die ganze Tegernseer Welt auf, sie gucken direkt auf den Wallberg – ein tolles Panorama. Selbst wenn man schon lange hier ist, weiß man es immer wieder zu schätzen. Das vergessen Sie nicht."

to be indispensable, but list the wonderful fruit brandies of Lantenhammer near Lake Schliersee, one of the most interesting brandy distillers in the German-speaking area. Stefan Klein's sophisticated culinary philosophy has earnt the Margarethenhof a reputation which now extends well beyond regional boundaries. Golf and exquisite cuisine, the combination is one of the finest features of the Golf and Country Club nearly 2,850 feet above Lake Tegernsee. It is wonderful for guests who are not members. While they do have to pay the green fee (70 Marks) – unlike the members – they too receive preferential treatment when booking tee times. Spring can be recommended for beginners and those who want coaching. In April and May the course is hardly used so it's a good time to work on one's weaker points or to have one's first experience as a new golfer. During this period beginners who lack experience of playing on a course are allowed to do one or two practice rounds. However, it really is well worth considering becoming a member of the Margarethenhof. One of the many advantages is green fee free access to more than seven associated partner clubs in Germany, a good reason to take the occasional break for a round of golf on the courses at Gut Kaden, St. Leon-Rot and Schloss Liebenstein. Yet all willingly return to their beautiful Bavarian home club, and no wonder. Even Golf Manager Achim Lehnstaedt who has been the pro at Margarethenhof for the last 10 years still goes into raptures about the landscape. "Take the view from the 17th hole for instance – we re-laid it last year. You look towards the green and behind it you see the new bridge which spans the ravine. When you go over the bridge to the 18th tee it gradually goes uphill and then suddenly you have a view of the whole of Tegernsee and its surrounds and straight ahead is the Wallberg – a fantastic panorama. Even when one has been here for a very long time you always appreciate it. You never forget it."

Das erfolgreiche Trio, das den Margarethenhof unter den führenden Golfanlagen Deutschlands etablierte: Direktor Günter Esterer, Küchenchef Stefan Klein und Head Pro Achim Lehnstaedt.

The successful trio whohave established Margarethenhof as one of the leading golf courses in Germany: General Manager Günter Esterer, Chef Stefan Klein and Head Pro Achim Lehnstaedt.

Sonnenalp
Hotel & Resort

HERAUSFORDERNDER ALPENKURS • AN ALPINE CHALLENGE

Die südlichste Ecke Deutschlands, das Oberallgäu, ist zugleich auch eine der bezaubernsten Naturlandschaften. In diese malerische Kulisse aus schneebedeckten Bergen, fruchtbaren Tälern, tiefdunklen Wäldern, saftigen Wiesen und Weiden eingebettet liegt die Sonnenalp, das facettenreiche Hotel & Resort mit außergewöhnlicher Erlebnisvielfalt. Dazu gehört auch der abwechslungsreiche Meisterschaftsgolfplatz, ein sportlich anspruchsvoller Alpenkurs für Individualisten.

Oberallgäu, the most southern corner of Germany, is one of the most enchanting landscapes in the country. Deep in the heart of these picturesque surroundings of snow-capped peaks, fertile valleys, dark green forests, lush meadows and pastures is the Sonnenalp, an Hotel & Resort offering an extraordinary range of facilities and experiences. One of them is its demanding championship golf course, a challenge for all classes of golfers.

Text: Gundula Luig · Fotos: Ydo Sol / Hotel Sonnenalp

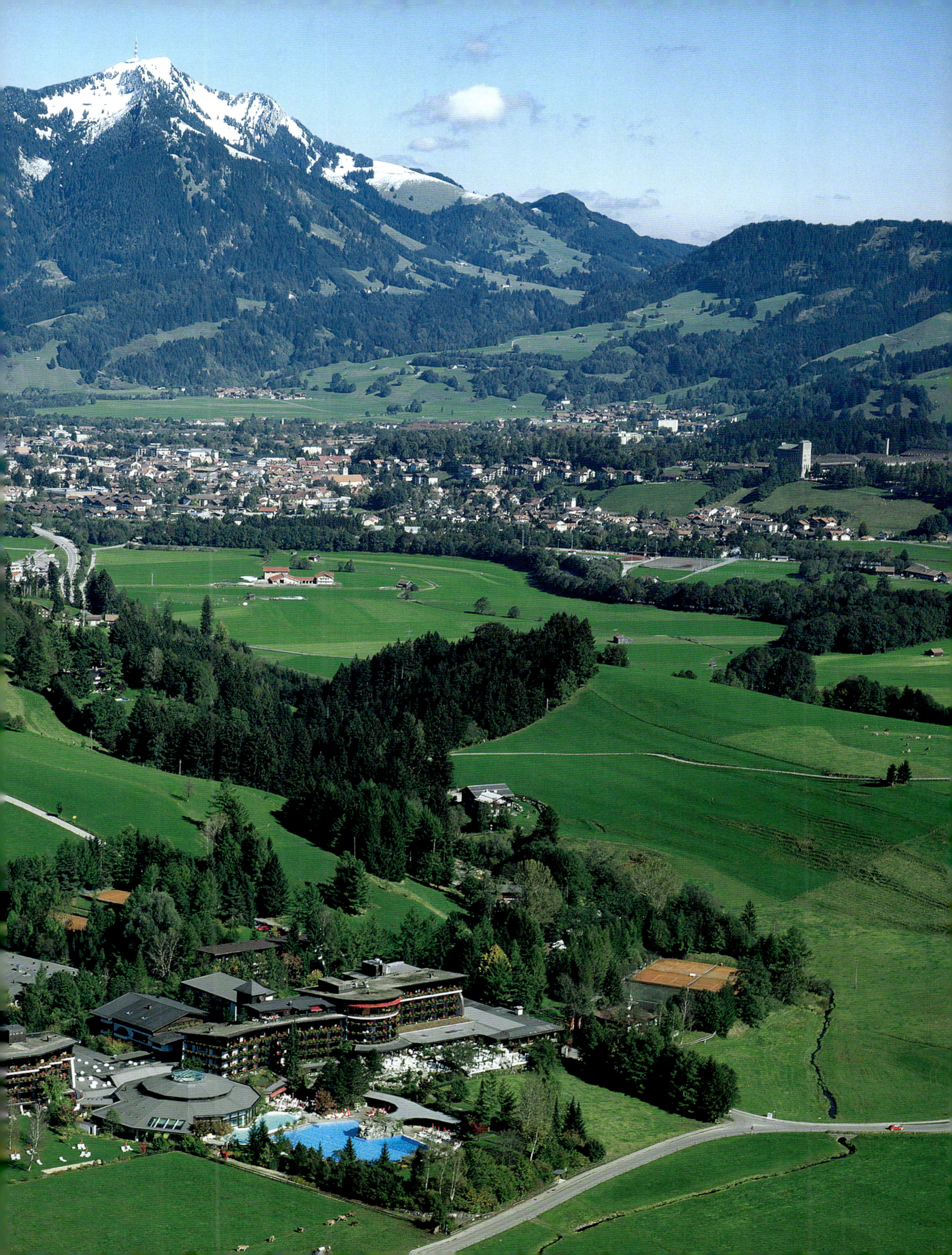

Alles, was das Golferherz begehrt, vom Golfball über den Spezialschläger bis zum modischen Outfit, hält der Pro-Shop bereit.
The Pro Shop stocks all the gear the golfer needs, from balls and special clubs to stylish clothing.

On first entering the main hall, one's initial impression is of space, elegance and good taste. The guest immediately warms to the Hotel because of its large, welcoming lounge which combines luxury and alpine charm. One's gaze wanders from the fine gallery with its substantial library to the comfortable upholstered furniture, then across to

Großzügigkeit, Eleganz und Gediegenheit bestimmen die ersten Eindrücke, wenn man die Halle der Sonnenalp betritt. Als Gast fühlt man sich sofort sympathisch angesprochen von der freundlichen Ästhetik der geräumigen, lebendigen Lounge, die eine schöne Kombination von Luxus und alpinem Charme widerspiegelt. Das Auge wandert von der stattlichen Galerie mit auswahlreicher Bibliothek zu den gemütlichen Polstergruppen, von den dekorativen Blumen-Bouquets zu den herzlichen Mitarbeitern an der Rezeption. Vom ersten „Grüß Gott!" an spürt man jene traditionelle Gastfreundschaft, die hier seit vier Generationen von der Familie Fäßler und deren Mitarbeitern gepflegt wird. Heute sind es Sabine und Michael Fäßler, die die Verantwortung für die mit den Jahren stetig gewachsene Resortanlage übernommen haben. Unter ihrer Regie präsentiert sich die Sonnenalp mit einer breiten Palette von Einrichtungen und Anlagen als ein Ferienparadies für den besonderen Anspruch. Dafür steht vorrangig die mit Konsequenz umgesetzte Resort-Idee: Die Hotelgäste sind unter sich, ungestört in einer privaten, niveauvollen Atmosphäre mit allen nur denkbaren Annehmlichkeiten. Und die sind ausschließlich den Hausgästen vorbehalten. Sogar auf dem Golfplatz, der naturgemäß eine gewisse Öffentlichkeit zulässt, genießt das Sonnenalp-Publikum Präferenz bei den Abschlagzeiten.

Apropos Golf – der Alpenparcours der Sonnenalp ist nicht nur liebstes Steckenpferd von Seniorchef Karlheinz Fäßler, der dort als Präsident vorsteht. Er gehört auch zu den attraktivsten Golfanlagen der Region, verbindet er doch faszinierende Naturromantik mit hohem sportlichen Anspruch. Sein Architekt, Donald Harradine, war bekannt dafür, Golfplätze unauffällig und harmonisch in die Natur zu integrieren. So gestaltete er auch 1975 den abwechslungsreichen Meisterschaftsplatz (18 Löcher, Par 71, 5938 Meter). Das anspruchsvolle Golfareal mit einem alten Baumbestand, naturbelassenen Teichen und Bächen sowie der Bergkulisse im Hintergrund hat alles, was Golfer glücklich macht: herausfordernde Fairways, Driving Range, Putting Green und eine neue Chipping Area, wo man die Feinheiten des Pitchens und Chippens unter realistischen Voraussetzungen (z. B. mit flachem und tiefem Bunker) üben kann. Head Pro Bernard Kennedy und seine PGA-Pros sind wahre Meister darin, Golf zu lehren – egal ob man gerade erst die Platzfreigabe erreicht hat, bereits ein erfahrener Handicap-Spieler ist oder noch nie einen Golfschläger in der Hand hatte. Mit Programmen wie dem fünftägigen Intensiv-Golfkurs, individuellen Übungseinheiten oder Turnier-Trainingswochen werden Kennedy & Co jedem Spieler-

the beautiful flower arrangements and the kindly staff at the reception desk. From the very first "Grüss Gott!", one is at the receiving end of the genuine hospitality which has been practised by four generations by the Fässler family and their staff. Over the years, the resort has grown steadily and today Sabine and Michael Fässler are running the business. Under their management the Sonnenalp offers a wide range of facilities which makes it a paradise for discerning holidaymakers. The idea of creating a resort has clearly been pursued single-mindedly. The hotel guests have their own private sphere, and every possible facility is reserved exclusively for them. At the golf course which is usually open to the public, house guests always have priority for tee times. Apropos golf – Sonnenalp's Alpine course is not only the favourite hobby horse of senior hotel owner and current president of the Sonnenalp Golf Club, Karlheinz Fässler. It is one of the most attractive golf courses in the whole region, combining the romance of nature with great sporting achievement. Its architect, Donald Harradine, was a well-known designer of golf course which blend harmoniously in with their surroun-

Das anspruchsvolle Golfareal mit einem alten Baumbestand, naturbelassenen Teichen und Bächen präsentiert sich vor einer eindrucksvollen Bergkulisse.

The demanding golf course has old trees, original ponds and streams and magnificent mountain scenery in the background.

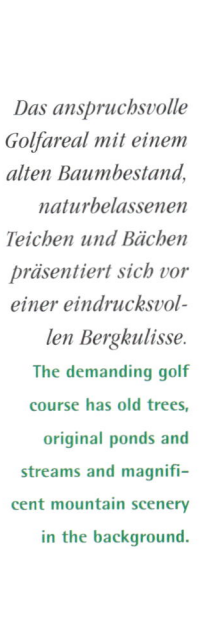

Head Pro Bernard Kennedy ist ein wahrer Meister darin, Anfängern die Faszination des Golfsports nahe zu bringen.

Head Pro Bernard Kennedy is a past master at bringing home the fascination of golf to beginners.

dings. He created this demanding championship course (18 holes, par 71, 6,493 yards) in 1975. The golf area which consist of old trees, original ponds and streams and a mountainous background has everything to make golfers happy. It has challenging fairways, a driving range, a putting green and a new chipping area where the golfer can practise chipping and putting in realistic conditions e.g. with flat and deep bunkers. Head pro, Bernard Kennedy, and his PGA pros are real masters at golf coaching, whether one has only just reached the standard required to play on a real golf course or is an experienced handi-

230 HIDEAWAYS

Level gerecht. Von April bis November finden Golfer einen vorbildlich gepflegten, wundervollen Kurs vor, mit schnellen, guten Grüns und Fairways, die es manchmal in sich haben. Das abenteuerliche „Sapperlot" (Hole 7) etwa, mit Wasser links vom erhöhten Grün und dazu ein mächtiger Bunker. Oder der „Kastanienbaum" (Hole 11), ein Par 4 mit über 400 Meter Länge und meistens Gegenwind. Dort ergibt sich die Herausforderung durch den Bach auf Drivelänge sowie einem See vor dem Grün, das sich zudem mehr nach rechts neigt, als es optisch den Anschein hat. Der Kurs erfordert also nicht nur rein technisches Geschick, sondern auch eine gehörige Portion Inspiration. Ebenso erstklassig wie der Parcours ist die Betreuung rund um das Golfspiel: Club-Managerin Renate Kraus und ihre Golf-Sekretärinnen kümmern sich um Termine, Buchung und Organisation ebenso wie um Ablauf und Auswertung der zahlreichen Turniere. Die größte Anziehungskraft im Clubhaus hat natürlich das zünftige kleine Restaurant mit der hübschen Sonnenterrasse und dem direkten Blick auf Loch 18. Und im Golfshop nebenan findet sich alles, was des Golfers Herz begehrt: eine reiche Auswahl an trendiger Mode, Accessoires und Spielgerät für den grünen Sport. Doch das ist nur ein Bruchteil von dem, was dieses so persönlich geführte Spitzenhotel an Freizeitaktivitäten zu bieten hat. Hier findet wirklich jeder sein ganz persönliches Paradies. Tennis-Cracks wählen unter zwei Hallen- und zwei Sandplätzen. Noch mehr Action verspricht der Squash-Court. Mit der neuen Reitanlage kommen endlich auch die Pferdefans unter den Sonnenalplern voll auf ihre Kosten. Der Reiterhof im Bauernhofstil beherbergt zehn eigene Island-Ponys für Kinder, Jugendliche und auch Erwachsene und bietet zudem Stallungen für weitere sechs Gästepferde. Überhaupt ist die Kinder- und Jugendfreundlichkeit des Hauses herausragend zu nennen. Selten findet man in Deutschland ein vergleichbares Angebot für Familien und Kids jeder Altersstufe. Ob Krippenkind oder Teen, kompetente Kindergärtnerinnen und Animateure organisieren erlebnisreiche, phantasievolle und unvergessliche Tage für den Nachwuchs. Vom Malspaß über das Zeltlager bis zu den aktuellsten Funsportarten. Und die Eltern werden zufrieden feststellen, dass ihre Kinder bald ebenso be-

cap player. Even if the aspiring golfer has never held a golf club before, Kennedy & Co. can cope with any level. They run courses – such as the five day intensive course – and give private instruction. They also organize week-long coaching session for golfers practising for tournaments. From April to November, golfers play on a wonderfully maintained course with fast, good greens and fairways which are sometimes very challenging. For instance, the exciting "Sapperlot" (7th hole) has a water hazard on the left, a plateau green and a huge bunker. And what about the "chestnut", the 11th hole par 4, and 437 yards long and usually played in a headwind! The challenge of this one is that there is a water hazard in the direct path of the drive, and yet another water hazard just

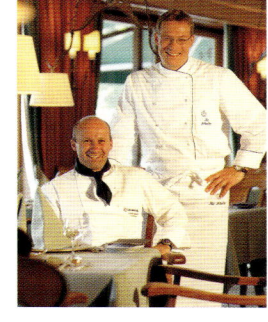

Zwei, die für die ausgezeichnete Cuisine Verantwortung tragen: Küchendirektor Jochen Schreieck (sitzend) mit Kai Schneller, dem Chefkoch des Gourmet-Restaurants „Silberdistel".

Jochen Schreieck, Maître de Cuisine (seated), and Kai Schneller, head chef at the Silberdistel gourmet restaurant, wich serves excellent cuisine.

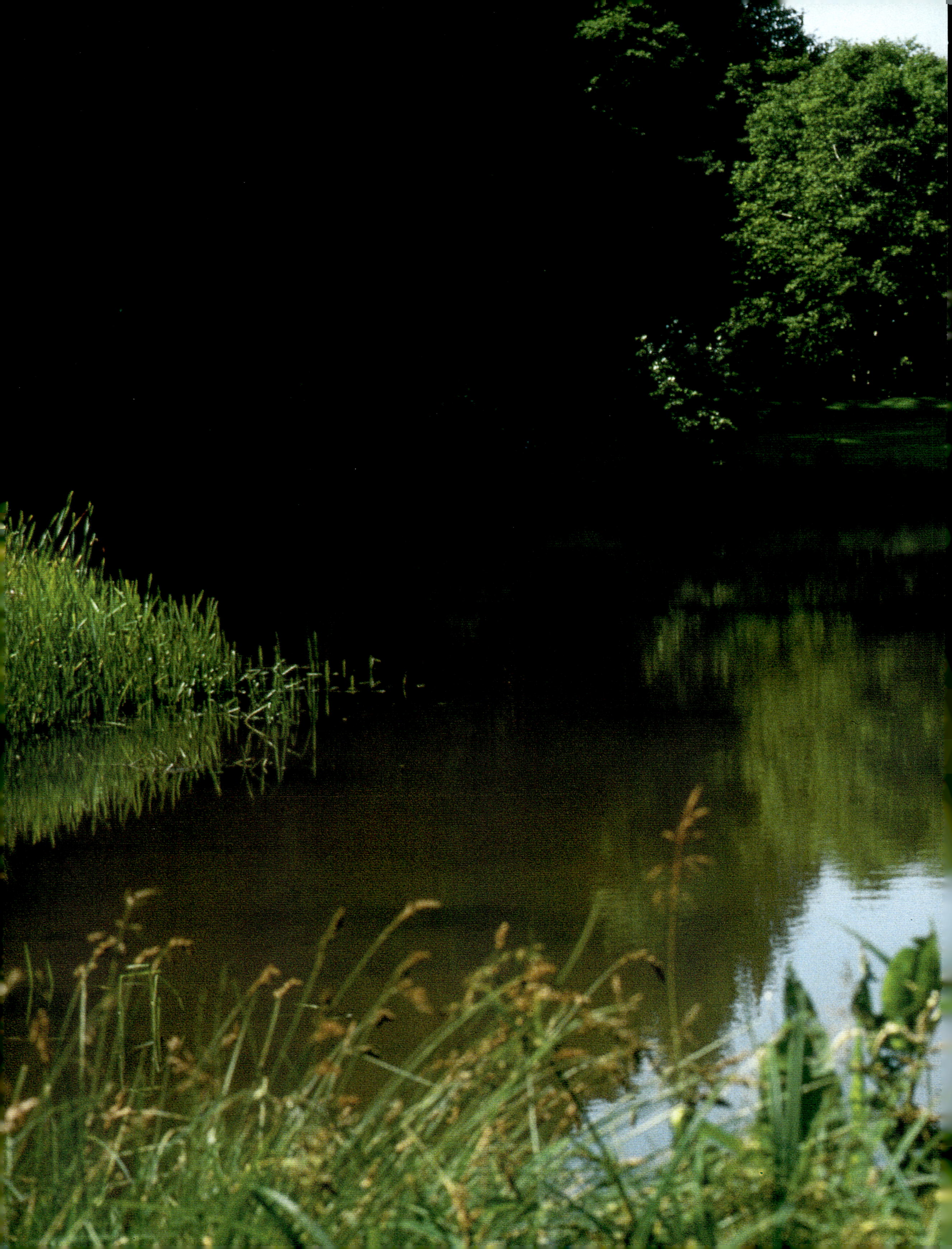

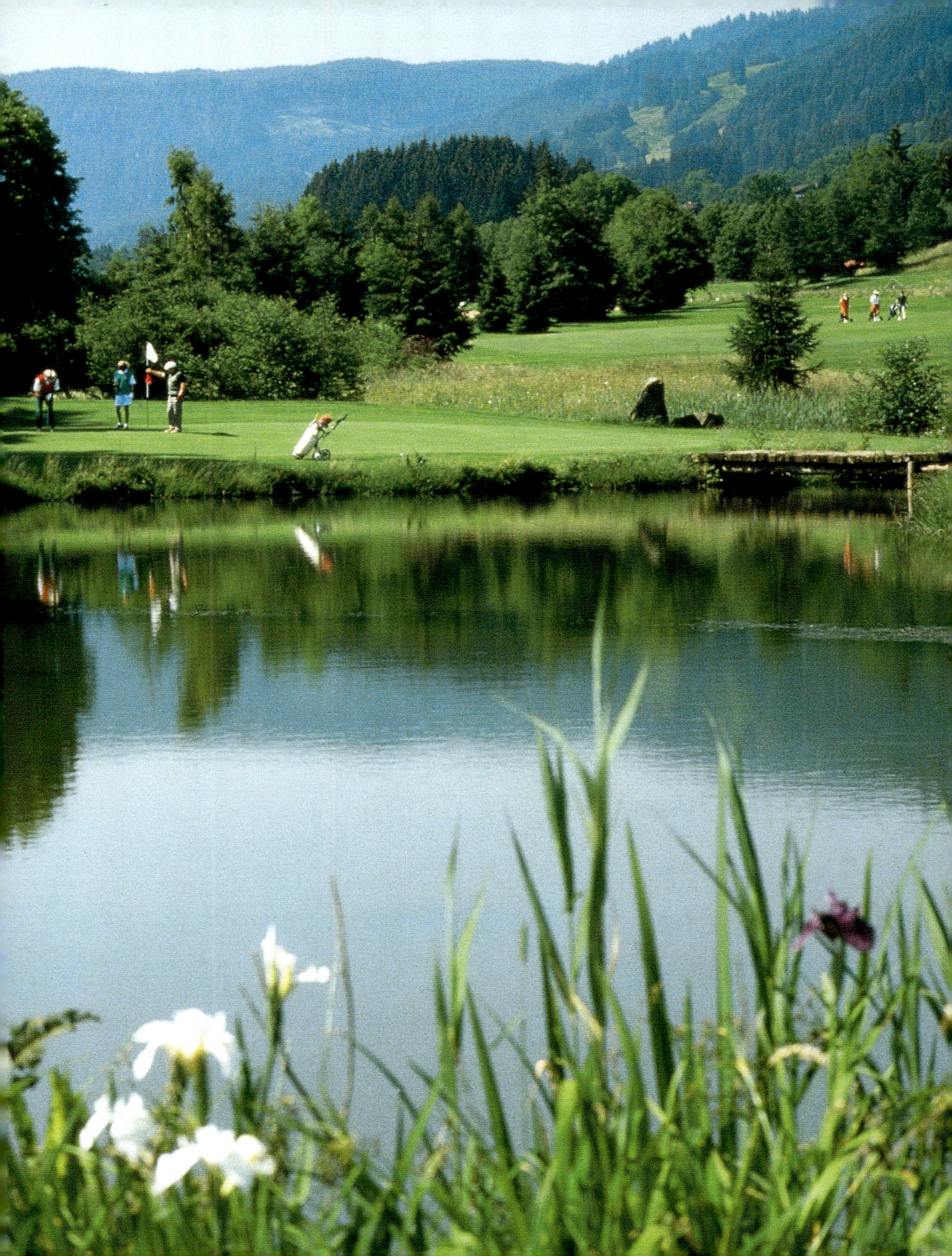

before the green which appears to lie more to the right than it actually is. The course not only requires technical ability but a lot of inspiration. The service associated with golf is equally superb. The Club Manager, Renate Kraus, and her golf secretaries record tee times and bookings, and do all the organization to ensure the smooth running of the many golf tournaments. The greatest attraction in the clubhouse is the little restaurant with the lovely sun terrace overlooking the 18th hole. The adjoining golf shop stocks a wide range of trendy fashion, accessories and equipment, in fact everything the golfer could wish for. Yet that is only a fraction of what this privately managed hotel has to offer in the way of sports and pastimes. There is something for absolutely everyone. Tennis fans have one hall two hard courts and two sand courts. The squash court attracts players who want more action, and the riding facilities provide the equestrians at Sonnenalp with everything they want too. The riding stables built in farmhouse style house ten of the hotel's own Island ponies for the youngsters and adults. But the stables have sample room for six more horses that guests might wish to bring along with them. The children's facilities and the hotel's child-friendly policy deserve a special mention because it is very rare to find a place in Germany where children of all ages are made to feel so welcome. Whether toddlers or teens, competent child-carers and entertainers organize exciting activities, imaginative events and unforgettable days for them. They have fun painting, go camping and play great games. Parents find that their offspring are as keen on Sonnenalp as they are themselves. The fountain of life is water, a central feature of the resort's Quellengarten. The oasis is marvellous owing to its dimensions and extravagance. The large (2,045 sq. ft) heated indoor pool (28 °C) and the outdoor pool (2,368 sq. ft) are linked together and provide a wonderful opportunity for bathing enthusiasts. Even more impressive is the vast adjoining outdoor pool (8,934 sq. ft) which is heated to 24 °C in summer. There is plenty to satisfy pleasure seekers in the aesthetic sauna world which has 2 Finnish saunas, a bio-sauna, solariums, steam grotto, a diving pool, a paddling pool and an exotic Japanese open air garden to regenerate vitality. At the Rainbow Club, the hotel's innovative centre for health, beauty and well-being, body, soul and mind can be restored to harmonious co-existence. There is certainly no shortage of superb restaurants at this outstanding resort – nine in all – to keep the gourmet happy. Each one has its own distinct character and the guest has the freedom to choose the ambience he prefers to sample the superlative cuisine. Under the aegis of maître de cuisine Jochen Schreieck, his ambitious chefs produce dishes using ingredients

geisterte Sonnenalpfans sind wie sie selbst. Der Quell allen Lebens ist das Wasser und dieses spielt im Quellengarten des Resorts eine zentrale Rolle. Die Wasseroase besticht durch Größe und Extravaganz. Dank der direkten Verbindung des 190 qm großen temperierten Hallenbeckens (28 °C) mit dem 220 qm messenden Außenpool ist das Naturerlebnis im nassen Element hautnah. Eine genussreiche Steigerung bietet das anschließende 830 qm weite Freibad, im Sommer auf 24 °C beheizt. Lebensfreude spendet ebenfalls die ästhetische Saunawelt mit zwei Finnischen Saunen, Biosauna, Solarien, Dampfgrotte, Tauchbecken, Wassertretbecken und exotischem japanischen Freiluftgarten zur vitalen Regeneration. Und im innovativen Zentrum für Schönheit, Gesundheit und Wohlgefühl, dem Sonnenalp Rainbow-Club, finden Körper, Seele und Geist auf harmonische Weise wieder zueinander.

Dass das einzigartige Refugium auch mit gastronomischen Highlights nicht geizt, beweist die Vielfalt seiner wunderschönen Restaurants, neun an der Zahl. Jedes hat seinen ureigenen Charakter und dem Gast steht frei, welches Ambiente er für die vorzügliche Cuisine auswählt. Unter der Ägide von Küchendirektor Jochen Schreieck und seinen ambitionierten Küchenchefs entsteht eine ehrliche, marktfrische Küche aus heimischen und internationalen Produkten. Man hat die Wahl zwischen dem täglich wechselnden 4-Gang-Halbpensionsmenü oder bedient sich in der Taverne am reichhaltigen Themenbuffet – mal asiatisch, mal heimisch oder mediterran. Für den besonderen Anlass empfiehlt sich die Silberdistel, das exquisite A-la-carte Gourmetrestaurant am höchsten Punkt der Sonnenalp. Dort verwöhnt Chefkoch Kai Schneller mit aufwändigen Kreationen wie der gebratenen Gänseleber auf Honigweißkraut mit Aprikosenessig, vielleicht gefolgt von einem Bärlauchsüpple mit Garnele vom Ofen. Während man sich auf das Leckerle vom Milchzicklein mit Artischockenragout freut, betört die Panoramasicht auf die Gebirgsformationen der Allgäuer Alpen. Ein herrliches Schauspiel hier oben sind auch die Sonnenuntergänge mit rot gefärbtem Himmel. Zum Käse mundet eine der erstklassigen roten Kreszenzen aus dem wohlsortierten Keller, und das Finale kann ein Sorbetteller in der Honigwabe bestreiten. Anschließend nimmt man noch einen letzten Drink an der Bar, bevor ein erlebnisreicher Tag auf der

Sonnenalp zu Ende geht. In der Geborgenheit der vielgestaltigen Doppelzimmer, Appartements, Familien- und Luxusappartements oder der Suiten erlebt man die Einzigartigkeit dieses familiären Hauses aufs Neue. Die Interieurs bezaubern durch höchsten Komfort und detailreiche Inszenierungen. Und bevor einen die Stille der Nacht in den Schlaf hinausträgt, planen die Gedanken schon den morgigen Tag: Shoppen in der traumhaften Shopping-Passage mit ihren 13 Edelboutiquen und -geschäften; mit der Harley kurvige Bergstraßen erkunden; Hüttenzauber auf der Alm; faszinierende Alpinwanderungen; Naturerkundung mit dem Förster!

Auch heute noch sehr engagiert: Seniorchef Karlheinz Fäßler und seine Frau Gretl.
Even today very occupied: Senior hotel owner Karlheinz Fäßler and his wife Gretl.

fresh from the market and local and international products. Guests have the choice between the half-board four-course menu which changes daily or they can they can go to the Taverne for the substantial theme buffet – sometimes home cooking, other times Asian or Mediterranean. The Silberdistel, the exquisite à la carte restaurant at the highest point of the Sonnenalp, can be recommended for special occasions. Guests can indulge in the cuisine of chef Kai Schneller, who produces extravagant dishes, for example a fried pâté de fois gras on a honey white cabbage with apricot vinegar. While you wait in expectation of the Kiogoat with artichoke ragout, you can take in the panoramic view of the Allgäu mountain scenery. The sight of the sun setting in a red sky is dramatic. The cheese course calls for a first class red wine from the well stocked cellar – as a prelude to the sorbet served in honeycomb. Finally guests go the bar for a nightcap after an eventful day. Back in the various double rooms, apartment and suites, one experiences the warmth of this house a new. The interiors are delightful down to last detail, and they provide the optimum in luxury and comfort. Before the quiet of the night transports you into slumberland, you find yourself already planning the next day. Maybe shopping in the fantastic shopping mall – it has 13 exquisite boutiques and shops. Or perhaps a ride on the Harley Davidson along the winding mountain roads? What about going to a mountain chalet, or maybe going on an alpine ramble, or the nature walk with the forest warden, or!

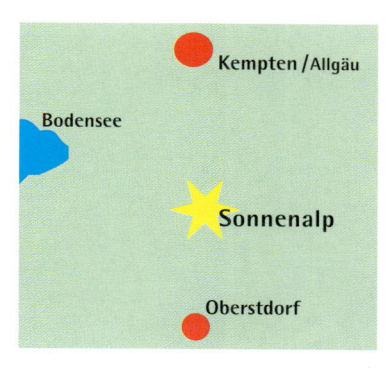

Pflegen niveauvolle und familiäre Gastlichkeit in vierter Generation: Sabine und Michael Fäßler mit ihrem Filius.
Sabine and Michael Fässler with son – fourth generation of hosts offering high class hospitality.

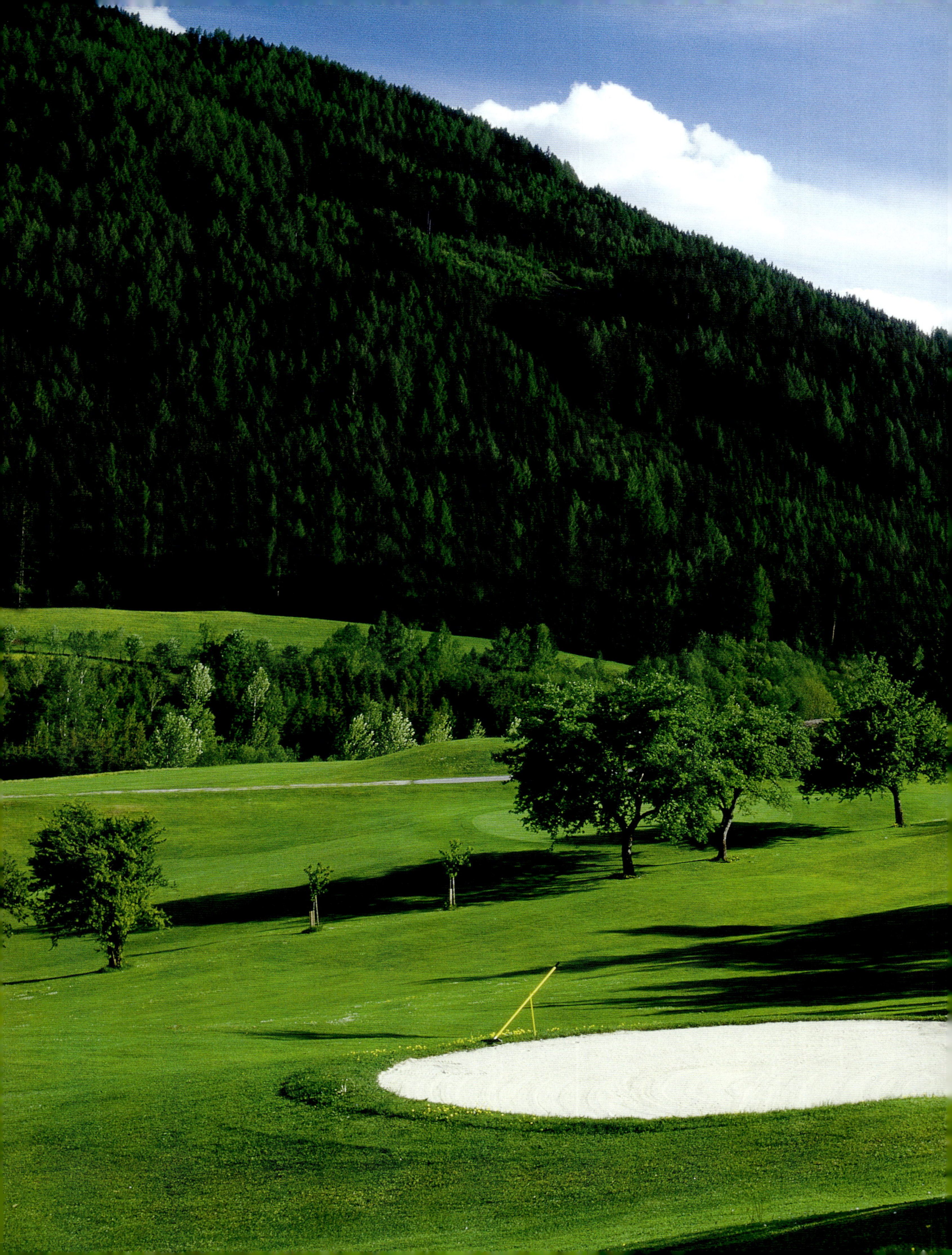

TRADITION UND LIFESTYLE

Tradition and lifestyle

GOLF IN ÖSTERREICH

Golf und Österreich haben vieles gemeinsam, nicht zuletzt ihr ausgeprägtes Verhältnis zur Tradition. Der Sport und das Alpenland haben aber auch längst ihre Offenheit für den modernen Lebensstil unter Beweis gestellt. Zwischen Donau und Gebirge ist eine attraktive Golfszene entstanden. Nicht selten hat sich die Natur dabei selbst zum Architekten der Plätze gemacht, oft trägt die Geschichte Österreichs nostalgisches Flair bei, so zum Beispiel beim Abschlag an einem alten Königsschloss in der Steiermark.

Golf and Austria have a lot in common not least its prominent bond with tradition. However the sport of golf and this alpine republic have long proved their openness for a more modern lifestyle as well. An attractive golfing scene has developed here between the Danube and the Alps. Quite often nature itself has become the principal architect of the courses. In addition Austria's history adds a nostalgic flair i.e. when one tees off next to a royal palace in the Steiermark.

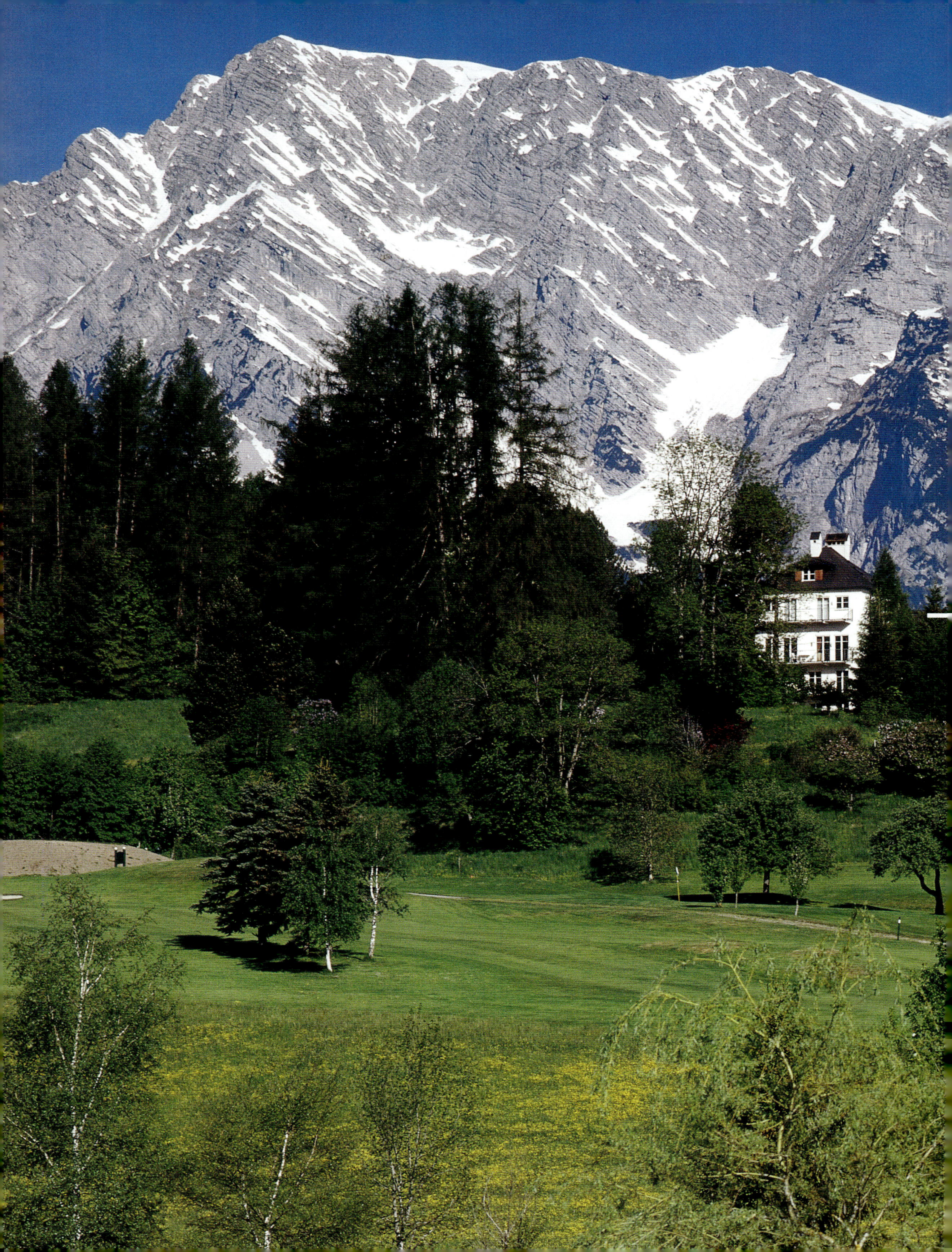

Hotel Schloss Pichlarn

GOLFERS GLÜCK IM SCHÖNEN ENNSTAL
GOLFERS JOY AT THE BEAUTIFUL ENNSTAL

Das exklusive Fünf-Sterne-Hotel Schloss Pichlarn liegt in einer der beeindruckendsten Gebirgs- und Kulturlandschaften Österreichs zwischen Schladming und dem Kloster Admont. Hier, in der Weite des wildromantischen Ennstals, verschmelzen Naturerlebnis, Gastlichkeit auf höchstem Niveau, Erholungssuche und sportliche Aktivitäten zu einem einzigartigen Ganzen. Insbesondere Golferherzen werden beim Anblick des Pichlarner 18-Loch-Platzes höher schlagen. Selbst Könner zollen dem Parcours gehörigen Respekt.

The exclusive five-star Hotel Schloss Pichlarn is in one of Austria's grandest and culturally most interesting mountain locations, between Schladming and the Admont Monastery. At the heart of the wildly romantic Ennstal, the beauty of nature, superb hospitality, relaxation and sporting activities are uniquely combined. Golfers will rejoice when they catch sight of the 18-hole course which commands a great deal of respect, even from experienced golfers.

TEXT: GUNDULA LUIG • FOTOS: YDO SOL

Eine wahrhaft königliche Residenz und eine der stilvollsten Hotelanlagen mit eigenem Meisterschaftsgolfplatz in Europa.

A truly regal residence with its own golf course. One of the most stylish hotel complexes in Europe.

It's one of those mornings one wants to last for ever, a cloudless sky and crystal clear air. One senses the day will be really warm. Nature is bursting out all over and there's the smell of freshly-mown grass. It's May. Very soon Steiermark, Austria's second largest state, will be an ocean of blue when the Iris Sibirica comes into bloom. This protected species of iris still is common to this largely unspoilt mountain region. The peak of Mt Grimming (7,711 ft) rises boldly into the sky. The massive mountain of numerous legends dominates the wild scenery of the Trog valley of the Enns. At its foot lies the unspoilt little market village of Irdning, and on a nearby hill one of the most beautiful golf resorts in the world welcomes its international clientèle – Schloss Pichlarn. The sunlight twinkles through the thick foliage of the 500 year-old linden tree in the palace yard. Standing beneath its boughs, I have the distinct feeling I'm drawing strength from it, such is its magical fascination. The tree is opposite the part of the building whose history reaches back into early mediaeval times, around 1074. Once upon a time the

Es ist einer dieser Morgen, die gar nicht lang genug andauern können. Wolkenloser Himmel, glasklare Luft, man spürt, dass es warm werden wird über Tag, die Natur strotzt vor Energie, der Duft frisch gemähten Grases steigt in die Nase – wir haben Mai. Nicht mehr lange, dann wird sich das Ennstal in Österreichs zweitgrößtem Bundesland, der Steiermark, in ein einziges blaues Blütenmeer verwandeln. Dann kommt die Zeit der Iris Sibirica, der unter Naturschutz stehenden Schwertlilie, die in dieser weitgehend noch intakten Gebirgslandschaft so reichlich anzutreffen ist. Kühn ragt der Felsklotz des Grimming 2351 Meter in die Höhe. Der mächtige, sagenumwobene Bergstock beherrscht mit seinen markanten Wandfluchten das wildromantische Trogtal der Enns. An seinem

Fuß liegt Irdning, ein ursprünglich gebliebenes Marktdorf, an dessen Ortsgrenze, auf einer Anhöhe, eines der weltweit schönsten Golfresorts seine internationalen Gäste empfängt: Schloss Pichlarn.

Die Sonne blinzelt durch das dichte Laubwerk der über 500-jährigen Linde im Schlosshof. Ich hab' das Gefühl, sie gibt mir Kraft, wenn ich drunterstehe. Eine faszinie-

nobility of Bavaria, Austria and Italy lived within these royal walls with their imposing round towers. Today this stylish hotel which combines tradition and contemporary hôtelérie at its very best, is one of the most sought-after residences in Europe. Whether the historic drawing rooms or the stylish restaurants, the elegant conference rooms or the romantic park, the unique ambience of the place is present in every corner. The historic cross-vaulting in entrance hall is an early indication of the hotel's majestic style. When you enter the "Red Drawing Room" you find a comfortable, palatial room with sumptuously upholstered red armchairs, old paintings on the walls and beautiful parquet flooring. It is an ideal place to relax with a good book and your afternoon coffee, or as a venue for a champagne reception before the main event. The drawing room opens out on to the sun-terrace of the bar which has a fantastic views of the valley, the golf course's driving range and the towering Mt. Grimming. Golf is central to Schloss Pichlarn. The 18-hole championship golf course is considered to be a real challenge in golf circles. It is a demanding course and is special because of the hills, valleys and woods of its terrain. Golf architect Donald Harradine had no trouble incorporating the natural environ-

Herrschaftlich residieren Gäste in der zauberhaften Präsidentensuite mit einmaligem Blick auf den majestätischen Grimming und die Driving Range.

Guests in the charming Presidential Suite live like royalty. The suite has wonderful views of the majestic Mt. Grimming and the driving range.

ment of Ennstal into his design for the golf course. It is true to say that nature itself was the architect. The resulting course (Par/SSS 72) was to prove a testing one, even for professionals. Incidentally the course record is currently held by Bernhard Langer who completed the course in 66, under par. The high points of the golf season which lasts from April to October, are the traditional events such as the Schloss Pichlarn Pro-Am and the Schloss Pichlarn Summer and Autumn Golf Week. The golf takes place within a framework of big events hosted by international companies including a whole range of other golf tournaments. Yet, Schloss Pichlarn is the right place to come for someone who has never even stood on a golf course. The hotel's own golf academy caters for beginners as well as for experienced golfers keen on improving their technique. The centrally located practice area has putting, chipping

rende Magie geht von diesem eindrucksvollen Baum aus. Vis-à-vis der historische Teil des Schlosses, dessen Geschichte bis ins frühe Mittelalter um 1074 zurückreicht. Einst residierten in dem königlichen Gemäuer mit den beiden prägnanten Rundtürmen höchste Würdenträger aus Bayern, Österreich und Italien. Heute zählt die stattliche Festung zu den gefragtesten und stilvollsten Hotelanlagen ihrer Art in Europa, denn sie verbindet Tradition mit zeitgemäßer Hotelkultur auf Top-Niveau. Ob in den historischen Salons oder in den stilvollen Restaurants, in den eleganten Konferenzräumlichkeiten bis hin zu den romantischen Parkanlagen – das außergewöhnliche Ambiente ist in jedem Winkel spürbar. Schon die Eingangshalle mit ihren historischen Kreuzgewölben lässt den königlichen Stil des Hauses erahnen. Man geht auf den „Roten Salon" zu, einen gemütlichen Raum mit Schlosscharakter, rot und üppig gepolsterten Fauteuilles, einer Galerie alter Exponate an den Wänden, herrlichem Parkett. Genau der richtige Ort zum Entspannen, für den Nachmittagskaffe, ein gutes Buch oder den kleinen Sektempfang bei Veranstaltungen. Vom Salon

tritt man auf die Sonnenterrasse der Bar, von wo aus sich ein traumhafter Blick auf das Tal, die Driving Range des Golfplatzes und den mächtigen Grimming auftut.

Der grüne Sport spielt auf Schloss Pichlarn eine wesentliche Rolle. Die 18-Loch-Meisterschaftsanlage gilt als Herausforderung in Golferkreisen. Sie ist anspruchsvoll zu spie-

Clubcharakter im englischen Stil: die elegante Cigar Lounge.

The elegant Cigar Lounge in the style of an English gentlemen's club.

242 HIDEAWAYS

len und besticht durch die natürliche Struktur ihrer Hügel, Täler und Wälder. Golfarchitekt Donald Harradine hatte Anfang der 70er Jahre keine Mühe, die ursprünglichen Gegebenheiten des Ennstals für seine Platzgestaltung zu nutzen. Die Natur selbst spielte „Baumeister" und gestaltete einen Kurs, der mit seinen Par/SSS 72 dafür sorgt, dass sich selbst Profis immer wieder beweisen müssen. Platzrekord hält übrigens Bernhard Langer mit 66 Schlägen. Die Höhepunkte jeder Golfsaison zwischen April und Oktober sind traditionelle Events wie das „Schloss Pichlarn Pro-Am" sowie die „Schloss Pichlarn Sommer- und Herbstgolfwoche". Umrahmt werden diese Hightlights durch Großveranstaltungen internationaler Firmen und sportlich abwechslungsreiche Golftournaments. Auch wer noch nie auf einem Green gestanden hat, ist im steirischen Schlosshotel goldrichtig. Denn die Golfakademie ermöglicht sowohl Anfängern als auch Fortgeschrittenen auf den zentral gelegenen Übungseinheiten wie Putting-, Chipping- und Pitching Greens, Bunkeranlagen und 10 geräumigen Abschlagboxen das Golfspiel zu erlernen bzw. zu verbessern. Drei PGA-geprüfte Pro's unter der Leitung von Head Pro Alan Mitchell bieten mit einem umfangreichen Unterrichtsprogramm Trainingsmodelle für alle Leistungs- und Alters-

Feinste Regionalküche à la Kuntner: Kalbsmedaillons in der Bärlauchkruste auf Portweinglacé mit Grammelroulade.
The best of regional cuisine à la Kuntner – veal médaillons with a Bärlauch crust served with potatoe dumplings on a port wine glacé.

and pitching greens, bunkers and 10 places with sample space to practise your drive. Three qualified PGA pros under head pro, Alan Mitchell, run a wide range of courses for all levels so that it is possible for anyone to achieve the standard required to manage the feared 12th hole. One needs three gentle but not timid strokes trough narrow woodland clearings to reach the green of this par 5 hole. As well as golf, Pichlarn guests can play tennis on the three open-air and two indoor tennis courts or take advantage of the riding stables. The Schloss itself has an open air and an indoor swimming pool, a sauna, a steam bath, a whirlpool and a solarium. For generations, Schloss Pichlarn has epitomized hospitality, luxury and exclusivity. This tradition is faithfully continued by the hotel's General Managers, Christine and Stefan Frenzel who, together with their charming local staff, are utterly committed to providing outstanding personal care and attention. The delightful rooms and suites contribute greatly to the total sense of well-being that one feels. Not only do the interiors radiate a warmth and harmony, they convey a regal milieu as do the grand Presidential Suites. Some are classically furnished, others are contemporary in style but all have the latest mod cons. A most successful architectural solution has been found to link the historic castle building of the hotel and the extension housing the accommodation and

Jung, dynamisch und erfolgreich: Küchenchef Rainhard Kuntner und Restaurantleiter Boris Janbay.
Young, dynamic and successful – head chef Rainhard Kuntner with Boris Janbay, restaurant manager.

Die runden Schlosstürme gelten als Stilelemente mittelalterlicher Baukunst. Architektonisch verbinden sie alt und neu.
Mediaeval in style, the round towers are the architectural elements linking the old with the new.

the new Royal Congress and Media Centre. It goes without saying that cuisine is an integral element of sophisticated living, and Rainhard Kuntner from Steiermark, provides it. The castle's dynamic young chef whose superb cooking has already been awarded two Gault Millau toques blanches, earned his laurels at such illustrious houses as Schloss Fuschl and Hotel Klosterbräu in Seefeld. His menus range from international dishes to local fare. He serves up Steiermark specialities as light tasty dishes with an imaginative touch. For instance, his filet of beef with boletus edulis in truffle butter served on a bed of mixed vegetables with potato dumplings, or fish on a celery purée with whipped apple-horseradish and little parcels of beetroot. The dishes are served in the Stüberl, Schloss Pichlarn's à la carte restaurant where hunting trophies on the walls and the obligatory tiled stove create a rustic elegance. In summer the big attraction is the garden terrace where guests can have light dishes such as tuna fish and a sesame sweet potato salsa served with Chinese noodles and king prawns. Obviously the menu includes all the classic Austrian dishes – Vienna soured boiled rump with apple-horseradish, chives sauce and creamed kohlrabi and fried potatoes. To accompany the meal, the castle's ancient cellar stocks a select choice of wine ranging from the best local wines to ones from France, Italy and even farther afield. The cellarer lavishes care on his great Austrian wines. Half-board guests are equally provided for. The Wintergarten restaurant is light and airy and has a terrace with lovely views of the forest. Schloss Pichlarn has one more feature which sets it apart – its exclusive Ayurveda health centre which offers the whole range of ayurvedic therapies. The Pancha Karma focuses on the cleansing and regeneration of the whole person. This set of gentle treatments administered under the guidance of the experienced ayurvedic practitioner, Dr. Hans Schäffler, bring relief from the stresses and strains of daily life and the frenzied world of work. Guests experience their stay at

gruppen. Damit man sich irgendwann auch einmal an das gefürchtete Loch 12 heranwagen kann. Man braucht drei gefühlvolle, aber nicht zaghafte Schläge, um letztendlich durch enge Waldpassagen hindurch das Green dieses Par-5-Loches zu erreichen. Als Ergänzung zum Golfsport und erweitertes Sportangebot stehen den Pichlarn-Gästen noch zusätzlich drei Tennisfrei- und zwei Tennishallenplätze sowie eine Reitanlage zur Verfügung. Im Schloss selbst befinden sich Frei- und Hallenbad, Sauna, Dampfsauna, Whirlpool und Solarium. Schloss Pichlarn ist seit Generationen Inbegriff für Gastlichkeit, Komfort und Exklusivität. Diese Tradition lebt mit dem engagierten Direktorenpaar Christine und Stefan Frenzel weiter, die zusammen mit ihren einheimischen Mitarbeitern und österreichischem Charme diese Form des Verwöhnt- und Umsorgtwerdens perfekt kultivieren. Einen entscheidenden Beitrag zum Rundumwohlfühlen leisten die zauberhaften Zimmer und Suiten. Sie strahlen Gemütlichkeit und Harmonie aus, vermitteln ein königliches Flair, wie die großzügige Präsidenten-Suite, sind mal mit klassischen, mal mit modernen Interieurs stilvoll eingerichtet und lassen an zeitgemäßem Komfort nicht mangeln. Auch die architektonische Gratwanderung zwischen historischem Schloss und dem Anbau von Zimmertrakt und dem neuen

Mit großem Aufwand wird die Pichlarner Golfanlage täglich von mehreren Greenkeepern gepflegt.

Several greenkeepers are occupied each day keeping the Pichlarn golf course in immaculate condition.

„Königlichen Kongress- & Medienzentrum" erscheint überaus gelungen. Denn die Stilelemente mittelalterlicher Baukunst (z. B. die runden Türme) werden im Neubau wieder aufgegriffen. Zur feinen Lebensart gehört selbstverständlich auch eine entsprechende Cuisine. Und die ist auf dem Schloss von zwei Gault-Millau-Hauben gekrönt. Rainhard Kuntner, der junge dynamische Steirer Küchenchef, der seine Lorbeeren in so renommierten Häusern wie Schloss Fuschl und Hotel Klosterbräu in Seefeld verdient hat, zelebriert eine feine Küche. Sie variiert zwischen international und heimisch. Vor allem steirische Spezialitäten setzt er phantasievoll, leicht und schmackhaft in Szene. So etwa das mit Steinpilzen gratinierte Rinderfiletsteak in Trüffelbutter an buntem Gemüse und Erdäpfel-Grammelroulade oder zweierlei Waller auf Selleriepüree in Apfel-Krenschaum mit rotem Rübentascherl. Man genießt sie im rustikal-eleganten „Stüberl", dem A-la-carte-Restaurant von Schloss Pichlarn, dessen Jagdtrophäen an den Wänden und der obligatorische Kachelofen für vollkommenes Steirer Flair sorgen. Im Sommer lockt der Terrassengarten nach draußen und während der heißen Tage bietet sich Leichtes wie gefüllter Thunfisch an Sesam-Süßkartoffelsalsa mit Glasnudeln und Riesengarnelen an. Natürlich fehlt auch der absolute Klassiker österreichischer Kochkunst nicht auf der Karte: gekochter Wiener Tafelspitz mit Apfelkren, Schnittlauchsauce, Rahmkohlrabi und Röstkartoffeln. Dazu hält der historische Schlosskeller Erlesenes aus besten heimischen, französischen, italienischen und Übersee-Lagen bereit. Mit besonderer Liebe pflegt der Kellermeister die großen Österreicher. Halbpensionsgäste speisen nicht weniger niveauvoll. Das Restaurant „Wintergarten" wartet mit freundlich heller Ambiance, Terrasse und wundervollem Waldblick auf. Und noch etwas macht Schloss Pichlarn einmalig: Sein exklusives Ayurveda-Gesundheitszentrum, das das gesamte Spektrum ayurvedischer Therapien anbietet. Im Mittelpunkt steht „Pancha Karma", ein Set sanfter Behandlungen zur Reinigung und Regeneration des gesamten Menschen. Die Behandlungen unter Leitung des erfahrenen Ayurveda-Arztes Dr. Hans Schäffler bringen weg vom Alltäglichen und vom Beruf, weg von Hektik und Stress. Kurgäste erleben einen Urlaub, der die Seele, den Körper und den Geist beflügelt, in einer der schönsten Regionen Europas. Und wieder zu Hause, wird man sich noch lange erinnern an die Morgen, die gar nicht lange genug andauern können, an den oft wolkenlosen Himmel, die glasklare Luft, den Duft frisch gemähten Grases und die alte Linde, der man magische Kräfte nachsagt.

Schloss Pichlarn as a vacation for body, soul and spirit in one of the most beautiful regions in Europe. When they leave they take with them cherished memories of mornings which were simply not long enough, cloudless skies, crystal clear air, freshly-mown grass and the old linden tree said to have magical powers.

Pflegen die Tradition von Gastlichkeit, Komfort und Exklusivität: Christine und Stefan Frenzel.

Christine and Stefan Frenzel continue the hotel's traditional hospitality in exclusive luxurious surroundings.

ÜBERSICHT DER HOTELS

Almenara Golf Hotel & Spa

Direktor: Santiago Cabré
Avenida Almenara s/n
E-11310 Sotogrande (Cadiz)
Telefon: 00 34 / 9 56 / 58 20 00
Telefax: 00 34 / 9 56 / 58 20 01
E-Mail: almenara.hotel@sotogrande.com

Meernah im Westen Andalusiens, eine Autostunde von den Flughäfen Malaga und Jerez de la Frontera sowie 15 Minuten vom Flughafen Gibraltar entfernt.

140 Standardzimmer und 10 Suiten. Zimmerpreise: DZ ab 144 Euro, Junior Suite ab 210 Euro, Suite ab 355 Euro, Frühstück 15 Euro, alle Preise zzgl. 7 % Steuern.

Voll ausgestatteter Spa auf 1000 m² Fläche, Spa Pool, Finnische Sauna, Türkisches Bad, Hairstylist, Gym & Kraftraum u.v.m. Außenpool, separater Kinderpool, 18-Loch-Golfplatz (27 im Laufe des Jahres), Golf Academy, Tennisplätze.

Drei Restaurants mit gesunder mediterraner Küche, in denen neben internationalen Gerichten lokale Spezialitäten frisch auf den Tisch kommen.

Das Klima ist mild und trocken bei Höchsttemperaturen über 30 °C im Juli/August, im Winter kaum unter 18 °C bei z. T. kalten Nächten.

Neben der LTU bedienen u.a. Condor, Hapag-Lloyd und Air Berlin die Strecke nach Malaga.

Auto- und Helikoptervermietung, 2 Banketträume von je 120 m².

Kempinski Estepona

Ctra. de Cádiz, Km. 159
Playa El Padrón
E-29680 Estepona (Málaga)
Telefon: 00 34 / 95 / 2 80 95 00
Telefax: 00 34 / 95 / 2 80 95 50
E-Mail: agp.reservation@kempinski.com
Internet: www.kempinski-spain.com

Im Westen Andalusiens, direkt am Strand der spanischen Costa del Sol.

Alle 131 Zimmer und Suiten haben einen privaten Balkon mit Meeresblick. Preis je nach Saison und Kategorie für ein Doppelzimmer von 29 000 – 50 000 Pesetas, Suiten von 46 500 – 300 000 Pesetas (100 Pesetas = 1,18 DM).

1 Innen- und 3 Außenpools, Tennisplatz, Wassersport-Center, Fitnessraum. Das Polly Mar bietet auf über 1000 m² ein breit gefächertes Angebot an Entspannungs- und Beautyprogrammen. Reitzentrum in direkter Nachbarschaft.

Im Kempinski-Restaurant wird eine gehobene „Cuisine légère" serviert.

Das subtropische Klima macht die Costa del Sol zu einem Ganzjahresziel, Hauptsaison von Ende April bis Mitte Oktober.

40 Fahrminuten vom Flughafen Malaga und 45 Fahrminuten vom Flughafen Gibraltar. Limousinen-Service auf Anfrage.

Angeschlossenes Medico-Center mit einer Vielzahl medizinischer Therapieangebote.

Las Dunas Beach Hotel & Spa

Crta. Cádiz, km 163,5
La Boladilla Baya
E-29689 Estepona (Málaga)
Telefon: 00 34 / 5 / 2 79 43 45
Telefax: 00 34 / 5 / 2 79 48 25

Las Dunas liegt unmittelbar am Strand zwischen Marbella und Estepona.

75 luxuriöse Zimmer und Suiten im mediterranen Stil mit Terrasse oder Balkon. Preise je nach Saison: Doppelzimmer mit Einzelbelegung 250,– bis 390,– DM, Doppelzimmer 320,– bis 480,– DM, Suiten 460,– bis 2 100,– DM, Las Dunas Suites: 28 Deluxe-Residenzen mit 1–3 Schlafzimmern, 1–2 Bädern und Küche, ab 140 000,– Pts. pro Woche.

27 Golfplätze in der näheren Umgebung, 40 Plätze an der gesamten Costa del Sol, besondere Konditionen im zehn Minuten entfernten La Quinta Golf & Country Club; Jet Skiing, Wasserski, Katamaransegeln, Paragliding; Regena Sol Clinic und Spa-Bereich.

Exquisite Gourmet-Cuisine, Supervisor: Zwei-Sterne-Koch Heinz Winkler, Residenz Aschau.

Das subtropische Klima macht die Costa del Sol zu einem Ganzjahresziel. Die Hauptsaison geht von Ende April bis Mitte Oktober. Golfer schätzen die hervorragende Bespielbarkeit der Plätze im Winter.

Zahlreiche Fluggesellschaften bieten von Frankfurt, Berlin, Düsseldorf, München, Wien und Zürich täglich Direktflüge nach Malaga an. Autotransfer von dort ca. 45 Minuten.

SUMMARY OF THE HOTELS

Almenara Golf Hotel & Spa

General Manager: Santiago Cabré
Avenida Almenara s/n
E-11310 Sotogrande (Cadiz)
Telephone: 00 34 / 9 56 / 58 20 00
Telefax: 00 34 / 9 56 / 58 20 01
E-mail: almenara.hotel@sotogrande.com

Near the sea in west Andalusia, an hour's drive from Malaga airports and Jerez de la Frontera, and 15 minutes from Gibraltar airport.

140 standard rooms and 10 suites. Double room from 144 Euro, Junior Suite from 210 Euro, Suite from 355 Euro, breakfast 15 Euro, all rates plus 7 % tax.

Fully equipped Spa with an area of nearly 11,000 sq. ft. Spa pool, Finnish sauna, Turkish bath, hair stylist, Gym and body-building studio and much else. Outdoor pool, 18-hole golf course (being extended to 27-hole this year), Golf Academy, tennis courts.

Three restaurants serving healthy Mediterranean cuisine including international and local dishes.

Dry, mild climate. Maximum temperature over 30 degree centigrade in July and August, in winter seldom below 18 degrees even when the nights are cold.

As well as LTU, Condor, Hapag-Lloyd and Air Berlin fly to Malaga.

Car and helicopter hire, 2 banqueting rooms each nearly 1,300 sq. ft. in area.

Kempinski Estepona

Ctra. de Cádiz Km. 159
Playa El Padrón
E-29680 Estepona (Málaga)
Telephone: 00 34 / 95 / 2 80 95 00
Telefax: 00 34 / 95 / 2 80 95 50
E-mail: agp.reservation@kempinski.com
Internet: www.kempinski-spain.com

Located in the West of Andalusia, directly on the beach of the Spanish Costa del Sol.

Each of the 131 rooms and 17 suites has a private balcony with a sea view. Depending on season and category, the price for a double room ranges from 29,000 – 50,000 pesetas and for a suite from 46,500 – 300,000 pesetas (100 peseta = DM 1.18).

Indoor and outdoor pools, tennis court, watersports centre, fitness room. The Polly Mar offers a wide range of relaxation and beauty programmes in an area of more than 10,000 square feet. Riding centre is in the direct vicinity.

The Kempinski Restaurant serves gourmet "Cuisine légère".

The subtropical climate makes the Costa del Sol an all-year-round destination. The main season lasts from mid-April to mid-October.

40 minutes' drive from Malaga Airport and 45 minutes' drive from Gibraltar airport. Limousine service on request.

Adjoining medical centre offering a wide range of therapies.

Las Dunas Beach Hotel & Spa

Crta. Cádiz, km 163,5
La Boladilla Baya
E-29689 Estepona (Málaga)
Telephone: 00 34 / 5 / 2 79 43 45
Telefax: 00 34 / 5 / 2 79 48 25

Las Dunas lies directly on the beach between Marbella and Estepona.

75 luxurious rooms and suites in the Mediterranean style with terrace or balcony. Price according to the season: Double room with single occupancy 250,– to 390,– DM. Double room 320,– to 480,– DM. Suites 460,– to 2,100,– DM. Las Dunas Suites: 28 deluxe residences, 1–3 bedrooms, 1–2 bathrooms and kitchen, from Pts. 140 000,– per week.

27 golf courses in the near vicinity, 40 courses on the whole of the Costa del Sol, special privileges for guests at La Quinta Golf & Country Club 10 minutes away; Jet skiing, Water skiing, Katamaran sailing, Paragliding; Regena Sol Clinic and Spa.

Exquisite gourmet cuisine, Supervisor: Two-star-chef Heinz Winkler, Residenz Aschau.

The subtropical climate makes the Costa del Sol an all year destination. The high season is from the end of April to the middle of October. Golfers appreciate the excellent opportunity to play on the courses in winter.

Numerous airlines fly directly to Malaga daily from Frankfurt, Berlin, Düsseldorf, Munich, Vienna and Zürich. Transfer from there by car approx. 45 minutes.

ÜBERSICHT DER HOTELS

Ofra Resort Hotel Mallorca

General Manager: Birgit Angele
C/Arquitecto Francisco Casas, 18
E-07181 Portals Nous (Mallorca)
Telefon: 00 34 / 9 71 / 70 77 77
Telefax: 00 34 / 9 71 / 70 76 76
E-Mail: golf@ofra-resort-hotel.com
Internet: www.ofra-resort-hotel.com

Rund sieben Kilometer von Palma Stadt und zwei Kilometer vom Hafen Puerto Portals entfernt, im Herzen der eleganten Villenurbanisation Bendinat.

100 Zimmer und Suiten mit Terrasse oder Balkon, individuell regelbare Aircondition, Safe, Sat-TV, ISDN-Telefon, Direktwahl, Internetanschluss, Minibar, beheizbare Badspiegel und Handtuchhalter, Fön.
EZ 14 000 – 18 000 Pts., DZ 22 500 – 35 500 Pts., Suiten 35 500 – 54 500 Pts.

Anspruchsvolle 18-Loch-Golfanlage Real Golf de Bendinat direkt vor der Tür; Außen- und Innenpool, Fitnessstudio, Jacuzzi, Sauna, Dampfbad, Caldarium, Solarium, Massage; Frisör- und Beautysalon Aileen Mees.

Gourmetrestaurant „Es Romaní": mediterran inspiriert, mit spanischer und internationaler Küche. Pool-Restaurant Chumbo mit mexikanischen Snacks und coolen Drinks.

Ganzjähriges Reiseziel.

Von allen deutschen Airports aus bis Palma de Mallorca, z. B. mit Air Berlin. Von dort ca. 18 km Autobahn Richtung Andratx, Ausfahrt Portals Nous. Dann weiter Richtung Urbanisation Bendinat.

Ausgezeichnete Kinderbetreuung im hauseigenen Bendiclub.

Son Vida

Carrer de la Vinagrella s/n
E-07013 Palma de Mallorca
Telefon: 00 34 / 9 71 / 79 99 99
Telefax: 00 34 / 9 71 / 79 99 97
Gebührenfreie Reservierung:
00 800 325 45 45 45
E-Mail: arabella@readysoft.es
Internet: www.sheraton.com

Oberhalb der Inselhauptstadt Palma im noblen Villenvorort Son Vida.

Preise: 93 Zimmer, davon 24 Suiten und eine Präsidentensuite je nach Reisezeit und Ausstattung von 230,25 Euro bis 859,33 Euro pro Tag und Zimmer inklusive Frühstück. Zuschlag Halbpension pro Person 28,94 Euro.

18-Loch-Golfplatz Son Vida direkt am Haus, neuer 18-Loch-Golfplatz Son Muntaner in unmittelbarer Nähe. Pitch & Put-Platz, 5 Quarzsand-Tennisplätze, Croquet-Platz, Jogging-Track. Beautyfarm mit Produkten von Shiseido und Mary Cohr.

Gourmetrestaurant „Plat d'Or" mit feiner Mittelmeerküche, Restaurant „Foravila" mit Blick auf den Golfplatz.

Mallorca ist eine Ganzjahresdestination. Attraktive Angebote vom 1. 1. – 26. 2. und 18. 11. bis 23. 12. Im August kann es sehr heiß werden.

LTU, Condor, Hapag-Lloyd, Aero Llyod und Air Berlin bieten Direktflüge nach Palma von fast allen deutschen Flughäfen an.

Mitglied der „Luxury Collection" von Sheraton.

Dorint Golfresort & Spa Camp de Mar

General Manager: Bernard Meyer
Carreterra Camp de Mar
E-07160 Camp de Mar (Mallorca)
Telefon: 00 34 / 9 71 / 13 65 65
Telefax: 00 34 / 9 71 / 13 60 70
E-Mail: info@dorint.com

Im Südwesten der Sonneninsel Mallorca, eine Bucht vor Andratx. Inmitten einer 18-Loch-Championsship-Golfanlage; nur 300 Meter vom Badestrand.

162 Superior Deluxe Suiten (ca. 50 m² inkl. Terrasse) mit Meer- oder Golfplatzblick; stilvolle Interieurs, vollklimatisiert, Telefon, Faxanschluss, Safe, Radio Sat-TV, Pay-TV etc. Preise von 284,87 bis 332,96 Euro pro Zimmer inkl. Frühstück. Zwei repräsentative Präsidentensuiten, Preis auf Anfrage.

18-Loch-Golfanlage; Tauchen, Tennis, Reiten, Wandern, Mountainbike; Beautyfarm nach Dr. med. Erich Schulte, ästhetische Chirurgie; Outdoor-Pool, 1400 qm Wellnessoase mit Pool- und Saunalandschaft, Massage- und Bäderabteilung, Fitnessstudio.

Restaurant „El Mallorquín" mit superben Spezialitäten der Insel und Showküche. International speist man im A-la-carte-Restaurant „Mediterránea".

Ganzjähriges Reiseziel.

Von fast allen deutschen Flughäfen gehen täglich Direktflüge nach Palma de Mallorca.

Die Golfanlage zählt zu den anspruchsvollsten Spaniens und birgt interessante spielerische Herausforderungen.

SUMMARY OF THE HOTELS

Ofra Resort Hotel Mallorca

General Manager: Birgit Angele
C/Arquitecto Francisco Casas, 18
E-07181 Portals Nous (Majorca)
Telephone: 00 34 / 9 71 / 70 77 77
Telefax: 00 34 / 9 71 / 70 76 76
E-mail: golf@ofra-resort-hotel.com
Internet: www.ofra-resort-hotel.com

Just over four miles from the city of Palma and roughly one mile from the port of Puerto Portals, in the centre of Bendinat, the elegant residential area.

100 rooms and suites with terrace or balcony, self-regulated air-conditioning, safe, Sat-TV, ISDN-telephone, DDI telephone, Internet connection, minibar, heated bathroom mirror and towel rack, hairdryer. Single room 14 000 – 18 000 Pts, double room 22 500 – 35 500 Pts, suites 35 500 – 54 500 Pts.

Challenging 18-hole golf course, Real Golf de Bendinat just outside the door. Outdoor and indoor pools, fitness room, jacuzzi, sauna, steam bath, caldarium, solarium, massage, Hairdressing & Beauty Salon Aileen Mees.

Gourmet restaurant „Es Romani": Mediterranean inspired cuisine. Chumbo, the relaxed pool restaurant, serves Mexican snacks.

Best time to travel: All the year round.

From all German airports to Palma de Majorca, e.g. by Air Berlin. From the airport approx. 18 km on the motorway in the direction of Andratx. Exit Portals Nous. Continue in the direction of the residential district of Bendinat.

Excellent childcare facilities at the hotel's own Bendiclub.

Son Vida

Carrer de la Vinagrella s/n
E-07013 Palma de Mallorca
Telephone: 00 34 / 9 71 / 79 99 99
Telefax: 00 34 / 9 71 / 79 99 97
Reservations freecall:
00 800 325 45 45 45
E-mail: arabella@readysoft.es
Internet: www.sheraton.com

High above the island's capital, Palma, in the elegant residential area of Son Vida.

93 rooms of which 24 are suites and one Presidential Suite depending on time of year and furnishings.
From 230.25 to 859.33 Euro per room per day breakfast included. Surcharge for half board per person 28.94 Euro.

18-hole golf course Son Vida next to the house and the new 18-hole golf course, Son Muntaner, is nearby. Pitch and putting green, five hotel silica tennis courts, a croquet lawn, a jogging track, beauty farm with Shiseido and Mary Cohr products.

Gourmet restaurant "Plat d'Or" with exquisite Mediterranean cuisine, restaurant "Foravila" overlooking the golf course.

Majorca is a destination for all the year round. Attractive packages from 1. 1.– 26. 2. and 18. 11.–23. 12. In August it can get very hot.

LTU, Condor, Hapag-Lloyd, Aero Lloyd and Air Berlin offer direct flights to Palma from nearly all German airports.

Member of Sheraton's "Luxury Collection".

Dorint Golfresort & Spa Camp de Mar

General Manager: Bernard Meyer
Carreterra Camp de Mar
E-07160 Camp de Mar (Majorca)
Telephone: 00 34 / 9 71 / 13 65 65
Telefax: 00 34 / 9 71 / 13 60 70
E-mail: info@dorint.com

In the south-west of the sunny island of Majorca, beside a bay near Andratx. In the centre of 18-hole championship links approx. 320 years from the beach.

162 Superior de Luxe suites (approx. 538 sq. ft.) with views of either the sea or the golf course. Stylish interiors, air-conditioned throughout, telephone, fax, safe, radio, Sat TV, pay TV etc. Rates from 284.87 to 332.96 Euro per room, including breakfast. Two prestigious Presidential Suites, rates on request.

18-hole links, skin diving, tennis, rambling, mountain biking; Beauty farm based on the methods of Dr. Erich Schulte, aesthetic surgery; outdoor pool, wellness oasis of over 15,000 sq. ft. including pool and sauna area, massage and baths and a fitness gym.

"El Mallorquín" restaurant serving superb island specialities and a show kitchen. International cuisine is served in the à la carte "Mediterránea" restaurant.

Best time to travel: All the year round.

Direct flights to Palma de Majorca daily from nearly all German airports.

The golf course, one of the most demanding in Spain, provides interesting challenges.

ÜBERSICHT DER HOTELS

La Reserva Rotana

Cami de S'Avall. K.M. 3
Apartado Correos 69
E-07500 Manacor (Mallorca)
Telefon: 00 34 / 71 / 84 56 85 - 84 56 86
Telefax: 00 34 / 71 / 55 52 58

La Reserva Rotana liegt drei Kilometer westlich von Manacor, zwanzig Autominuten von Portocristo und der Ostküste entfernt.

14 Einzel- und Doppelzimmer, Suiten und Juniorsuiten im exklusiven mallorquinischen Landhausstil, teilweise mit eigenem Garten oder mit Terrasse zum Außenpool.
Preise von ca. 360,– bis 600,– DM inklusive Frühstück.

Innen- und Außenpool, Reiten, privater 9-Loch-Golfplatz exklusiv für Hausgäste, eigener Pro, fünf 18-Loch-Golfplätze in nächster Umgebung.

Mediterrane Gourmet-Cuisine, Weinkarte mit spanischem Schwerpunkt und mallorquinischen Kreszenzen. Das Restaurant mit Patio zählt zu Mallorcas feinen Adressen.

Mediterranes Klima mit trockenen heißen Sommern und milden Wintern. Als Ganzjahresziel speziell auch für Golfer attraktiv.

LTU, Lufthansa, Condor, Hapag-Lloyd, Aero Lloyd und Air Berlin decken Direktflüge nach Palma von fast allen deutschen Flughäfen ab. Auch im Winter mehrmals wöchentlich. Im Sommer fliegen LTU und Hapag-Lloyd von Düsseldorf aus täglich. Vom Airport in ca. 45 Minuten mit dem Mietwagen zum Hotel.

Exklusive Zuflucht im authentisch restaurierten Finca-Stil. Geheimtipp für Golfer.

Quinta do Lago

General Manager: Sandro Fabris
P-8135-024 Almancil (Algarve)
Telefon: 00 351 / 2 89 / 35 03 50
Telefax: 00 351 / 2 89 / 39 63 93
E-Mail: info@quintadolagohotel.com
Internet: www.quintadolagohotel.com

Etwa 30 Autominuten vom Flughafen Faro entfernt an der Lagune des Naturschutzgebietes Ria Formosa.

141 elegant im mediterranen Stil gestaltete Zimmer und Suiten. Alle mit großen Terrassen und Balkonen, größtenteils mit Meeresblick. Zimmer je nach Saison von 175 – 409 Euro; Suiten von 434 – 758 Euro.

3 Golfplätze auf der Quinta-do-Lago-Anlage, eigener PGA Golf Pro vom Hotel, 7 weitere Plätze in nächster Umgebung; 2 beheizte Pools (innen und außen), 1 Strandbasis, Tennis, Wasserski; Sauna, Massage; Beauty-Behandlungen.

Ein Gourmetrestaurant mit superber venezianischer Küche. Ein elegantes Restaurant mit internationaler und portugiesischer Küche.

Die Algarve ist aufgrund ihrer 3 000 Sonnenstunden jährlich und wegen der milden Wintertemperaturen ganzjährig ein angenehmes Reiseziel.

Von Düsseldorf direkt mit LTU nach Faro. Anschließend ca. 30 Minuten Limousinen-Transfer zum Hotel, wenn gewünscht.

Mitglied der „Leading Hotels of the World".

Vila Joya

Buchungen:
Vila Joya
Postfach 80 09 44
D-81609 München
Telefon: 0 89 / 6 49 33 37
Telefax: 0 89 / 6 49 26 36

Portugiesische Algarveküste, eine halbe Autostunde vom Flughafen Faro entfernt.

Maurisch anmutender Palazzo mit 12 Doppelzimmern und 5 Suiten. Doppelzimmer von 300,– DM bis 350,– DM, 3 Junior Suiten von 390,– bis 510,– DM, die „1001-Nacht-Suite", „Royal Suite 2001" jeweils ab 600,– DM. Preise pro Person im Doppelzimmer, inklusive Frühstück und (Gala-) Dinner.

Großer Swimmingpool. Angeln, segeln, tauchen, Wasserski, Parasegeln im Atlantik. Einige der 15 schönsten Golfplätze Portugals (18–36 Holes) liegen in der Nähe.

Klassische französische Gourmet-Cuisine mit täglich wechselndem Menü, mit Akzent auf frischem Fisch der Region.

Ganzjährig subtropisches, durch ständige Brisen gemildertes Klima. Über dreihundert Sonnentage.

Sowohl Hapag-Lloyd als auch Condor und LTU fliegen Faro an.

Bestes Restautrant Portugals, 2-Michelin-Sterne. Konferenzraum ab 25 Personen.

SUMMARY OF THE HOTELS

La Reserva Rotana

Cami de S'Avall. K.M. 3
Apartado Correos 69
E-07500 Manacor (Majorca)
Telephone:
00 34 / 71 / 84 56 85 - 84 56 86
Telefax: 00 34 / 71 / 55 52 58

La Reserva Rotana is located three kilometres west of Manacor, twenty minutes drive from Portocristo and the east coast.

14 single and double rooms, suites and junior suites in exclusive Majorcan country house style, some with their own gardens or with a terrace leading to the outdoor pool.
Prices from approx. DM 360,- to DM 600,- including breakfast.

Indoor and outdoor pools, riding, private 9-hole golf course for the exclusive use of residents, own professional golf coach, five 18-hole golf courses in the immediate vicinity.

Mediterranean gourmet cuisine, wine list with a Spanish flavour and Majorcan wines. The restaurant with patio is one of Majorca's most exclusive culinary venues.

Mediterranean climate with dry, hot summers and mild winters. Attractive for golfers all the year round.

LTU, Lufthansa, Condor, Hapag-Lloyd, Aero Lloyd and Air Berlin all offer direct flights to Palma from nearly all German airports. Also in winter flights several times weekly. In the summer LTU and Hapag-Lloyd fly daily from Düsseldorf. The journey from the airport to the hotel takes about 45 minutes in a hired car.

Exclusive refuge in authentically restored Spanish country house style.
Confidential tip for golfers.

Quinta do Lago

General Manager: Sandro Fabris
P-8135-024 Almancil (Algarve)
Telephone: 00 351 / 2 89 / 35 03 50
Telefax: 00 351 / 2 89 / 39 63 93
E-mail: info@quintadolagohotel.com
Internet: www.quintadolagohotel.com

About 30 minutes by car from Faro Airport, beside a lagoon of the Ria Formosa nature conservancy area.

141 elegant rooms in Mediterranean style, all with large terraces and balconies, most with sea views. Rooms depending on season from 175 to 409 Euro; suites from 434 to 758 Euro.

3 golf courses on the Quinta do Lago estate, hotel's own PGA golf pro, 7 more courses in the vicinity; 2 heated pool (indoor and outside), 1 beach base, tennis, water skiing; sauna, massage; beauty treatments.

A gourmet restaurant serving superb Venetian dishes. Elegant restaurant with international and Portuguese cuisine.

Owing to its 3000 hours of sun a year and its mild winter temperatures, it is a pleasant holiday destination all the year round.

Direct LTU flight from Düsseldorf to Faro, then a 30 minute transfer to the hotel in a limousine if required.

Member of "The Leading Hotels of the World".

Vila Joya

Reservations:
Vila Joya
P. O. Box 80 09 44
D-81609 Munich
Telephone: 00 49 89 / 6 49 33 37
Telefax: 00 49 89 / 6 49 26 36

Beachside location in the Portugese Algarve, half an hour's drive from Faro Airport.

Moorish style Palazzo with 12 double rooms and 5 suites. Prices: double room from DM 300,- to DM 350,-, 3 Junior Suites from DM 390,- to DM 510,-, "1001 Nights Suite", "Royal Suite 2001", each from DM 600,-. All prices are per person and include breakfast, (Gala) dinner.

Large heated swimming pool. Angling, sailing, skin-diving, water skiing, parasailing in the Atlantic close by. Some of the 15 best golf courses (18–36 holes) in Portugal are in the immediate vicinity.

Classical French cuisine, daily charge of menue, accent in fresh fish of the region.

Subtropical climate moderated by steady breezes all the year round. Over 300 sunny days.

As well as Hapag-Lloyd, Condor and LTU also fly to Faro.

Best restaurant in Portugal, 2 Michelin stars, Confèrence room.

ÜBERSICHT DER HOTELS

Vila Vita Parc

General Manager: Luís de Camões
Apartado 196
P-8365-911 Armação de Pêra (Algarve)
Telefon: 00 351 / 2 82 / 31 01 00
Telefax: 00 351 / 2 82 / 31 53 33
E-Mail: vilavitaparc@mail.telepac.pt
Internet: www.vilavitaparc.com
& vilavitahotels.com

An der algarvischen Steilküste zwischen Portimão und Faro auf einem 24 Hektar großen Privatgrundstück.

189 Zimmer, Suiten und Appartements in sechs verschiedenen Anlagen, die ein weitläufiges Dorf bilden. Je nach gewählter Unterkunft und Saison von 117 – 276 Euro (Einzelzimmer) und 146 – 1035 Euro pro Person.

2 Badestrände, beheiztes Hallenbad, Pools, Jacuzzis; Golf, Tennis, Squash, Boccia, Minigolf, Wasserski, Windsurfen, Katamaran; Vila Vita Vital Center.

6 Restaurants präsentieren eine unschlagbare Vielfalt an Gerichten und Weinen. 7 Bars, sehenswerter Weinkeller.

Durchschnittliche Wintertemperatur liegt bei 15 °C und ist für passionierte Golfer besonders reizvoll.

Der Flughafen Faro hat internationale Anbindung. Von Düsseldorf fliegt LTU. Abholung vom Airport mit hoteleigener Limousine möglich.

Die Anlage ist sehr familienfreundlich.

Burj Al Arab

P.O. Box 74147
Dubai
Vereinigte Arabische Emirate, U.A.E.
Telefon: 00 971 / 4 / 3 01 77 77
Telefax: 00 971 / 4 / 3 01 70 00
Internet: www.burj-al-arab.com

Burj Al Arab, 321 Meter hoch, liegt in Dubai, einem der sieben Vereinigten Arabischen Emirate, 15 Kilometer südlich der Stadt Dubai.

202 prachtvolle doppelstöckige Suiten mit allem erdenklichen Luxus vom persönlichen Butler bis zum Check-in/Checkout in der Suite. Die beiden Royal Suiten im 25. Stock bieten das Optimum, 780 qm Wohnfläche, eigenen Lift, eigenes Kino, drehbare Betten, goldene Treppen etc. Preise von 3 300 Dirhams bis 25 000 Dirhams (1 US $ = 3,50 Dirhams).

Der Healthclub geht über zwei Etagen, ist verschwenderisch dekoriert im Stil traditioneller arabischer Bäder. Top-professionelle Crew bietet alles an Entspannungs-, Vitalisierungs- und Beautybehandlungen.

Feine mediterrane Küche im Al Muntaha, 220 m über dem Meer; ausgezeichnetes Seafood im Al Mahara, unter dem Meeresspiegel; libanesische und internationale Gourmet-Cuisine im Al Iwan.

Subtropisches Klima mit Sonne und wolkenlosem Himmel übers ganze Jahr. Nur wenige Tage Regen. Beste Reisezeit im Winter, das heißt von Oktober bis Ende April.

HIDEAWAYS empfiehlt Emirates, z. B. von Frankfurt, München, Manchester täglich einmal, London täglich viermal, Paris, Mailand und Athen dreimal wöchentlich, Zürich fünfmal wöchentlich, Rom sechsmal wöchentlich.

Das derzeit höchste und eines der spektakulärsten Hotels der Welt.

Fancourt Hotel

Buchungen:
Fancourt Hotel and Country Club Estate
P.O. Box 2266
George 6530, South Africa
Telefon: 00 27 / 44 / 8 04 00 00
Telefax: 00 27 / 44 / 8 04 07 00
E-Mail: hotel@fancourt.co.za
Internet: www.fancourt.co.za

In der Nähe von George in Südafrika, eine halbe Autostunde von den bildschönen Stränden des Indischen Ozeans entfernt.

30 Zimmer und Suiten im historischen Manor House, ausgestattet mit antikem Mobiliar (1000 – 1500 Rand), 70 Garden-Suiten mit bis zu drei Schlafzimmern, zweckmäßig mit Küche ausgestattet (1 540 – 3 465 Rand).
Ein Rand entspricht ca. DM 0,30.

Fancourt ist der Inbegriff für Golf in Südafrika schlechthin. 3 x 18 Lochplatz auf mehr als 500 Hektar Gelände. Hervorragendes Health & Beauty Centre mit modernem Fitness-Gym für gesundheitsbewusste Gäste.

Fünf Restaurants mit lokalen und internationalen Kreationen erster Güte, darunter südafrikanische, asiatische, italienische und französische Küche.

Ausgeglichenes klares „kanarisches" Klima das ganze Jahr hindurch: Heiße Sommer (Weihnachten) und milde Winter, durchschnittliche Tageshöchsttemperaturen: Juli bis 20 °C, Dezember um 30 °C.

Neben South African Airways wird Kapstadt von zahlreichen namhaften Fluggesellschaften angeflogen, darunter Lufthansa, KLM, Air France, British Airways und LTU.

Kostenloser 24-Stunden-Internetzugang für die Gäste.

SUMMARY OF THE HOTELS

Vila Vita Parc

General Manager: Luís de Camões
Apartado 196
P-8365-911 Armação de Péra (Algarve)
Telephone: 00 3 51 / 2 82 / 31 01 00
Telefax: 00 351 / 2 82 / 31 53 33
E-mail: vilavitaparc@mail.telepac.pt
Internet: www.vilavitaparc.com
& www.vilavitahotels.com

Situated on the cliffs of the Algarve coast between Portimão and Faro in sixty acres of private grounds.

189 rooms and apartments at six luxurious, individual sites form a sprawling village. Depending on type of accommodation and season, 117 – 276 Euros (single rooms) and 146 – 1035 Euro per person.

2 beaches, heated indoor swimming pool, pools, jacuzzis; golf, tennis, squash, boccia, minigolf, water skiing, windsurfing, catamaran, deep sea fishing; Vila Vita Vital Center.

6 restaurants offer an unbeatable diversity of dishes and wines. 7 bars, a wine cellar worth seeing.

The average temperature in winter is 15 °C so is particularly good for passionate golfers.

Faro Airport has international links. LTU flies from Düsseldorf. Collection from the airport by the hotel's own limousine is possible.

The resort is very family-friendly.

Burj Al Arab

P.O. Box 74147
Dubai
United Arab Emirates, U.A.E.
Telephone: 00 971 / 4 / 3 01 77 77
Telefax: 00 971 / 4 / 3 01 70 00
Internet: www.burj-al-arab.com

The 321 metre-high Burj Al Arab is in Dubai, one of the seven United Arab Emirates, and is 15 kms south of Dubai.

202 magnificent two-storey suites equipped with every conceivable luxury, from a personal butler, check-in and checkout in the suite. Each of the Royal Suites on the 25th floor has optimum space – 780 square metres, its own lift, a cinema, revolving bed and a golden staircase etc. Rates from 3,300 Dirhams to 25,000 Dirhams (1 US $ = 3.50 Dirhams).

The Health Club is on two floors and is lavishly decorated in the style of traditional Arab baths. Top professionals offer every conceivable treatment for relaxation and vitalization.

Excellent Mediterranean cuisine is served in the Al Muntaha, 220 metres above the sea. Below sea level seafood is available in the Al Mahara. Al Iwan has a menu of Lebanese dishes and international gourmet cuisine.

Subtropical climate with sunshine and cloudless skies all the year round. Rainfall is limited to a few days only. The best time to travel is winter, from October to the end of April.

HIDEAWAYS recommends flying Emirates, i.e. from Frankfurt, Munich, Manchester one daily flight; from London 4 flights a day; from Paris, Milan and Athens 3 x weekly; from Zurich 5 x weekly and from Rome 6 x weekly.

Currently the tallest hotel building in the world and one of the most spectacular.

Fancourt Hotel

Reservations:
Fancourt Hotel and Country Club Estate
P.O. Box 2266
George 6530, South Africa
Telephone: 00 27 / 44 / 8 04 00 00
Telefax: 00 27 / 44 / 8 04 07 00
E-mail: hotel@fancourt.co.za
Internet: www.fancourt.co.za

Near George in South Africa, a half hour drive from the stunning beaches of the Indian Ocean.

30 rooms and suites in the historic Manor House, furnished with antiques (1,000 – 1,500 Rand), 70 Garden Suites with up to three bedrooms and kitchen (1,540 – 3,465 Rand).
One Rand = approx. DM 0.30.

Fancourt is the epitome of golf in South Africa. 3 x 18-hole golf courses across about 1,300 acres. Superb Health & Beauty Centre equipped with the latest fitness gym for health conscious guests.

Five restaurants serving first class local and international dishes including South African, Asian, Italian and French cuisine.

Temperate clear Canaries-type climate throughout the year. Hot summer (Christmas) and mild winter. Average daily temperatures: July up to 20 °C and December about 30 °C.

Many well-known airlines fly to Cape Town as well as South African Airways, including Air France, British Airways, KLM, Lufthansa and LTU.

Guests enjoy free 24-hour Internet access.

ÜBERSICHT DER HOTELS

Las Ventanas al Paraiso

Rosewood Hotels & Resorts
Direktor: Edward T. Steiner
KM 19,5 Carretera Transpeninsular –
Cabo San Lucas
San José del Cabo, Baja California Sur
23400 Mexico
Telefon: 00 52 / 1 14 / 4 03 00
Telefax: 00 52 / 1 14 / 4 03 01
Verkaufszentrale Los Angeles:
Telefon: 0 01 / 3 10 / 8 24 77 81
Telefax: 0 01 / 3 10 / 8 24 12 18

Mexiko, Südspitze der Baja California, an der Küste der Cortez-See zwischen San José del Cabo und Cabo San Lucas.

61 Suiten mit Meer- und Gartenblick von US $ 475 – 3 000. Luxuriöses Innendesign in kunstbetontem mexikanisch-mediterranen Stil.

5 Meisterschafts-Golfplätze: El Dorado, Cabo del Sol, Palmilla, Cabo Real, Cabo San Lucas Country Club; Poollandschaft; Wassersport: Schnorcheln, Tauchen, Windsurfen, Kajak, Sportfischen u. ä.; Tennis, Reiten; Beautyfarm und Fitnesscenter.

Kreative mexikanisch-mediterrane Cuisine, Grillküche mit frischem Meeresfang, Ceviche-Bar.

Extrem regenarmes Wüstenklima mit kühlen Kaminabenden im Winter. Hochsaison ist von Dezember bis Februar, die beste Reisezeit geht von November bis April.

Empfehlenswert: Direktflug nach Los Angeles (Lufthansa von Frankfurt täglich in ca. 11 1/2 Stunden). Dann mit Aero California im Zwei-Stunden-Flug die ganze Baja entlang nach San José del Cabo.

Sonnenreiches Luxusresort mit kunstvollem Außen- und Innendesign. Erstklassiger Service.

Litchfield Plantation

Direktor: Karl W. Friedrich
P.O. Box 290, Kings River Road
Pawleys Island, South Carolina 29585
Reservierung:
Telefon: 0 01 / 8 00 / 8 69 / 14 10
oder 0 01 / 8 43 / 2 37-91 21
Telefax: 0 01 / 8 43 / 2 37-10 41
E-Mail: vacation@lichtfieldplantation.com
Internet: www.litchfieldplantation.com

Litchfield Plantation liegt in South Carolina am Waccamaw River, 15 Autominuten nördlich von Georgetown.

38 luxuriöse Suiten und Zimmer, gestaltet mit dem Charme und der Eleganz der alten Südstaaten. Man wohnt im Plantagenhaus, im Guest House und in Villen. Preise je nach Saison und Kategorie von US$ 148,– bis US$ 582,–.

100 Golfplätze im Umkreis von 80 km, 10 der reizvollsten davon wenige Autominuten von der Plantage entfernt. Zwei Tennisplätze, ein großzügiger geheizter Pool auf der Plantage.

Chefkoch Orobosa Uwagbai bietet im Carriage House Club verfeinerte typische Küche auf Gourmet-Niveau.

Der Küstenstrich von South Carolina ist wegen seiner milden Winter und nicht zu heißen, trockenen Sommer ein Ganzjahresziel, vor allem für Golfer.

Man fliegt nach Atlanta, Georgia, (etwa mit Delta Airlines oder Lufthansa direkt von Frankfurt, ca. neuneinhalb Stunden), dann mit dem kleinen Jet ca. eine Stunde nach Myrtle Beach.

Litchfield Plantation liegt mitten in einem Golfparadies.

Cambridge Beaches

Präsident und Geschäftsführer:
Michael J. Winfield
30 Kings Point, Sandys
Bermuda MA 02
Telefon: 0 01 / 4 41 / 2 34 03 31
Telefax: 0 01 / 4 41 / 2 34 33 52
E-Mail: cambridgebeaches@ibl.bm

Rund 1500 Kilometer östlich der USA und ebensoweit nördlich der Karibik im golfstromerwärmten Atlantik.

82 individuell eingerichtete Bungalows und Suiten, alle vor kurzem renoviert. Alle Zimmer mit Terrasse, die meisten mit Meeresblick, Klimaanlage, Telefon, Radio, Fön. US$ 335,– bis 1 075,–. Tax, Gratuity extra.

3 Tennisplätze, Putting Green, Croquet Lawn, Schnorcheln, Tauchen, Hochseefischen. Vollausgestattete Marina mit Segel- und Motorbooten, Health and Beauty Center.

Internationale Haute Cuisine, täglich wechselndes 5-Gang-Dinner. Hervorragend sortierter Weinkeller. Zimmerservice bis 22.00 Uhr.

Sonniges Ganzjahresziel, heiße Sommer (über 30 °C im Juli/August), milde Winter (ca. 15 °C zu Weihnachten).

Neben Delta Air Lines wird Bermuda auch von Condor, British Airways, USAir, American Airlines und Continental Airlines angeflogen.

Reiseschecks werden problemlos akzeptiert, Kreditkarten nicht.

SUMMARY OF THE HOTELS

Las Ventanas al Paraiso

Rosewood Hotels & Resorts
General Manager: Edward T. Steiner
KM 19,5, Carretera Transpeninsular –
Cabo San Lucas
San José del Cabo, Baja California Sur
23400 Mexico
Telephone: 00 52 / 1 14 / 4 03 00
Telefax: 00 52 / 1 14 / 4 03 01
Sales centre Los Angeles:
Telephone: 0 01 / 3 10 / 8 24 77 81
Telefax: 0 01 / 3 10 / 8 24 12 18

Mexico, at the most southerly point of Baja California on the coast of the Sea of Cortez, between San José del Cabo and Cabo San Lucas.

61 suites with sea or garden views from US $ 475 – 3,000. Luxurious interior décor in artistic Mexican style.

5 championship golf courses: El Dorado, Cabo del Sol, Palmilla, Cabo Real, Cabo San Lucas Country Club. Pool area, water sports, snorkelling, skin-diving, windsurfing, kayak, fishing and more. Riding, beauty farm and fitness centre.

Creative Mexican-Mediterranean cuisine, grill with fresh fish, ceviche bar.

Extremely dry desert climate with cool evenings around the fire in winter. High season is from December to February, best time travel – from November to April.

The direct Lufthansa flight to Los Angeles from Frankfurt (approx. 11 1/2 hours) can also be recommended. Then a 2-hour Aero California flight down the whole of the Baja to San José del Cabo.

Sun-drenched luxury resort of artistic exterior and interior design. First class service.

Litchfield Plantation

General Manager: Karl W. Friedrich
P.O. Box 290, Kings River Road
Pawley's Island, South Carolina 29585
Reservations:
Telephone: 0 01 / 8 00 / 8 69-14 10
and 0 01 / 8 43 / 2 37-91 21
Telefax: 0 01 / 8 43 / 2 37-10 41
E-mail: vacation@litchfieldplantation.com
Internet: www.litchfieldplantation.com

Litchfield Plantation is in South Carolina on the Waccamaw River, a 15 minute drive north of Georgetown.

38 luxurious suites and room furnished with the charm and elegance of the old Southern States. Guests stay at the Plantation House, at the Guest House or in villas. Rates according to season and category from US$ 148.– to US$ 582.–.

100 golf courses within an 80 mile radius, 10 of best only a few minutes drive away from the plantation. Two tennis courts, a large heated pool on the plantation.

Head Chef Orobosa Uwagbai serves a fine cuisine based on typical Lowland dishes at gourmet standard.

South Carolina's coast is an all-year destination, especially for golfers, because of its mild winters and dry summers which never get too hot.

Direct flights from Frankfurt to Atlanta, Georgia, for instance by Delta Airlines or Lufthansa, approx. nine and a half hour flying time. Then a half-hour flight by small jet to Myrtle Beach.

Litchfield Plantation lies at the centre of a golf paradise.

Cambridge Beaches

President and Chief Executive Officer:
Michael J. Winfield
Kings Point, Sandys
Bermuda MA 02
Telephone: 0 01 / 4 41 / 2 34 03 31
Telefax: 0 01 / 4 41 / 2 34 33 52
E-mail: cambridgebeaches@ibl.bm

Around 1,500 kilometers east of the USA and equally as far north of the Caribbean in the Gulf Stream warmed Atlantic.

82 individually furnished bungalows and suites, all recently renovated. All rooms have a terrace and most have a sea view. Air conditioning, telephone, radio, hair drier. US$ 335.– to US$ 1,075.–.
Tax and gratuity extra.

3 tennis courts, putting green, croquet lawn, snorkeling, diving, high sea fishing, a fully equipped marina with sailing and motor boats, Health and Beauty Centre.

International haute cuisine. The 5 course dinner changes daily. Excellently assorted wine cellar. Room service until 22.00 h.

Sunny all year, hot summers (over 30 °C in July/August), mild winters (approx. 15 °C at Christmas).

As well as Delta Air Lines, Condor, British Airways, USAir, American Airlines and Continental Airlines also fly to Bermuda.

Travellers cheques are accepted, credit cards not.

ÜBERSICHT DER HOTELS

Old Course Hotel St. Andrews

Old Course Hotel Golf Resort & Spa
Direktor: Andrew Phelan
St. Andrews, Kingdom of Fife
Scotland KY16 9SP
Telefon: 00 44 / 13 34 / 47 43 71
Telefax: 00 44 / 13 34 / 47 76 68
Internet: www.oldcoursehotel.co.uk
E-Mail: info@oldcoursehotel.co.uk

St. Andrews liegt rund 20 Kilometer südöstlich von Dundee auf einer Halbinsel direkt an der schottischen Nordseeküste.

114 Zimmer und 32 Suiten, 5-Sterne-Komfort; besonders luxuriös, großzügig geschnitten die Zimmer und Suiten im neuen, 2000 angebauten Flügel. Preise je nach Kategorie und Saison von £ 180 bis £ 520 mit Frühstück inklusive kostenloses, unbegrenztes Golfen am Duke's Course.

Fünf öffentliche Links Courses von St. Andrews, darunter der legendäre Old Course; Dukes's Course (18-Loch-Championship-Inland-Platz des Hotels); Spa mit Indoor-Pool, Jacuzzi, Sauna, Fitness, 4 Behandlungsräumen.

Feine, klassische Grill-Cuisine im Road Hole Grill, unkomplizierte Brasserie-Küche im modern gestylten Sands, einmaliges Whiskyangebot in der Road-Hole Bar (über 170 verschiedene Sorten, jede schottische Destillerie ist vertreten), typische Pub-Snacks im Jigger Inn, herzhafte Golfküche im Duke's Course Clubhouse.

Günstiges Mikroklima mit viel Sonne und wenig Niederschlägen, frische Nordseeluft; Hochsaison im Sommer, gute Golfbedingungen auch im Herbst und Winter.

Internationaler Flughafen von Edinburgh, von dort einstündiger, landschaftlich reizvoller Limousinentransfer durch das Hotel.

Mitglied der Leading Hotels of the World.

Skibo Castle

Eigentümer: Peter de Savary
Direktor: Charles P. Oak
Dornoch, Sutherland, Scotland
IV25 3RQ
Telefon: 00 44 / 18 62 / 89 46 00
Telefax: 00 44 / 18 62 / 89 46 01
Internet: www.carnegieclub.co.uk
E-Mail: skibo@carnegieclub.com

Skibo Castle liegt an der Ostküste der nördlichen schottischen Highlands an der Mündung des Dornoch Firth.

21 Schlosszimmer und 12 Lodges im luxuriös-eleganten Landhausstil der Edwardianischen Ära. Aufenthalt: Mitglieder £ 275,00 pro Person und Tag, Gäste von Mitgliedern: £ 325,00 pro Person und Tag, Gäste: £ 375,00 pro Person und Tag.

18 Hole Championship Links Course, Par 72, 9 Hole Parkland Course, Par 35, Fischen (Lachs und Forellen), Tontaubenschießen, Jagen (auch mit dem Falkner), Croquet, Tennis; geheizter Swimmingpool, Fitnesscenter, Sauna, Dampfbad, Spa.

Dinner an der Table d'hôte im Schloss (20.00 Uhr, Herren tragen Jackett und Krawatte), Lunch 12.30–15.00 Uhr an der Table d'hôte im Golf House am 18-Loch-Platz. Küchenchef John McMahon kocht mit besten einheimischen Produkten.

Das milde Mikroklima ist vom Golfstrom beeinflusst. Die Gegend am Dornoch Firth hat die meisten Sonnen- und die wenigsten Regentage der schottischen Highlands.

Man fliegt von London mit British Airways nach Inverness. Von dort im Club-Shuttle eine knappe Stunde zum Schloss.

Einer der schönsten und exklusivsten Golfclubs der Grünen Insel.

Loch Lomond Golf Club

Rossdhu House, Luss
Dunbartonshire
G83 8NT Scotland
Telefon: 00 44 / 14 36 / 65 55 55
Telefax: 00 44 / 14 36 / 65 55 00

Tee-Times nur für Mitglieder und ihre Gäste nach Reservierung.
Eintrittsbeitrag:
£ 20 000 für Großbritannien,
£ 8 000 für außerhalb,
jährlicher Mitgliedsbeitrag
£ 925, kein Greenfee für Mitglieder, für Gäste £ 150 pro Person und Runde.

SUMMARY OF THE HOTELS

Old Course Hotel St. Andrews

Old Course Hotel Golf Resort & Spa
General Manager: Andrew Phelan
St. Andrews
Kingdom of Fife
Scotland KY16 9SP
Telephone: 00 44 / 13 34 / 47 43 71
Telefax: 00 44 / 13 34 / 47 76 68
Internet: www.oldcoursehotel.co.uk
E-mail: info@oldcoursehotel.co.uk

St. Andrews is about 12 miles southeast of Dundee on a peninsula in the North Sea coast of Scotland.

114 rooms and 32 suites, 5-star luxury; very luxurious spacious too and suites in a new wing built in 2000. Rates depending on category and season from £ 180 – £ 520 inclusive of breakfast. Unlimited golf on the Duke's course free of charge.

5 public links courses of St. Andrews, including the legendary Old Course; Duke's Course (18-hole championship inland course belonging to the hotel); spa with indoor pool, Jacuzzi, sauna, fitness room, 4 treatment rooms.

Sophisticated classic grill cuisine at the Road Hole Grill, plain brasserie cooking in the modern Sands, unique range of whiskies at the Road Hole Bar (over 170 different kinds, every Scottish distillery is represented), typical pub snacks at the Jigger Inn, tasty golf food at the Duke's Course Clubhouse.

Favourable micro climate with a lot of sun and few showers, fresh North Sea air. High season in summer. Favourable Autumn and winter conditions for golf.

International airport in Edinburgh. From there one hour's drive by hotel limousine through beautiful scenery.

Member of the Leading Hotels of the World.

Skibo Castle

Proprietor: Peter de Savary
General Manager: Charles P. Oak
Dornoch, Sutherland
Scotland IV25 3RQ
Telephone: 00 44 / 18 62 / 89 46 00
Telefax: 00 44 / 18 62 / 89 46 01
Internet: www.carnegieclub.co.uk
E-mail: skibo@carnegieclubs.com

Skibo Castle is located on the eastern coast of the Scottish Highlands at the mouth of the Dornoch Firth.

21 castle rooms and 12 lodges built in the grand luxurious style of an Edwardian country mansion. Accommodation: members £ 275.– per person per day; members' guests daily £ 325.– per person. Guests £ 375.– per person per day.

18-hole championship links, par 72; 9-hole parkland course, par 35. Fishing (salmon and trout). Clay pigeon shooting, hunting (also with a falconer) croquet, tennis. Roofed-over heated swimming pool, fitness centre, sauna, steam bath, spa.

Dinner, table d'hôte, at the hotel (8 pm, men jacket and tie), lunch 12.30–3.30 pm, table d'hôte at the golf house on the 18-hole links, chef John McMahon cooks with the very best local ingredients.

The mild local climate is affected by the Gulf Stream. The area around Dornoch Firth has the most sunny days and the fewest rainy days in the Scottish Highlands.

British Airways flight to Inverness. From there by Club shuttle it is just under an hour's drive to the Castle.

One of the most beautiful and most exclusive golf clubs in the British Isles.

Loch Lomond Golf Club

Rossdhu House, Luss
Dunbartonshire
G83 8NT Scotland
Telephone: 00 44 / 14 36 / 65 55 55
Telefax: 00 44 / 14 36 / 65 55 00

Tee times members only and their guests after booking.
Membership fee £ 20,000 for the United Kingdom, £ 8,000 for members from abroad. Annual subscription: members £ 925, no green fee; guests £ 150 per person per round.

ÜBERSICHT DER HOTELS

Les Bordes

Direktor: Brian Sparks
F-41220 Saint-Laurent-Nouan
Telefon: 00 33 / 2 54 87 72 13
Telefax: 00 33 / 2 54 87 78 61
E-Mail: info@lesbordes.com
Internet: www.lesbordes.com

In der Nähe des Städtchens Saint-Laurent-Nouan, wenige Autominuten von der Loire entfernt, in der Sologne, der Landschaft des Loirebogens.

10 Cottages mit 80 Zimmern, die Hälfte davon direkt am 18. Loch, Doppelzimmer können zu Suiten verbunden werden, rustikal-eleganter Jagdhausstil, moderner Topkomfort.
Preise: 1150 Franc (Einzelbelegung), 1250 Franc (Doppelbelegung).

18-Loch-Championship-Platz Les Bordes, in unmittelbarer Nachbarschaft 36-Loch-Platz Prieure de Ganay, Spa & Health Club in Orléans, 30 Autominuten entfernt.

Erstklassige französische Küche mit Produkten und Einflüssen aus der Sologne, mittags Buffet und à la carte, gute Karte mit Bar-Snacks.

Les Bordes ist das ganze Jahr über geöffnet. Hauptsaison April bis Oktober.

Man fährt vom internationalen Flughafen Paris-Orly 1,5 Stunden mit dem Auto an, vom internationalen Flughafen Paris-Charles de Gaulle 2 Stunden.

Gästebetreuung zweisprachig: englisch und französisch.

Grand Hotels Quellenhof

Direktion: Silvia und Hans Geiger
CH-7310 Bad Ragaz
Telefon: 00 41 / 81 / 3 03 30 30
Telefax: 00 41 / 81 / 3 03 30 33
E-Mail: reservation@resortragaz.ch
Internet: www.resortragaz.ch
Reservierung: gebührenfrei aus CH/A/B/D/F/NL/UK
Telefon: 00 800 / 80 12 11 10
aus allen übrigen Ländern
Telefon: 00 41 / 81 / 3 03 20 60
Telefax: 00 41 / 81 / 3 03 20 66

Inmitten der sanften voralpinen Landschaft des schweizerischen Rheintals, am Tor zu Graubünden.

Grand Hotel Quellenhof: 97 sehr großzügige und luxuriöse Juniorsuiten, 8 Suiten und eine 200 m$_2$ große Royal Suite mit eigenem Thermalwasser-Whirlpool, allesamt mit eigenem Balkon, Preis je nach Saison und Aufenthaltsdauer 370,– bis 710,–, Suiten 710,– bis 2 300,– Schweizer Franken.

Healthclub To B.: auf über 2100 m$_2$ Aktivbereich mit modernsten Geräten, Wasserwelt mit Sauna-, Dampf- und Duftlandschaften, hoteleigenes Thermalbad mit römisch-irischem Bad, Schönheitsoase.

Im Quellenhof Halbpensionsrestaurant Bel Air mit Gartenterrasse. Gourmetrestaurant Äbtestube, typische Schweizer Gerichte in der Dorfbeiz Zollstube.

In 500 Meter Höhe gelegen, hat Bad Ragaz das ganze Jahr ein gesundes Klima zu bieten. Golfsaison von März bis November.

Internationale Flughäfen: Zürich 110 km, München 250 km, Mailand 230 km. Von dort mit dem Zug nach Bad Ragaz. Limousinen-Service auf Anfrage.

Leading Hotel of the World. Einziges Hotel in der Schweiz mit eigenem 18-Loch-Golfplatz.

Margarethenhof

Geschäftsführer: Günter F. Esterer
Postfach 11 01
D-83701 Gmund am Tegernsee
Telefon: 00 49 / 80 22 / 7 50 60
Telefax: 00 49 / 80 22 / 7 48 18
E-Mail: margarethenhof@gmx.de
Internet: www.margarethenhof.com.

Im bayerischen Voralpenland, 868 m hoch über dem Tegernsee, 48 km von München, 96 km von Salzburg entfernt.

38 Juniorsuiten und zweistöckige Galerie-Appartements mit allem modernen Komfort im geschmackvollen Landhausstil. Preise nach Kategorie und Saison von DM 168,– bis 395,–.

18-Loch-Championship-Kurs, Par 72, Chipping Green, Driving Range, 2 Putting Greens, Übungsbunker; Sauna, Fitness, Solarium, Mountainbikes im Hotel.

Kreative mediterrane Feinschmecker-Cuisine und herzhafte bayerisch-österreichische Schmankerl- und Brotzeitküche. Gute Weine.

Golfsaison mit viel Sonne und milden Temperaturen von Juni bis Mitte Oktober. April und Mai eignen sich gut fürs intensive Training.

Man fliegt nach München oder Salzburg. Von dort mit dem Auto (München ca. 50 Min., Salzburg ca. 1 Std. 10 Min.) zum Golfplatz.

Hotel und Clubhaus mitten im Golfplatz.

SUMMARY OF THE HOTELS

Les Bordes

General Manager: Brian Sparks
F-41220 Saint Laurent-Nouan
Telephone: 00 33 / 2 54 87 72 13
Telefax: 00 33 / 2 54 97 78 61
E-mail: info@lesbordes.com
Internet: www.lesbordes.com

Near the little town of Saint-Laurent-Nouan, a few minutes drive from the Loire, in Sologne, the region of the Loire river bend.

10 cottages with 80 rooms half of which at the 18th hole. Double rooms can be combined with suites. Elegant rustic hunting lodge style, extremely luxurious with the latest mod cons.
Rates: Single room 1,150 francs, double room 1,250 francs.

Les Bordes 18-hole championship golf course is close to the 36-hole Prieure de Ganay Course with Spa & Health Club in Orléans, 30 minutes by car.

First class French cuisine using ingredients from the Sologne to produce dishes influenced by regional cooking. Midday buffet and good à la carte menu and bar snacks.

Les Bordes in open all the year rounds. High season from April to October.

From Paris-Orly International Airport it is 1,5 hour drive, from Paris-Charles de Gaulle Airport 2 hours.

Bilingual hospitality: English and French.

Grand Hotels Quellenhof

Direction: Silvia und Hans Geiger
CH-7310 Bad Ragaz
Telephone: 00 41 / 81 / 3 03 30 30
Telefax: 00 41 / 81 / 3 03 30 33
E-mail: reservation@resortragaz.ch
Internet: www.resortragaz.ch
Reservations: toll free from
CH/A/B/D/F/NL/UK
Telephone: 00 800 / 80 12 11 10
All others:
Telephone: 00 41 / 81 / 3 03 20 60
Telefax: 00 41 / 81 / 3 03 20 66

In the middle of the gently undulating alpine foothills of the Swiss Rhine valley close to Graubünden.

Grand Hotel Quellenhof: 97 very spacious, luxurious Junior Suites, 8 suites and a Royal Suite 2,150 square feet in area with its own thermal water whirlpool, all with a private balcony, rates according to season 370.– to 710.–, Suites 710.– to 2,300.– Swiss francs.

Health Club To B. with an area of 22,600 square feet has the most up-to-date equipment. Waterworld with sauna, steam bath, aroma landscapes, hotel thermal bath with a Roman-Irish bath, beauty oasis.

At the Quellenhof half board restaurant Bel Air with a garden terrace. At the Ragaz half-board restaurant Hof Ragaz, gourmet restaurant Äbtestube, typical Swiss dishes in the Dorfbeiz Zollstube.

At an altitude of nearly 5,400 feet Bad Ragaz has a bracing climate all the year round. Golf season from March to November.

International airports: Zurich 68 miles, Munich 155 miles, Milan 142 miles. From there by train to Bad Ragaz. Limousine service on request.

Leading Hotel of the World. Only hotel in Switzerland with its own 18-hole golf course.

Margarethenhof

General Manager: Günter F. Esterer
Postfach 11 01
D-83701 Gmund am Tegernsee
Telephone: 00 49 / 80 22 / 7 50 60
Telefax: 00 49 / 80 22 / 7 48 18
E-mail: margarethenhof@gmx.de
Internet: www.margarethenhof.com

Located in the alpine foot-hills, 2,850 feet above Lake Tegernsee, 30 miles from Munich and 60 miles from Salzburg.

38 junior suites and two-storey galleried apartments with all mod cons tastefully presented in country house style. Rates depending on category and season, from DM 168.– to DM 395.–

18-hole championship golf course, par 72, chipping green, driving range, 2 putting greens, practice bunkers; sauna, fitness room, solarium and mountain bikes in the hotel.

Creative Mediterranean cuisine and tasty Austro-Bavarian snacks and open sandwiches. Good wines.

Golf season with plenty of sun and mild temperatures from June to the middle of October. April and May are great for intensive training.

There are flights from Munich or Salzburg. From there by car (from Munich about 50 minutes and from Salzburg 1 hour ten minutes) to the golf course.

The Hotel is in the middle of the course.

ÜBERSICHT DER HOTELS

Sonnenalp Hotel & Resort

Besitz und Leitung: Familie Fäßler
D-87527 Ofterschwang/Oberallgäu
Telefon: 0 83 21 / 27 20
Telefax: 0 83 21 / 27 22 42
E-Mail: info@sonnenalp.de
Internet: www.sonnenalp.de

Absolut ruhige Lage zwischen Wäldern und Wiesen in der herrlichen Naturlandschaft des Oberallgäus. Nur wenige Kilometer von Sonthofen entfernt.

41 Einzelzimmer, 142 Doppelzimmer, 17 Appartements, 23 Luxus-Appartements und Suiten. Alle sehr komfortabel, großzügig und ruhig, mit Balkon oder Terrasse zumeist nach Süden. Safe, Kabel-TV, ISDN-Telefon, Direktwahl, Minibar, Fön. Preise pro Person und Tag inkl. HP von 371,61 bis 733,44 DM.

Anspruchsvolle 18-Loch-Golfanlage gehört zum Hotel; Außen- und Innenpool, Freibad, Außen-Whirlpools, Tennishalle und -freiplätze, Squash, Sporthalle, Fahrräder, Wandern u. v. m.; Fitnessstudio, Saunaparadies, Solarium; Beautysalon, Friseur, Massagen und Kuranwendungen.

Neun Restaurants mit heimischen und internationalen Spezialitäten: Ludwigs-Restaurant, Alpenterrasse, Sonnenstube, Jägerstube, Alte Stube (4-Gang-Pensionsmenü), Taverne (Kalt-warmes Buffet mit Grillgerichten, Pizza, Themenabende), Wirt's-Stuben (alpenländische Spezialitäten), Seepferd'l (Snacks und Italienisches am Pool), Restaurant Silberdistel (feine, leichte A-la-carte-Zubereitungen).

Ganzjähriges Reiseziel.

Gute Flugverbindungen nach München, Stuttgart, Augsburg und Friedrichshafen. Pkw-Anreise: Von Kempten auf der B19 Richtung Oberstdorf, 3 km nach Sonthofen, Direktabfahrt Sonnenalp.

Kinderbetreuung durch geschultes Personal.

Schloss Pichlarn

Direktion: Christine & Stefan Frenzel
A-8952 Irdning/Steiermark
Telefon: 00 43 / 36 82 / 22 84 10
Telefax: 00 43 / 36 82 / 22 84 16
E-Mail: reservierung@pichlarn.at
Internet: www.pichlarn.at

Etwas außerhalb des Ortes Irdning auf einer Anhöhe gelegen. Umgeben von einer herrlichen Park- und Golfanlage. Sehr ruhige Alleinlage im romantischen Ennstal.

Äußerst komfortable, in unterschiedlichen, sehr ansprechenden Stilrichtungen eingerichtete Einzelzimmer, Doppelzimmer und Suiten mit traumhaftem Blick auf das Ennstal und/oder den Golfplatz. Größtenteils mit Balkon. Annehmlichkeiten wie Safe, Sat-TV, ISDN-Telefon, Direktwahl, Minibar, Fön. Preise pro Person und Tag inkl. HP von 1490,– bis 4230,– ATS.

18-Loch-Golfanlage, 3-Loch-Übungsplatz; Hallenschwimmbad, Freibad, Liegewiese, Tennishalle und -freiplätze, Reitstall, Mountainbikes, Jagd, Fischerei, komplettes Wintersportangebot; Fitnessstudio, Sauna, Solarium; Ayurveda-Kurabteilung, Bade-, Beauty- und Massagezentrum.

Von zwei Gault-Millau-Hauben gekrönte Schlossküche mit internationalen und österreichischen Spezialitäten. Restaurant Wintergarten mit großer Terrasse, A-la-carte-Restaurant Schloss-Stüberl, Golfstüberl während der Golfsaison.

Ganzjähriges Reiseziel.

Nächstgelegener Flughafen ist Salzburg-Maxglan in 130 km Entfernung oder Graz-Thalerhof in 145 km Entfernung. Limousinen-, Bus- und Helikopterservice.

Das Ennstal ist eine der schönsten Gebirgs- und Kulturlandschaften Europas.

SUMMARY OF THE HOTELS

Sonnenalp Hotel & Resort

Managing proprietors: Fäßler Family
D-87527 Ofterschwang/Oberallgäu
Telephone: 0 83 21 / 27 20
Telefax: 0 83 21 / 27 22 42
E-mail: info@sonnenalp.de
Internet: www.sonnenalp.de

The hotel stands alone in a very peaceful location surrounded by the woods and meadows of the beautiful region of Oberallgäu, a few miles from Sonthofen.

41 single rooms, 142 double rooms, 17 appartements, 23 luxury appartements and suites, all very comfortable, spacious and peaceful, most with a south facing balcony or terrace. Safe, cable-TV, ISDN, telephone, DDI, minibar, hairdryer. Rates per person per day including HP from DM 371.61 – 733.44.

Challenging golf course belonging to the hotel. Outdoor and indoor swimming pools, indoor and outdoor tennis courts, squash, sports halls, cycles, rambling and much else. Fitness room, sauna, solarium, beauty salon, hairdresser, massage and various treatments.

Nine restaurants with local and international specialities: Ludwig's Restaurant, Alpenterrasse, Sonnenstube, Jägerstube, Alte Stube (plain 4-course menu), Taverne (warm and cold buffet with grilled dishes, pizza, theme evenings), Wirt's-Stuben (Alpine specialities), Seepferd'l (snacks and Italian fare by the pool), Restaurant Silberdistel (light sophisticated dishes à la carte).

Best time to travel: All the year round.

Favourable connections to Munich, Stuttgart, Augsburg and Friedrichshafen. By car: from Kempten take the B19 in the direction of Oberstdorf. About 2 miles after Sonthofen the Sonnenalp exit.

Excellent child care for tots to teens. Trained child carers.

Schloss Pichlarn

Direction: Christine & Stefan Frenzel
A-8952 Irdning/Steiermark
Telephone: 00 43 / 36 82 / 22 84 10
Telefax: 00 43 / 36 82 / 22 84 16
E-mail: reservierung@pichlarn.at
Internet: www.pichlarn.at

On a hill on the outskirts of Irdning, surrounded by a wonderful park and golf course. Very peaceful location in the middle of the romantic Ennstal.

Extremely comfortable single rooms, double rooms and suites with different styles of décor in very good taste. Most of the rooms have balconies. Fantastic views over Ennstal and/or the golf course. Mod cons include safe, Sat-TV, ISDN-telephone, DDI, minibar and hairdryer. Rates per person, incl. HP from ATS 1,490 – 4,230.

18-hole golf course, 3-hole practice course, indoor swimming bath, outdoor swimming bath, sunbathing lawn, indoor and outdoor tennis courts, riding stables, mountain bikes, fishing, full range of winter sports, fitness room, sauna, solarium, Ayurveda system, baths, beauty and massage centre.

Awarded two Gault Millau toques blanches, international and Austrian specialities. Wintergarten restaurant with a large terrace, à la carte restaurant Schloss-Stüberl, Golfstüberl during the golf season.

Best time to travel: All the year round.

Nearest airport: Salzburg-Maxglan 80 miles away or Graz-Thalerhof Airport 90 miles away. Limousine, bus and helicopter service.

Ennstal is one of the most beautiful, and culturally most interesting regions in Europe.

Genießen Sie auch unsere weiteren exklusiven Bildbände

Hideaways – eine zutreffende Beschreibung für den Charakter der Hotels, die diese exklusiven Bildbände präsentierten, gibt es nicht: es sind Verstecke an den atemberaubendsten Plätzen und Metropolen der Welt, Refugien für die Seele und Kleinode des erlesenen Geschmacks. Zahlreiche dieser persönlich geführten Domizile befinden sich an Destinationen, an denen die Natur faszinierende Szenarien kreiert hat, deren Eindrücke für immer der Erinnerung verschrieben bleiben.

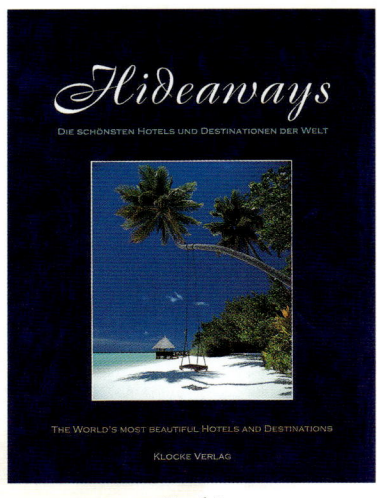

Band I
Malediven, Südafrika, Bali, Karibik
248 Seiten, 23,5 x 32 cm, 98,– DM

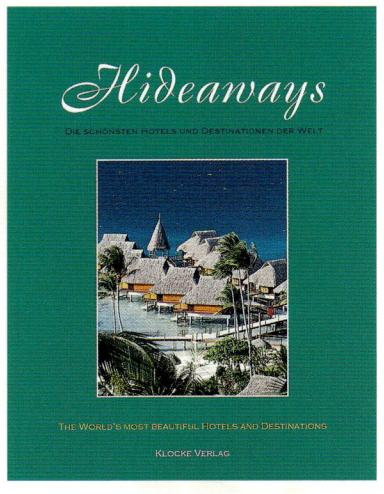

Band II
Südsee, Neuseeland, Kalifornien, Mexiko
240 Seiten, 23,5 x 32 cm, 98,– DM

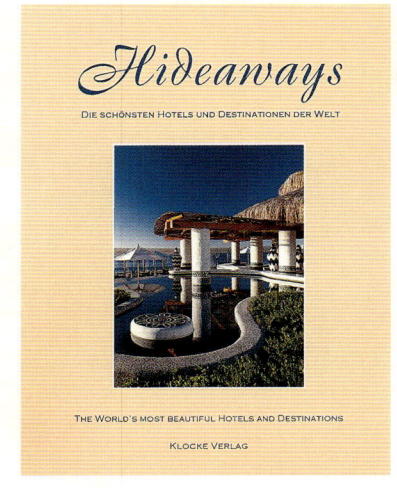

Band III
Karibik, Australien, Mallorca, Südafrika
240 Seiten, 23,5 x 32 cm, 98,– DM

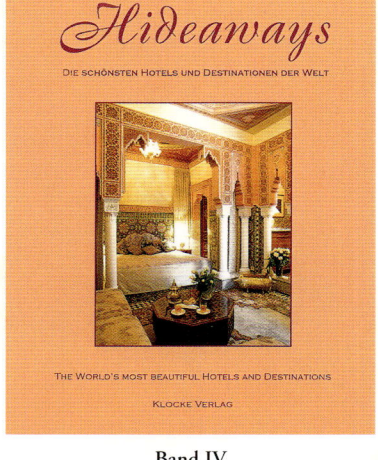

Band IV
Mauritius, Seychellen, Europa, Dubai
240 Seiten, 23,5 x 32 cm, 98,– DM

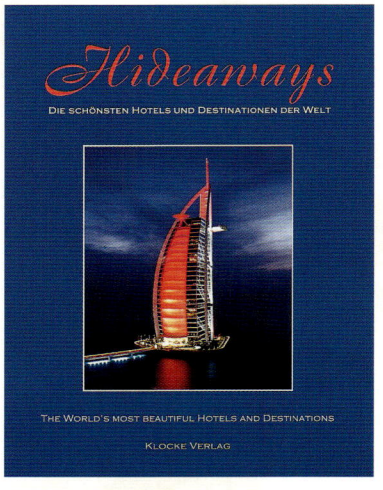

Band V
Südsee, Dubai, Karibik, Schweiz
240 Seiten, 23,5 x 32 cm, 98,– DM

Sternstunden ist eine Reise zu den besten Köchen der Welt. Erleben Sie bei Paul Bocuse, Alain Ducasse, Paul Haeberlin, Pierre Gagnaire, Jean-Claude Bourgueil, Dieter Müller, Heinz Winkler, Hans Haas, Gualtiero Marchesi, Eckart Witzigmann und vielen anderen kulinarische Sternstunden, festgehalten in faszinierenden Bildern.

STERNSTUNDEN –
Zu Gast bei den besten Köchen Europas
216 Seiten, 23,5 x 25,5 cm
98,– DM

Reisen, Wohnkultur und erlesene Gourmandise

Dieses Buch ist Pflichtlektüre für jeden Genießer, Hobby- und auch Profikoch. In humorvoller Art und Weise erzählt der ehemalige Zwei-Sterne-Koch Gerhard Gartner von seiner beruflichen Laufbahn: angefangen von der ersten Watschn als Lehrjunge bis zu Highlights wie zum Beispiel der Ausrichtung der Hochzeitsfeier für das niederländische Königshaus. Einzigartig ist der Rückblick in die deutsche Kochgeschichte, die Gartner anhand seiner historischen Kochbuchsammlung bis zurück in das Jahr 1350 aufblättert.

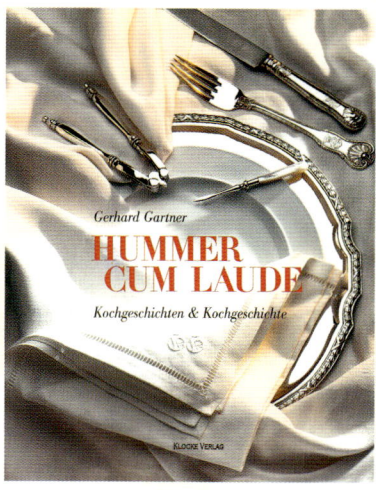

HUMMER CUM LAUDE
Kochgeschichten & Kochgeschichte von Gerhard Gartner
216 Seiten, 23,5 x 32 cm, 98,– DM

Landpartie. Schon der Name dieses exklusiven Bildbandes weckt die Sehnsucht, dem Alltagsstress für ein paar Tage zu entfliehen, wieder einmal die Schönheit der Natur zu genießen oder vielleicht in idyllischen Dörfchen romantische Stunden zu zweit zu verleben. Thomas und Martina Klocke haben zahlreiche liebenswerte Zufluchten ausfindig gemacht, wo man umgeben von schönstem *country style* logieren und sich kulinarisch verwöhnen lassen kann.

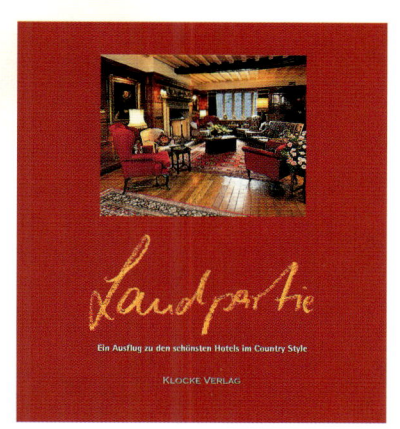

LANDPARTIE I
Ein Ausflug zu den schönsten Hotels im *country style*
216 Seiten, 23,5 x 25,5 cm, 78,– DM

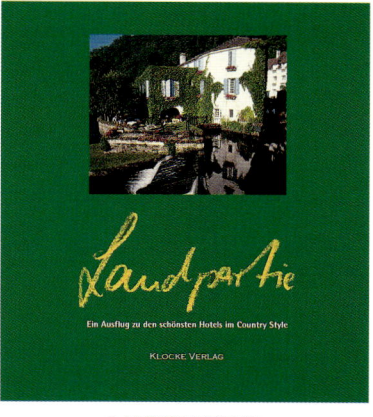

LANDPARTIE II
Ein Ausflug zu den schönsten Hotels im *country style*
216 Seiten, 23,5 x 25,5 cm, 98,– DM

Country Style Living gewährt Einblicke in die schönsten Häuser im Landhausstil. Genießen Sie ländliche Ambiancen in Deutschland, aber auch internationale Wohnkultur in England und mediterrane Inspirationen in der Provence. Natürlich laden wir Sie auch ein in einige der stilvollsten Fincas auf Mallorca, die geprägt werden von südlicher Sonne und der Leichtigkeit des Seins am Mittelmeer. Martina und Thomas Klocke haben mit ihrem Redaktionsteam Refugien besucht, die mit erstklassigen, meist großformatigen Fotos Lust auf ländliche Lebensart machen und Sie in diesem Bildband zum Träumen einladen.

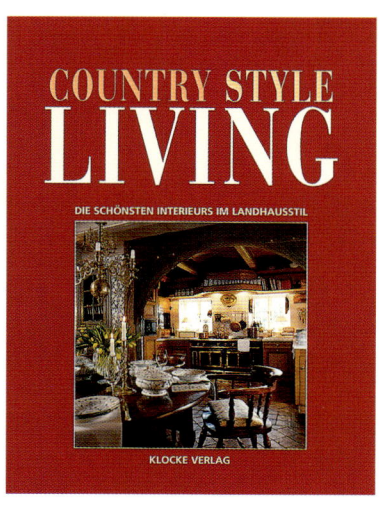

COUNTRY STYLE LIVING
Die schönsten Interieurs im Landhausstil
228 Seiten, 23,5 x 32 cm, 98,– DM

Restaurant-Guides im praktischen Taschenbuchformat

ELSASS A LA CARTE	MALLORCA A LA CARTE	SYLT KULINARISCH	BERLIN A LA CARTE
Ein kulinarischer Wegweiser zu den schönsten Restaurants und Hotels Mit Sonderteil Luxemburg	Die schönsten Fincas, Hotels und Restaurants der Baleareninsel Mit Rezepten von Eckart Witzigmann	Der ultimative Hotel- und Restaurantführer für die Nordseeperle	Ein kulinarischer Wegweiser zu den besten Hotels und Restaurants der Hauptstadt
176 Seiten mit zahlreichen Farbfotos Format: 10,5 x 21 cm, Hardcover 34,80 DM ISBN 3-934 170-03-X	256 Seiten mit zahlreichen Farbfotos Format: 10,5 x 21 cm, Hardcover 39,80 DM ISBN 3-934 170-02-1	272 Seiten mit zahlreichen Farbfotos Format: 10,5 x 21 cm, Hardcover 34,80 DM ISBN 3-934 170-07-2	272 Seiten mit zahlreichen Farbfotos Format: 10,5 x 21 cm, Hardcover 34,80 DM ISBN 3-934 170-06-4

Telefonische Bestell-Hotline: 0800 / 9 11 11 10 ■ Internet: www.klocke-verlag.de ■ Shop E-Mail: info@klocke-verlag.de
LIEFERUNGEN innerhalb Deutschlands frei Haus, innerhalb der EU 18,– DM, außerhalb der EU 30,– DM Versandkosten.